W9-DGO-873

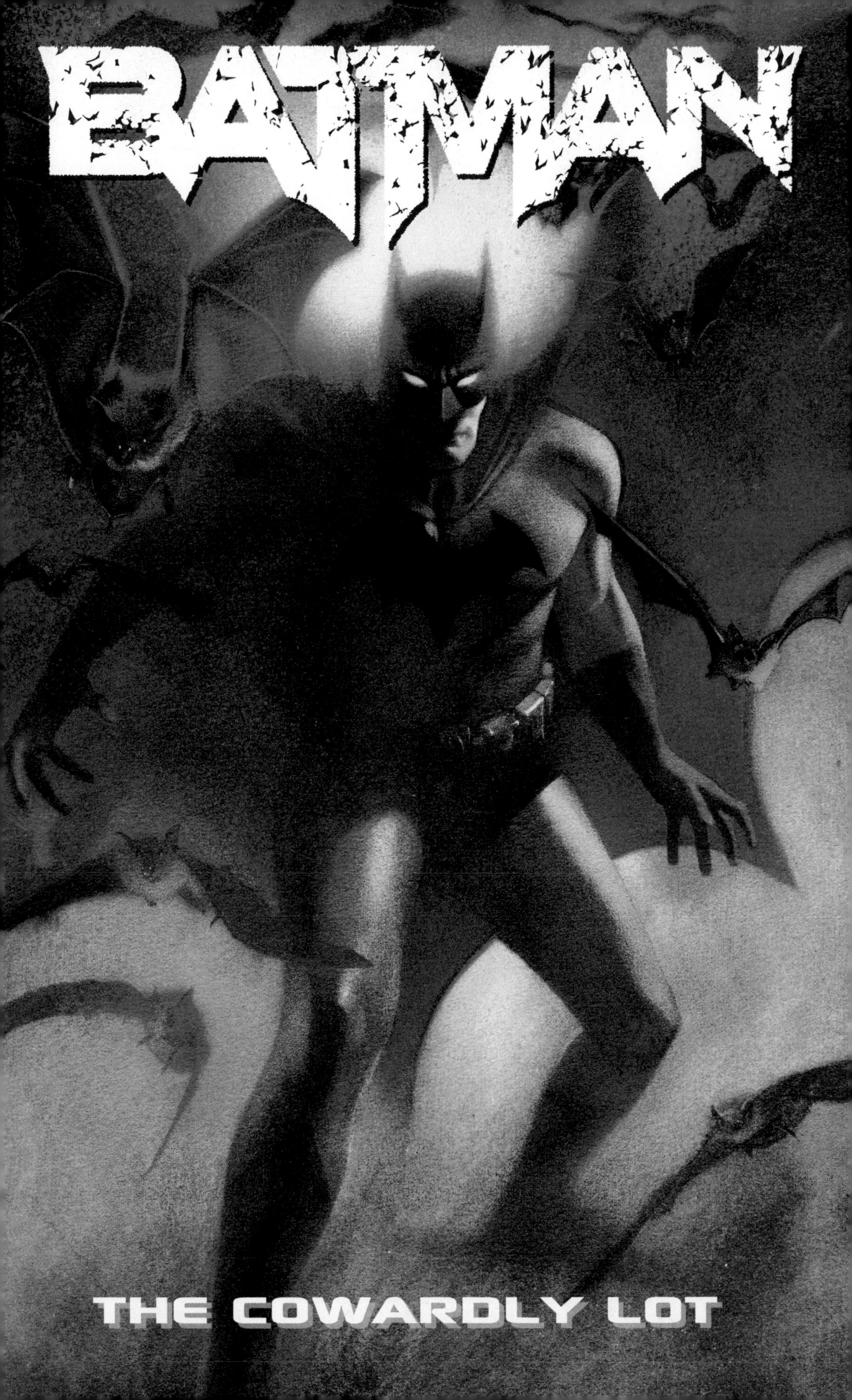
BATMAN
THE COWARDLY LOT

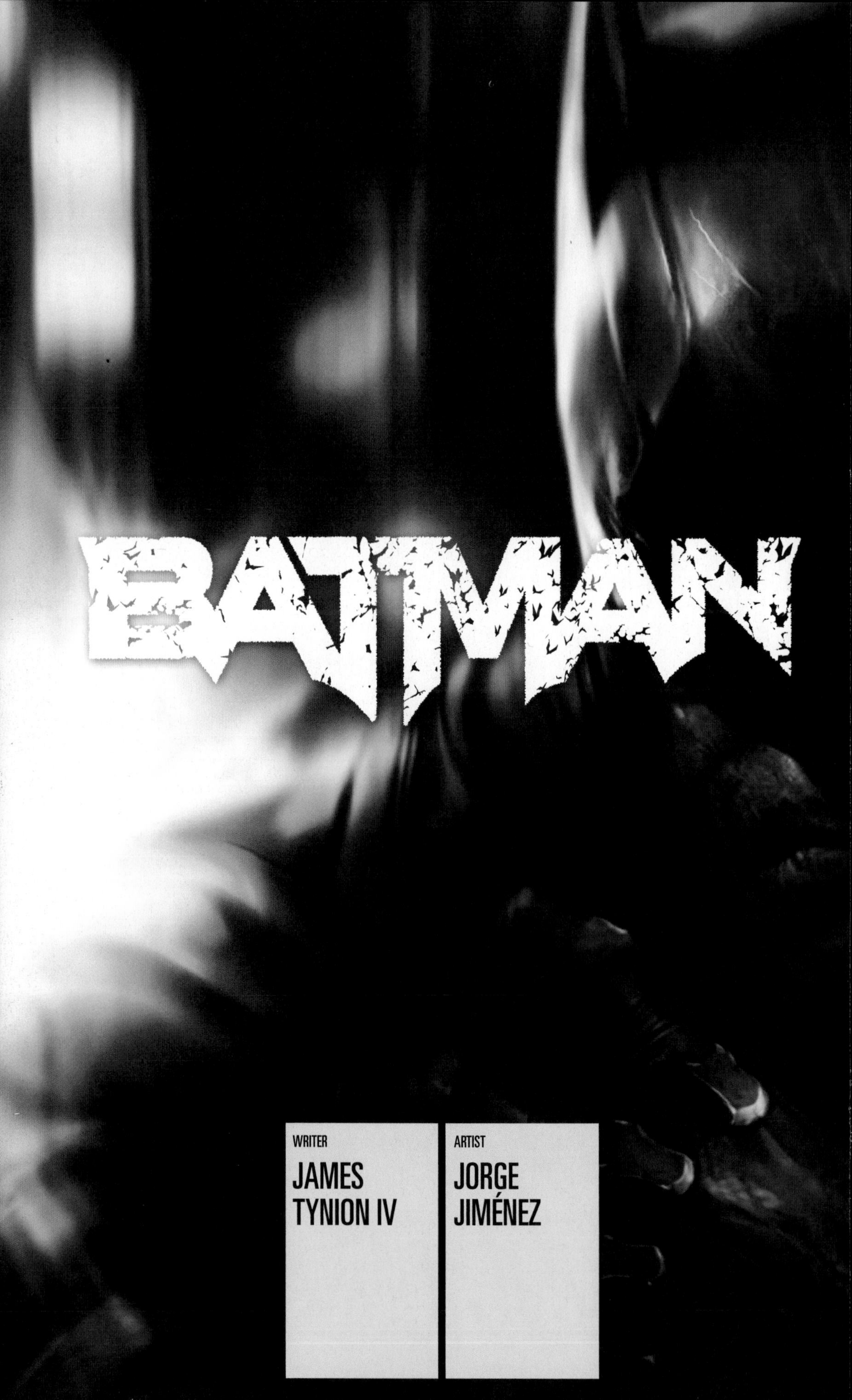

BATMAN

WRITER
JAMES TYNION IV

ARTIST
JORGE JIMÉNEZ

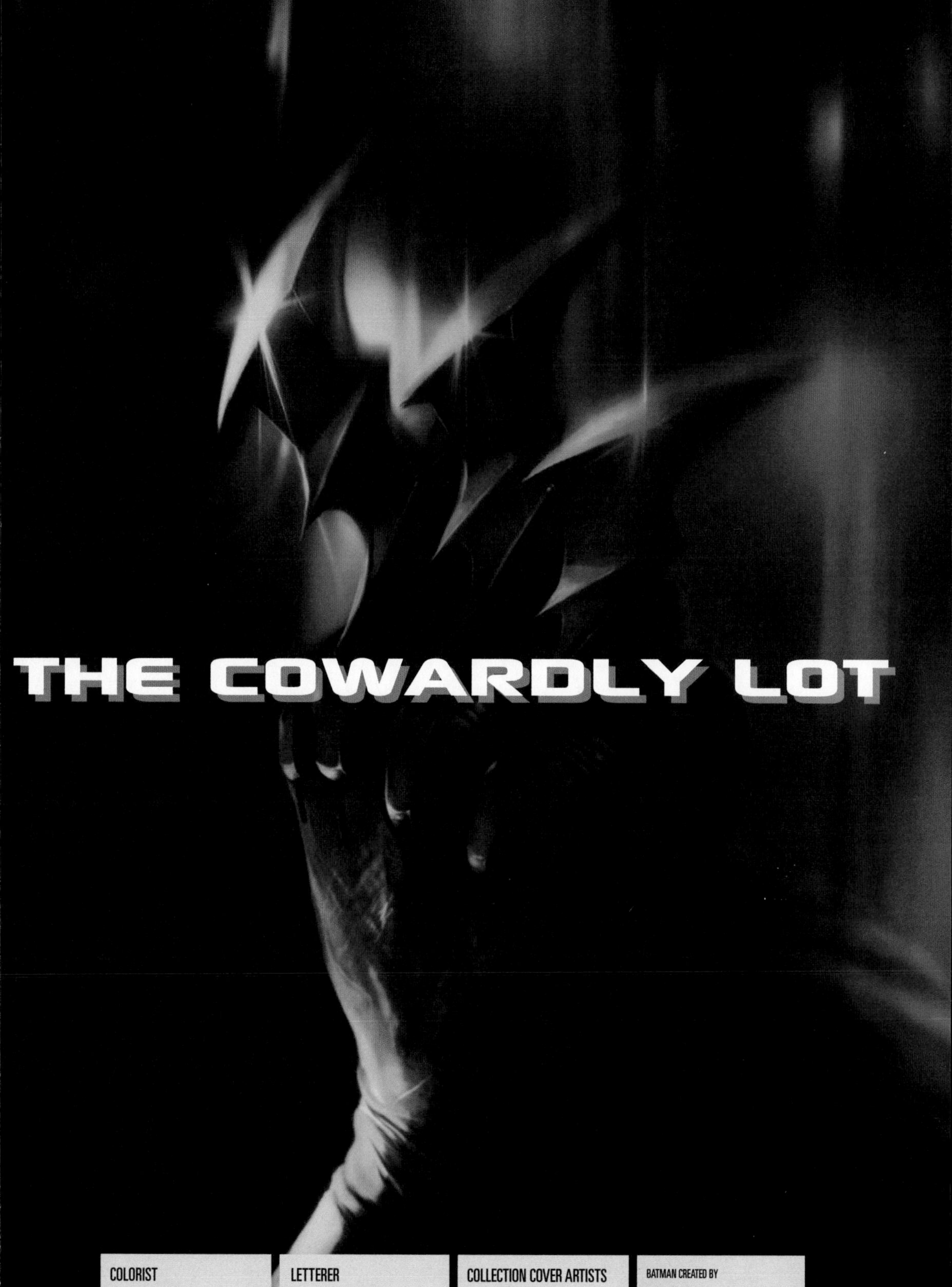

THE COWARDLY LOT

COLORIST
TOMEU MOREY

LETTERER
CLAYTON COWLES
TROY PETERI

COLLECTION COVER ARTISTS
JORGE JIMÉNEZ & TOMEU MOREY

BATMAN CREATED BY
BOB KANE WITH BILL FINGER

BEN ABERNATHY
Editor – Original Series &
Collected Edition
DAVE WIELGOSZ
Associate Editor – Original Series
STEVE COOK
Design Director – Books
LOUIS PRANDI
Publication Design
ERIN VANOVER
Publication Production

MARIE JAVINS
Editor-in-Chief, DC Comics

DANIEL CHERRY III
Senior VP – General Manager
JIM LEE
Publisher & Chief Creative Officer
JOEN CHOE
VP – Global Brand & Creative Services
DON FALLETTI
VP – Manufacturing Operations &
Workflow Management
LAWRENCE GANEM
VP – Talent Services
ALISON GILL
Senior VP – Manufacturing & Operations
NICK J. NAPOLITANO
VP – Manufacturing Administration & Design
NANCY SPEARS
VP – Revenue

BATMAN VOL. 4: THE COWARDLY LOT

Published by DC Comics. Compilation and all new material
Copyright © 2021 DC Comics. All Rights Reserved.
Originally published in single magazine form in *Batman*
#106-111 and *Infinite Frontier* #0. Copyright © 2021
DC Comics. All Rights Reserved. All characters, their
distinctive likenesses, and related elements featured in
this publication are trademarks of DC Comics. The stories,
characters, and incidents featured in this publication are
entirely fictional. DC Comics does not read or accept
unsolicited submissions of ideas, stories, or artwork.
DC – a WarnerMedia Company.

DC Comics, 2900 West Alameda Ave., Burbank, CA 91505
Printed by Transcontinental Interglobe, Beauceville, QC,
Canada. 9/14/21. First Printing.
ISBN: 978-1-77951-198-0

Library of Congress Cataloging-in-
Publication Data is available.

PEFC Certified

This product is
from sustainably
managed forests and
controlled sources

PEFC/01-31-106   www.pefc.org

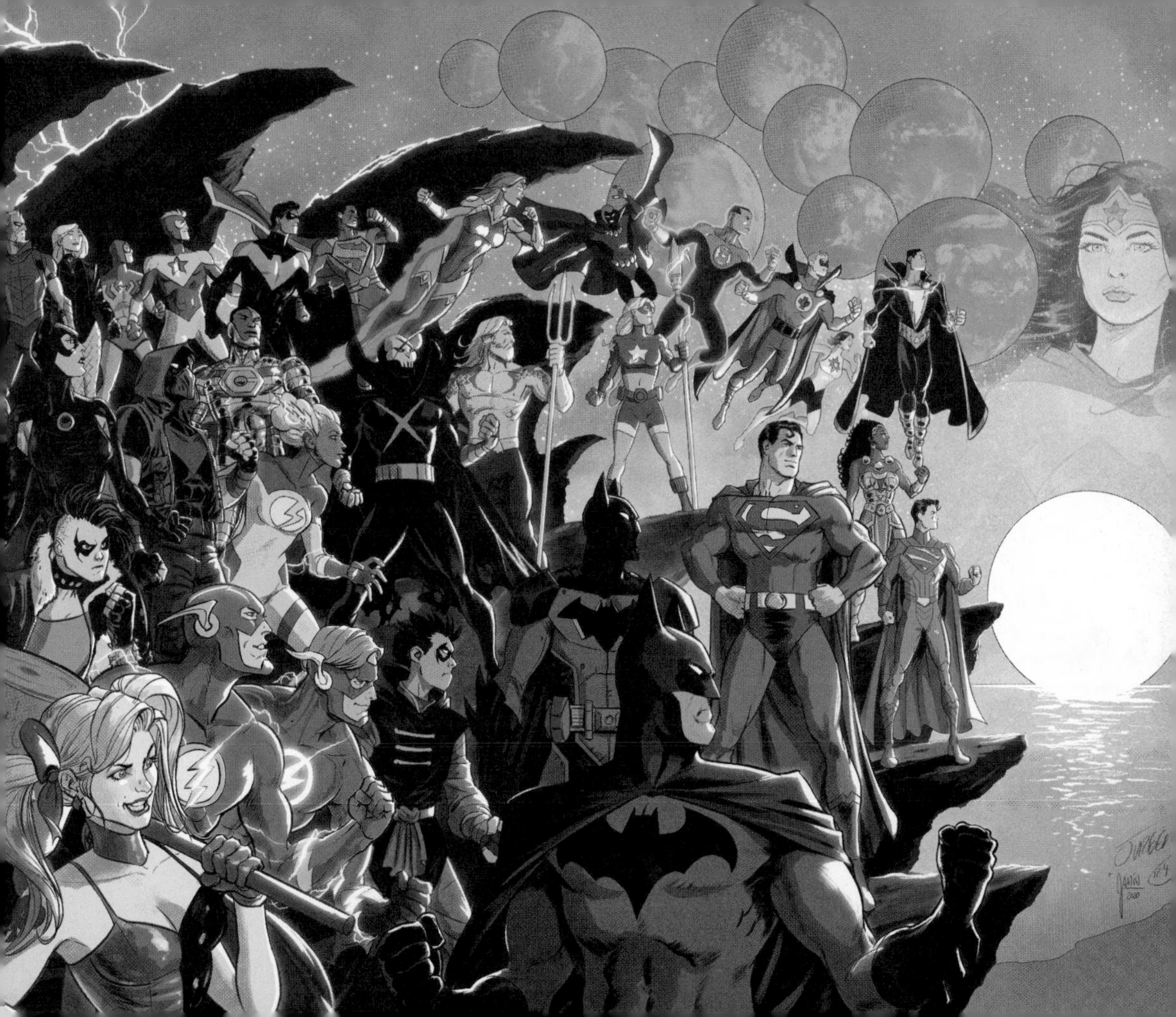

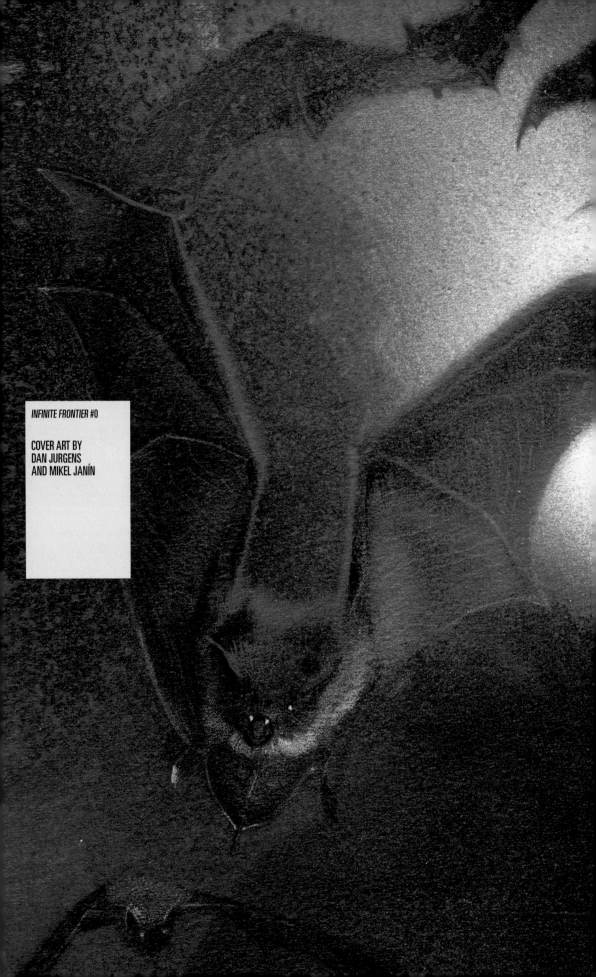

INFINITE FRONTIER #0

COVER ART BY
DAN JURGENS
AND MIKEL JANÍN

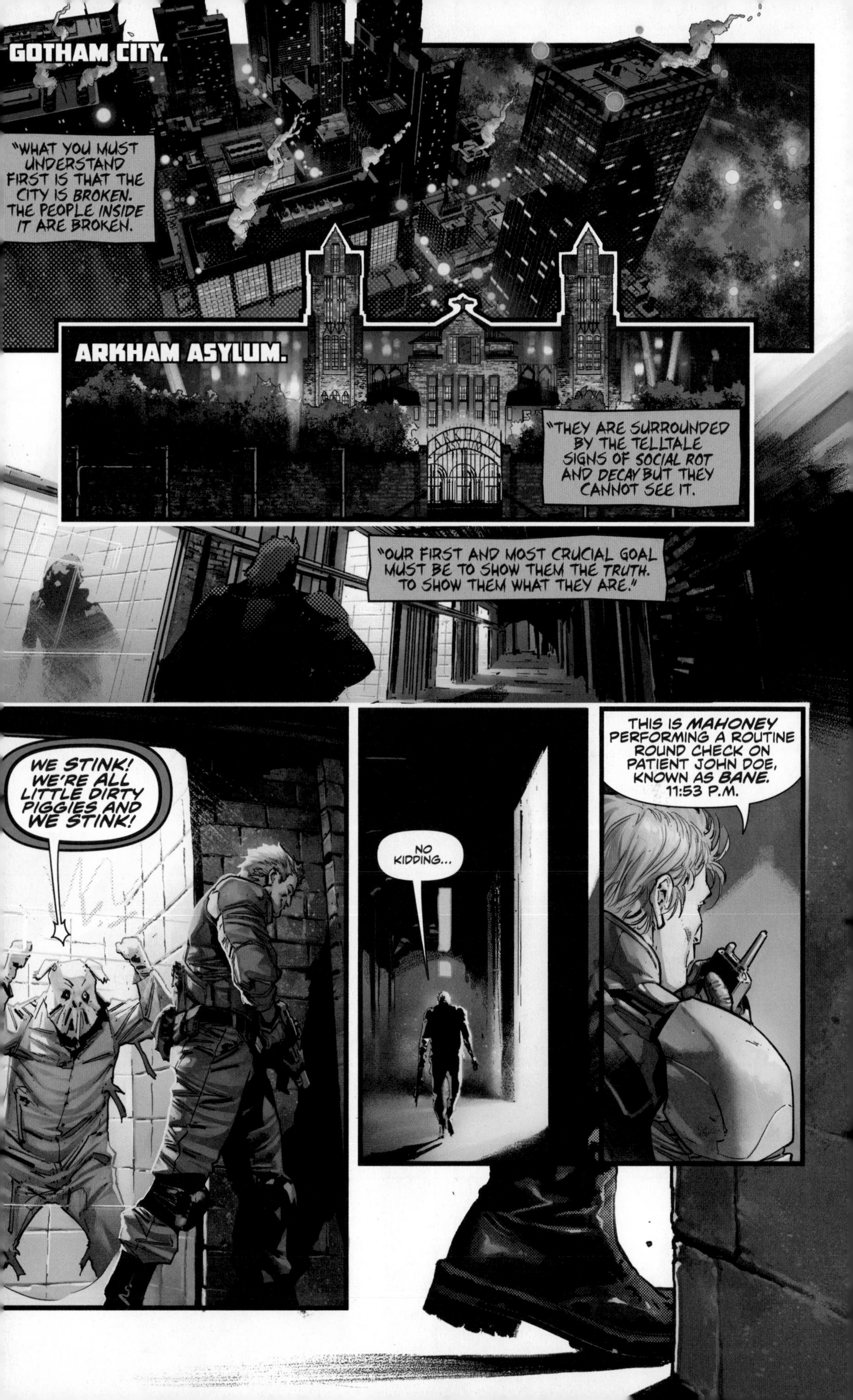
GOTHAM CITY.
"WHAT YOU MUST UNDERSTAND FIRST IS THAT THE CITY IS BROKEN. THE PEOPLE INSIDE IT ARE BROKEN.
ARKHAM ASYLUM.
"THEY ARE SURROUNDED BY THE TELLTALE SIGNS OF SOCIAL ROT AND DECAY BUT THEY CANNOT SEE IT.
"OUR FIRST AND MOST CRUCIAL GOAL MUST BE TO SHOW THEM THE TRUTH. TO SHOW THEM WHAT THEY ARE."
WE STINK! WE'RE ALL LITTLE DIRTY PIGGIES AND WE STINK!
NO KIDDING...
THIS IS MAHONEY PERFORMING A ROUTINE ROUND CHECK ON PATIENT JOHN DOE, KNOWN AS BANE. 11:53 P.M.

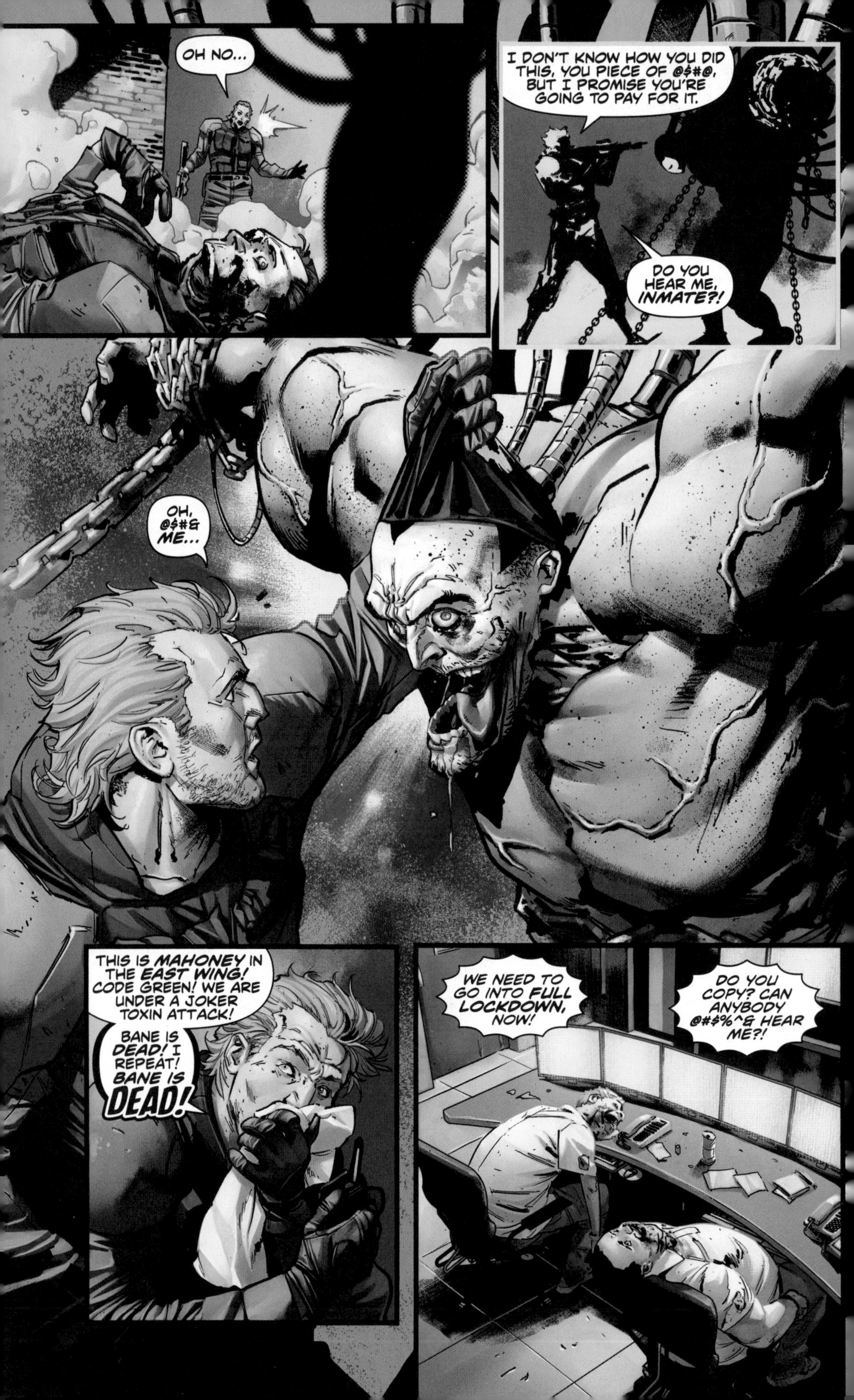
OH NO...
I DON'T KNOW HOW YOU DID THIS, YOU PIECE OF @$#@, BUT I PROMISE YOU'RE GOING TO PAY FOR IT.
DO YOU HEAR ME, INMATE?!
OH, @$#& ME...
THIS IS MAHONEY IN THE EAST WING! CODE GREEN! WE ARE UNDER A JOKER TOXIN ATTACK!
BANE IS DEAD! I REPEAT! BANE IS DEAD!
WE NEED TO GO INTO FULL LOCKDOWN, NOW!
DO YOU COPY? CAN ANYBODY @#$%^& HEAR ME?!

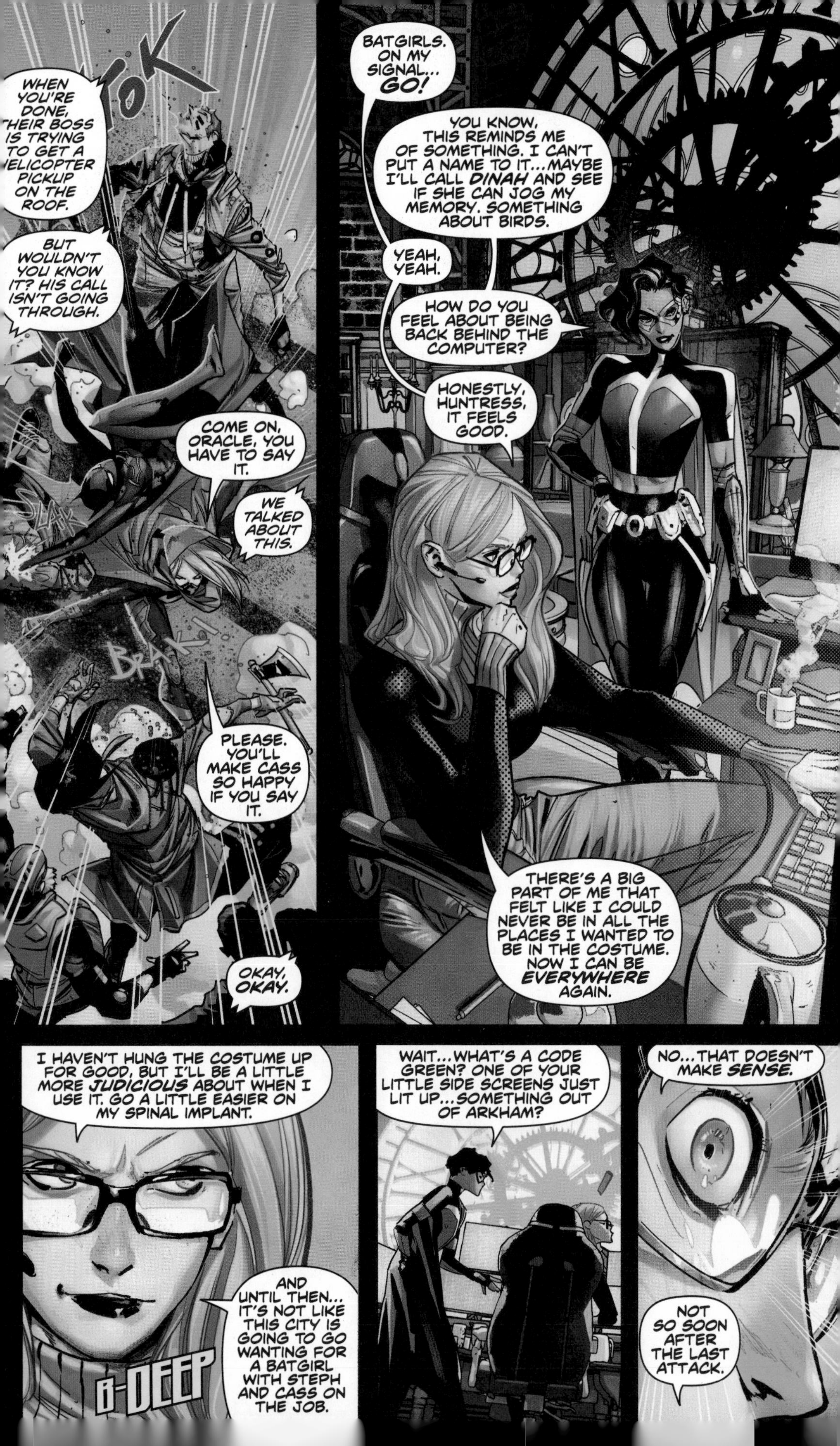

TOK
WHEN YOU'RE DONE, THEIR BOSS IS TRYING TO GET A HELICOPTER PICKUP ON THE ROOF.
BUT WOULDN'T YOU KNOW IT? HIS CALL ISN'T GOING THROUGH.
COME ON, ORACLE, YOU HAVE TO SAY IT.
WE TALKED ABOUT THIS.
BRAK
PLEASE. YOU'LL MAKE CASS SO HAPPY IF YOU SAY IT.
OKAY, OKAY.
BATGIRLS. ON MY SIGNAL... GO!
YOU KNOW, THIS REMINDS ME OF SOMETHING. I CAN'T PUT A NAME TO IT... MAYBE I'LL CALL DINAH AND SEE IF SHE CAN JOG MY MEMORY. SOMETHING ABOUT BIRDS.
YEAH, YEAH.
HOW DO YOU FEEL ABOUT BEING BACK BEHIND THE COMPUTER?
HONESTLY, HUNTRESS, IT FEELS GOOD.
THERE'S A BIG PART OF ME THAT FELT LIKE I COULD NEVER BE IN ALL THE PLACES I WANTED TO BE IN THE COSTUME. NOW I CAN BE EVERYWHERE AGAIN.
I HAVEN'T HUNG THE COSTUME UP FOR GOOD, BUT I'LL BE A LITTLE MORE JUDICIOUS ABOUT WHEN I USE IT. GO A LITTLE EASIER ON MY SPINAL IMPLANT.
AND UNTIL THEN... IT'S NOT LIKE THIS CITY IS GOING TO GO WANTING FOR A BATGIRL WITH STEPH AND CASS ON THE JOB.
B-DEEP
WAIT... WHAT'S A CODE GREEN? ONE OF YOUR LITTLE SIDE SCREENS JUST LIT UP... SOMETHING OUT OF ARKHAM?
NO... THAT DOESN'T MAKE SENSE.
NOT SO SOON AFTER THE LAST ATTACK.

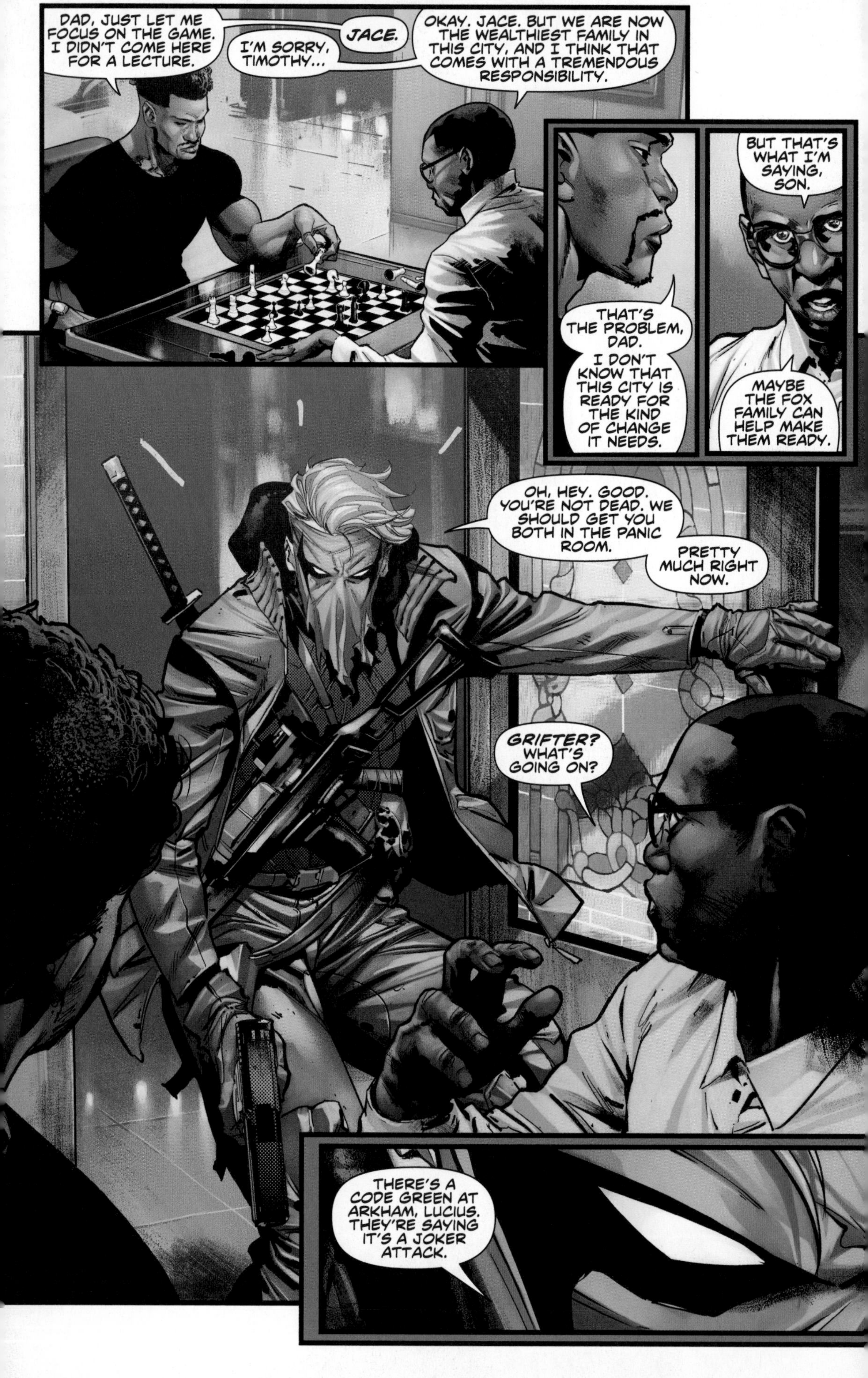
DAD, JUST LET ME FOCUS ON THE GAME. I DIDN'T COME HERE FOR A LECTURE.
JACE.
I'M SORRY, TIMOTHY...
OKAY. JACE. BUT WE ARE NOW THE WEALTHIEST FAMILY IN THIS CITY, AND I THINK THAT COMES WITH A TREMENDOUS RESPONSIBILITY.
THAT'S THE PROBLEM, DAD.
I DON'T KNOW THAT THIS CITY IS READY FOR THE KIND OF CHANGE IT NEEDS.
BUT THAT'S WHAT I'M SAYING, SON.
MAYBE THE FOX FAMILY CAN HELP MAKE THEM READY.
OH, HEY. GOOD. YOU'RE NOT DEAD. WE SHOULD GET YOU BOTH IN THE PANIC ROOM.
PRETTY MUCH RIGHT NOW.
GRIFTER? WHAT'S GOING ON?
THERE'S A CODE GREEN AT ARKHAM, LUCIUS. THEY'RE SAYING IT'S A JOKER ATTACK.

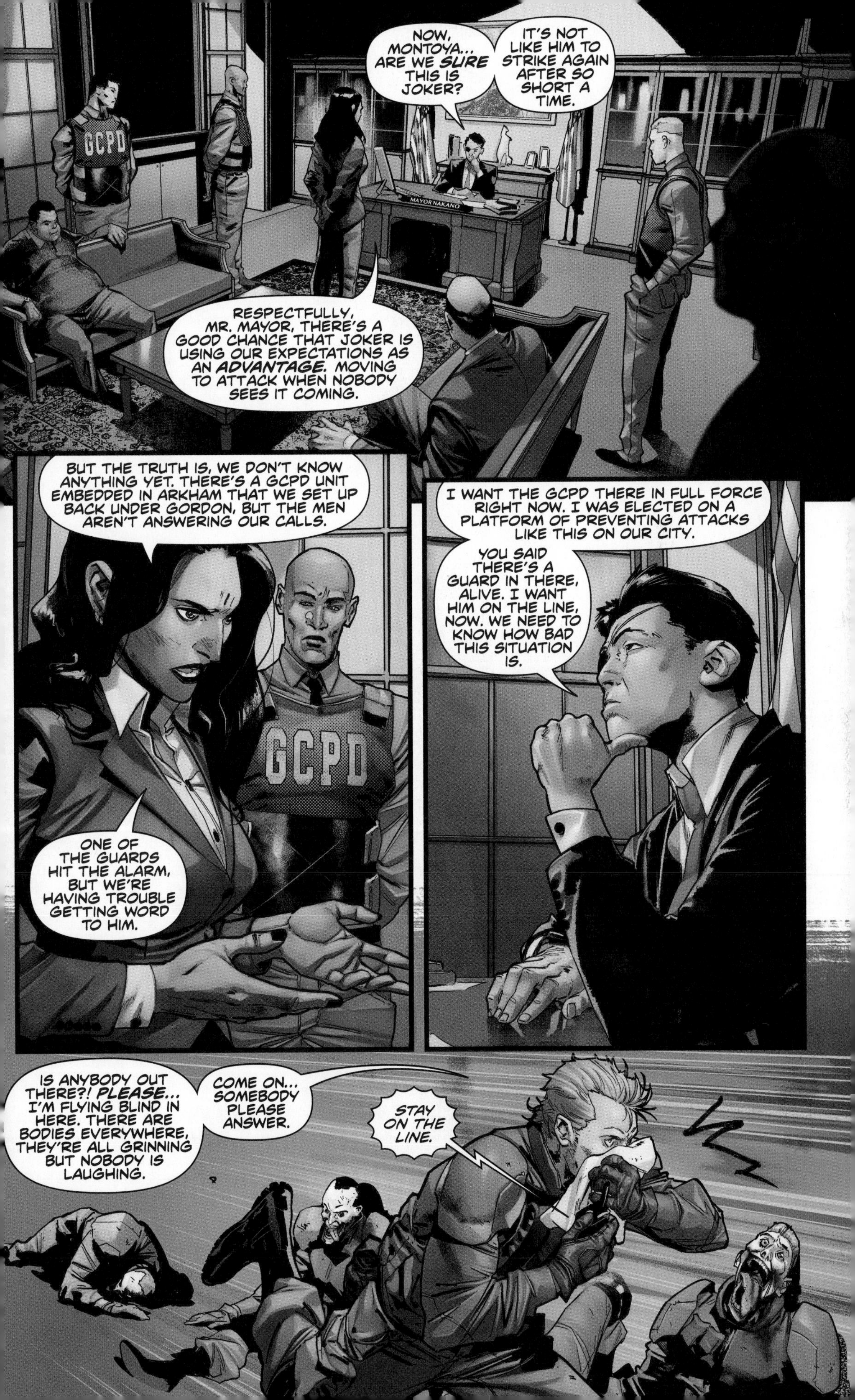
NOW, MONTOYA... ARE WE SURE THIS IS JOKER?
IT'S NOT LIKE HIM TO STRIKE AGAIN AFTER SO SHORT A TIME.
MAYOR NAKANO
RESPECTFULLY, MR. MAYOR, THERE'S A GOOD CHANCE THAT JOKER IS USING OUR EXPECTATIONS AS AN ADVANTAGE. MOVING TO ATTACK WHEN NOBODY SEES IT COMING.
BUT THE TRUTH IS, WE DON'T KNOW ANYTHING YET. THERE'S A GCPD UNIT EMBEDDED IN ARKHAM THAT WE SET UP BACK UNDER GORDON, BUT THE MEN AREN'T ANSWERING OUR CALLS.
ONE OF THE GUARDS HIT THE ALARM, BUT WE'RE HAVING TROUBLE GETTING WORD TO HIM.
GCPD
I WANT THE GCPD THERE IN FULL FORCE RIGHT NOW. I WAS ELECTED ON A PLATFORM OF PREVENTING ATTACKS LIKE THIS ON OUR CITY.
YOU SAID THERE'S A GUARD IN THERE, ALIVE. I WANT HIM ON THE LINE, NOW. WE NEED TO KNOW HOW BAD THIS SITUATION IS.
IS ANYBODY OUT THERE?! PLEASE... I'M FLYING BLIND IN HERE. THERE ARE BODIES EVERYWHERE, THEY'RE ALL GRINNING BUT NOBODY IS LAUGHING.
COME ON... SOMEBODY PLEASE ANSWER.
STAY ON THE LINE.

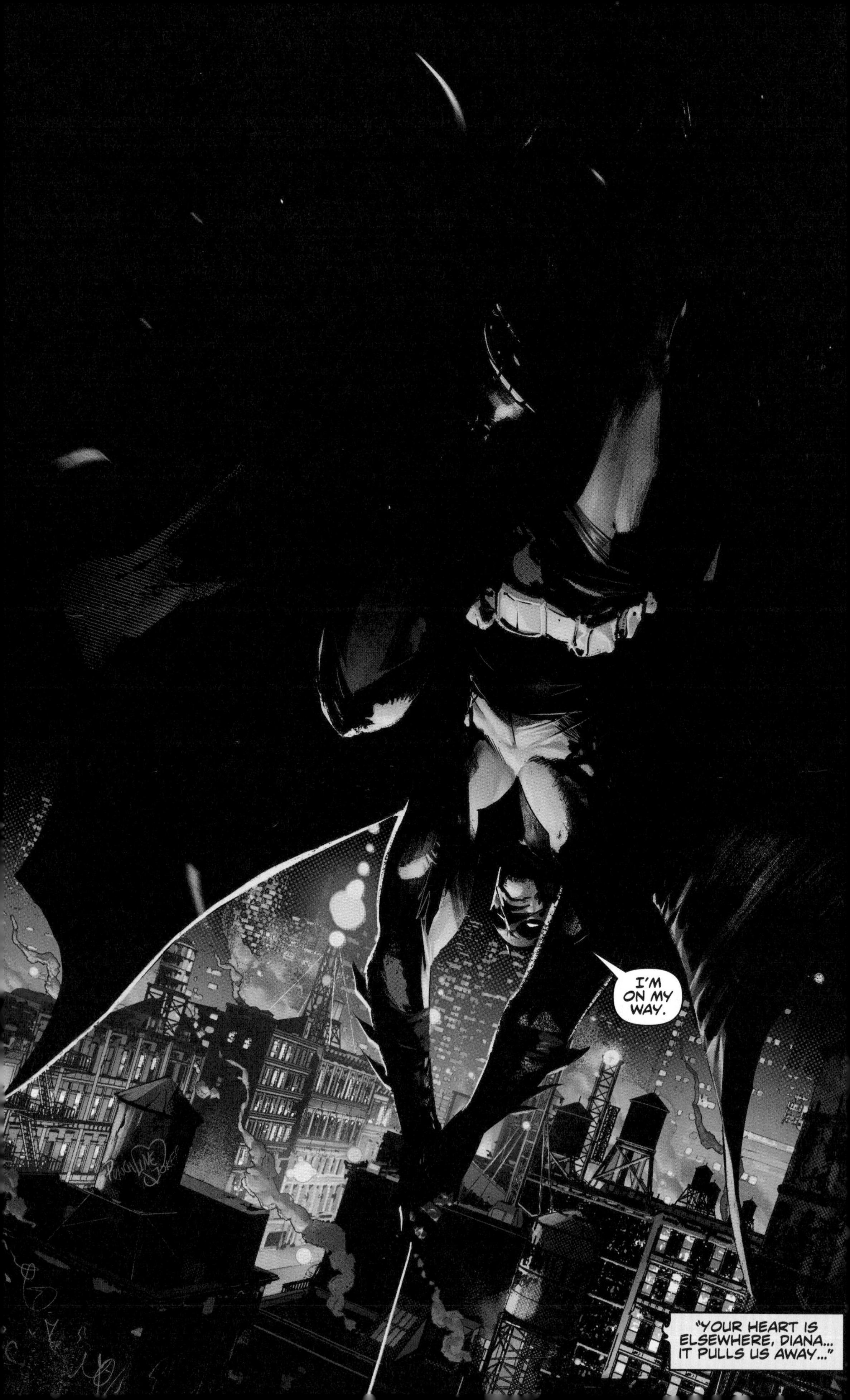

I'M ON MY WAY.
"YOUR HEART IS ELSEWHERE, DIANA... IT PULLS US AWAY..."

SEAN MAHONEY. I NEED YOU TO KEEP TALKING TO ME.

Y-YEAH. OKAY. SORRY...I'VE NEVER SEEN SO MANY BODIES.

IT'S OKAY. YOU'RE GOING TO BE OKAY. KEEP YOUR MOUTH COVERED AND TELL ME WHAT YOU SEE.

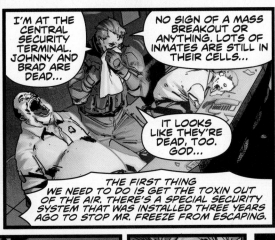

I'M AT THE CENTRAL SECURITY TERMINAL. JOHNNY AND BRAD ARE DEAD...

NO SIGN OF A MASS BREAKOUT OR ANYTHING. LOTS OF INMATES ARE STILL IN THEIR CELLS...

IT LOOKS LIKE THEY'RE DEAD, TOO. GOD...

THE FIRST THING WE NEED TO DO IS GET THE TOXIN OUT OF THE AIR. THERE'S A SPECIAL SECURITY SYSTEM THAT WAS INSTALLED THREE YEARS AGO TO STOP MR. FREEZE FROM ESCAPING.

IT'S A PROTOCOL TO SUPERHEAT THE AIR, AND IT SHOULD BURN OUT THE EXCESS TOXIN. ENTER THE COMMAND CODE 121.

OKAY, DONE.

NOW GET OUTSIDE... I'M ON MY WAY.

WAIT... CRAP, I DIDN'T SEE THEM...

SOME NURSES, THEY'RE USING OXYGEN IN A STORAGE ROOM TO STAY ALIVE. BUT WHEN THE FIRE GETS TO THEM... OH GOD, BATMAN...

BROOMM BROMM!

TELL ME YOU'RE ALMOST HERE!

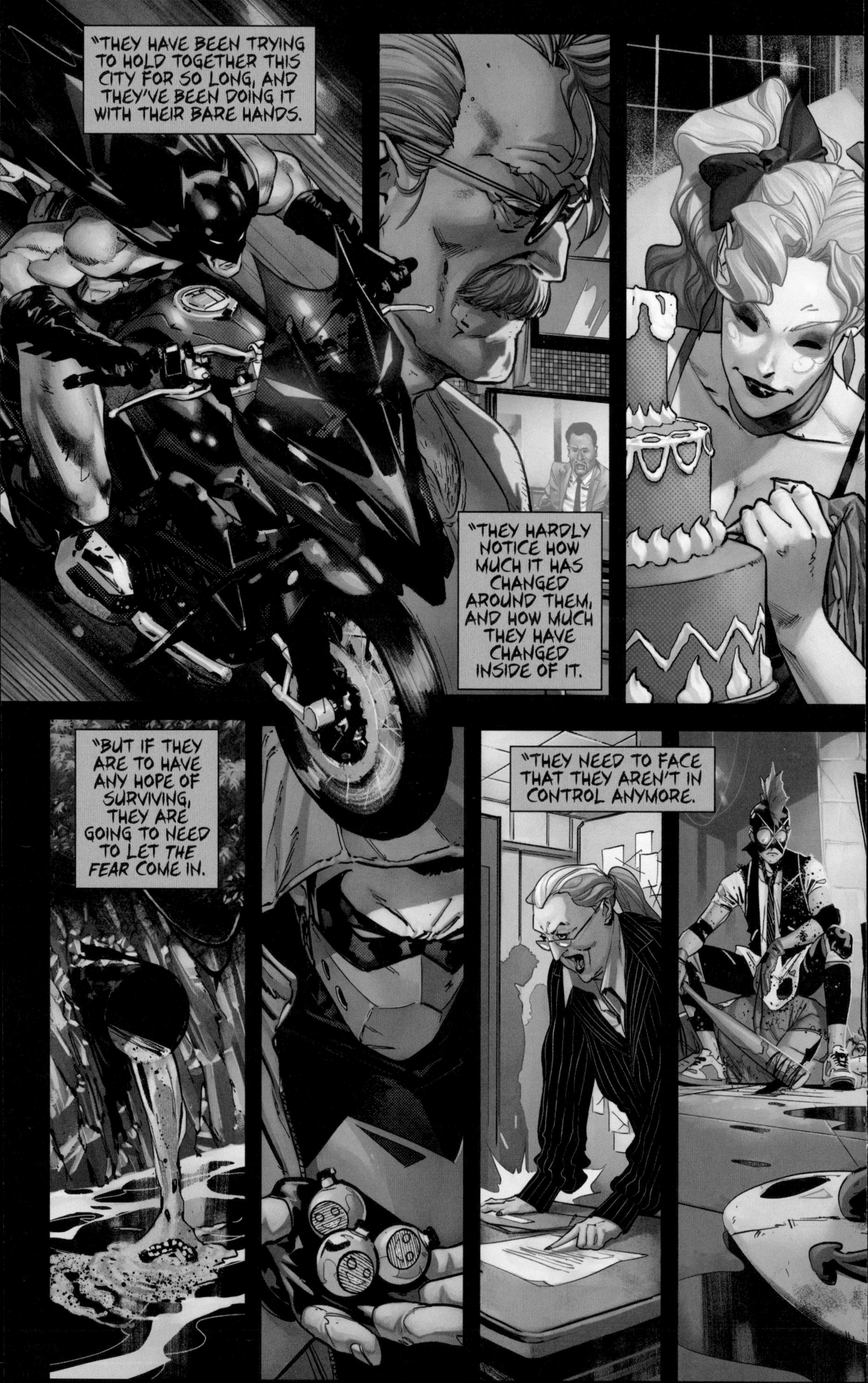
"THEY HAVE BEEN TRYING TO HOLD TOGETHER THIS CITY FOR SO LONG, AND THEY'VE BEEN DOING IT WITH THEIR BARE HANDS.
"THEY HARDLY NOTICE HOW MUCH IT HAS CHANGED AROUND THEM, AND HOW MUCH THEY HAVE CHANGED INSIDE OF IT.
"BUT IF THEY ARE TO HAVE ANY HOPE OF SURVIVING, THEY ARE GOING TO NEED TO LET THE FEAR COME IN.
"THEY NEED TO FACE THAT THEY AREN'T IN CONTROL ANYMORE.

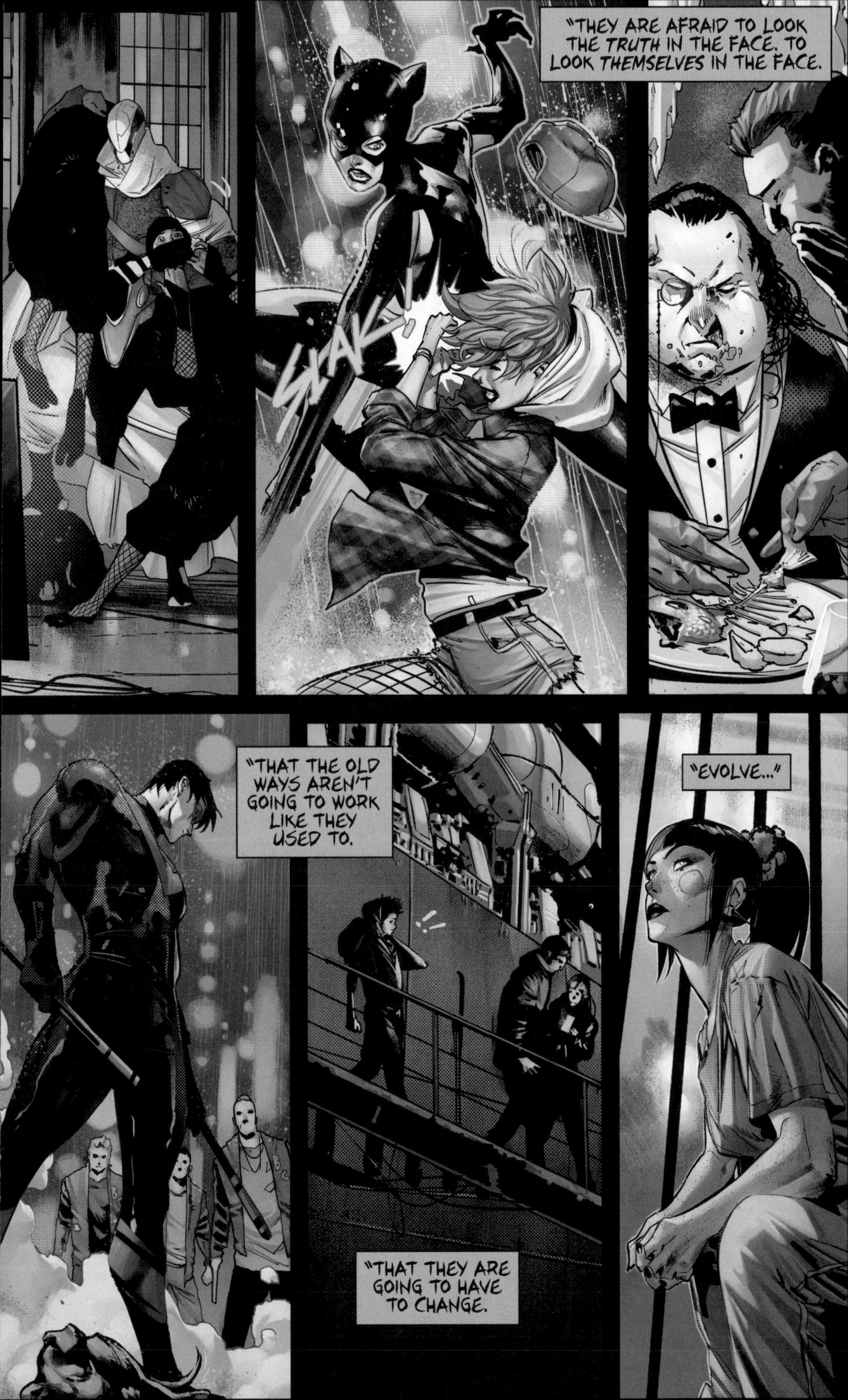
"THEY ARE AFRAID TO LOOK THE TRUTH IN THE FACE. TO LOOK THEMSELVES IN THE FACE.
SKAK!
"THAT THE OLD WAYS AREN'T GOING TO WORK LIKE THEY USED TO.
"THAT THEY ARE GOING TO HAVE TO CHANGE.
"EVOLVE..."

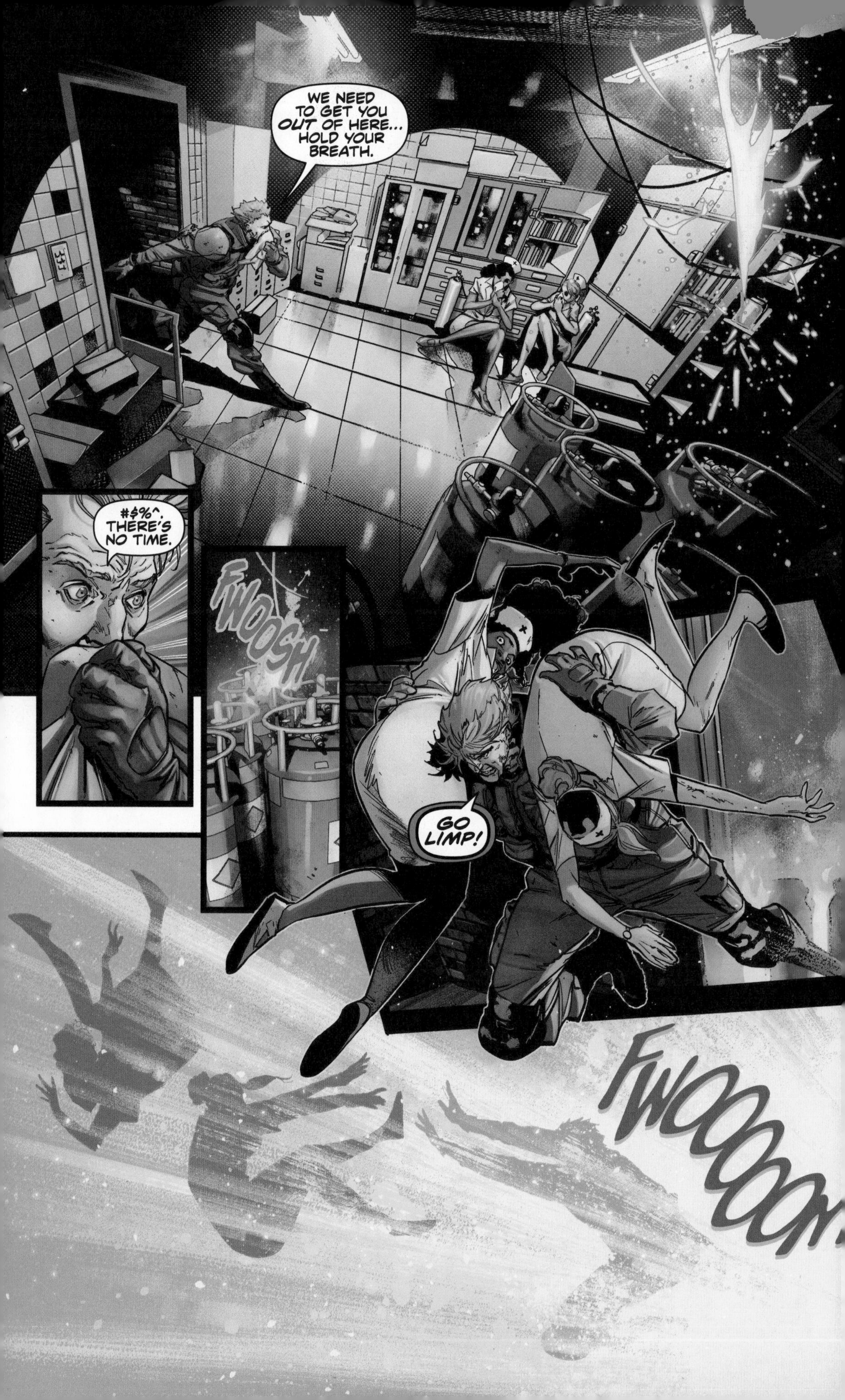
WE NEED TO GET YOU OUT OF HERE... HOLD YOUR BREATH.
#$%^. THERE'S NO TIME.
FWOOSH
GO LIMP!
FWOOOOM!

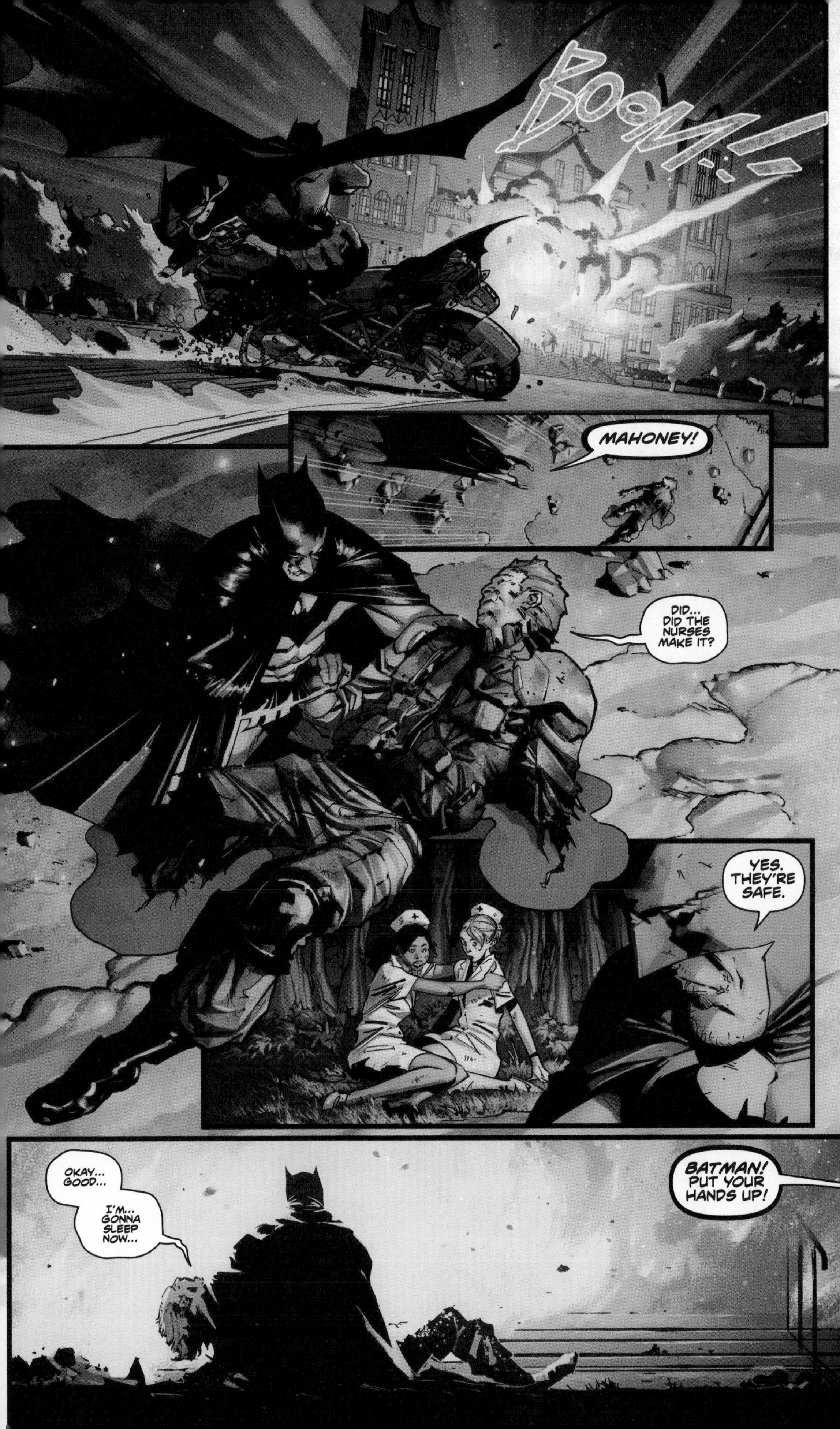
BOOM!!
MAHONEY!
DID... DID THE NURSES MAKE IT?
YES. THEY'RE SAFE.
OKAY... GOOD...
I'M... GONNA SLEEP NOW...
BATMAN! PUT YOUR HANDS UP!

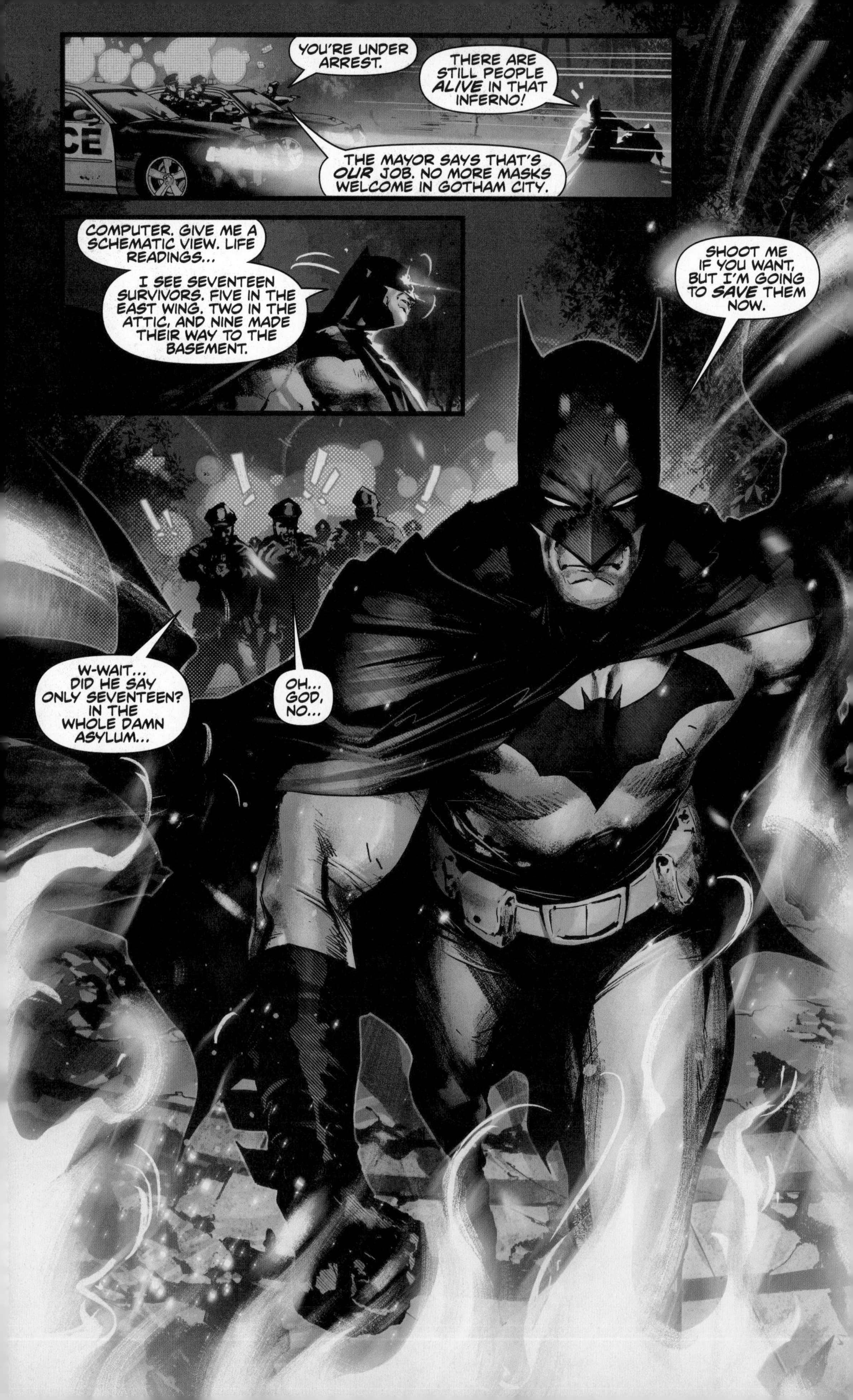
YOU'RE UNDER ARREST.
THERE ARE STILL PEOPLE *ALIVE* IN THAT INFERNO!
THE MAYOR SAYS THAT'S *OUR* JOB. NO MORE MASKS WELCOME IN GOTHAM CITY.
COMPUTER. GIVE ME A SCHEMATIC VIEW. LIFE READINGS...
I SEE SEVENTEEN SURVIVORS. FIVE IN THE EAST WING. TWO IN THE ATTIC, AND NINE MADE THEIR WAY TO THE BASEMENT.
SHOOT ME IF YOU WANT, BUT I'M GOING TO *SAVE* THEM NOW.
W-WAIT... DID HE SAY ONLY SEVENTEEN? IN THE WHOLE DAMN ASYLUM...
OH... GOD, NO...

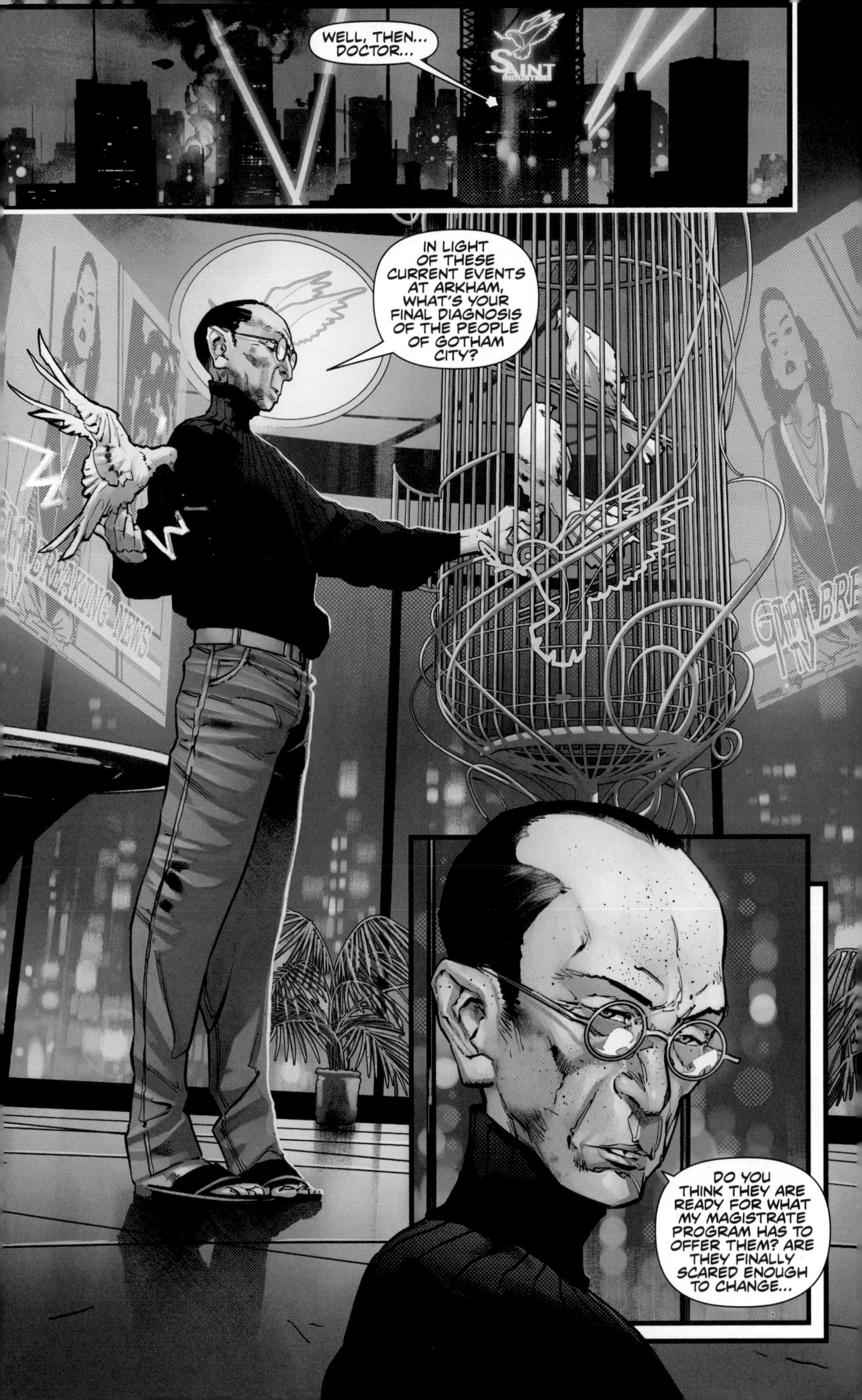
WELL, THEN... DOCTOR...
SAINT INDUSTRIES
IN LIGHT OF THESE CURRENT EVENTS AT ARKHAM, WHAT'S YOUR FINAL DIAGNOSIS OF THE PEOPLE OF GOTHAM CITY?
BREAKING NEWS
DO YOU THINK THEY ARE READY FOR WHAT MY MAGISTRATE PROGRAM HAS TO OFFER THEM? ARE THEY FINALLY SCARED ENOUGH TO CHANGE...

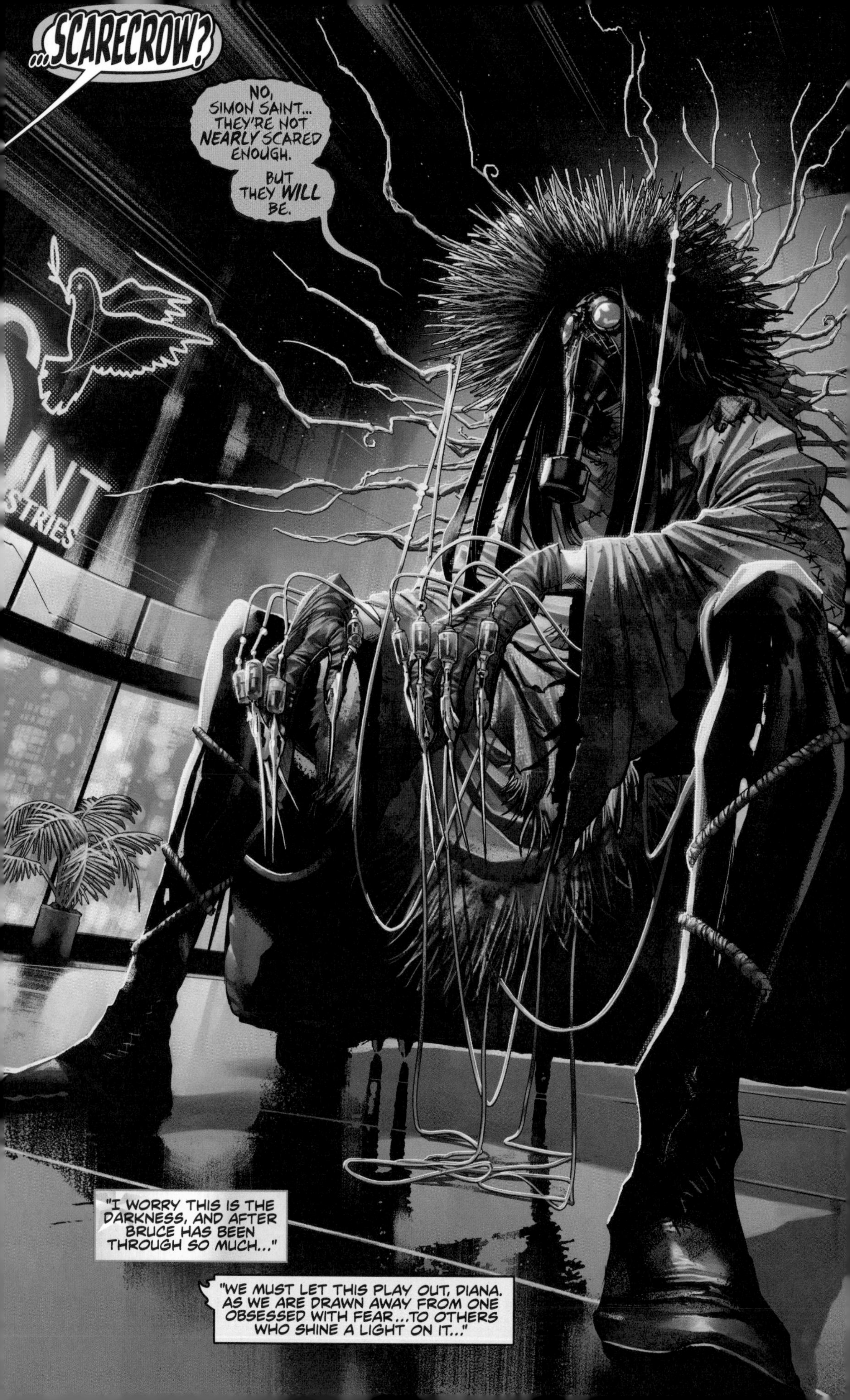
...SCARECROW?
NO, SIMON SAINT... THEY'RE NOT NEARLY SCARED ENOUGH.
BUT THEY WILL BE.
"I WORRY THIS IS THE DARKNESS, AND AFTER BRUCE HAS BEEN THROUGH SO MUCH..."
"WE MUST LET THIS PLAY OUT, DIANA. AS WE ARE DRAWN AWAY FROM ONE OBSESSED WITH FEAR...TO OTHERS WHO SHINE A LIGHT ON IT..."

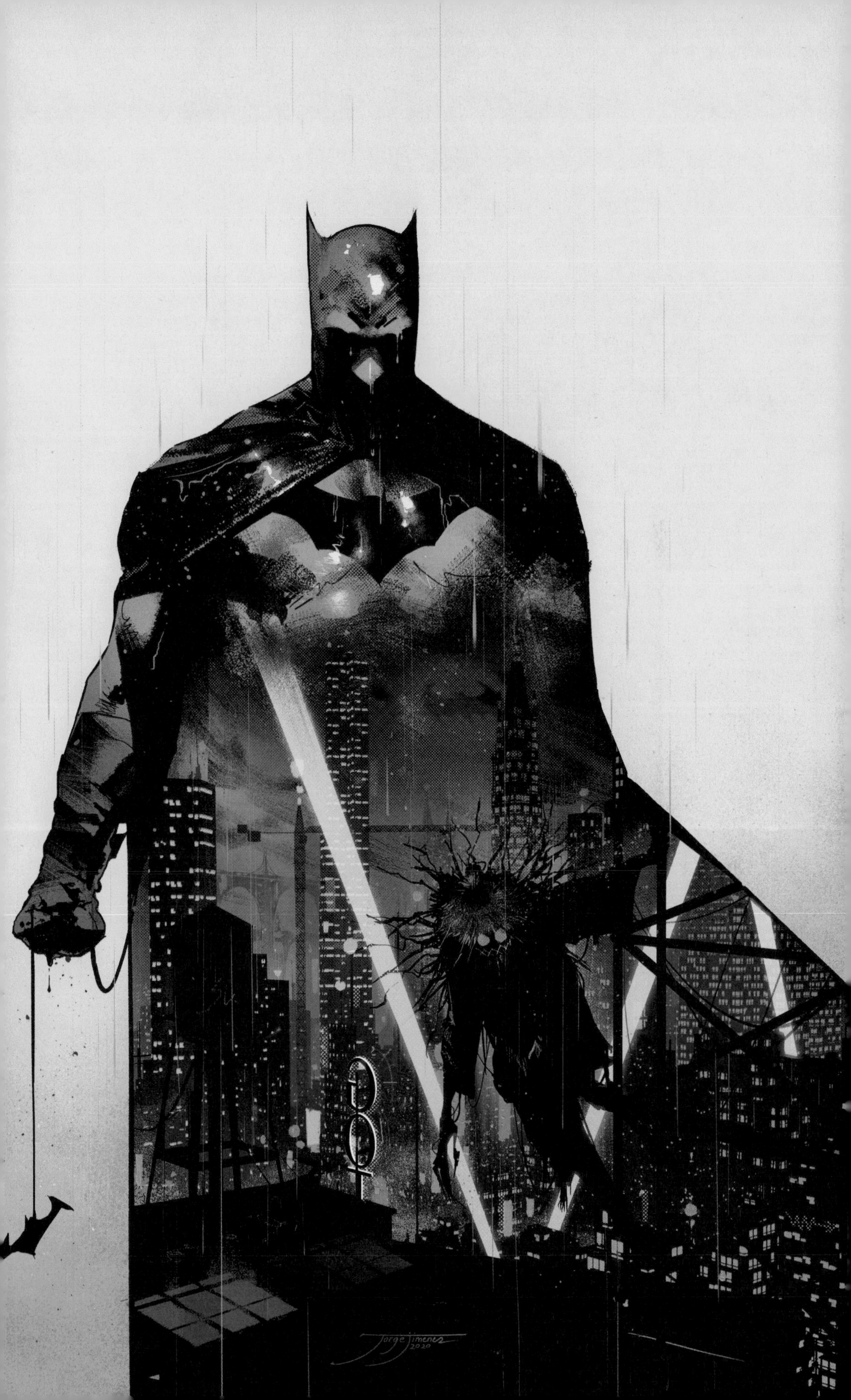
Jorge Jimenez
2020

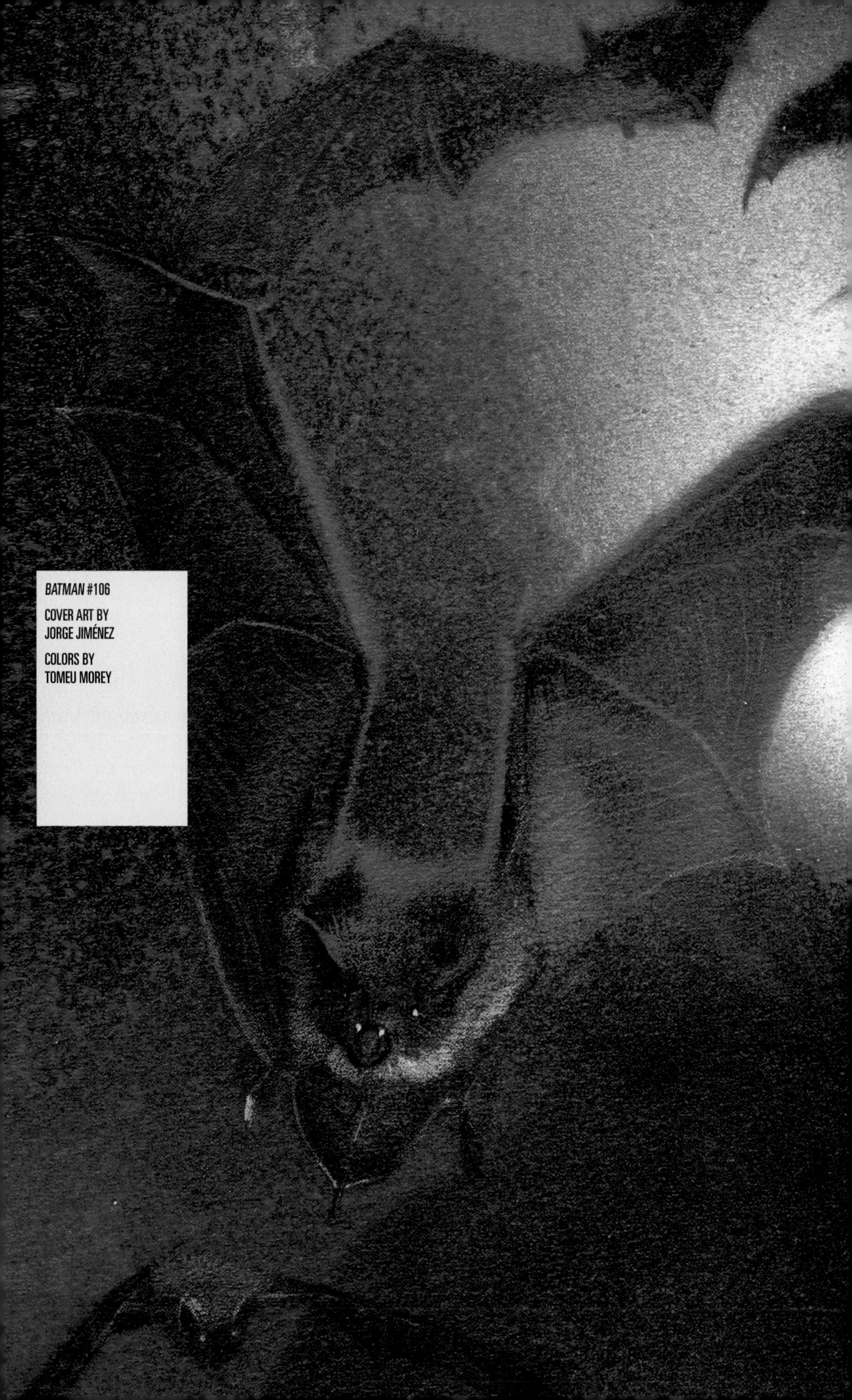

BATMAN #106

COVER ART BY
JORGE JIMÉNEZ

COLORS BY
TOMEU MOREY

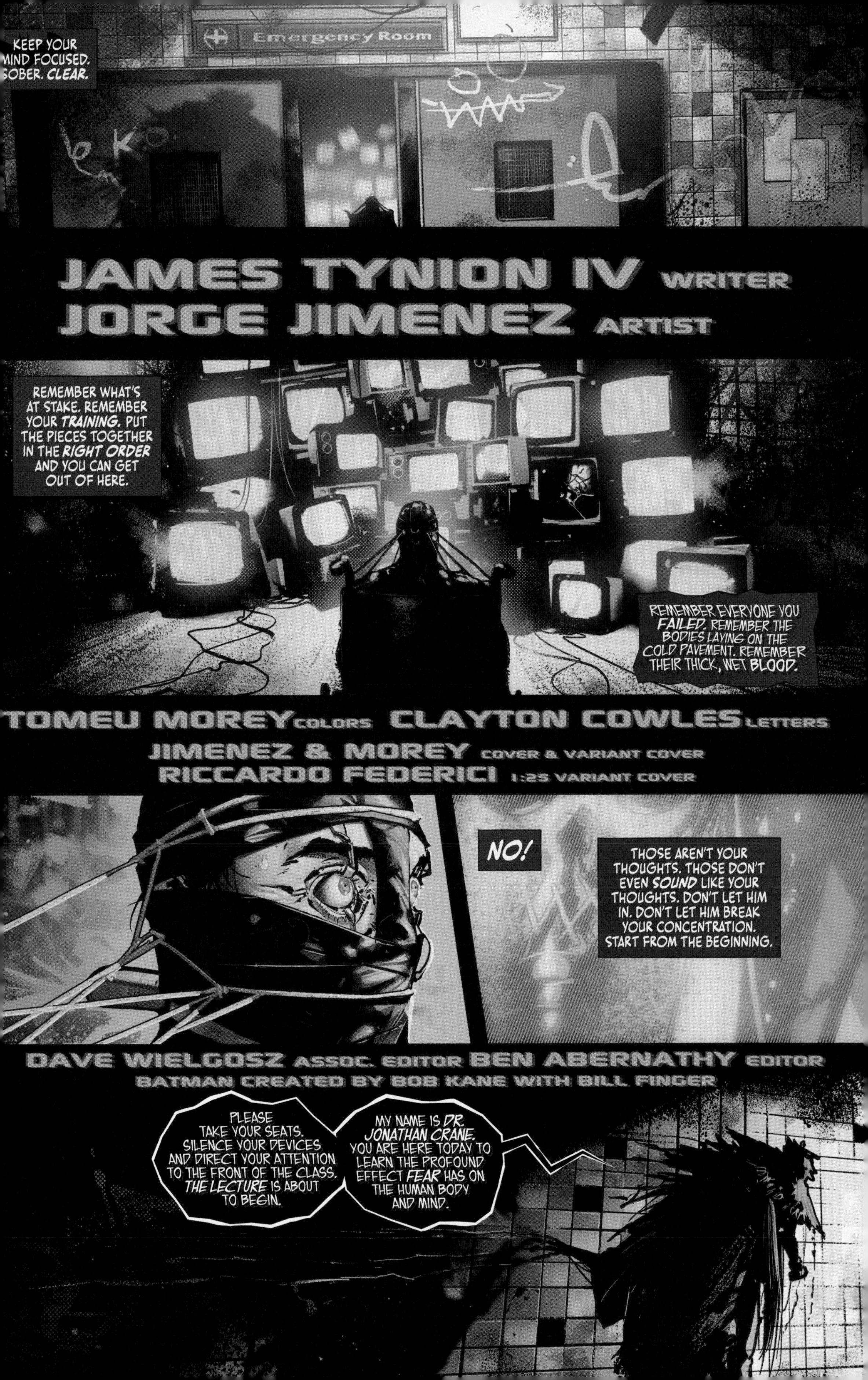

Emergency Room
KEEP YOUR MIND FOCUSED. SOBER. CLEAR.
JAMES TYNION IV WRITER
JORGE JIMENEZ ARTIST
REMEMBER WHAT'S AT STAKE. REMEMBER YOUR TRAINING. PUT THE PIECES TOGETHER IN THE RIGHT ORDER AND YOU CAN GET OUT OF HERE.
REMEMBER EVERYONE YOU FAILED. REMEMBER THE BODIES LAYING ON THE COLD PAVEMENT. REMEMBER THEIR THICK, WET BLOOD.
TOMEU MOREY COLORS CLAYTON COWLES LETTERS
JIMENEZ & MOREY COVER & VARIANT COVER
RICCARDO FEDERICI 1:25 VARIANT COVER
NO!
THOSE AREN'T YOUR THOUGHTS. THOSE DON'T EVEN SOUND LIKE YOUR THOUGHTS. DON'T LET HIM IN. DON'T LET HIM BREAK YOUR CONCENTRATION. START FROM THE BEGINNING.
DAVE WIELGOSZ ASSOC. EDITOR BEN ABERNATHY EDITOR
BATMAN CREATED BY BOB KANE WITH BILL FINGER
PLEASE TAKE YOUR SEATS. SILENCE YOUR DEVICES AND DIRECT YOUR ATTENTION TO THE FRONT OF THE CLASS. THE LECTURE IS ABOUT TO BEGIN.
MY NAME IS DR. JONATHAN CRANE. YOU ARE HERE TODAY TO LEARN THE PROFOUND EFFECT FEAR HAS ON THE HUMAN BODY AND MIND.

WE START OUR LESSON WITH THE MOST IMPORTANT QUESTION.
WHY DO WE FEAR?
Occupational therapy
TOILETS
TUNE HIM OUT. DON'T LET HIS VOICE INTO YOUR HEAD. YOU JUST NEED TO FOCUS. WHERE DID IT START...WAS IT ARKHAM? THE GAS ATTACK? THE EXPLOSION?
NO. THAT WAS *BEFORE*... I WAS DRIVING. I WAS DRIVING AND A WOMAN'S VOICE ASKED IF I WAS SURE THIS WAS MY CITY ANYMORE.
OR WAS THAT ANOTHER VOICE? ANOTHER WOMAN?
OR WAS IT **HIM?** HIS VOICE SOUNDS LIKE NEEDLES SCRAPING ON THE INSIDE OF MY SKULL...I *CAN'T* STOP MYSELF FROM LISTENING.
BATMAN
THE COWARDLY LOT
PART ONE

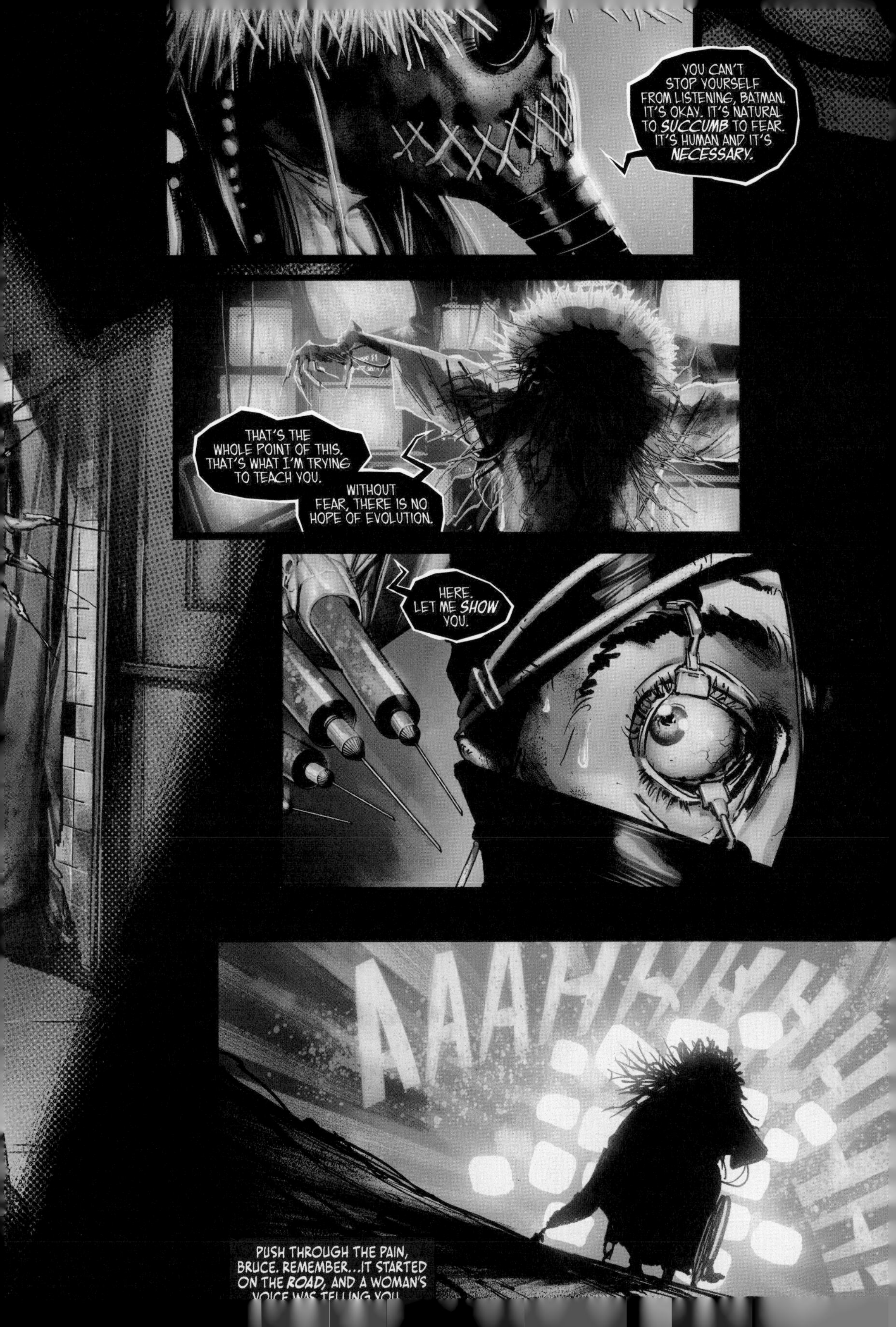
YOU CAN'T STOP YOURSELF FROM LISTENING, BATMAN. IT'S OKAY. IT'S NATURAL TO SUCCUMB TO FEAR. IT'S HUMAN AND IT'S NECESSARY.
THAT'S THE WHOLE POINT OF THIS. THAT'S WHAT I'M TRYING TO TEACH YOU.
WITHOUT FEAR, THERE IS NO HOPE OF EVOLUTION.
HERE. LET ME SHOW YOU.
AAAHHHHH
PUSH THROUGH THE PAIN, BRUCE. REMEMBER...IT STARTED ON THE ROAD, AND A WOMAN'S

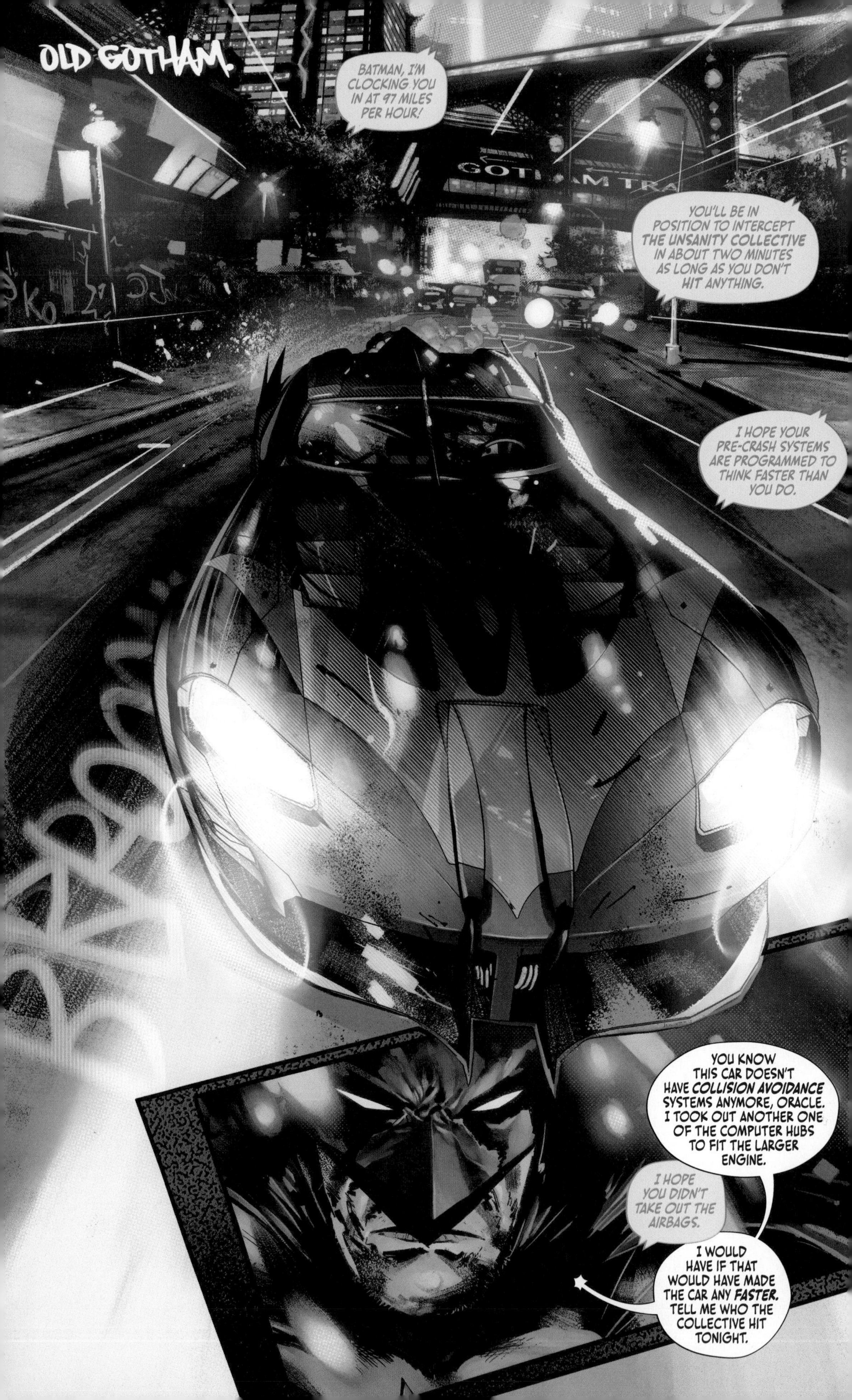
OLD GOTHAM.
BATMAN, I'M CLOCKING YOU IN AT 97 MILES PER HOUR!
GOTHAM TRA
YOU'LL BE IN POSITION TO INTERCEPT THE UNSANITY COLLECTIVE IN ABOUT TWO MINUTES AS LONG AS YOU DON'T HIT ANYTHING.
I HOPE YOUR PRE-CRASH SYSTEMS ARE PROGRAMMED TO THINK FASTER THAN YOU DO.
YOU KNOW THIS CAR DOESN'T HAVE COLLISION AVOIDANCE SYSTEMS ANYMORE, ORACLE. I TOOK OUT ANOTHER ONE OF THE COMPUTER HUBS TO FIT THE LARGER ENGINE.
I HOPE YOU DIDN'T TAKE OUT THE AIRBAGS.
I WOULD HAVE IF THAT WOULD HAVE MADE THE CAR ANY FASTER. TELL ME WHO THE COLLECTIVE HIT TONIGHT.

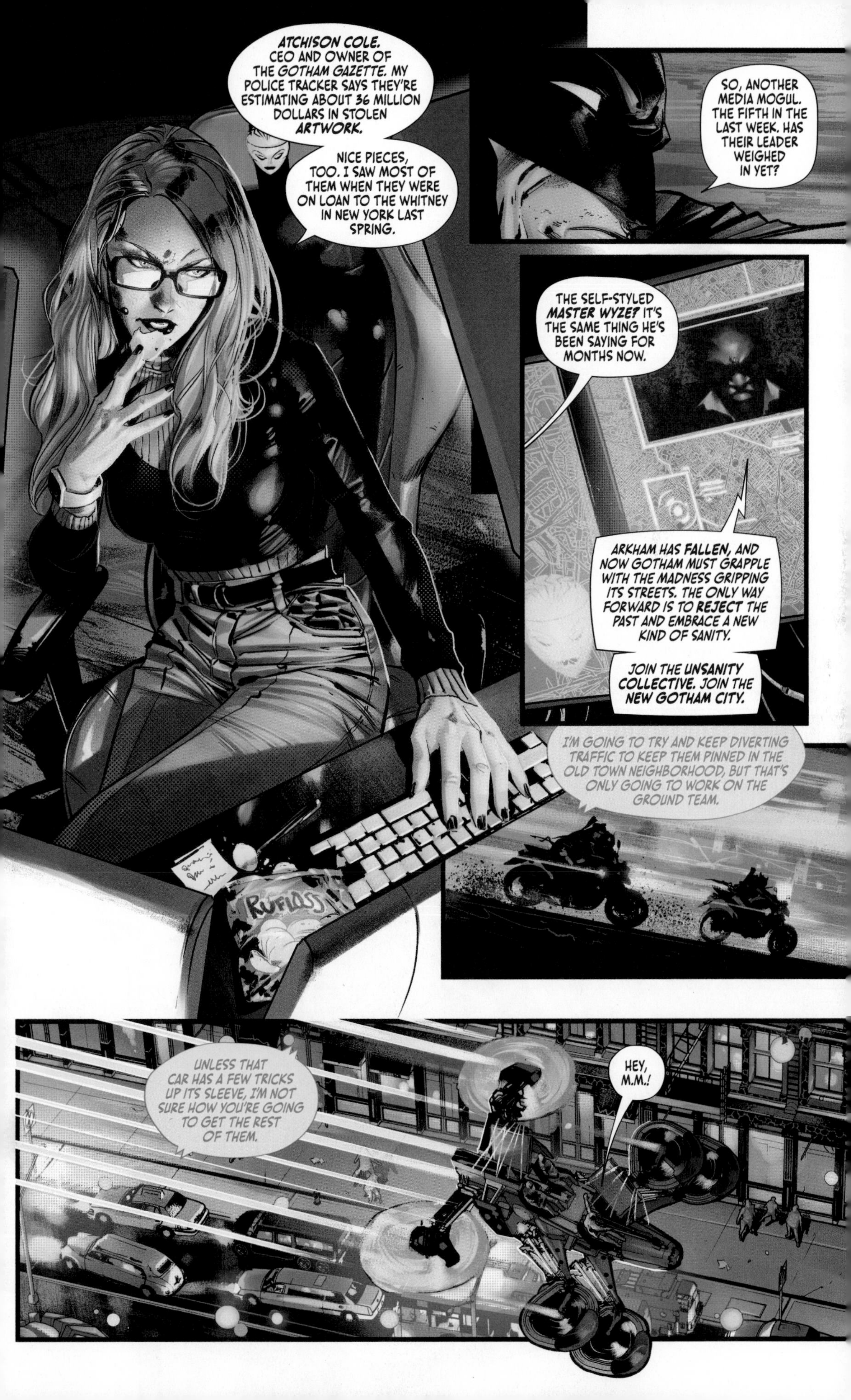
ATCHISON COLE. CEO AND OWNER OF THE GOTHAM GAZETTE. MY POLICE TRACKER SAYS THEY'RE ESTIMATING ABOUT 36 MILLION DOLLARS IN STOLEN ARTWORK.
NICE PIECES, TOO. I SAW MOST OF THEM WHEN THEY WERE ON LOAN TO THE WHITNEY IN NEW YORK LAST SPRING.
SO, ANOTHER MEDIA MOGUL. THE FIFTH IN THE LAST WEEK. HAS THEIR LEADER WEIGHED IN YET?
THE SELF-STYLED MASTER WYZE? IT'S THE SAME THING HE'S BEEN SAYING FOR MONTHS NOW.
ARKHAM HAS FALLEN, AND NOW GOTHAM MUST GRAPPLE WITH THE MADNESS GRIPPING ITS STREETS. THE ONLY WAY FORWARD IS TO REJECT THE PAST AND EMBRACE A NEW KIND OF SANITY.
JOIN THE UNSANITY COLLECTIVE. JOIN THE NEW GOTHAM CITY.
I'M GOING TO TRY AND KEEP DIVERTING TRAFFIC TO KEEP THEM PINNED IN THE OLD TOWN NEIGHBORHOOD, BUT THAT'S ONLY GOING TO WORK ON THE GROUND TEAM.
RUFLOSS
UNLESS THAT CAR HAS A FEW TRICKS UP ITS SLEEVE, I'M NOT SURE HOW YOU'RE GOING TO GET THE REST OF THEM.
HEY, M.M.!

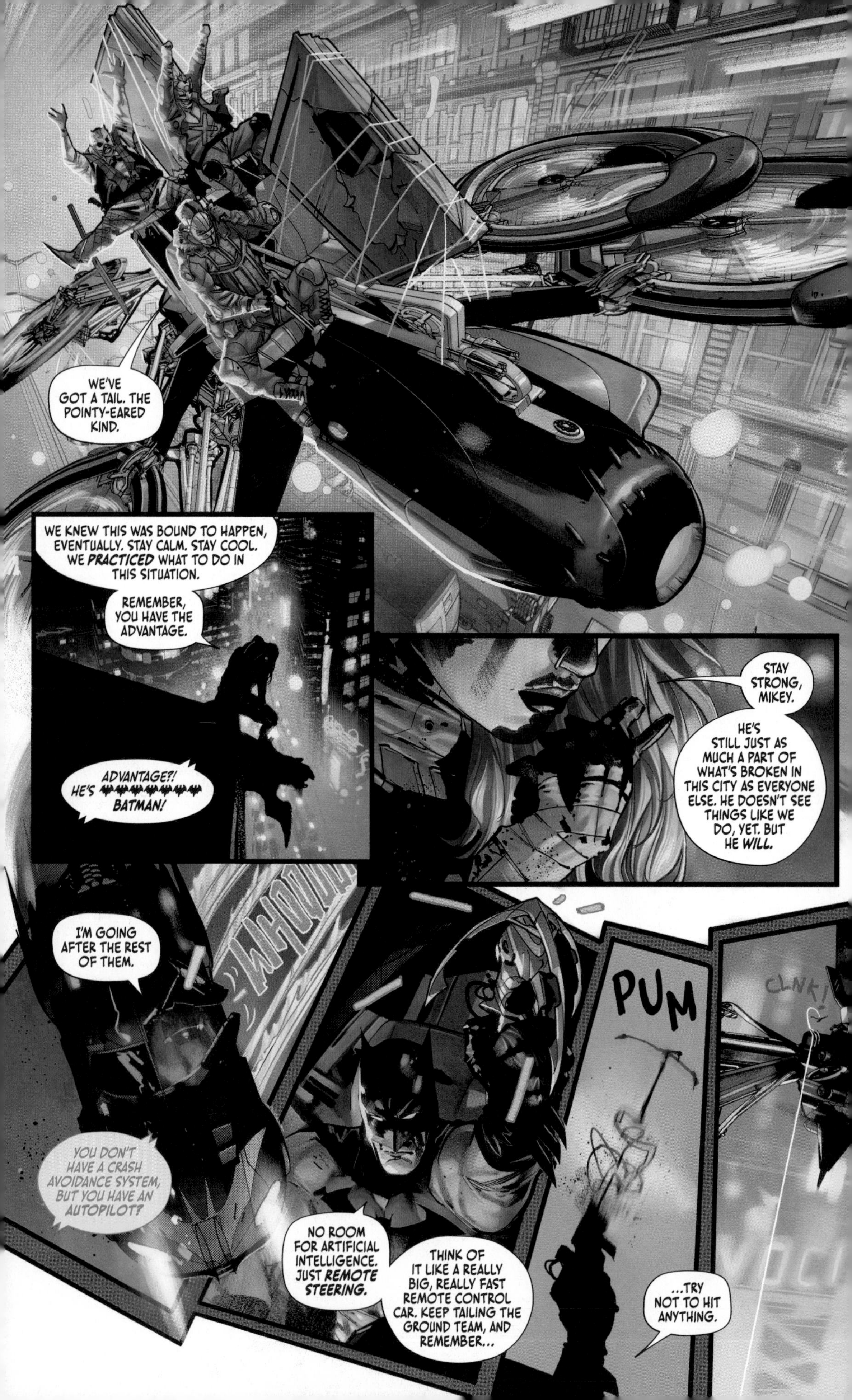
WE'VE GOT A TAIL. THE POINTY-EARED KIND.
WE KNEW THIS WAS BOUND TO HAPPEN, EVENTUALLY. STAY CALM. STAY COOL. WE *PRACTICED* WHAT TO DO IN THIS SITUATION.
REMEMBER, YOU HAVE THE ADVANTAGE.
ADVANTAGE?! HE'S BATMAN!
STAY STRONG, MIKEY.
HE'S STILL JUST AS MUCH A PART OF WHAT'S BROKEN IN THIS CITY AS EVERYONE ELSE. HE DOESN'T SEE THINGS LIKE WE DO, YET. BUT HE *WILL.*
I'M GOING AFTER THE REST OF THEM.
PUM
CLNK!
YOU DON'T HAVE A CRASH AVOIDANCE SYSTEM, BUT YOU HAVE AN AUTOPILOT?
NO ROOM FOR ARTIFICIAL INTELLIGENCE. JUST *REMOTE STEERING.*
THINK OF IT LIKE A REALLY BIG, REALLY FAST REMOTE CONTROL CAR. KEEP TAILING THE GROUND TEAM, AND REMEMBER...
...TRY NOT TO HIT ANYTHING.

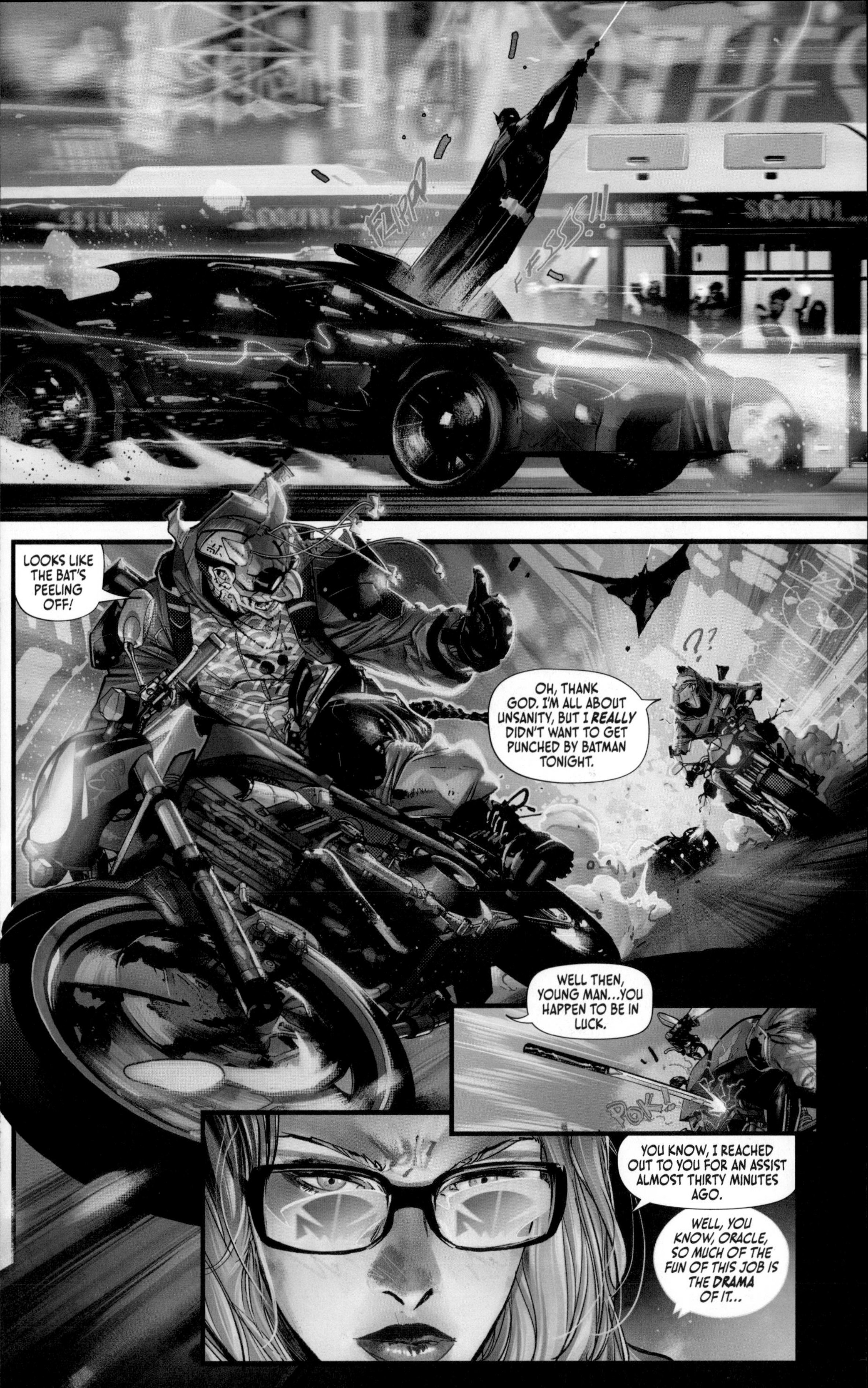
FLIPP
FSSSS!!
LOOKS LIKE THE BAT'S PEELING OFF!
??
OH, THANK GOD. I'M ALL ABOUT UNSANITY, BUT I REALLY DIDN'T WANT TO GET PUNCHED BY BATMAN TONIGHT.
WELL THEN, YOUNG MAN...YOU HAPPEN TO BE IN LUCK.
POK!
YOU KNOW, I REACHED OUT TO YOU FOR AN ASSIST ALMOST THIRTY MINUTES AGO.
WELL, YOU KNOW, ORACLE, SO MUCH OF THE FUN OF THIS JOB IS THE DRAMA OF IT...

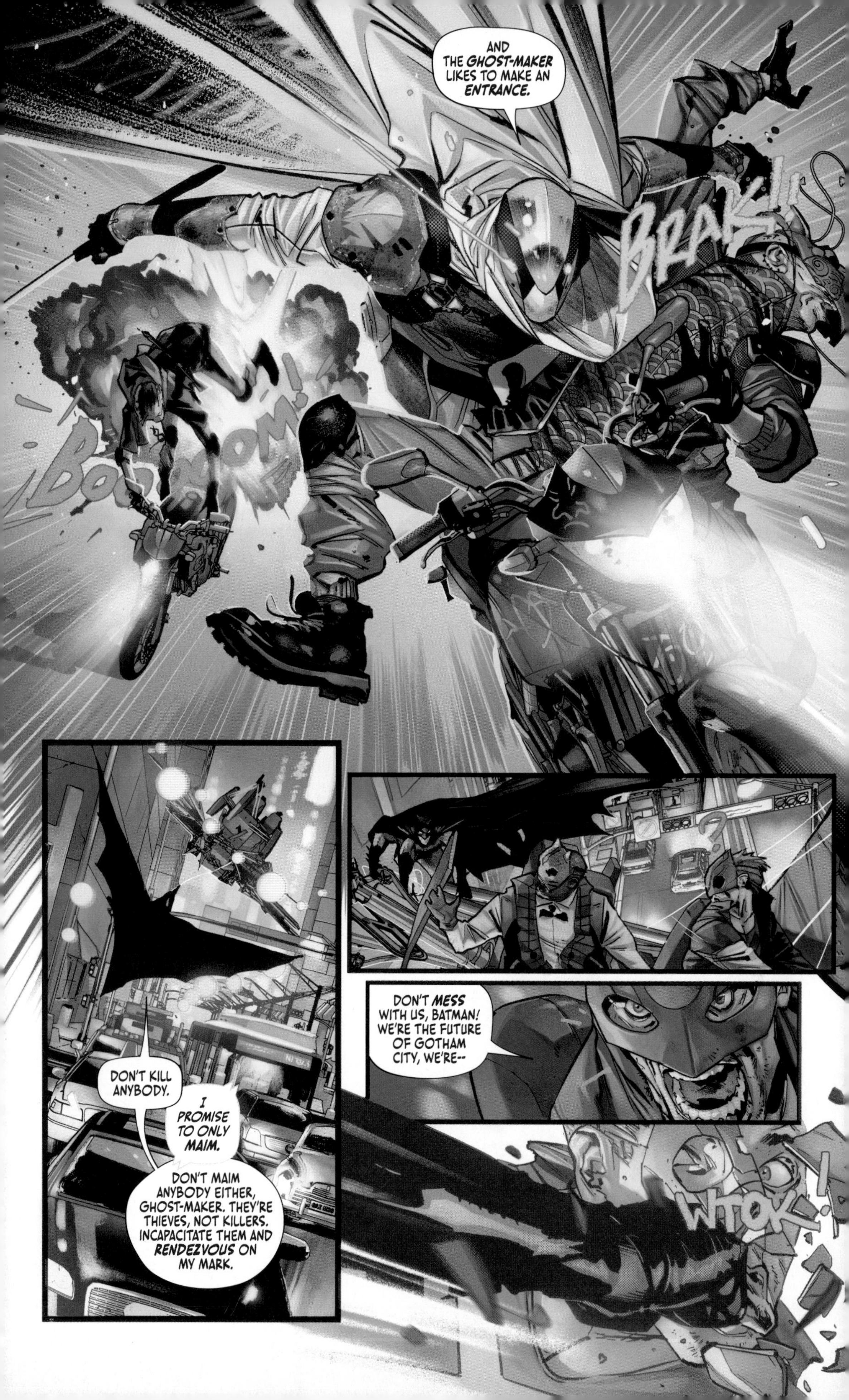
AND THE GHOST-MAKER LIKES TO MAKE AN ENTRANCE.
BRAK!!
BOOOOOM!
DON'T KILL ANYBODY.
I PROMISE TO ONLY MAIM.
DON'T MAIM ANYBODY EITHER, GHOST-MAKER. THEY'RE THIEVES, NOT KILLERS. INCAPACITATE THEM AND RENDEZVOUS ON MY MARK.
DON'T MESS WITH US, BATMAN! WE'RE THE FUTURE OF GOTHAM CITY, WE'RE--
WTOK!

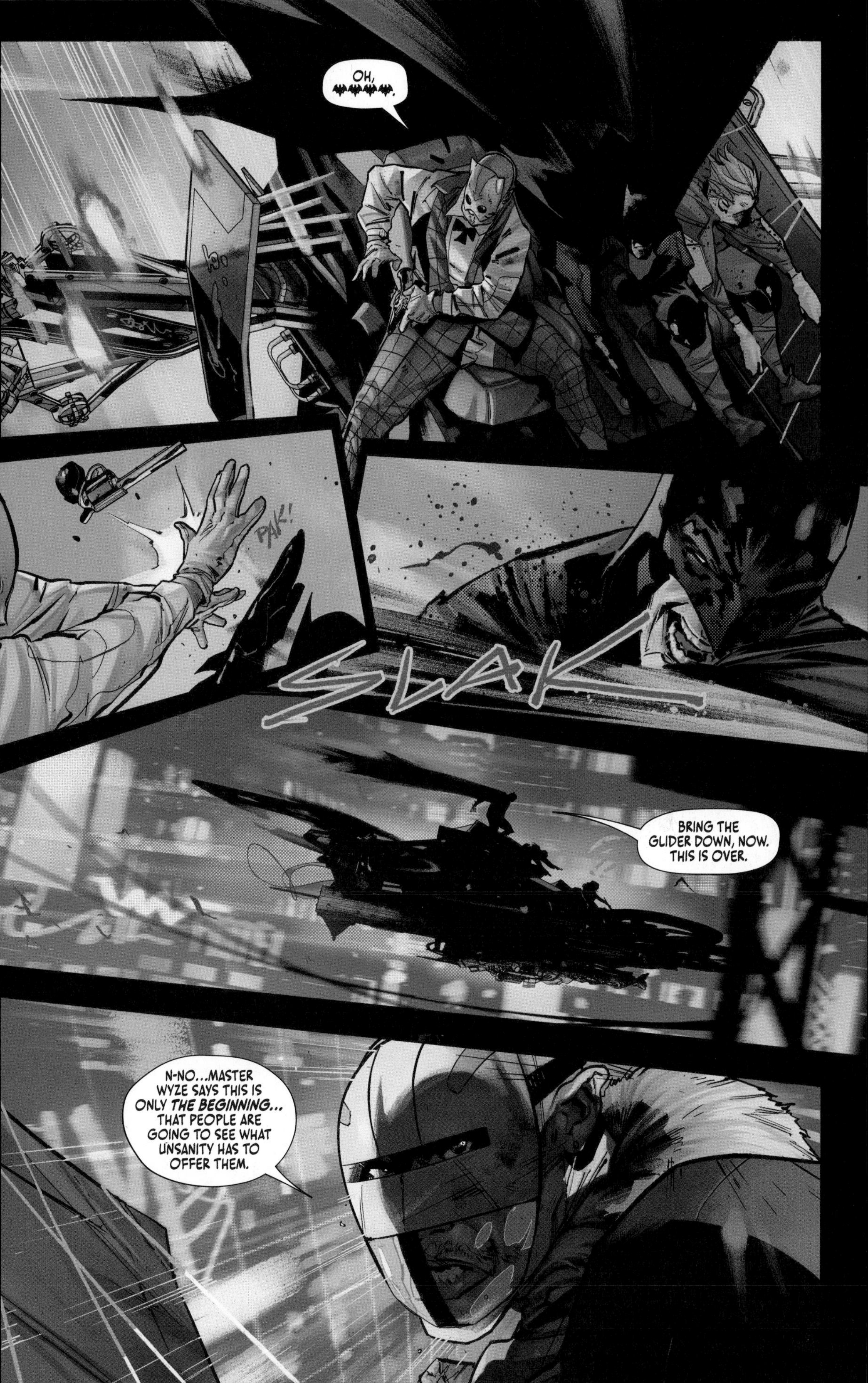
OH, [bat symbols].
PAK!
SLAK
BRING THE GLIDER DOWN, NOW. THIS IS OVER.
N-NO...MASTER WYZE SAYS THIS IS ONLY *THE BEGINNING*... THAT PEOPLE ARE GOING TO SEE WHAT UNSANITY HAS TO OFFER THEM.

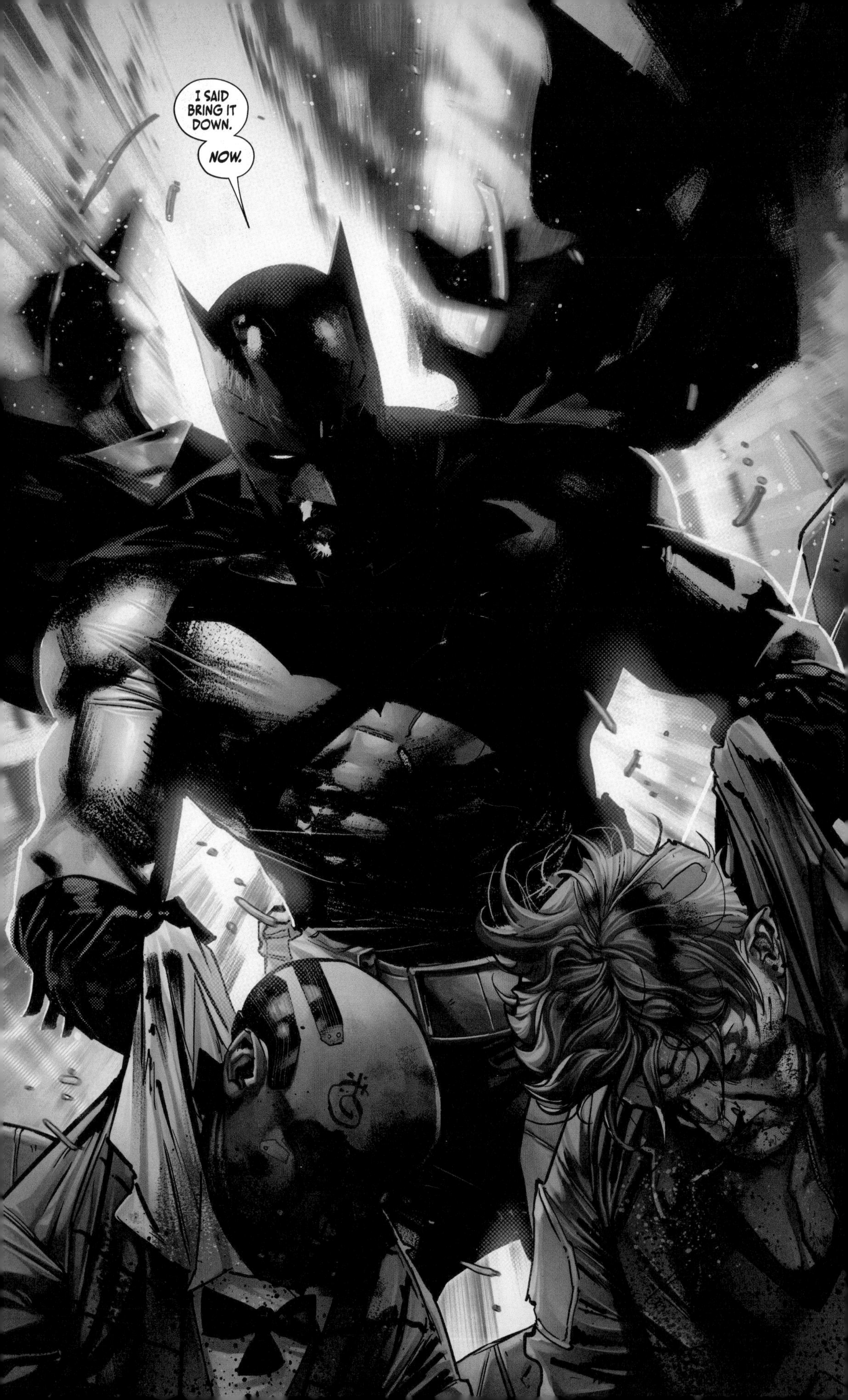
I SAID BRING IT DOWN.
NOW.

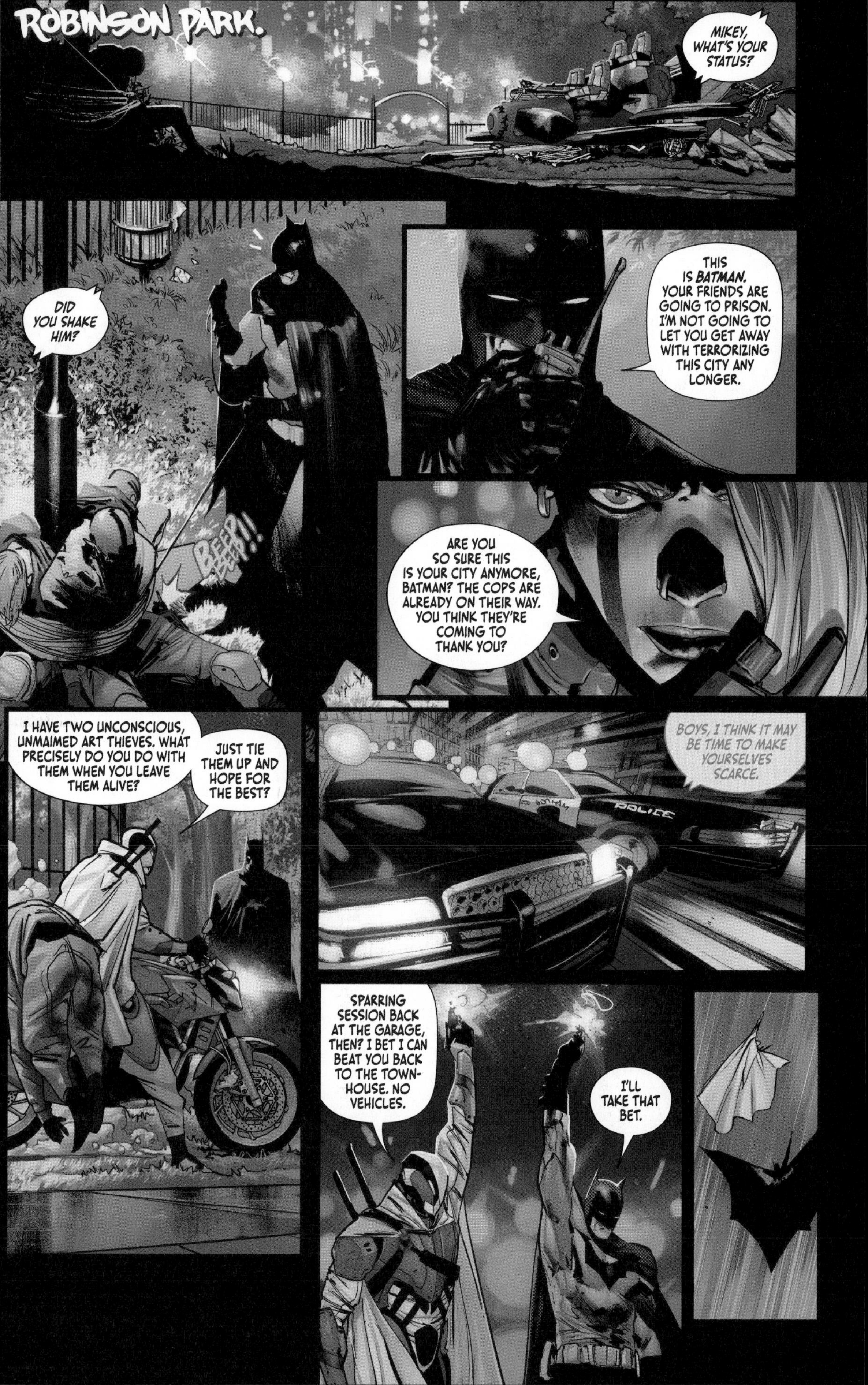
ROBINSON PARK.
MIKEY, WHAT'S YOUR STATUS?
DID YOU SHAKE HIM?
BEEP BEEP!!
THIS IS BATMAN. YOUR FRIENDS ARE GOING TO PRISON. I'M NOT GOING TO LET YOU GET AWAY WITH TERRORIZING THIS CITY ANY LONGER.
ARE YOU SO SURE THIS IS YOUR CITY ANYMORE, BATMAN? THE COPS ARE ALREADY ON THEIR WAY. YOU THINK THEY'RE COMING TO THANK YOU?
I HAVE TWO UNCONSCIOUS, UNMAIMED ART THIEVES. WHAT PRECISELY DO YOU DO WITH THEM WHEN YOU LEAVE THEM ALIVE?
JUST TIE THEM UP AND HOPE FOR THE BEST?
BOYS, I THINK IT MAY BE TIME TO MAKE YOURSELVES SCARCE.
POLICE
SPARRING SESSION BACK AT THE GARAGE, THEN? I BET I CAN BEAT YOU BACK TO THE TOWN-HOUSE. NO VEHICLES.
I'LL TAKE THAT BET.

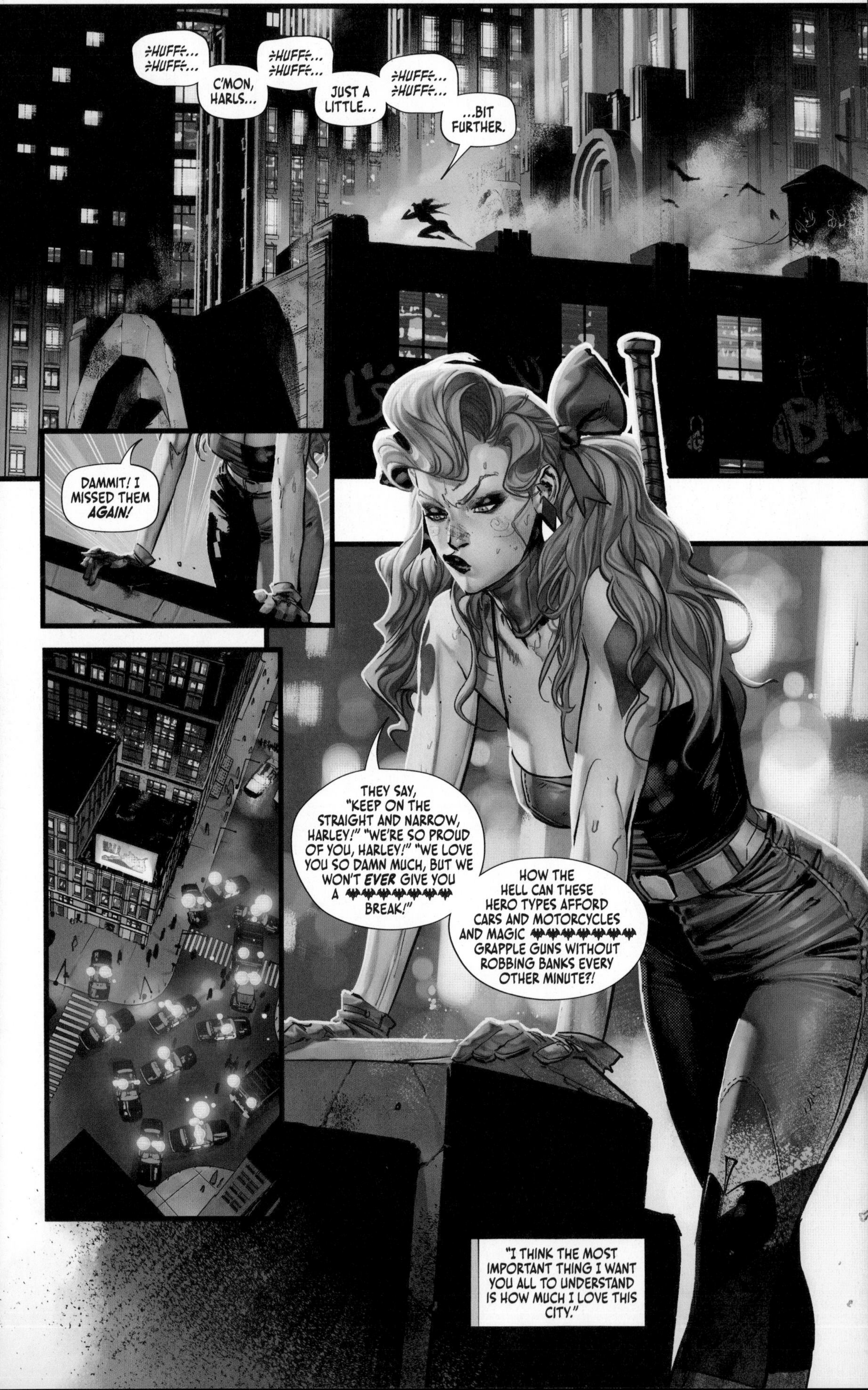

HUFF... *HUFF*...
C'MON, HARLS...
HUFF... *HUFF*...
JUST A LITTLE...
HUFF... *HUFF*...
...BIT FURTHER.
DAMMIT! I MISSED THEM *AGAIN!*
THEY SAY, "KEEP ON THE STRAIGHT AND NARROW, HARLEY!" "WE'RE SO PROUD OF YOU, HARLEY!" "WE LOVE YOU SO DAMN MUCH, BUT WE WON'T *EVER* GIVE YOU A BREAK!"
HOW THE HELL CAN THESE HERO TYPES AFFORD CARS AND MOTORCYCLES AND MAGIC GRAPPLE GUNS WITHOUT ROBBING BANKS EVERY OTHER MINUTE?!
"I THINK THE MOST IMPORTANT THING I WANT YOU ALL TO UNDERSTAND IS HOW MUCH I LOVE THIS CITY."

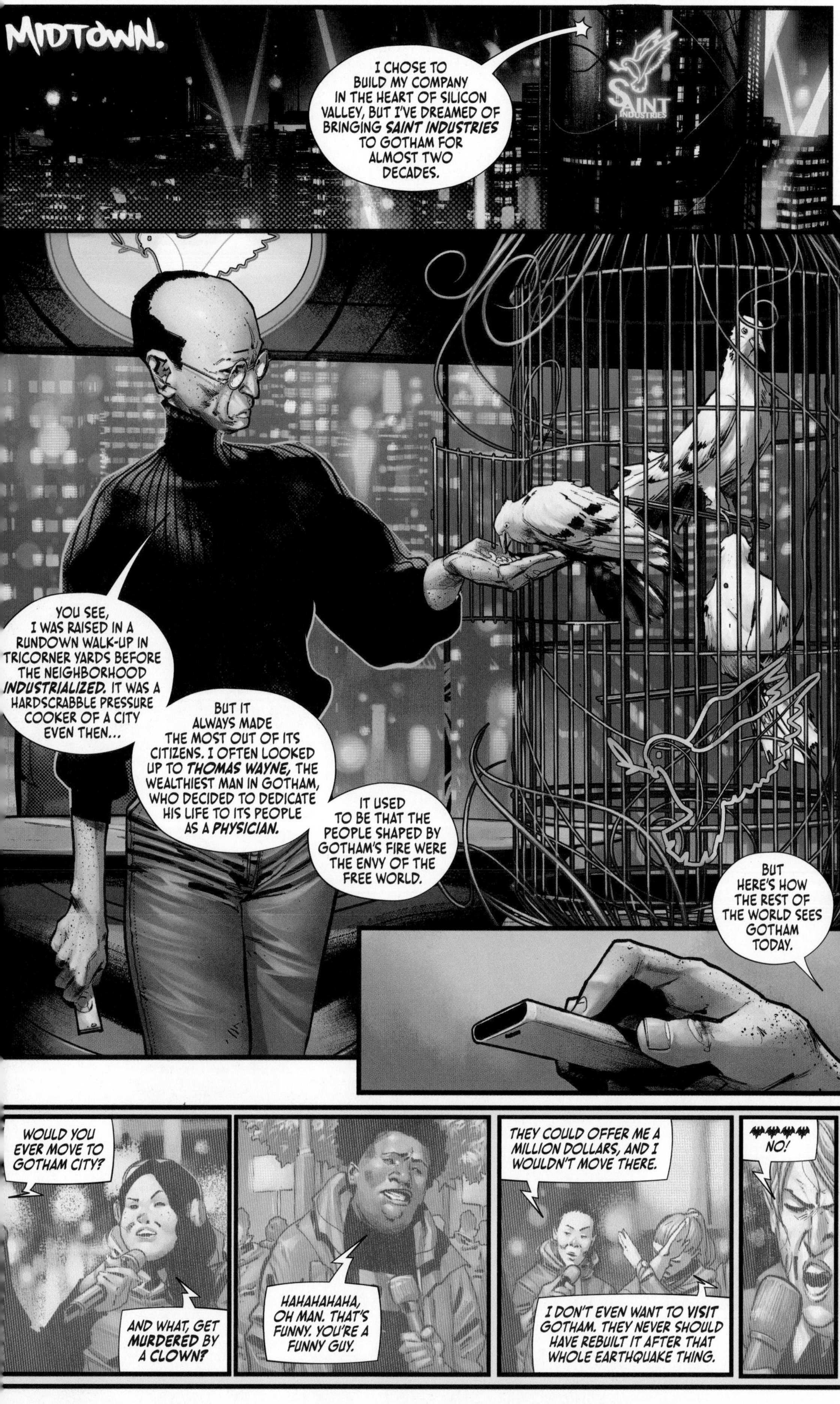
MIDTOWN.
I CHOSE TO BUILD MY COMPANY IN THE HEART OF SILICON VALLEY, BUT I'VE DREAMED OF BRINGING SAINT INDUSTRIES TO GOTHAM FOR ALMOST TWO DECADES.
SAINT INDUSTRIES
YOU SEE, I WAS RAISED IN A RUNDOWN WALK-UP IN TRICORNER YARDS BEFORE THE NEIGHBORHOOD INDUSTRIALIZED. IT WAS A HARDSCRABBLE PRESSURE COOKER OF A CITY EVEN THEN...
BUT IT ALWAYS MADE THE MOST OUT OF ITS CITIZENS. I OFTEN LOOKED UP TO THOMAS WAYNE, THE WEALTHIEST MAN IN GOTHAM, WHO DECIDED TO DEDICATE HIS LIFE TO ITS PEOPLE AS A PHYSICIAN.
IT USED TO BE THAT THE PEOPLE SHAPED BY GOTHAM'S FIRE WERE THE ENVY OF THE FREE WORLD.
BUT HERE'S HOW THE REST OF THE WORLD SEES GOTHAM TODAY.
WOULD YOU EVER MOVE TO GOTHAM CITY?
AND WHAT, GET MURDERED BY A CLOWN?
HAHAHAHAHA, OH MAN. THAT'S FUNNY. YOU'RE A FUNNY GUY.
THEY COULD OFFER ME A MILLION DOLLARS, AND I WOULDN'T MOVE THERE.
I DON'T EVEN WANT TO VISIT GOTHAM. THEY NEVER SHOULD HAVE REBUILT IT AFTER THAT WHOLE EARTHQUAKE THING.
NO!

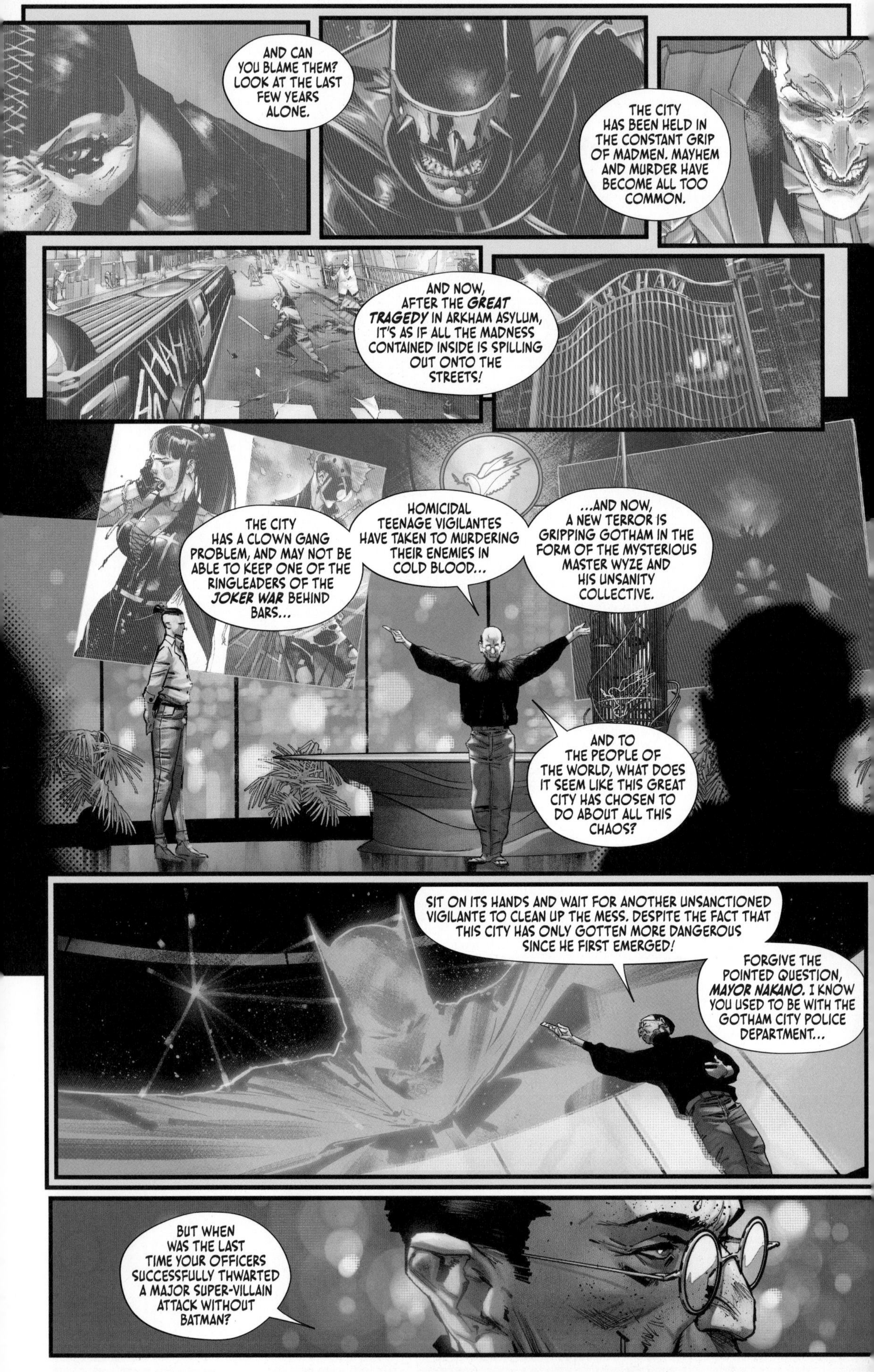
AND CAN YOU BLAME THEM? LOOK AT THE LAST FEW YEARS ALONE.
THE CITY HAS BEEN HELD IN THE CONSTANT GRIP OF MADMEN. MAYHEM AND MURDER HAVE BECOME ALL TOO COMMON.
AND NOW, AFTER THE *GREAT TRAGEDY* IN ARKHAM ASYLUM, IT'S AS IF ALL THE MADNESS CONTAINED INSIDE IS SPILLING OUT ONTO THE STREETS!
THE CITY HAS A CLOWN GANG PROBLEM, AND MAY NOT BE ABLE TO KEEP ONE OF THE RINGLEADERS OF THE *JOKER WAR* BEHIND BARS...
HOMICIDAL TEENAGE VIGILANTES HAVE TAKEN TO MURDERING THEIR ENEMIES IN COLD BLOOD...
...AND NOW, A NEW TERROR IS GRIPPING GOTHAM IN THE FORM OF THE MYSTERIOUS MASTER WYZE AND HIS UNSANITY COLLECTIVE.
AND TO THE PEOPLE OF THE WORLD, WHAT DOES IT SEEM LIKE THIS GREAT CITY HAS CHOSEN TO DO ABOUT ALL THIS CHAOS?
SIT ON ITS HANDS AND WAIT FOR ANOTHER UNSANCTIONED VIGILANTE TO CLEAN UP THE MESS. DESPITE THE FACT THAT THIS CITY HAS ONLY GOTTEN MORE DANGEROUS SINCE HE FIRST EMERGED!
FORGIVE THE POINTED QUESTION, *MAYOR NAKANO.* I KNOW YOU USED TO BE WITH THE GOTHAM CITY POLICE DEPARTMENT...
BUT WHEN WAS THE LAST TIME YOUR OFFICERS SUCCESSFULLY THWARTED A MAJOR SUPER-VILLAIN ATTACK WITHOUT BATMAN?

BATMAN RARELY GAVE US THE OPPORTUNITY TO DO WHAT WE COULD, MR. SAINT.

RESPECTFULLY... *I DISAGREE.* THE GCPD, LIKE EVERY POLICE FORCE IN THE COUNTRY, WAS CREATED TO HELP PEOPLE AND STOP MUNDANE CRIMES.

IF YOU'RE GOING TO STOP EXTRAORDINARY CRIMES, YOU ARE GOING TO NEED EXTRAORDINARY, ACCOUNTABLE CRIME-FIGHTERS.

WHICH IS WHY I HAVE DESIGNED WHAT I CALL *THE MAGISTRATE PROGRAM.* IT FEATURES A DEDICATED GROUP OF ONE TO FIVE SPECIALLY CHOSEN *PEACEKEEPERS,* DEPUTIZED BY THE CITY.

AND IT GIVES THEM THE SUPPORT AND RESOURCES TO STOP A BANE, OR A JOKER, OR *WHOEVER* MIGHT TRY TO DESTROY GOTHAM CITY NEXT.

MY PROGRAM WOULD ALLOW THE GCPD TO FOCUS ON THE SORT OF PETTY CRIME A POLICE FORCE WAS *DESIGNED* TO FACE. LEAVING ALL OF THE COSTUMED VILLAINY TO US.

THIS CITY IS GROWING *FAST,* MAYOR NAKANO. THE REBUILD OF GOTHAM THAT STARTED LAST YEAR CREATED THOUSANDS OF NEW JOBS IN THE METROPOLITAN CENTER.

THE CITY IS EXPANDING FASTER THAN IT HAS IN FIFTY YEARS.

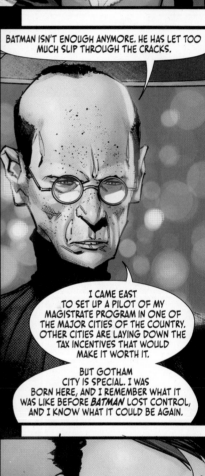

BATMAN ISN'T ENOUGH ANYMORE. HE HAS LET TOO MUCH SLIP THROUGH THE CRACKS.

I CAME EAST TO SET UP A PILOT OF MY MAGISTRATE PROGRAM IN ONE OF THE MAJOR CITIES OF THE COUNTRY. OTHER CITIES ARE LAYING DOWN THE TAX INCENTIVES THAT WOULD MAKE IT WORTH IT.

BUT GOTHAM CITY IS SPECIAL. I WAS BORN HERE, AND I REMEMBER WHAT IT WAS LIKE BEFORE *BATMAN* LOST CONTROL, AND I KNOW WHAT IT COULD BE AGAIN.

WELL, MR. SAINT... I WISH YOUR ARGUMENT WASN'T AS COMPELLING AS IT IS.

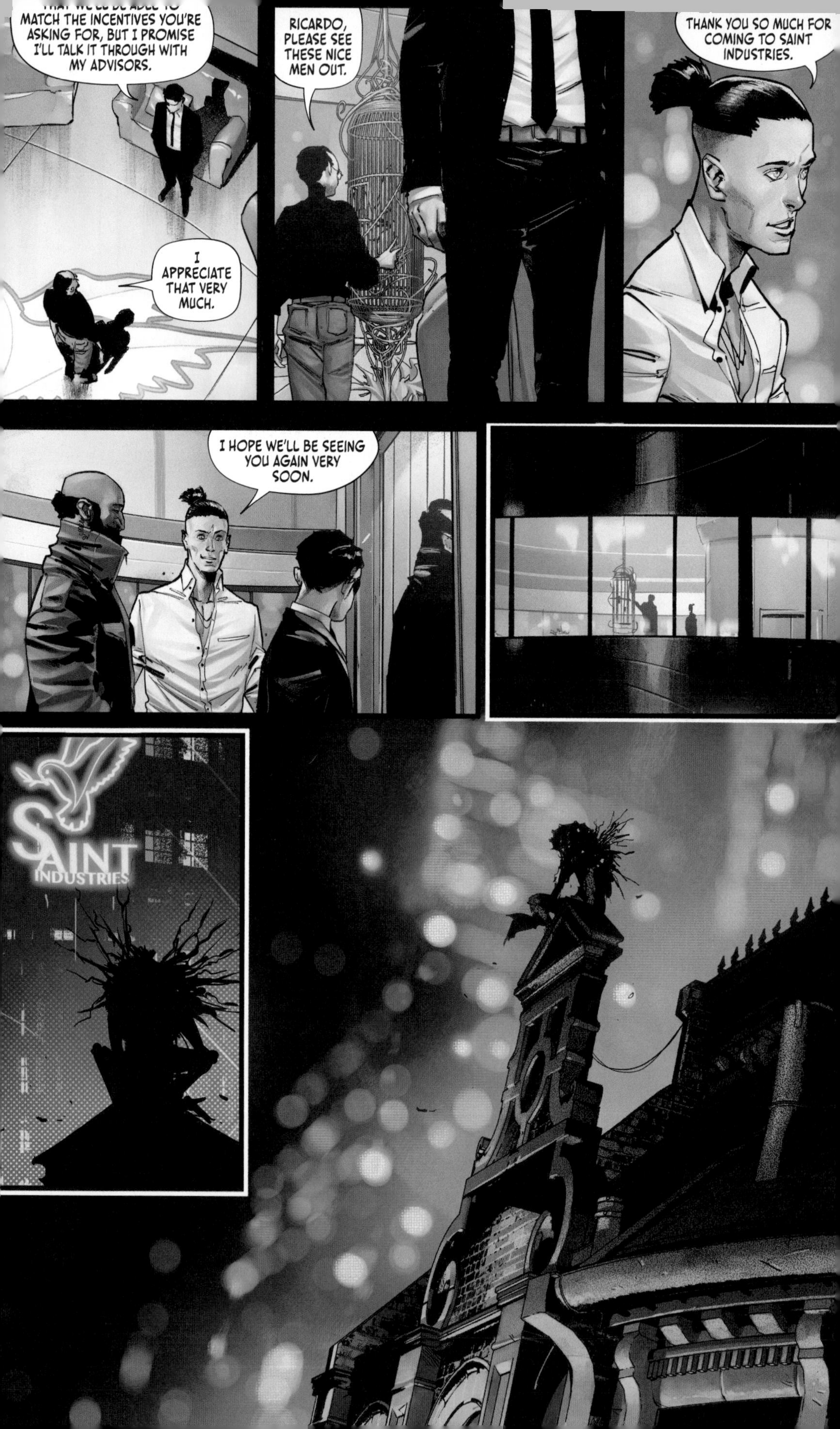
MATCH THE INCENTIVES YOU'RE ASKING FOR, BUT I PROMISE I'LL TALK IT THROUGH WITH MY ADVISORS.
I APPRECIATE THAT VERY MUCH.
RICARDO, PLEASE SEE THESE NICE MEN OUT.
THANK YOU SO MUCH FOR COMING TO SAINT INDUSTRIES.
I HOPE WE'LL BE SEEING YOU AGAIN VERY SOON.
SAINT INDUSTRIES

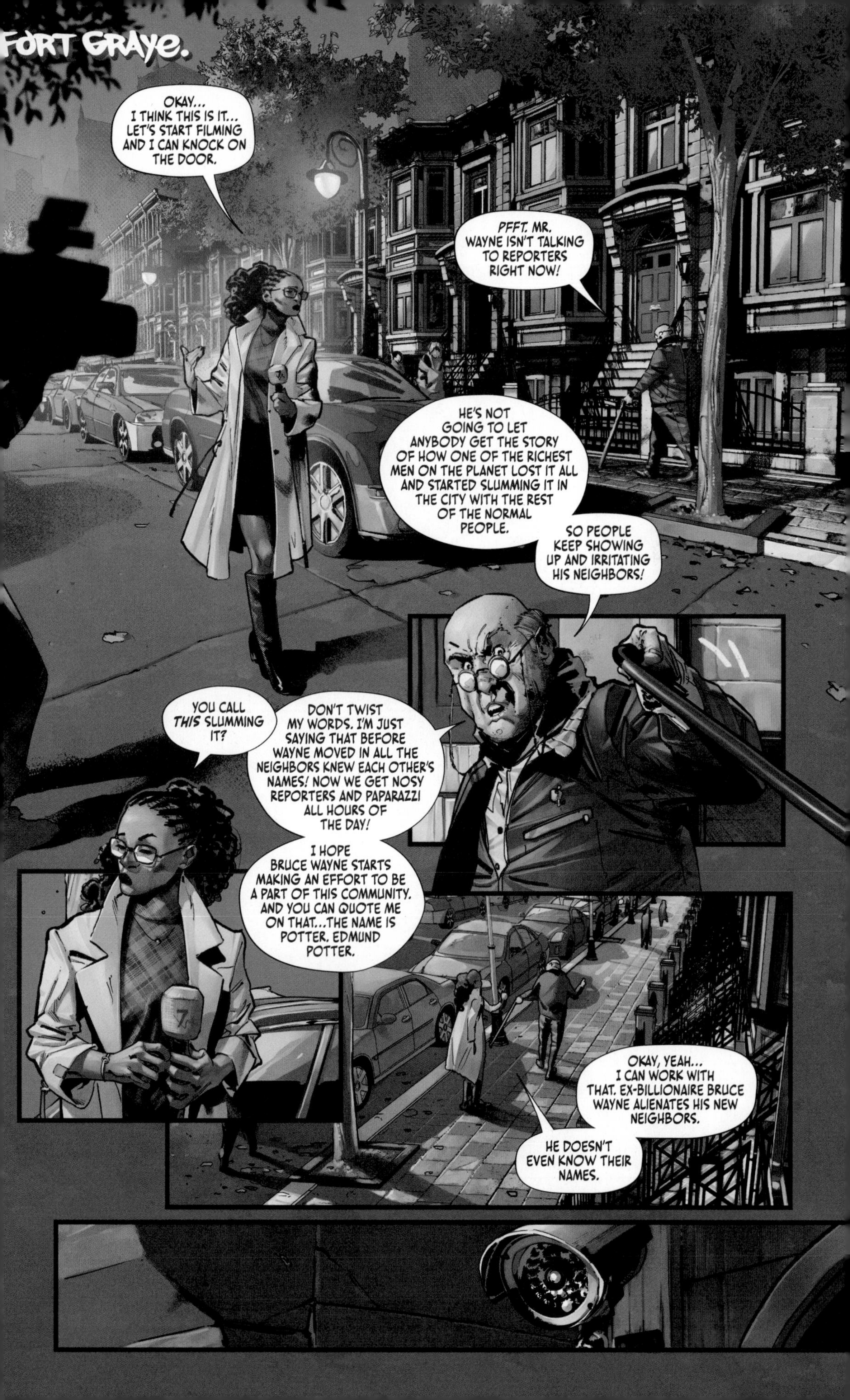
FORT GRAYE.
OKAY... I THINK THIS IS IT... LET'S START FILMING AND I CAN KNOCK ON THE DOOR.
PFFT. MR. WAYNE ISN'T TALKING TO REPORTERS RIGHT NOW!
HE'S NOT GOING TO LET ANYBODY GET THE STORY OF HOW ONE OF THE RICHEST MEN ON THE PLANET LOST IT ALL AND STARTED SLUMMING IT IN THE CITY WITH THE REST OF THE NORMAL PEOPLE.
SO PEOPLE KEEP SHOWING UP AND IRRITATING HIS NEIGHBORS!
YOU CALL *THIS* SLUMMING IT?
DON'T TWIST MY WORDS. I'M JUST SAYING THAT BEFORE WAYNE MOVED IN ALL THE NEIGHBORS KNEW EACH OTHER'S NAMES! NOW WE GET NOSY REPORTERS AND PAPARAZZI ALL HOURS OF THE DAY!
I HOPE BRUCE WAYNE STARTS MAKING AN EFFORT TO BE A PART OF THIS COMMUNITY. AND YOU CAN QUOTE ME ON THAT...THE NAME IS POTTER. EDMUND POTTER.
OKAY, YEAH... I CAN WORK WITH THAT. EX-BILLIONAIRE BRUCE WAYNE ALIENATES HIS NEW NEIGHBORS.
HE DOESN'T EVEN KNOW THEIR NAMES.

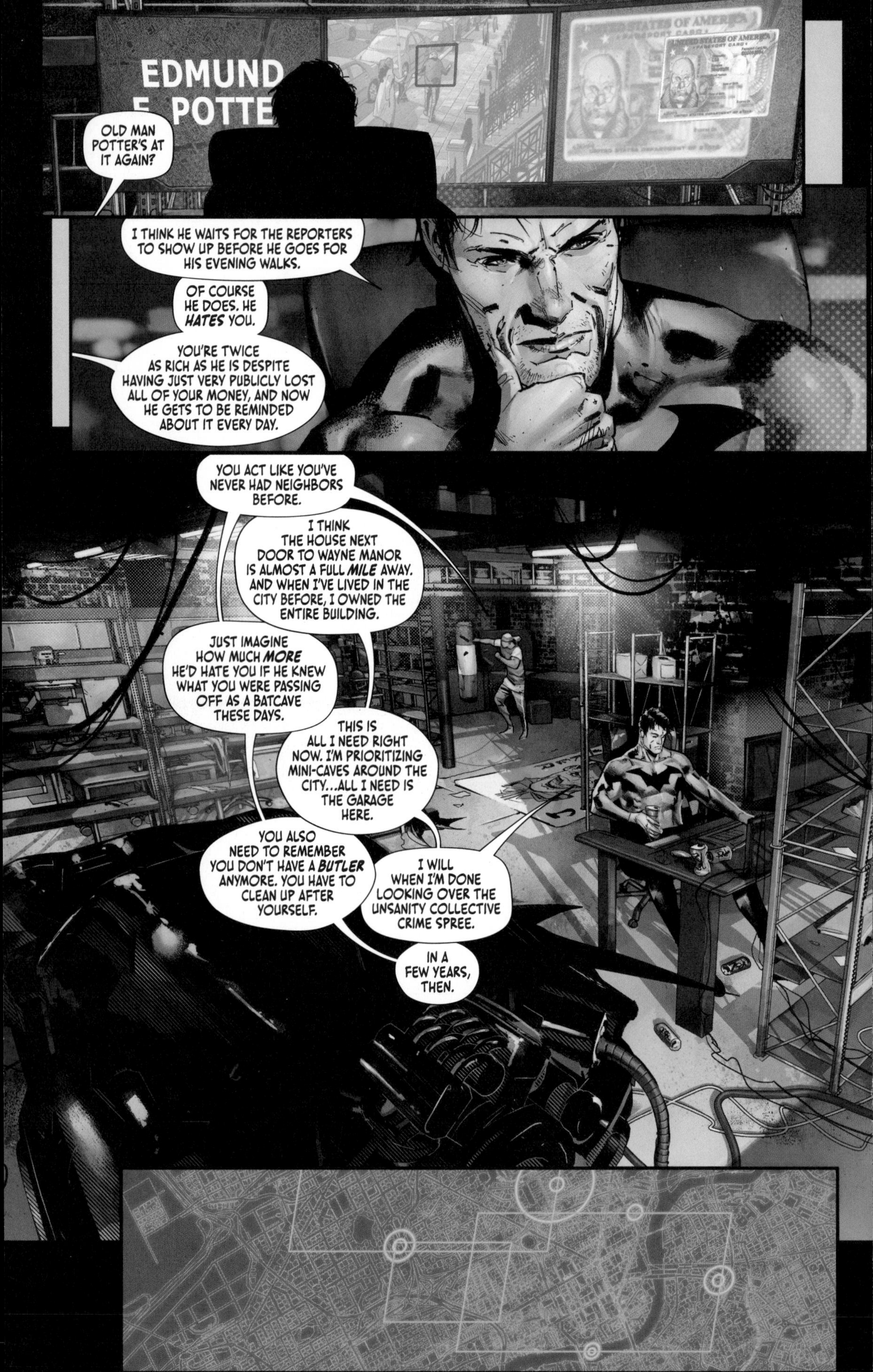
EDMUND E. POTTE
OLD MAN POTTER'S AT IT AGAIN?
I THINK HE WAITS FOR THE REPORTERS TO SHOW UP BEFORE HE GOES FOR HIS EVENING WALKS.
OF COURSE HE DOES. HE *HATES* YOU.
YOU'RE TWICE AS RICH AS HE IS DESPITE HAVING JUST VERY PUBLICLY LOST ALL OF YOUR MONEY, AND NOW HE GETS TO BE REMINDED ABOUT IT EVERY DAY.
YOU ACT LIKE YOU'VE NEVER HAD NEIGHBORS BEFORE.
I THINK THE HOUSE NEXT DOOR TO WAYNE MANOR IS ALMOST A FULL *MILE* AWAY. AND WHEN I'VE LIVED IN THE CITY BEFORE, I OWNED THE ENTIRE BUILDING.
JUST IMAGINE HOW MUCH *MORE* HE'D HATE YOU IF HE KNEW WHAT YOU WERE PASSING OFF AS A BATCAVE THESE DAYS.
THIS IS ALL I NEED RIGHT NOW. I'M PRIORITIZING MINI-CAVES AROUND THE CITY...ALL I NEED IS THE GARAGE HERE.
YOU ALSO NEED TO REMEMBER YOU DON'T HAVE A *BUTLER* ANYMORE. YOU HAVE TO CLEAN UP AFTER YOURSELF.
I WILL WHEN I'M DONE LOOKING OVER THE UNSANITY COLLECTIVE CRIME SPREE.
IN A FEW YEARS, THEN.

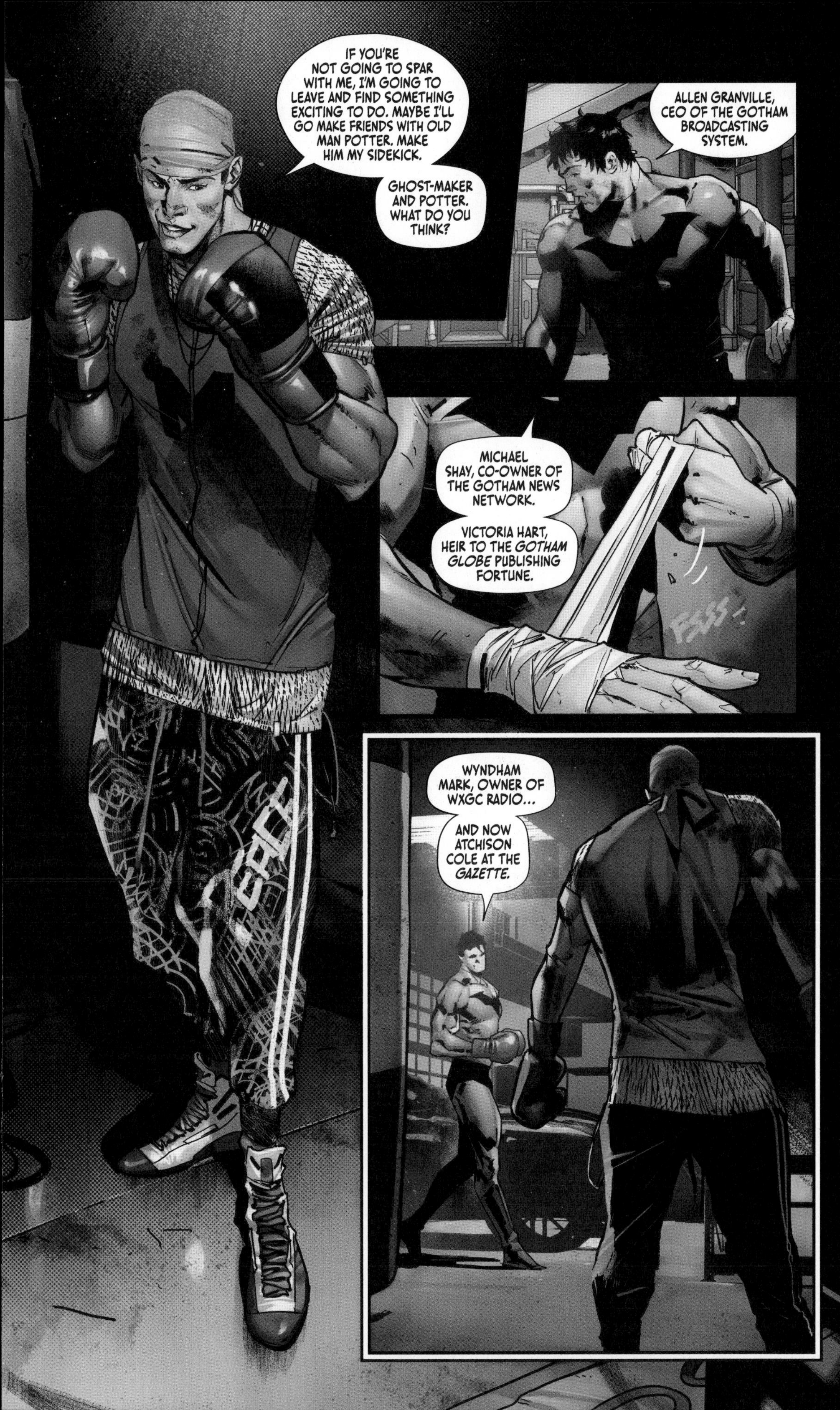
IF YOU'RE NOT GOING TO SPAR WITH ME, I'M GOING TO LEAVE AND FIND SOMETHING EXCITING TO DO. MAYBE I'LL GO MAKE FRIENDS WITH OLD MAN POTTER. MAKE HIM MY SIDEKICK.
GHOST-MAKER AND POTTER. WHAT DO YOU THINK?
ALLEN GRANVILLE, CEO OF THE GOTHAM BROADCASTING SYSTEM.
MICHAEL SHAY, CO-OWNER OF THE GOTHAM NEWS NETWORK.
VICTORIA HART, HEIR TO THE *GOTHAM GLOBE* PUBLISHING FORTUNE.
FSSS!
WYNDHAM MARK, OWNER OF WXGC RADIO...
AND NOW ATCHISON COLE AT THE *GAZETTE.*

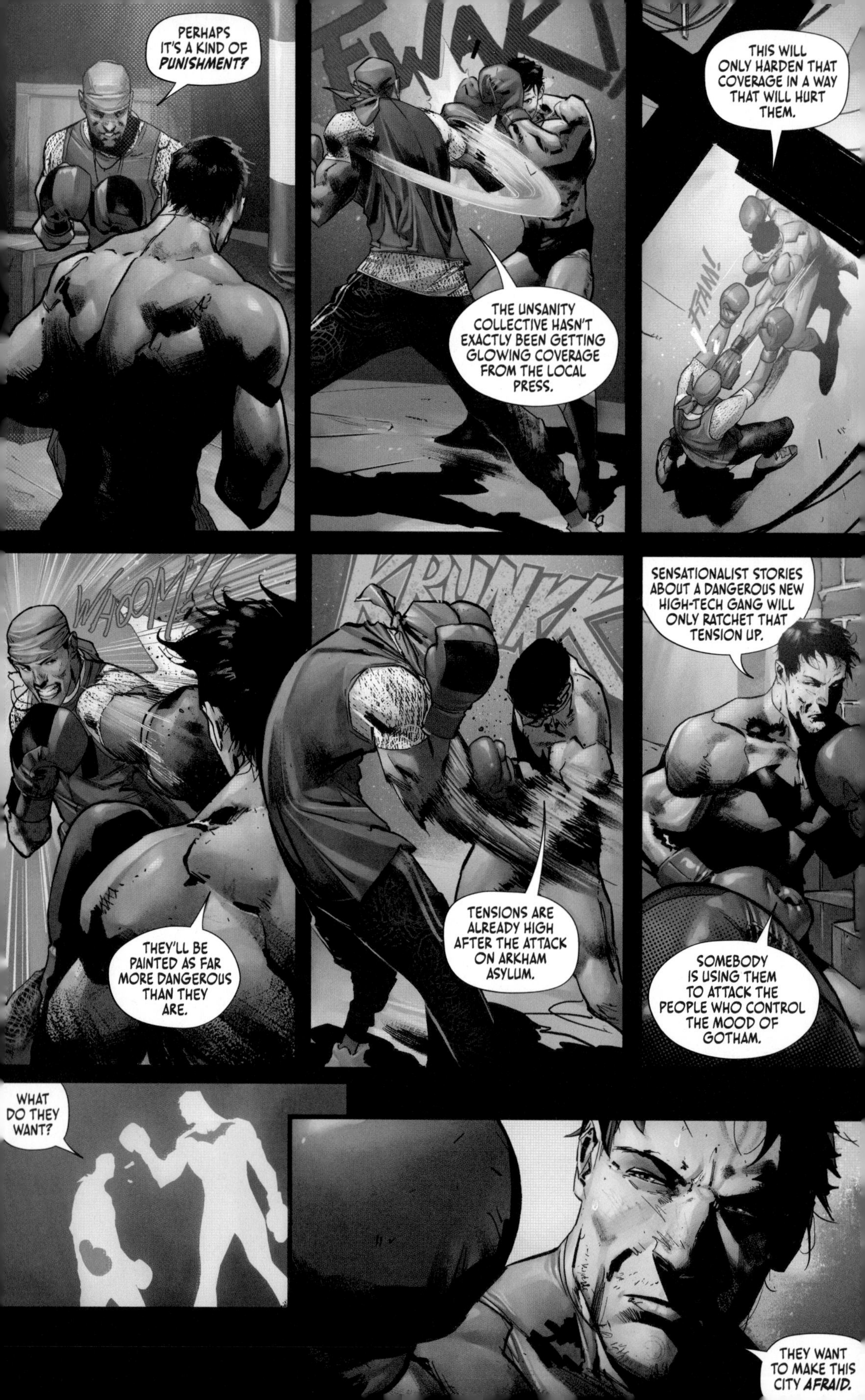
PERHAPS IT'S A KIND OF *PUNISHMENT?*
FWAK!!
THE UNSANITY COLLECTIVE HASN'T EXACTLY BEEN GETTING GLOWING COVERAGE FROM THE LOCAL PRESS.
THIS WILL ONLY HARDEN THAT COVERAGE IN A WAY THAT WILL HURT THEM.
FTAM!
WHOOM!!
THEY'LL BE PAINTED AS FAR MORE DANGEROUS THAN THEY ARE.
TENSIONS ARE ALREADY HIGH AFTER THE ATTACK ON ARKHAM ASYLUM.
SENSATIONALIST STORIES ABOUT A DANGEROUS NEW HIGH-TECH GANG WILL ONLY RATCHET THAT TENSION UP.
SOMEBODY IS USING THEM TO ATTACK THE PEOPLE WHO CONTROL THE MOOD OF GOTHAM.
WHAT DO THEY WANT?
THEY WANT TO MAKE THIS CITY *AFRAID*.

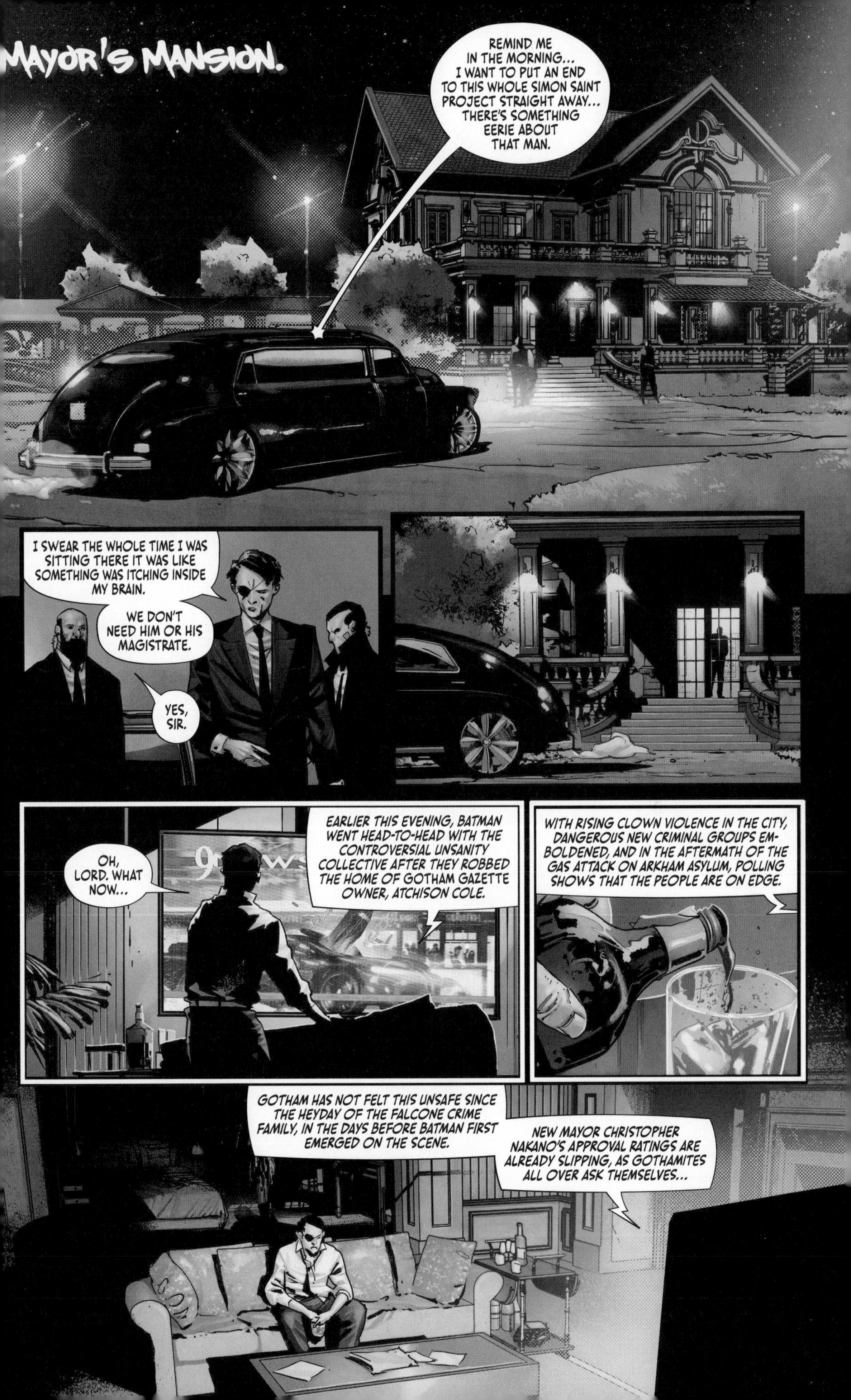
MAYOR'S MANSION.
REMIND ME IN THE MORNING... I WANT TO PUT AN END TO THIS WHOLE SIMON SAINT PROJECT STRAIGHT AWAY... THERE'S SOMETHING EERIE ABOUT THAT MAN.
I SWEAR THE WHOLE TIME I WAS SITTING THERE IT WAS LIKE SOMETHING WAS ITCHING INSIDE MY BRAIN.
WE DON'T NEED HIM OR HIS MAGISTRATE.
YES, SIR.
OH, LORD. WHAT NOW...
EARLIER THIS EVENING, BATMAN WENT HEAD-TO-HEAD WITH THE CONTROVERSIAL UNSANITY COLLECTIVE AFTER THEY ROBBED THE HOME OF GOTHAM GAZETTE OWNER, ATCHISON COLE.
WITH RISING CLOWN VIOLENCE IN THE CITY, DANGEROUS NEW CRIMINAL GROUPS EMBOLDENED, AND IN THE AFTERMATH OF THE GAS ATTACK ON ARKHAM ASYLUM, POLLING SHOWS THAT THE PEOPLE ARE ON EDGE.
GOTHAM HAS NOT FELT THIS UNSAFE SINCE THE HEYDAY OF THE FALCONE CRIME FAMILY, IN THE DAYS BEFORE BATMAN FIRST EMERGED ON THE SCENE.
NEW MAYOR CHRISTOPHER NAKANO'S APPROVAL RATINGS ARE ALREADY SLIPPING, AS GOTHAMITES ALL OVER ASK THEMSELVES...

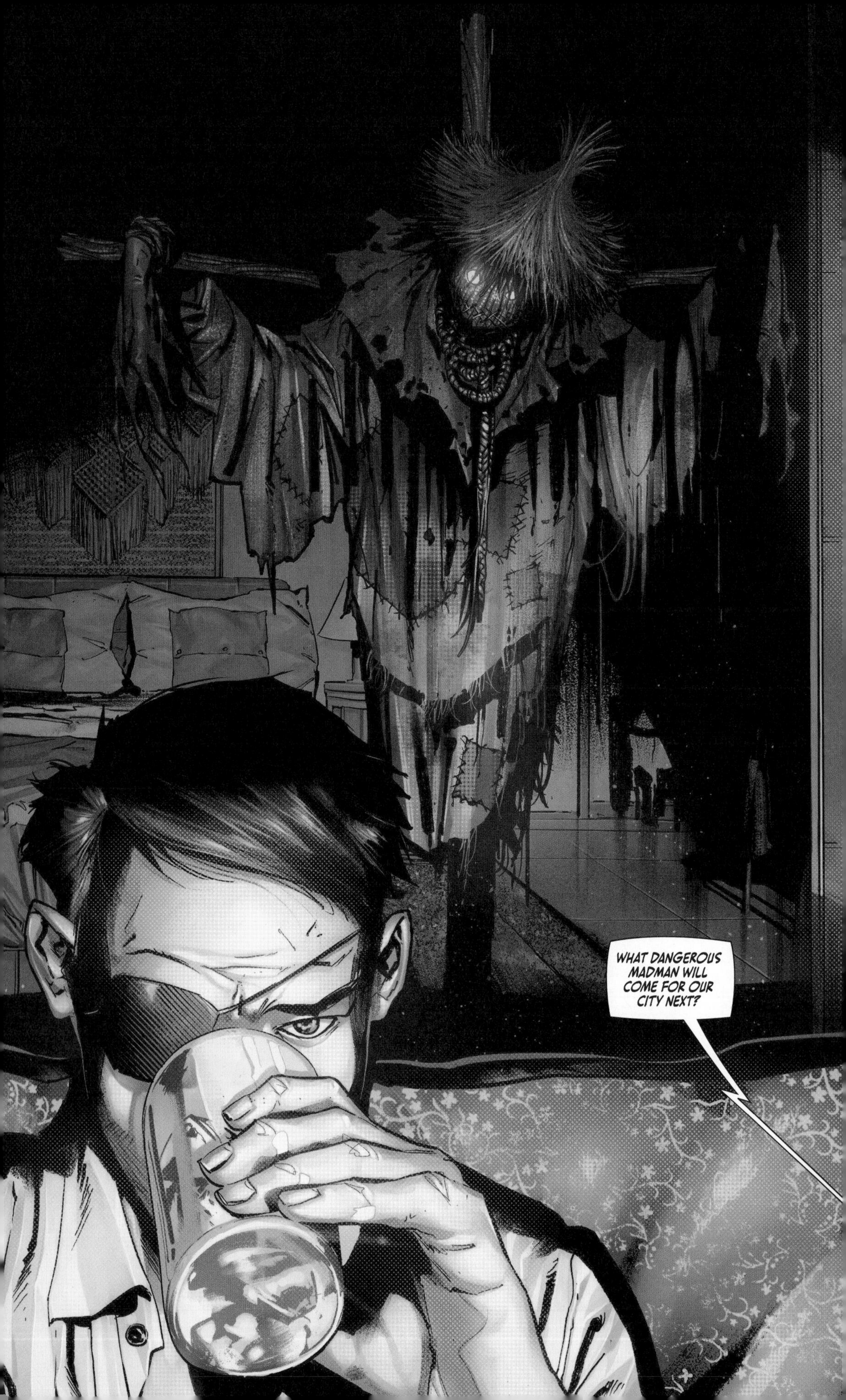
WHAT DANGEROUS MADMAN WILL COME FOR OUR CITY NEXT?

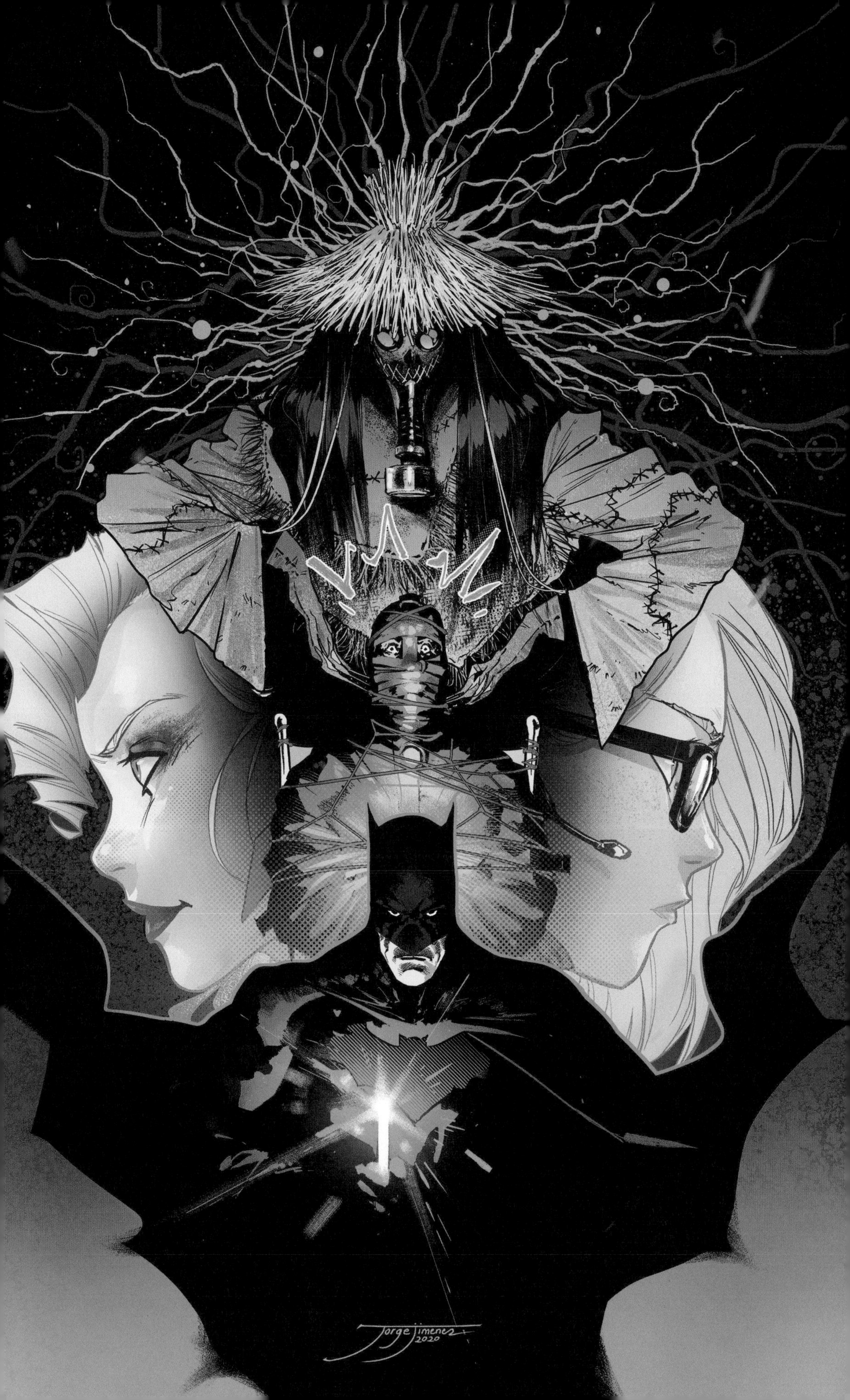
Jorge Jimenez
2020

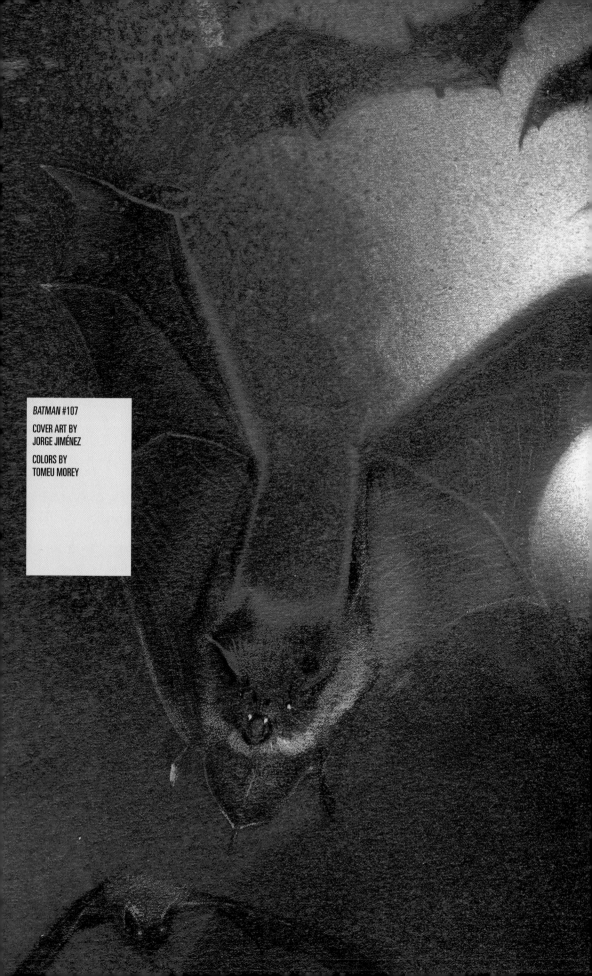

BATMAN #107
COVER ART BY
JORGE JIMÉNEZ

COLORS BY
TOMEU MOREY

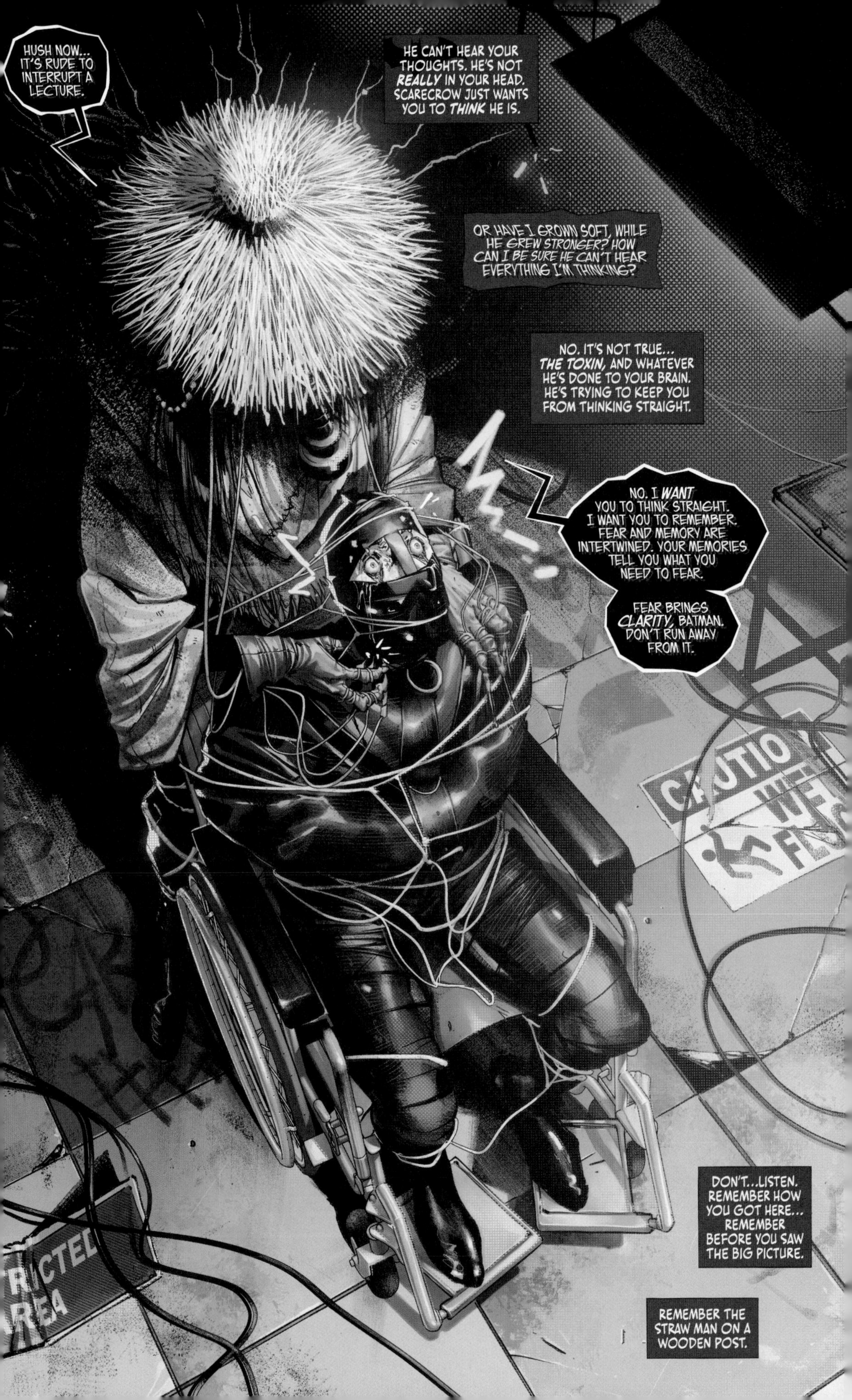
HUSH NOW... IT'S RUDE TO INTERRUPT A LECTURE.
HE CAN'T HEAR YOUR THOUGHTS. HE'S NOT *REALLY* IN YOUR HEAD. SCARECROW JUST WANTS YOU TO *THINK* HE IS.
OR HAVE I GROWN SOFT, WHILE HE GREW STRONGER? HOW CAN I BE SURE HE CAN'T HEAR EVERYTHING I'M THINKING?
NO. IT'S NOT TRUE... *THE TOXIN,* AND WHATEVER HE'S DONE TO YOUR BRAIN. HE'S TRYING TO KEEP YOU FROM THINKING STRAIGHT.
NO. I *WANT* YOU TO THINK STRAIGHT. I WANT YOU TO REMEMBER. FEAR AND MEMORY ARE INTERTWINED. YOUR MEMORIES TELL YOU WHAT YOU NEED TO FEAR.
FEAR BRINGS *CLARITY,* BATMAN. DON'T RUN AWAY FROM IT.
DON'T...LISTEN. REMEMBER HOW YOU GOT HERE... REMEMBER BEFORE YOU SAW THE BIG PICTURE.
REMEMBER THE STRAW MAN ON A WOODEN POST.

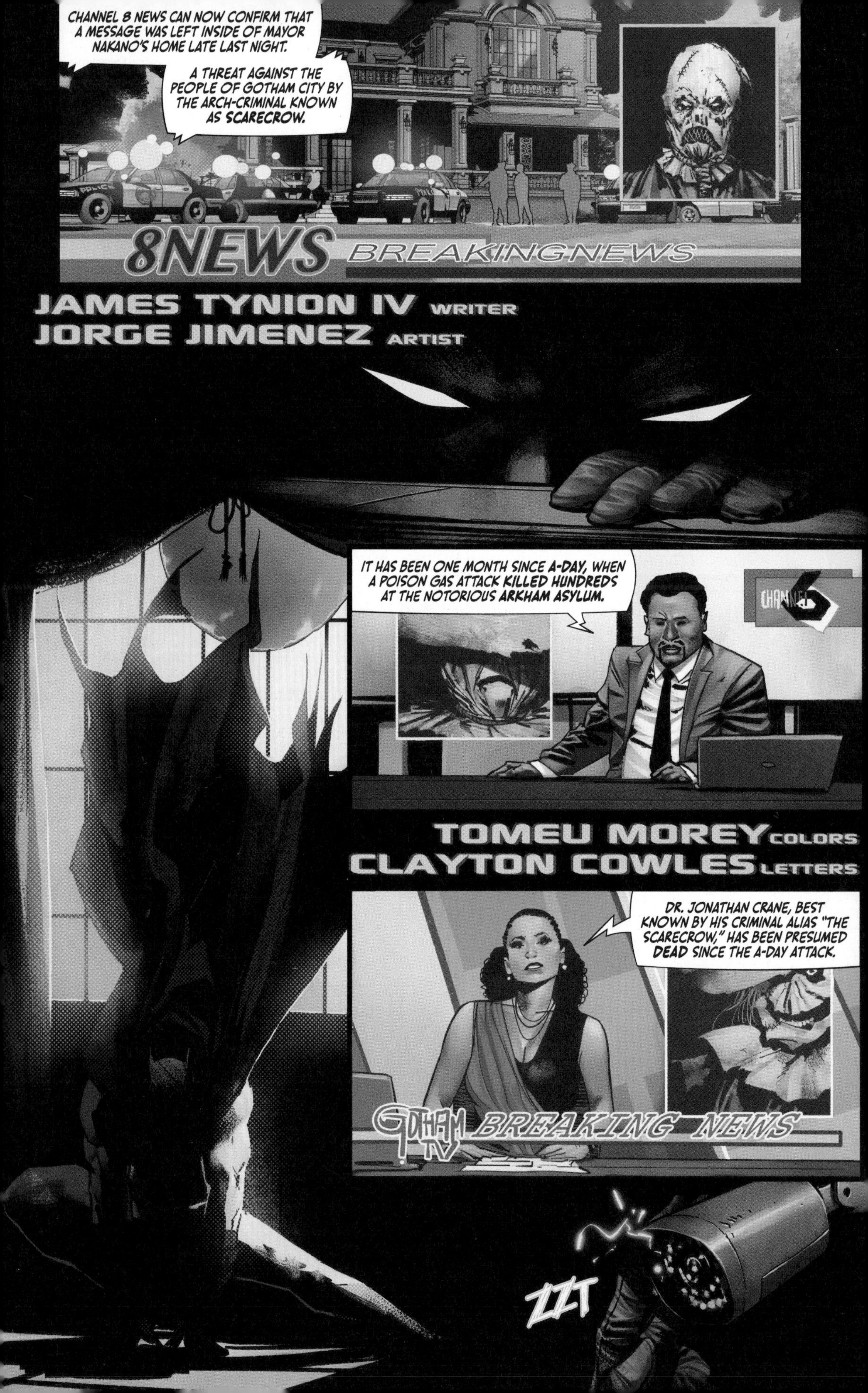
CHANNEL 8 NEWS CAN NOW CONFIRM THAT A MESSAGE WAS LEFT INSIDE OF MAYOR NAKANO'S HOME LATE LAST NIGHT.
A THREAT AGAINST THE PEOPLE OF GOTHAM CITY BY THE ARCH-CRIMINAL KNOWN AS SCARECROW.
8NEWS BREAKINGNEWS
JAMES TYNION IV WRITER
JORGE JIMENEZ ARTIST
IT HAS BEEN ONE MONTH SINCE A-DAY, WHEN A POISON GAS ATTACK KILLED HUNDREDS AT THE NOTORIOUS ARKHAM ASYLUM.
TOMEU MOREY COLORS
CLAYTON COWLES LETTERS
DR. JONATHAN CRANE, BEST KNOWN BY HIS CRIMINAL ALIAS "THE SCARECROW," HAS BEEN PRESUMED DEAD SINCE THE A-DAY ATTACK.
GOTHAM TV BREAKING NEWS
ZZT

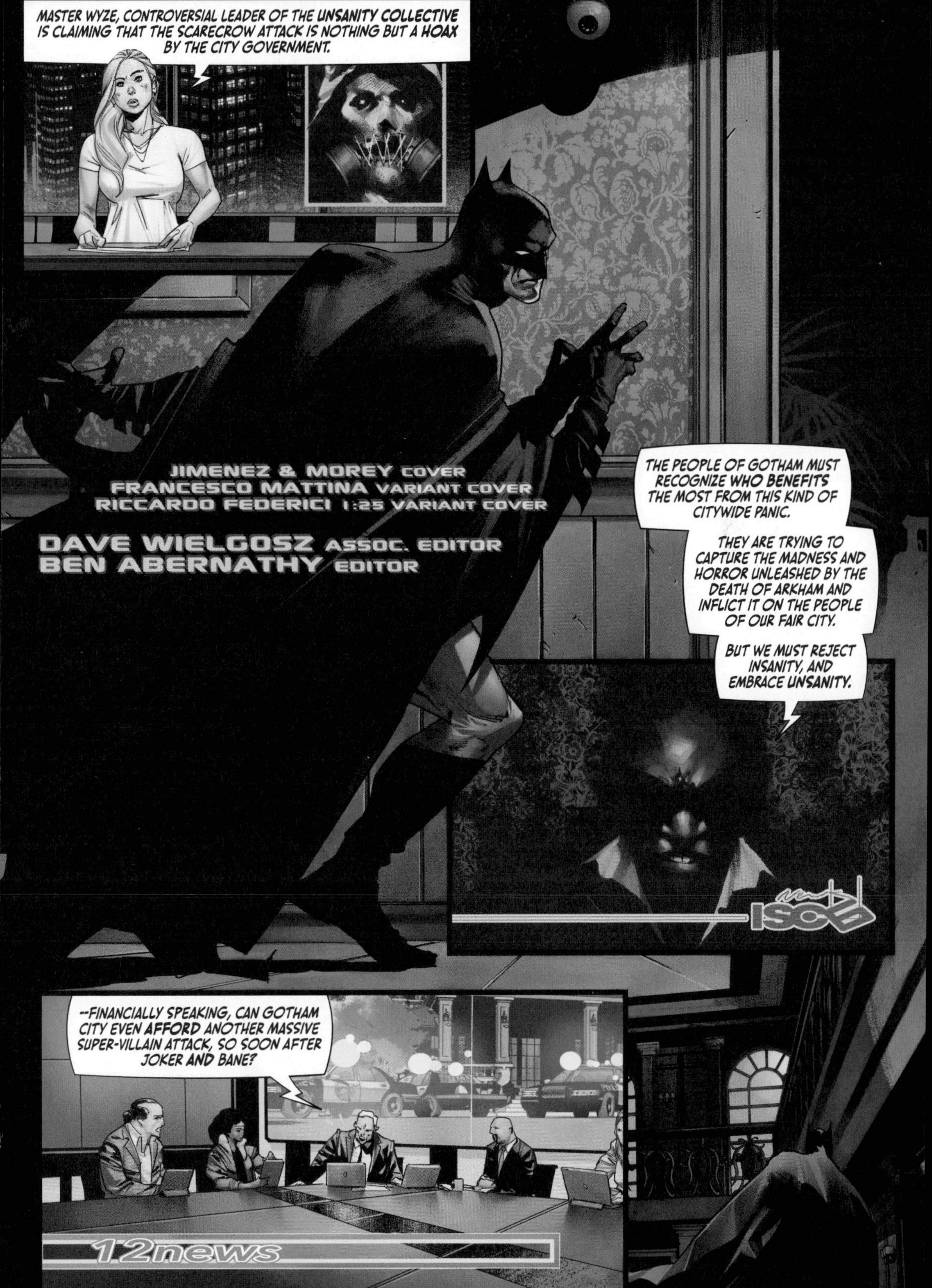

MASTER WYZE, CONTROVERSIAL LEADER OF THE UNSANITY COLLECTIVE IS CLAIMING THAT THE SCARECROW ATTACK IS NOTHING BUT A HOAX BY THE CITY GOVERNMENT.
JIMENEZ & MOREY COVER
FRANCESCO MATTINA VARIANT COVER
RICCARDO FEDERICI 1:25 VARIANT COVER
DAVE WIELGOSZ ASSOC. EDITOR
BEN ABERNATHY EDITOR
THE PEOPLE OF GOTHAM MUST RECOGNIZE WHO BENEFITS THE MOST FROM THIS KIND OF CITYWIDE PANIC.
THEY ARE TRYING TO CAPTURE THE MADNESS AND HORROR UNLEASHED BY THE DEATH OF ARKHAM AND INFLICT IT ON THE PEOPLE OF OUR FAIR CITY.
BUT WE MUST REJECT INSANITY, AND EMBRACE UNSANITY.
ISCB
--FINANCIALLY SPEAKING, CAN GOTHAM CITY EVEN AFFORD ANOTHER MASSIVE SUPER-VILLAIN ATTACK, SO SOON AFTER JOKER AND BANE?
12news

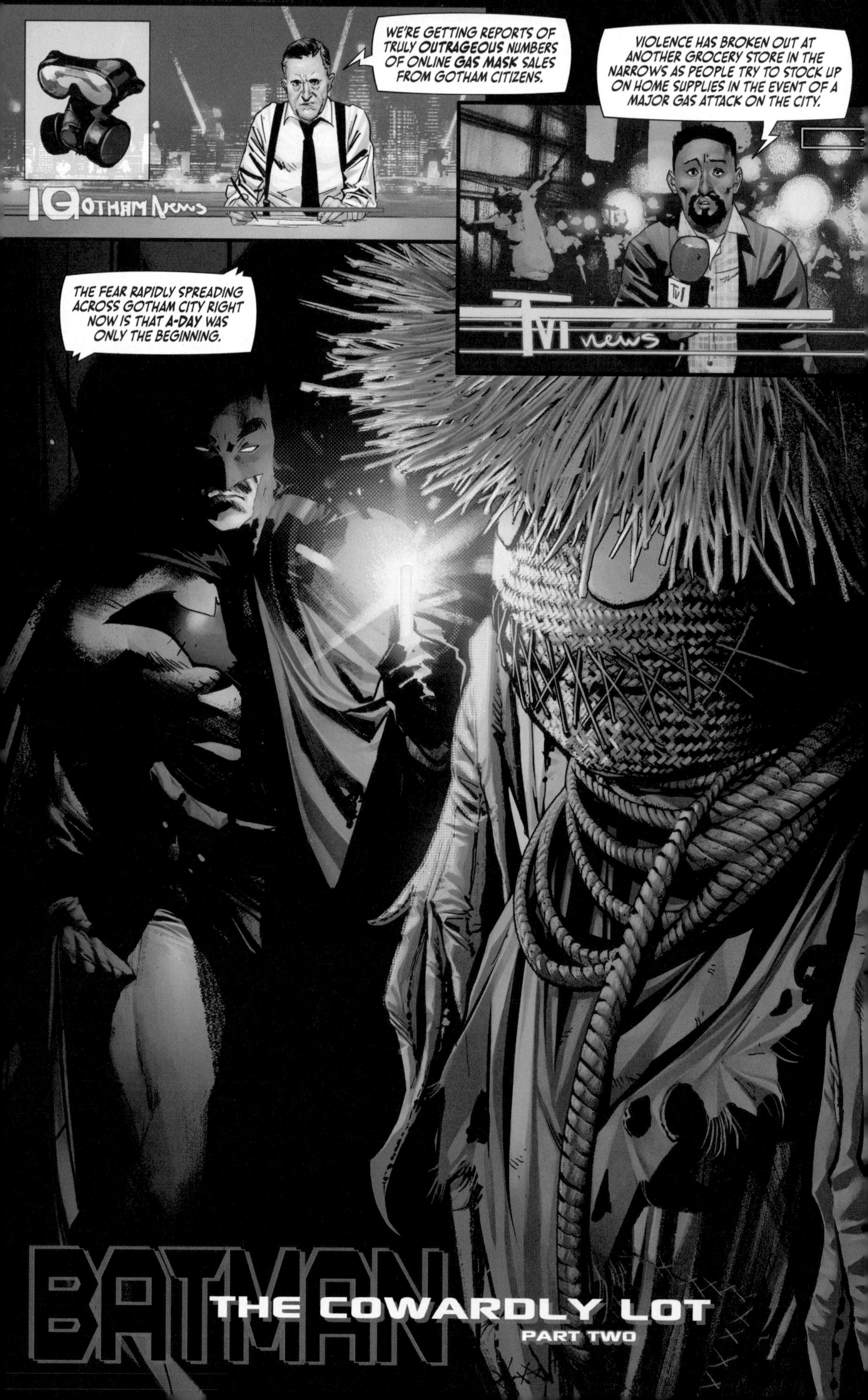
WE'RE GETTING REPORTS OF TRULY OUTRAGEOUS NUMBERS OF ONLINE GAS MASK SALES FROM GOTHAM CITIZENS.
VIOLENCE HAS BROKEN OUT AT ANOTHER GROCERY STORE IN THE NARROWS AS PEOPLE TRY TO STOCK UP ON HOME SUPPLIES IN THE EVENT OF A MAJOR GAS ATTACK ON THE CITY.
GOTHAM NEWS
TVI NEWS
THE FEAR RAPIDLY SPREADING ACROSS GOTHAM CITY RIGHT NOW IS THAT A-DAY WAS ONLY THE BEGINNING.
BATMAN
THE COWARDLY LOT
PART TWO

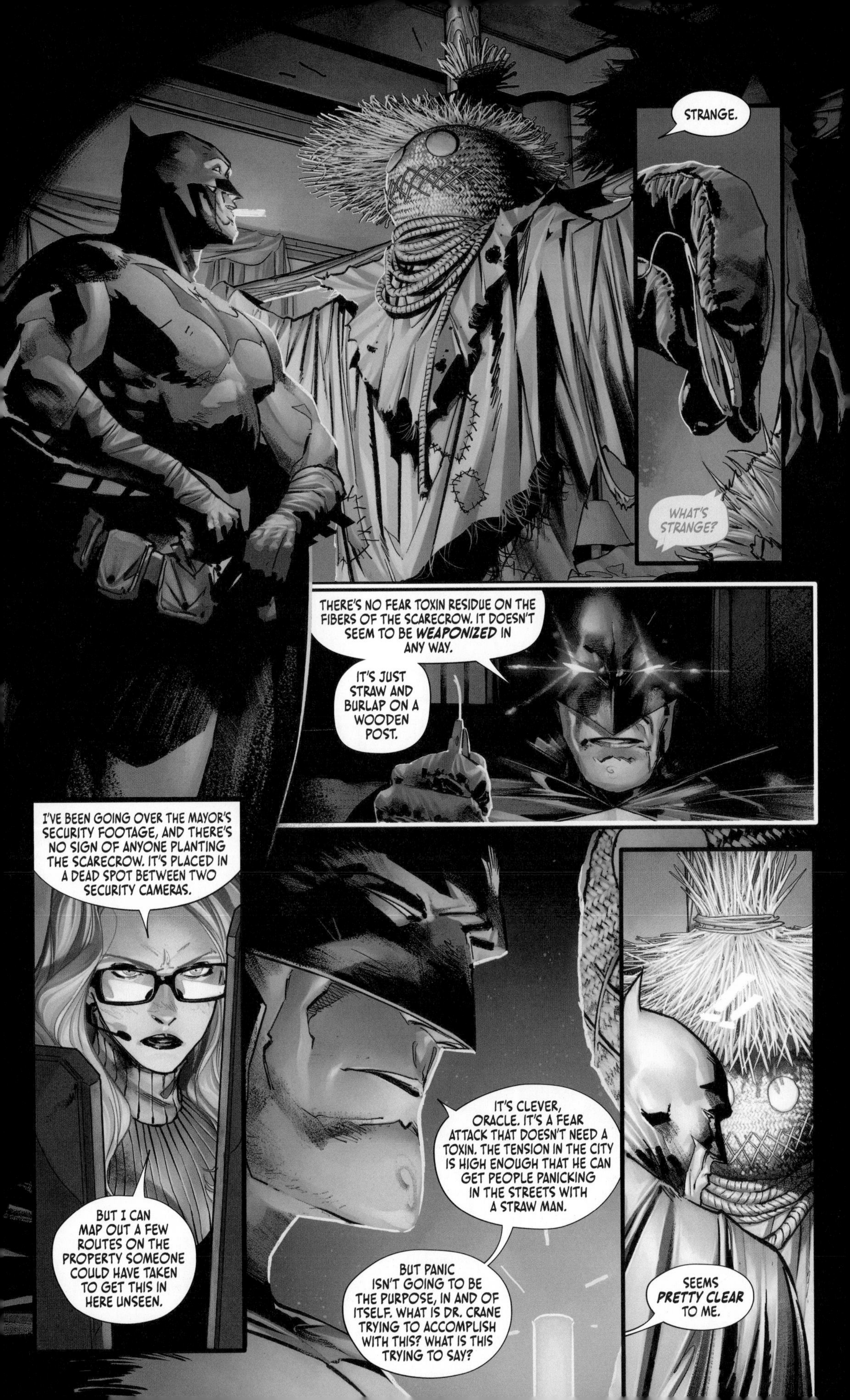
STRANGE.
WHAT'S STRANGE?
THERE'S NO FEAR TOXIN RESIDUE ON THE FIBERS OF THE SCARECROW. IT DOESN'T SEEM TO BE WEAPONIZED IN ANY WAY.
IT'S JUST STRAW AND BURLAP ON A WOODEN POST.
I'VE BEEN GOING OVER THE MAYOR'S SECURITY FOOTAGE, AND THERE'S NO SIGN OF ANYONE PLANTING THE SCARECROW. IT'S PLACED IN A DEAD SPOT BETWEEN TWO SECURITY CAMERAS.
BUT I CAN MAP OUT A FEW ROUTES ON THE PROPERTY SOMEONE COULD HAVE TAKEN TO GET THIS IN HERE UNSEEN.
IT'S CLEVER, ORACLE. IT'S A FEAR ATTACK THAT DOESN'T NEED A TOXIN. THE TENSION IN THE CITY IS HIGH ENOUGH THAT HE CAN GET PEOPLE PANICKING IN THE STREETS WITH A STRAW MAN.
BUT PANIC ISN'T GOING TO BE THE PURPOSE, IN AND OF ITSELF. WHAT IS DR. CRANE TRYING TO ACCOMPLISH WITH THIS? WHAT IS THIS TRYING TO SAY?
SEEMS PRETTY CLEAR TO ME.

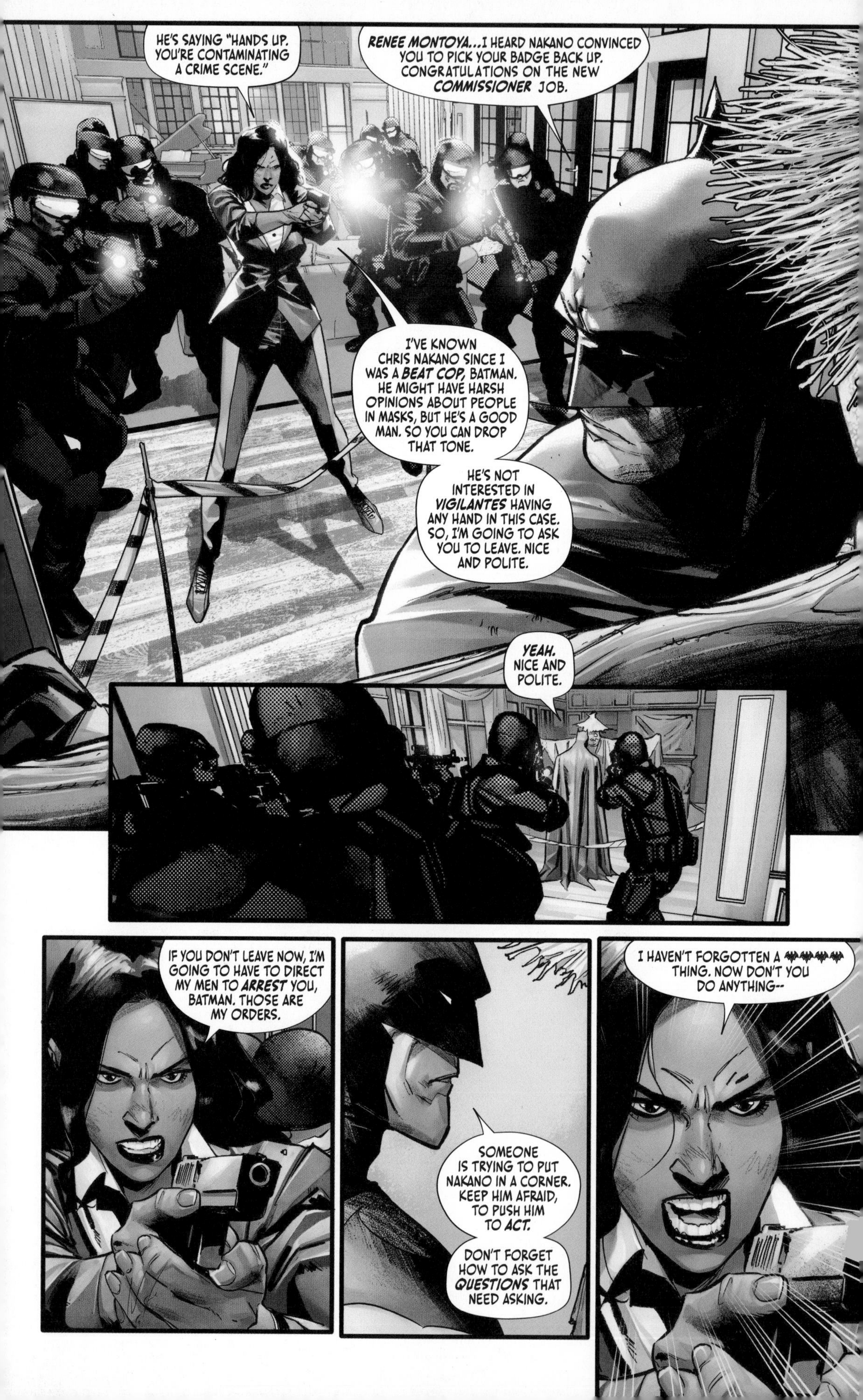
HE'S SAYING "HANDS UP. YOU'RE CONTAMINATING A CRIME SCENE."
RENEE MONTOYA...I HEARD NAKANO CONVINCED YOU TO PICK YOUR BADGE BACK UP. CONGRATULATIONS ON THE NEW COMMISSIONER JOB.
I'VE KNOWN CHRIS NAKANO SINCE I WAS A BEAT COP, BATMAN. HE MIGHT HAVE HARSH OPINIONS ABOUT PEOPLE IN MASKS, BUT HE'S A GOOD MAN. SO YOU CAN DROP THAT TONE.
HE'S NOT INTERESTED IN VIGILANTES HAVING ANY HAND IN THIS CASE. SO, I'M GOING TO ASK YOU TO LEAVE. NICE AND POLITE.
YEAH. NICE AND POLITE.
IF YOU DON'T LEAVE NOW, I'M GOING TO HAVE TO DIRECT MY MEN TO ARREST YOU, BATMAN. THOSE ARE MY ORDERS.
SOMEONE IS TRYING TO PUT NAKANO IN A CORNER. KEEP HIM AFRAID, TO PUSH HIM TO ACT.
DON'T FORGET HOW TO ASK THE QUESTIONS THAT NEED ASKING.
I HAVEN'T FORGOTTEN A THING. NOW DON'T YOU DO ANYTHING--

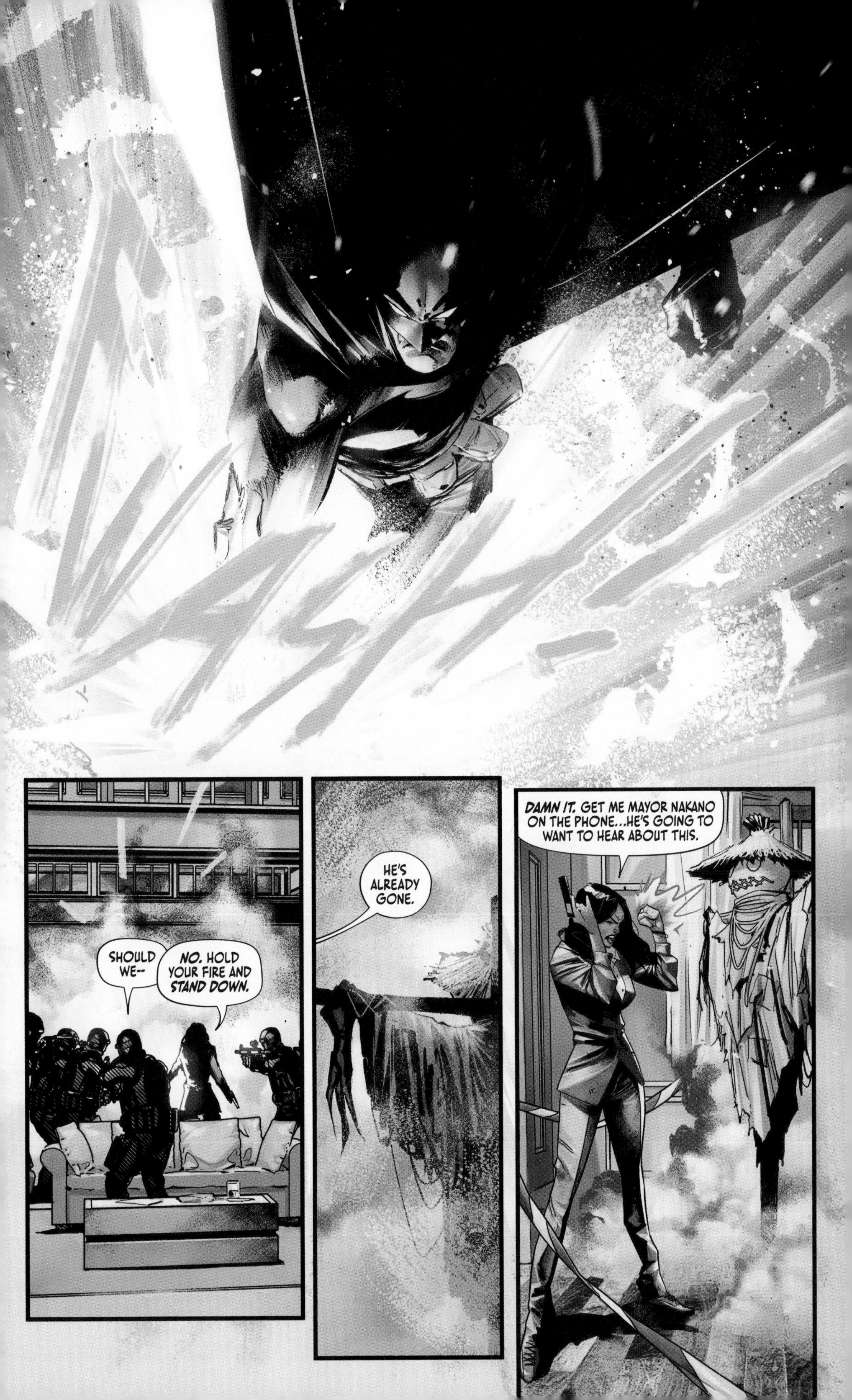
SHOULD WE--
NO. HOLD YOUR FIRE AND STAND DOWN.
HE'S ALREADY GONE.
DAMN IT. GET ME MAYOR NAKANO ON THE PHONE...HE'S GOING TO WANT TO HEAR ABOUT THIS.

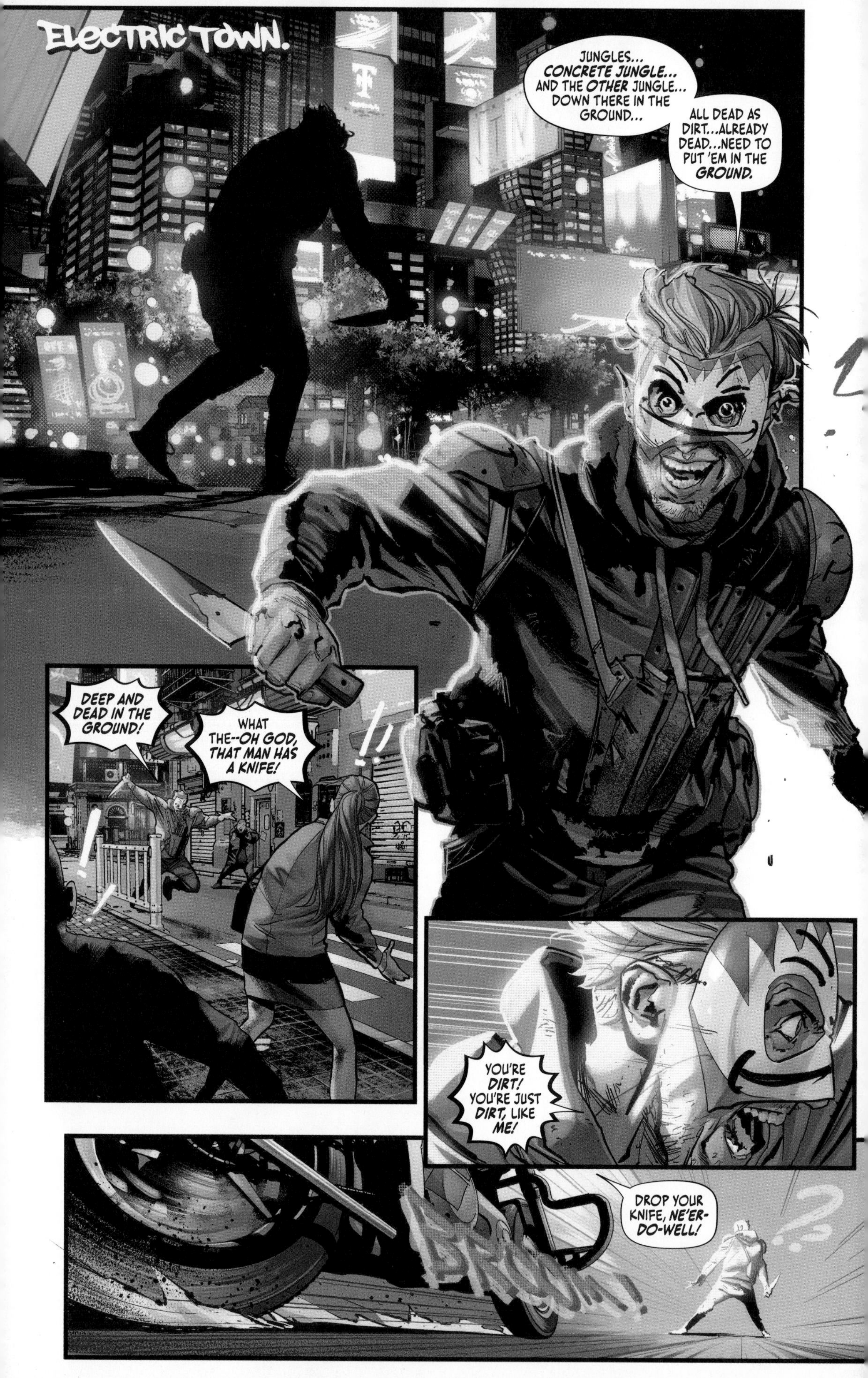
ELECTRIC TOWN.
JUNGLES... CONCRETE JUNGLE... AND THE OTHER JUNGLE... DOWN THERE IN THE GROUND...
ALL DEAD AS DIRT...ALREADY DEAD...NEED TO PUT 'EM IN THE GROUND.
DEEP AND DEAD IN THE GROUND!
WHAT THE--OH GOD, THAT MAN HAS A KNIFE!
YOU'RE DIRT! YOU'RE JUST DIRT, LIKE ME!
DROP YOUR KNIFE, NE'ER-DO-WELL!

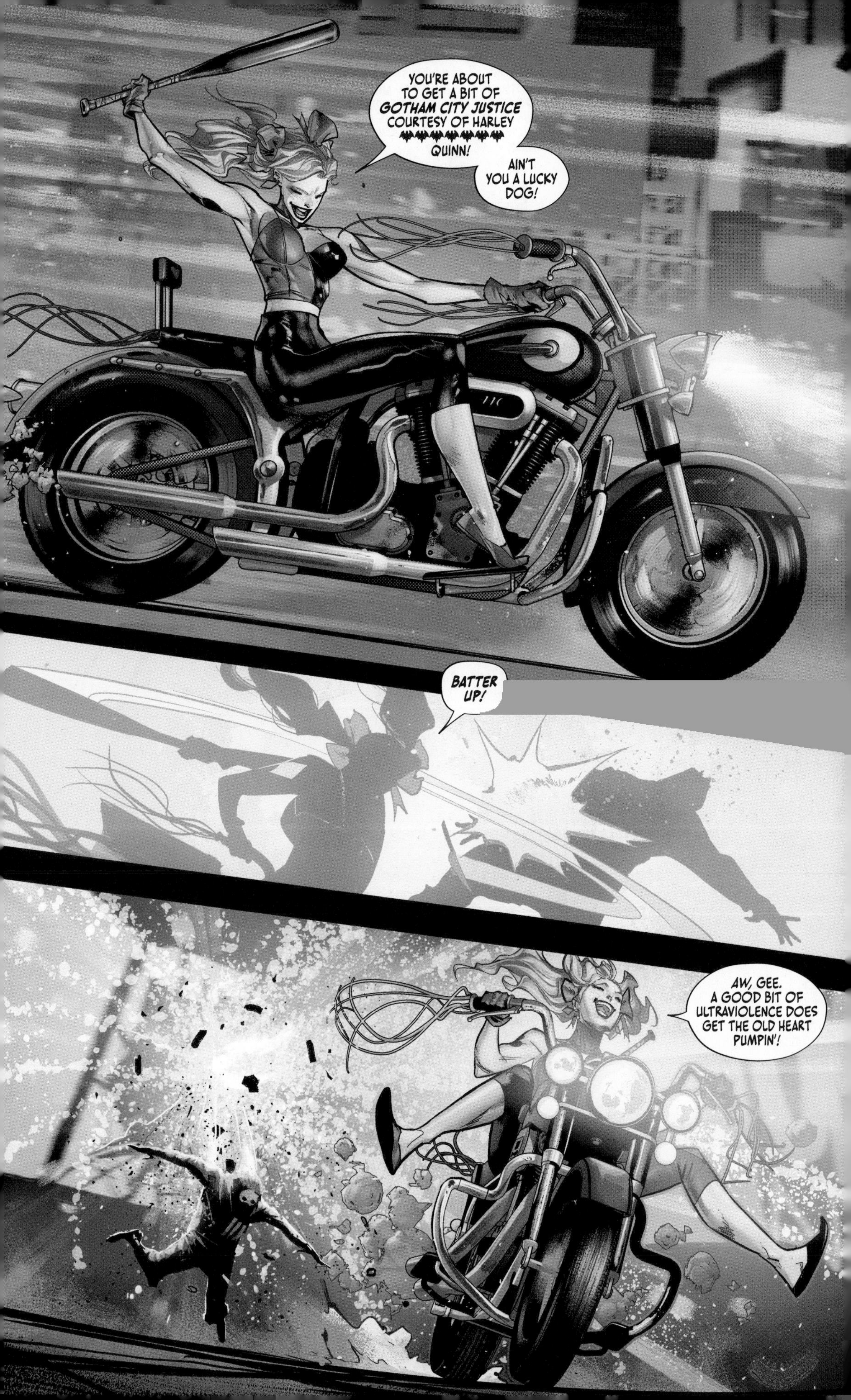
YOU'RE ABOUT TO GET A BIT OF *GOTHAM CITY JUSTICE* COURTESY OF HARLEY QUINN!
AIN'T YOU A LUCKY DOG!
BATTER UP!
AW, GEE. A GOOD BIT OF ULTRAVIOLENCE DOES GET THE OLD HEART PUMPIN'!

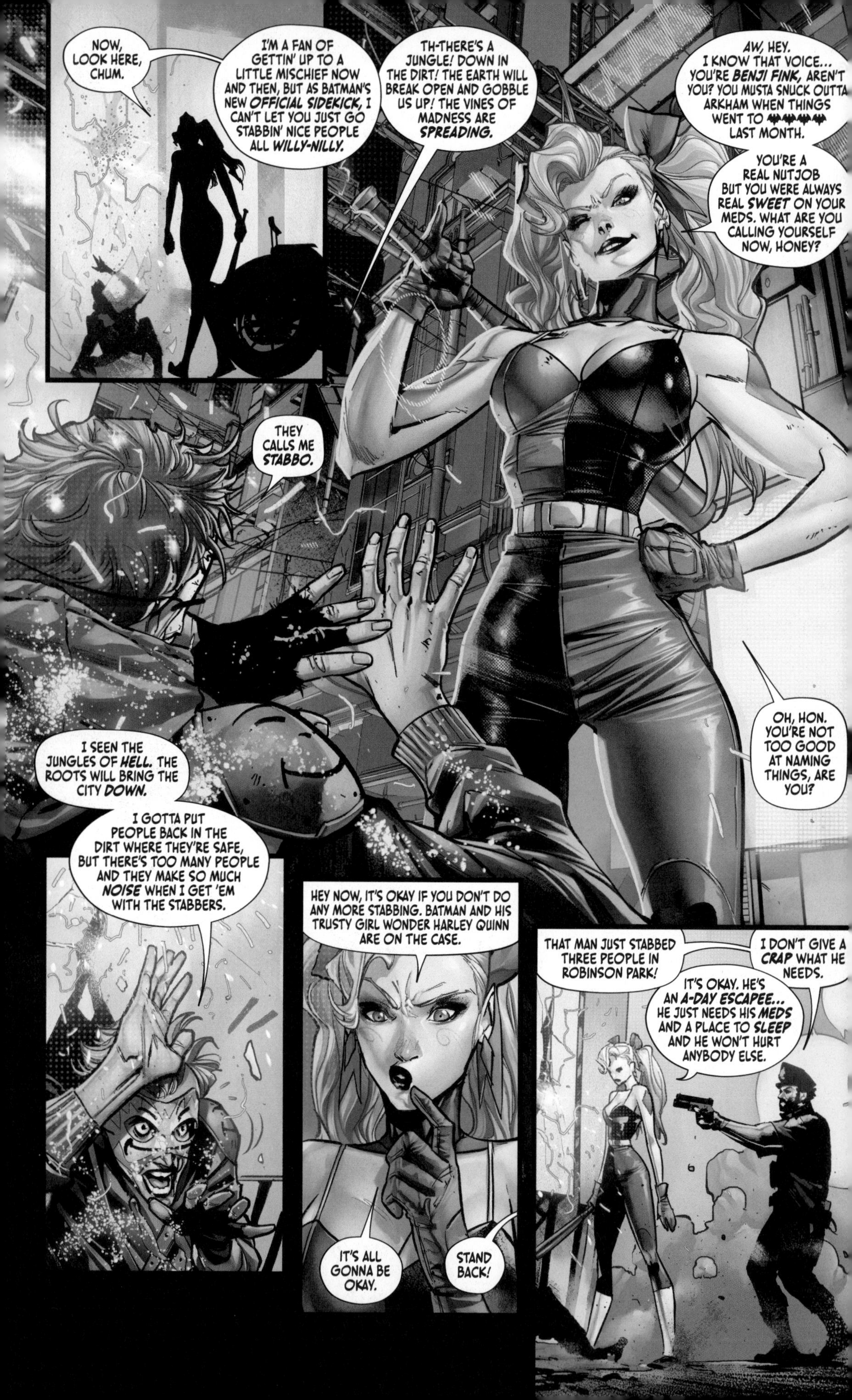
NOW, LOOK HERE, CHUM.
I'M A FAN OF GETTIN' UP TO A LITTLE MISCHIEF NOW AND THEN, BUT AS BATMAN'S NEW *OFFICIAL SIDEKICK*, I CAN'T LET YOU JUST GO STABBIN' NICE PEOPLE ALL *WILLY-NILLY.*
TH-THERE'S A JUNGLE! DOWN IN THE DIRT! THE EARTH WILL BREAK OPEN AND GOBBLE US UP! THE VINES OF MADNESS ARE *SPREADING.*
AW, HEY. I KNOW THAT VOICE... YOU'RE *BENJI FINK*, AREN'T YOU? YOU MUSTA SNUCK OUTTA ARKHAM WHEN THINGS WENT TO LAST MONTH.
YOU'RE A REAL NUTJOB BUT YOU WERE ALWAYS REAL *SWEET* ON YOUR MEDS. WHAT ARE YOU CALLING YOURSELF NOW, HONEY?
THEY CALLS ME *STABBO.*
OH, HON. YOU'RE NOT TOO GOOD AT NAMING THINGS, ARE YOU?
I SEEN THE JUNGLES OF *HELL*. THE ROOTS WILL BRING THE CITY *DOWN.*
I GOTTA PUT PEOPLE BACK IN THE DIRT WHERE THEY'RE SAFE, BUT THERE'S TOO MANY PEOPLE AND THEY MAKE SO MUCH *NOISE* WHEN I GET 'EM WITH THE STABBERS.
HEY NOW, IT'S OKAY IF YOU DON'T DO ANY MORE STABBING. BATMAN AND HIS TRUSTY GIRL WONDER HARLEY QUINN ARE ON THE CASE.
IT'S ALL GONNA BE OKAY.
STAND BACK!
THAT MAN JUST STABBED THREE PEOPLE IN ROBINSON PARK!
IT'S OKAY. HE'S AN *A-DAY ESCAPEE*... HE JUST NEEDS HIS *MEDS* AND A PLACE TO *SLEEP* AND HE WON'T HURT ANYBODY ELSE.
I DON'T GIVE A *CRAP* WHAT HE NEEDS.

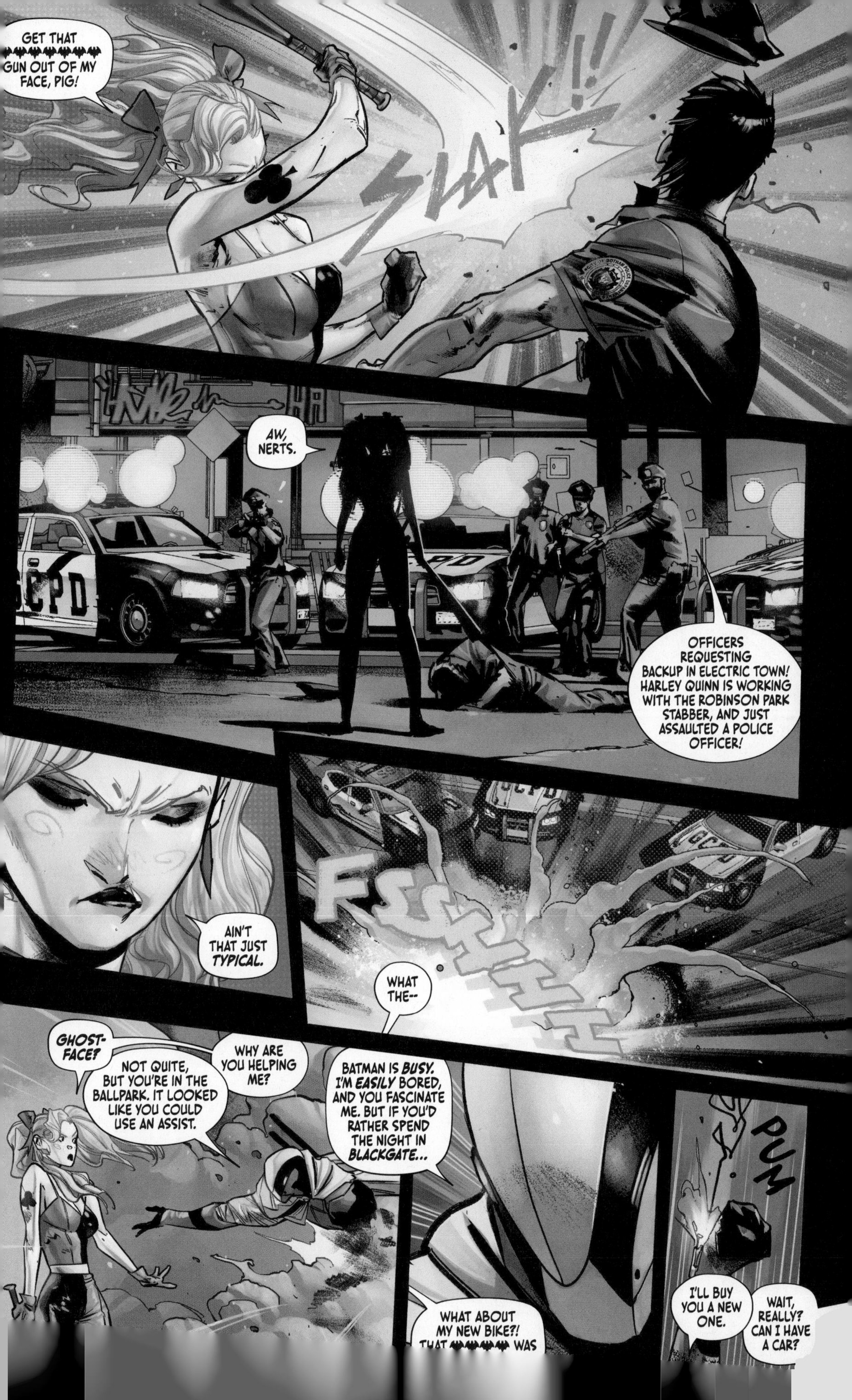

GET THAT GUN OUT OF MY FACE, PIG!
SLAK!!
AW, NERTS.
OFFICERS REQUESTING BACKUP IN ELECTRIC TOWN! HARLEY QUINN IS WORKING WITH THE ROBINSON PARK STABBER, AND JUST ASSAULTED A POLICE OFFICER!
AIN'T THAT JUST TYPICAL.
FSSHHH
WHAT THE--
GHOST-FACE?
NOT QUITE, BUT YOU'RE IN THE BALLPARK. IT LOOKED LIKE YOU COULD USE AN ASSIST.
WHY ARE YOU HELPING ME?
BATMAN IS BUSY. I'M EASILY BORED, AND YOU FASCINATE ME. BUT IF YOU'D RATHER SPEND THE NIGHT IN BLACKGATE...
WHAT ABOUT MY NEW BIKE?! THAT WAS
PUM
I'LL BUY YOU A NEW ONE.
WAIT, REALLY? CAN I HAVE A CAR?

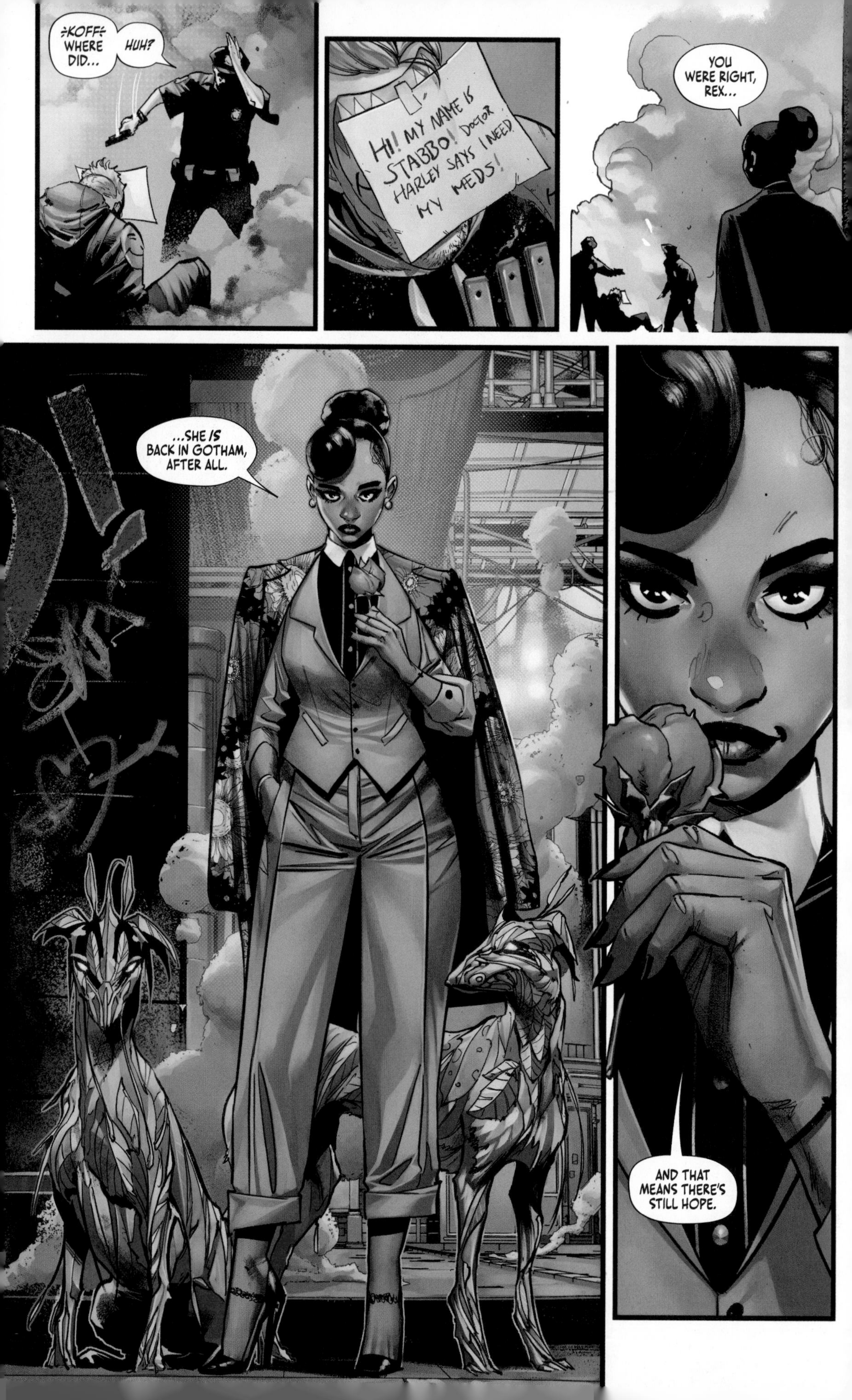

KOFF WHERE DID...
HUH?
HI! MY NAME IS STABBO! DOCTOR HARLEY SAYS I NEED MY MEDS!
YOU WERE RIGHT, REX...
...SHE *IS* BACK IN GOTHAM, AFTER ALL.
AND THAT MEANS THERE'S STILL HOPE.

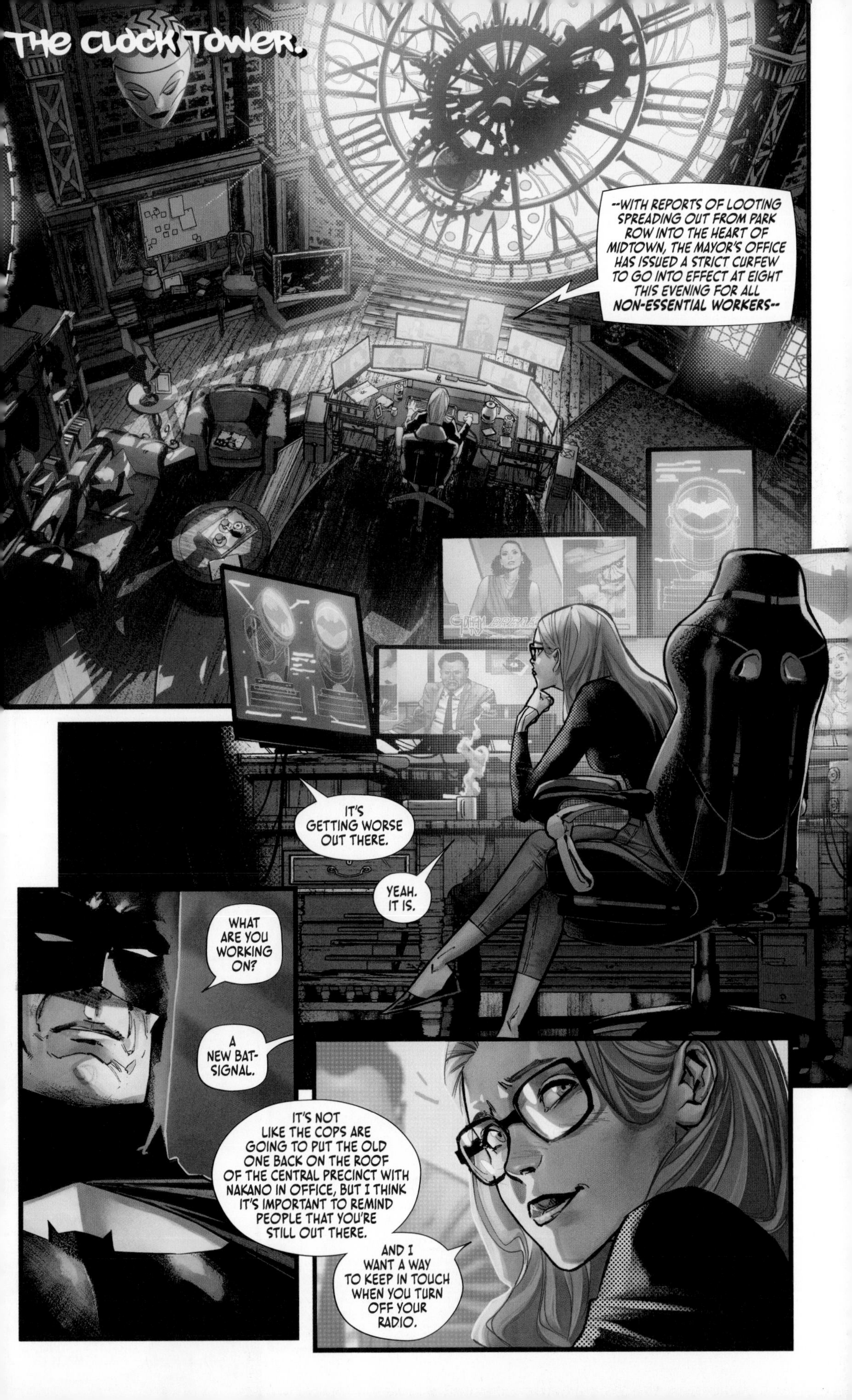
THE CLOCK TOWER.
--WITH REPORTS OF LOOTING SPREADING OUT FROM PARK ROW INTO THE HEART OF MIDTOWN, THE MAYOR'S OFFICE HAS ISSUED A STRICT CURFEW TO GO INTO EFFECT AT EIGHT THIS EVENING FOR ALL NON-ESSENTIAL WORKERS--
IT'S GETTING WORSE OUT THERE.
YEAH. IT IS.
WHAT ARE YOU WORKING ON?
A NEW BAT-SIGNAL.
IT'S NOT LIKE THE COPS ARE GOING TO PUT THE OLD ONE BACK ON THE ROOF OF THE CENTRAL PRECINCT WITH NAKANO IN OFFICE, BUT I THINK IT'S IMPORTANT TO REMIND PEOPLE THAT YOU'RE STILL OUT THERE.
AND I WANT A WAY TO KEEP IN TOUCH WHEN YOU TURN OFF YOUR RADIO.

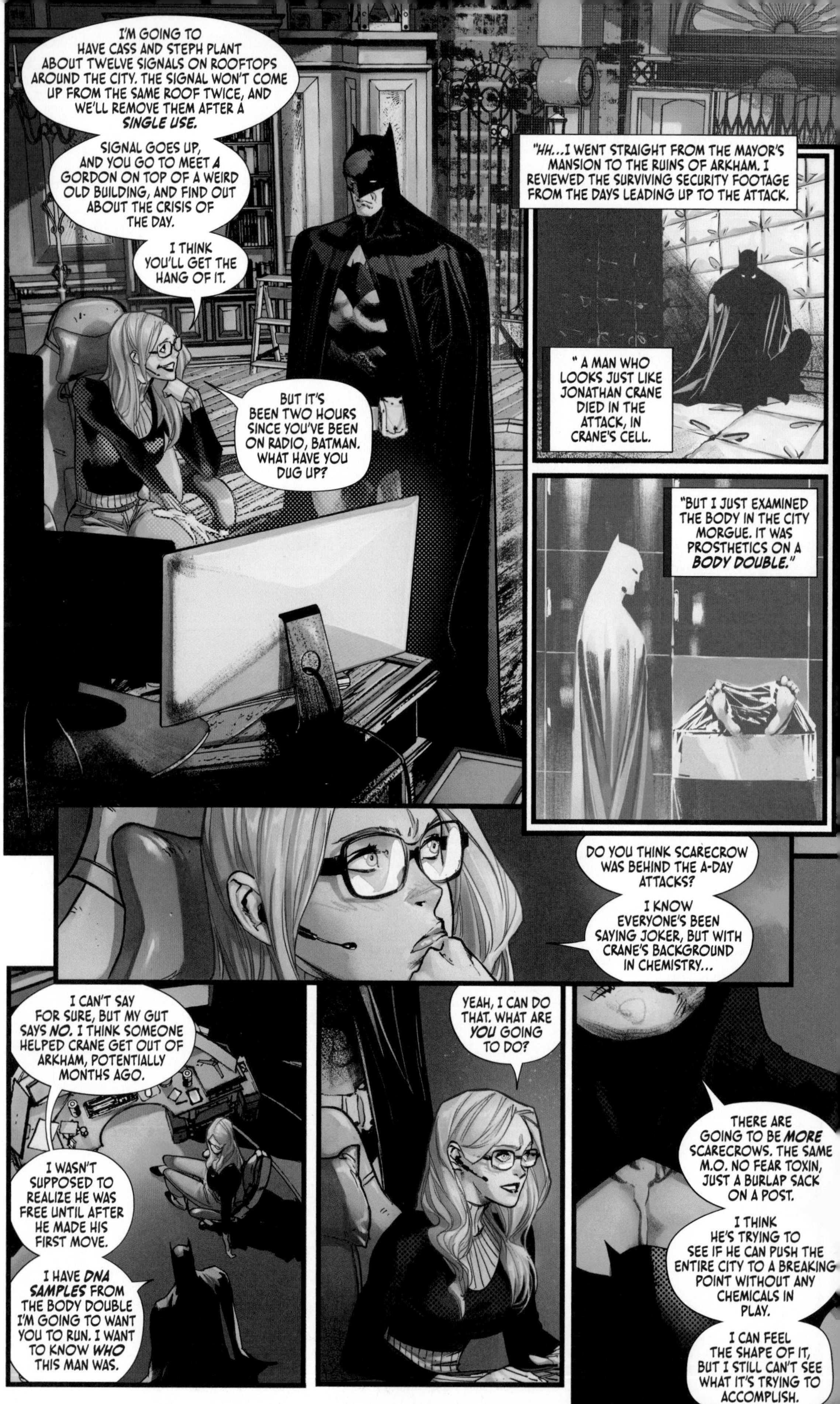
I'M GOING TO HAVE CASS AND STEPH PLANT ABOUT TWELVE SIGNALS ON ROOFTOPS AROUND THE CITY. THE SIGNAL WON'T COME UP FROM THE SAME ROOF TWICE, AND WE'LL REMOVE THEM AFTER A SINGLE USE.
SIGNAL GOES UP, AND YOU GO TO MEET A GORDON ON TOP OF A WEIRD OLD BUILDING, AND FIND OUT ABOUT THE CRISIS OF THE DAY.
I THINK YOU'LL GET THE HANG OF IT.
BUT IT'S BEEN TWO HOURS SINCE YOU'VE BEEN ON RADIO, BATMAN. WHAT HAVE YOU DUG UP?
"HH...I WENT STRAIGHT FROM THE MAYOR'S MANSION TO THE RUINS OF ARKHAM. I REVIEWED THE SURVIVING SECURITY FOOTAGE FROM THE DAYS LEADING UP TO THE ATTACK.
" A MAN WHO LOOKS JUST LIKE JONATHAN CRANE DIED IN THE ATTACK, IN CRANE'S CELL.
"BUT I JUST EXAMINED THE BODY IN THE CITY MORGUE. IT WAS PROSTHETICS ON A BODY DOUBLE."
DO YOU THINK SCARECROW WAS BEHIND THE A-DAY ATTACKS?
I KNOW EVERYONE'S BEEN SAYING JOKER, BUT WITH CRANE'S BACKGROUND IN CHEMISTRY...
I CAN'T SAY FOR SURE, BUT MY GUT SAYS NO. I THINK SOMEONE HELPED CRANE GET OUT OF ARKHAM, POTENTIALLY MONTHS AGO.
I WASN'T SUPPOSED TO REALIZE HE WAS FREE UNTIL AFTER HE MADE HIS FIRST MOVE.
I HAVE DNA SAMPLES FROM THE BODY DOUBLE I'M GOING TO WANT YOU TO RUN. I WANT TO KNOW WHO THIS MAN WAS.
YEAH, I CAN DO THAT. WHAT ARE YOU GOING TO DO?
THERE ARE GOING TO BE MORE SCARECROWS. THE SAME M.O. NO FEAR TOXIN, JUST A BURLAP SACK ON A POST.
I THINK HE'S TRYING TO SEE IF HE CAN PUSH THE ENTIRE CITY TO A BREAKING POINT WITHOUT ANY CHEMICALS IN PLAY.
I CAN FEEL THE SHAPE OF IT, BUT I STILL CAN'T SEE WHAT IT'S TRYING TO ACCOMPLISH.

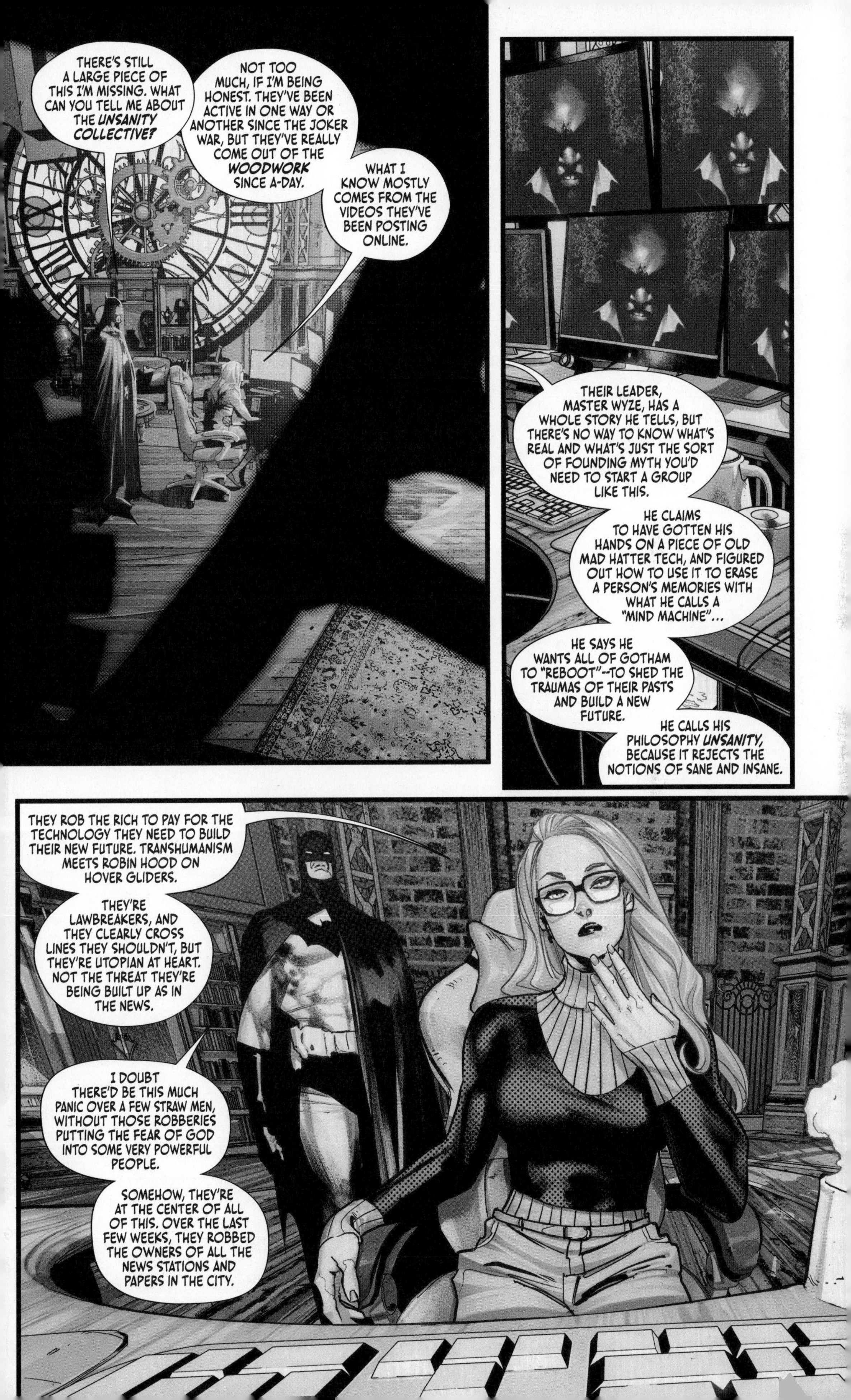
THERE'S STILL A LARGE PIECE OF THIS I'M MISSING. WHAT CAN YOU TELL ME ABOUT THE UNSANITY COLLECTIVE?
NOT TOO MUCH, IF I'M BEING HONEST. THEY'VE BEEN ACTIVE IN ONE WAY OR ANOTHER SINCE THE JOKER WAR, BUT THEY'VE REALLY COME OUT OF THE WOODWORK SINCE A-DAY.
WHAT I KNOW MOSTLY COMES FROM THE VIDEOS THEY'VE BEEN POSTING ONLINE.
THEIR LEADER, MASTER WYZE, HAS A WHOLE STORY HE TELLS, BUT THERE'S NO WAY TO KNOW WHAT'S REAL AND WHAT'S JUST THE SORT OF FOUNDING MYTH YOU'D NEED TO START A GROUP LIKE THIS.
HE CLAIMS TO HAVE GOTTEN HIS HANDS ON A PIECE OF OLD MAD HATTER TECH, AND FIGURED OUT HOW TO USE IT TO ERASE A PERSON'S MEMORIES WITH WHAT HE CALLS A "MIND MACHINE"...
HE SAYS HE WANTS ALL OF GOTHAM TO "REBOOT"--TO SHED THE TRAUMAS OF THEIR PASTS AND BUILD A NEW FUTURE.
HE CALLS HIS PHILOSOPHY UNSANITY, BECAUSE IT REJECTS THE NOTIONS OF SANE AND INSANE.
THEY ROB THE RICH TO PAY FOR THE TECHNOLOGY THEY NEED TO BUILD THEIR NEW FUTURE. TRANSHUMANISM MEETS ROBIN HOOD ON HOVER GLIDERS.
THEY'RE LAWBREAKERS, AND THEY CLEARLY CROSS LINES THEY SHOULDN'T, BUT THEY'RE UTOPIAN AT HEART. NOT THE THREAT THEY'RE BEING BUILT UP AS IN THE NEWS.
I DOUBT THERE'D BE THIS MUCH PANIC OVER A FEW STRAW MEN, WITHOUT THOSE ROBBERIES PUTTING THE FEAR OF GOD INTO SOME VERY POWERFUL PEOPLE.
SOMEHOW, THEY'RE AT THE CENTER OF ALL OF THIS. OVER THE LAST FEW WEEKS, THEY ROBBED THE OWNERS OF ALL THE NEWS STATIONS AND PAPERS IN THE CITY.

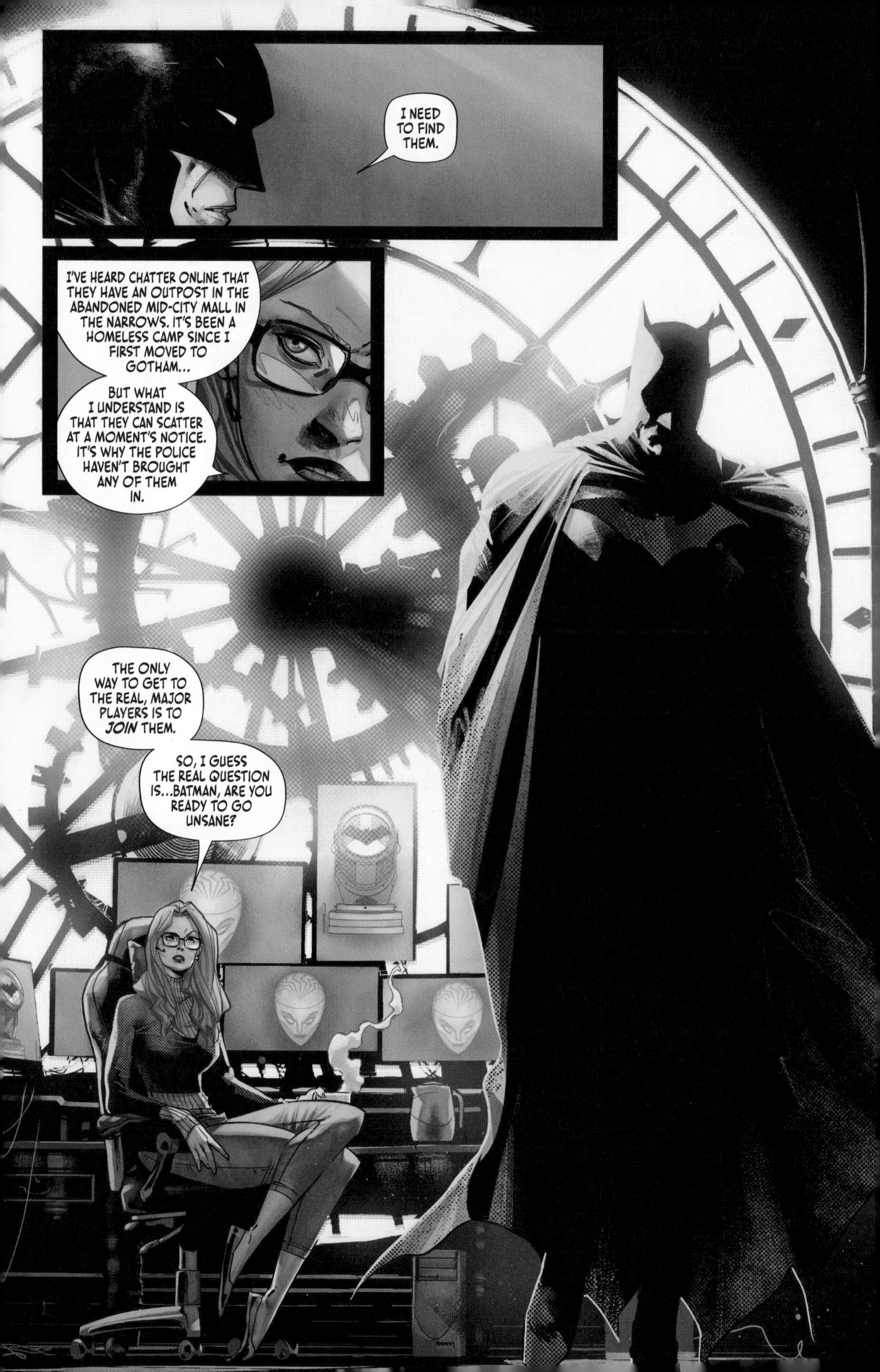
I NEED TO FIND THEM.
I'VE HEARD CHATTER ONLINE THAT THEY HAVE AN OUTPOST IN THE ABANDONED MID-CITY MALL IN THE NARROWS. IT'S BEEN A HOMELESS CAMP SINCE I FIRST MOVED TO GOTHAM...
BUT WHAT I UNDERSTAND IS THAT THEY CAN SCATTER AT A MOMENT'S NOTICE. IT'S WHY THE POLICE HAVEN'T BROUGHT ANY OF THEM IN.
THE ONLY WAY TO GET TO THE REAL, MAJOR PLAYERS IS TO *JOIN* THEM.
SO, I GUESS THE REAL QUESTION IS...BATMAN, ARE YOU READY TO GO UNSANE?

SAINT
INDUSTRIES

MIDTOWN.

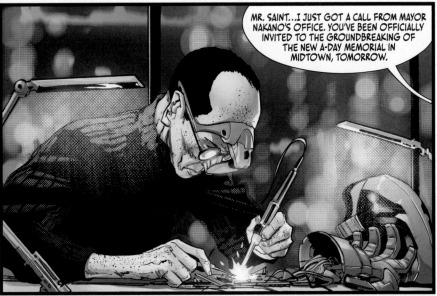

MR. SAINT...I JUST GOT A CALL FROM MAYOR NAKANO'S OFFICE. YOU'VE BEEN OFFICIALLY INVITED TO THE GROUNDBREAKING OF THE NEW A-DAY MEMORIAL IN MIDTOWN, TOMORROW.

THEY'RE GOING TO BE HONORING THE GUARD YOU'RE EYING UP. SEAN MAHONEY.

THANK YOU, RICARDO...THAT'S EXCELLENT NEWS.

SIMON SAYS... GOODBYE.

P-PLEASE ACCEPT THE INVITATION AND GET ON HOME. I'LL BE UP LATE.

OF COURSE, MR. SAINT. I'LL SEE YOU IN THE MORNING.

THE BOY IS GONE.

I'M ALONE.

YOU'RE NEVER ALONE. NOT IN THIS CITY. NOT ANYMORE.

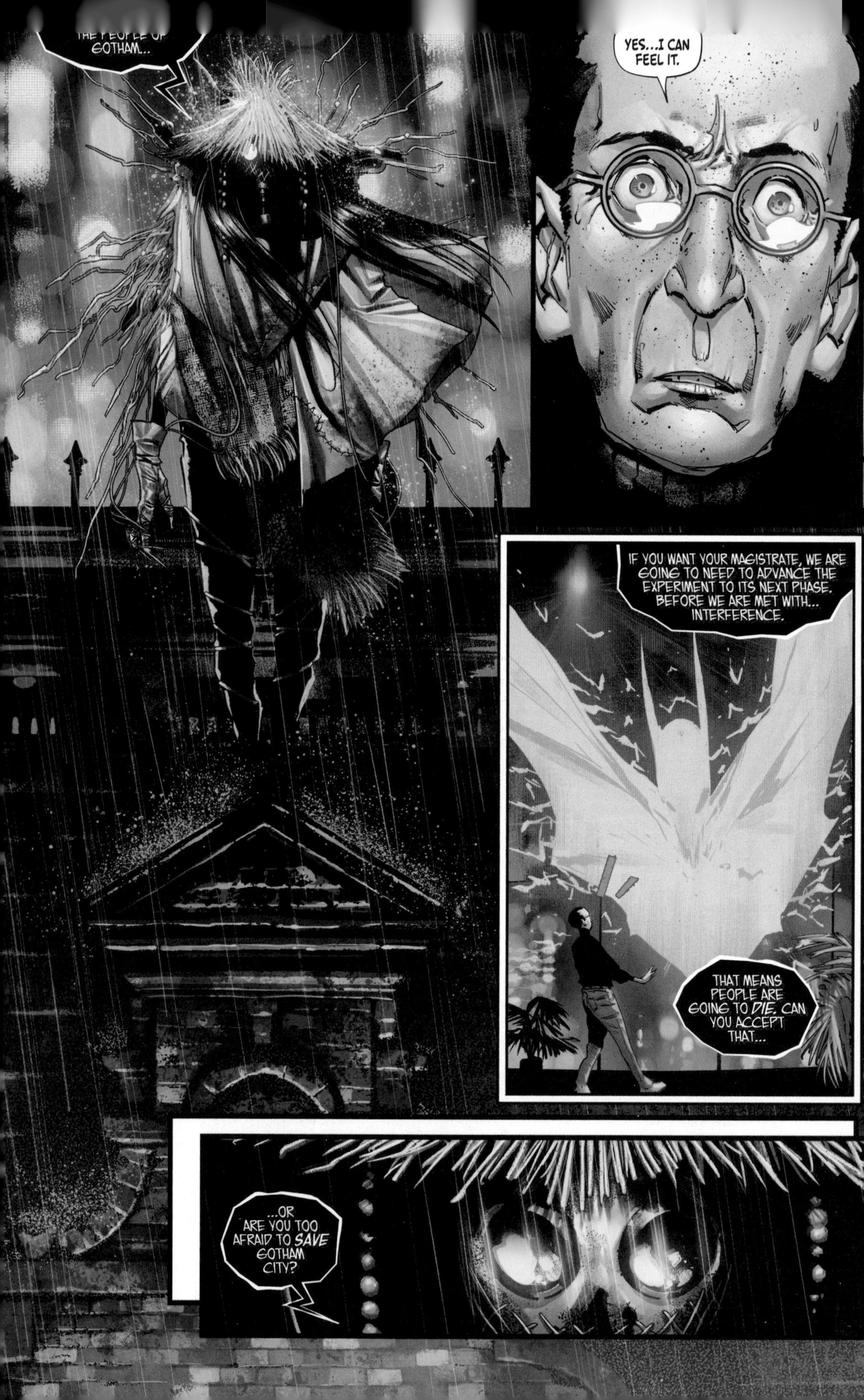
THE PEOPLE OF GOTHAM...
YES...I CAN FEEL IT.
IF YOU WANT YOUR MAGISTRATE, WE ARE GOING TO NEED TO ADVANCE THE EXPERIMENT TO ITS NEXT PHASE. BEFORE WE ARE MET WITH... INTERFERENCE.
THAT MEANS PEOPLE ARE GOING TO DIE. CAN YOU ACCEPT THAT...
...OR ARE YOU TOO AFRAID TO SAVE GOTHAM CITY?

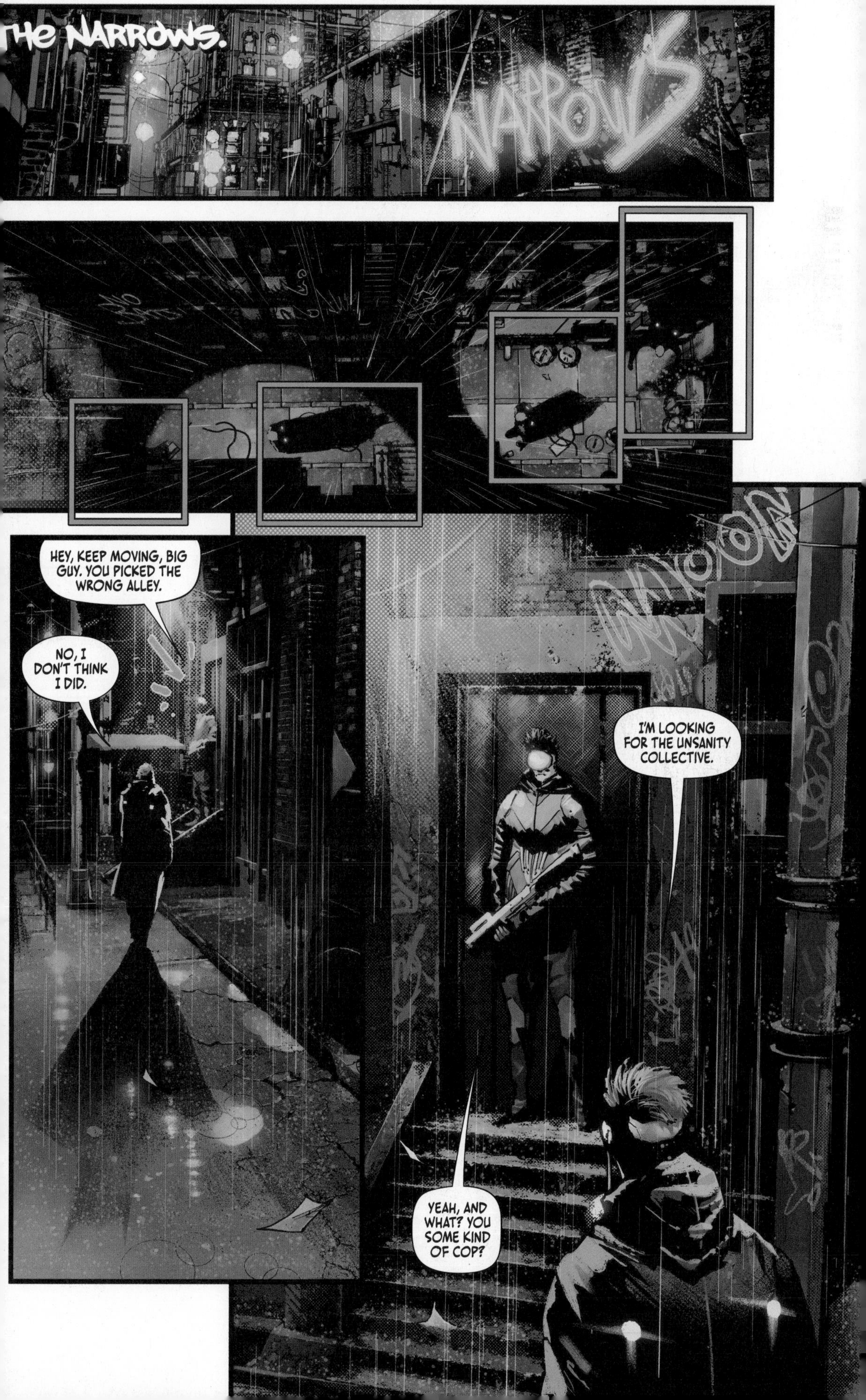
THE NARROWS.
NARROWS
HEY, KEEP MOVING, BIG GUY. YOU PICKED THE WRONG ALLEY.
NO, I DON'T THINK I DID.
I'M LOOKING FOR THE UNSANITY COLLECTIVE.
YEAH, AND WHAT? YOU SOME KIND OF COP?

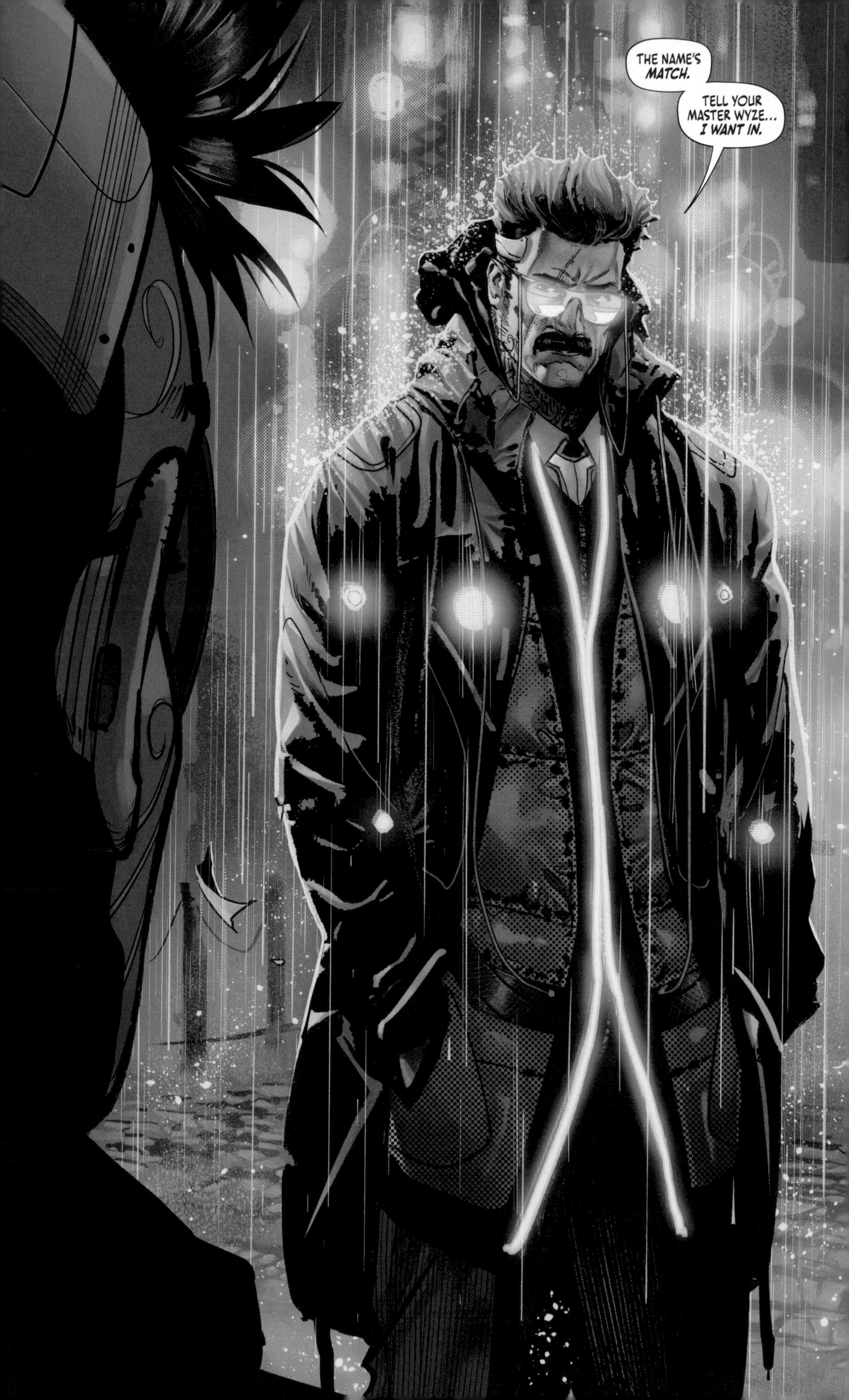
THE NAME'S *MATCH.*
TELL YOUR MASTER WYZE... *I WANT IN.*

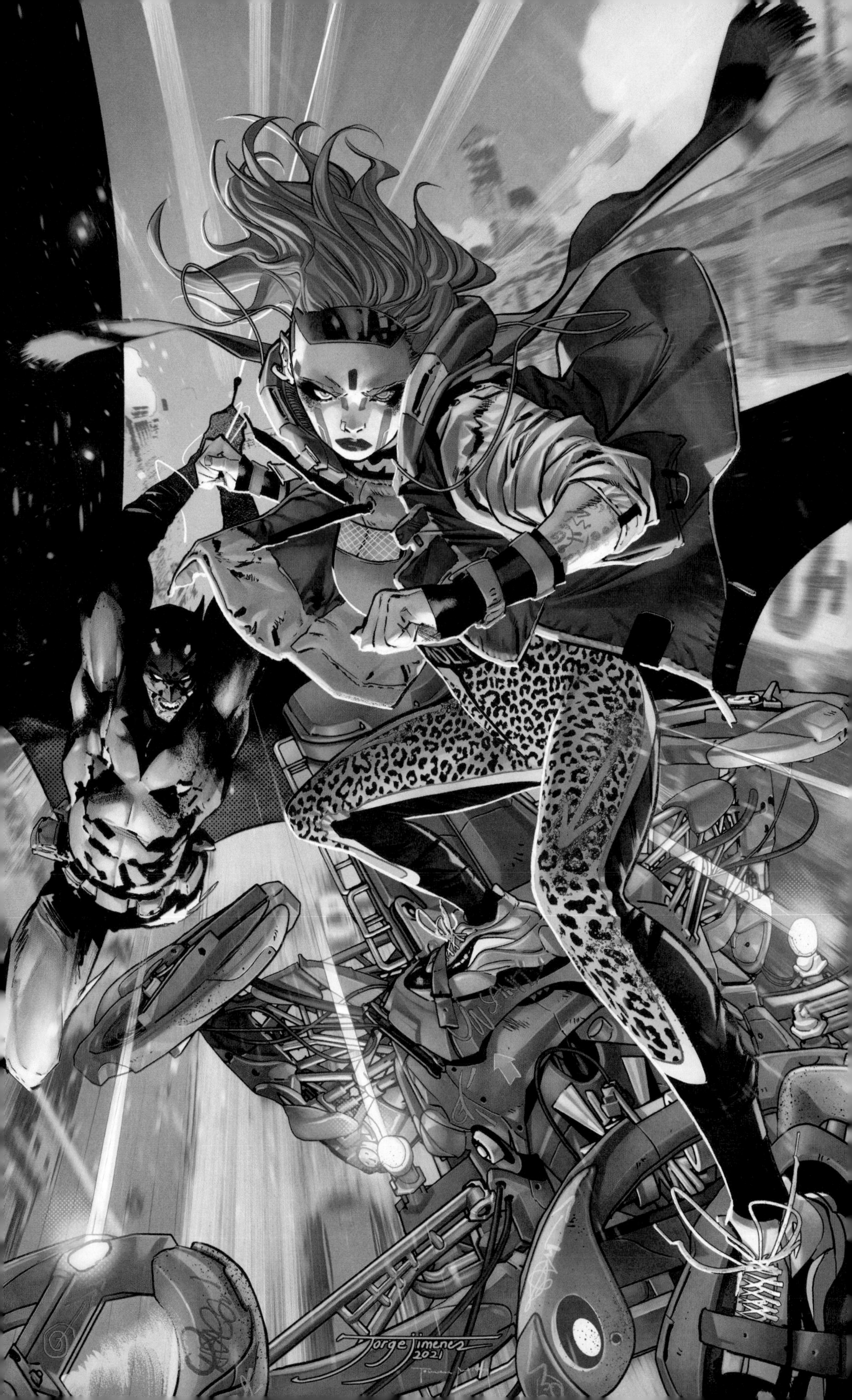
Jorge Jimenez
2021

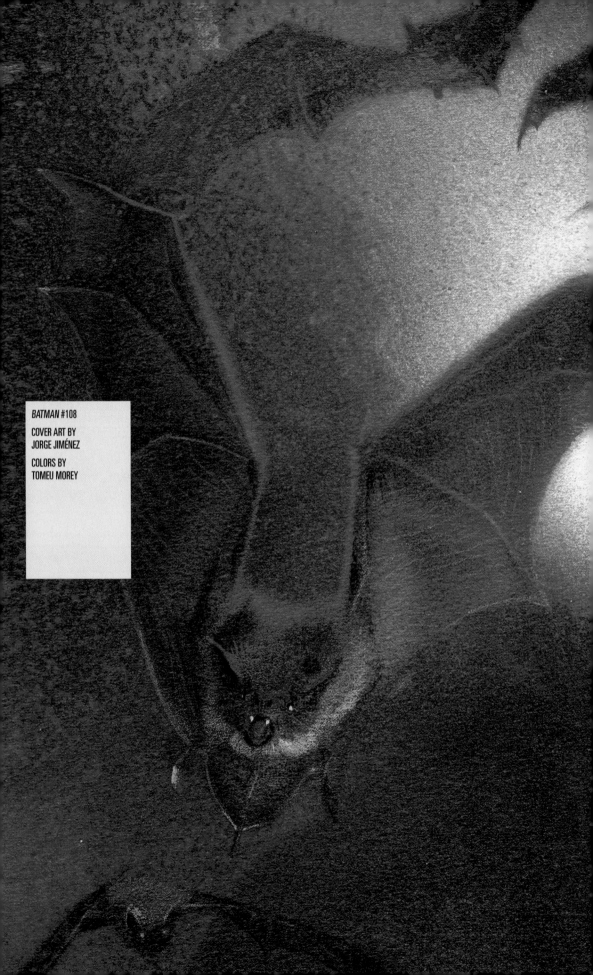

BATMAN #108
COVER ART BY
JORGE JIMÉNEZ

COLORS BY
TOMEU MOREY

IT'S USELESS TO RESIST, BATMAN.
THE TOXINS ARE WARPING YOUR SENSE OF REALITY. DON'T LET YOURSELF GET LOST IN IT.
GROUND YOURSELF IN WHAT YOU KNOW IS REAL. LET GO OF THE FEAR.
YOU CAN'T LET GO. I WON'T LET YOU. THIS IS HAPPENING WHETHER YOU WANT IT TO OR NOT.
REMEMBER HOW YOU PUT IT ALL TOGETHER. REMEMBER HOW YOU GOT HERE. SHE ASKED YOU A QUESTION.
REMEMBER HER SCREAMING. REMEMBER THE HORROR IN HER EYES.
NO. NOT YET. THAT CAME LATER. REMEMBER HER VOICE.
NO, REMEMBER WHO HURT HER. REMEMBER HOW YOU FAILED TO STOP HIM.

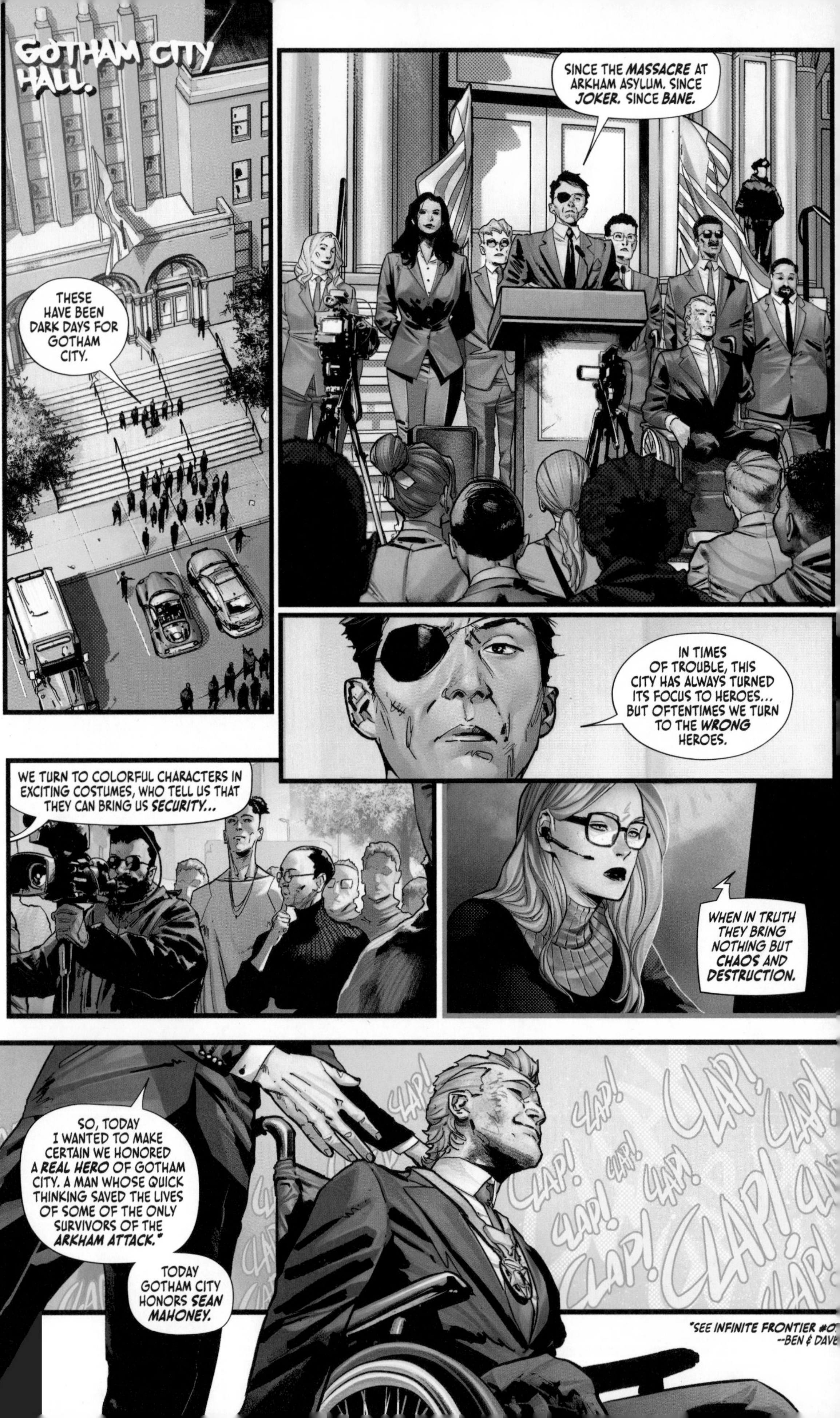

GOTHAM CITY HALL.
THESE HAVE BEEN DARK DAYS FOR GOTHAM CITY.
SINCE THE MASSACRE AT ARKHAM ASYLUM. SINCE JOKER. SINCE BANE.
IN TIMES OF TROUBLE, THIS CITY HAS ALWAYS TURNED ITS FOCUS TO HEROES... BUT OFTENTIMES WE TURN TO THE WRONG HEROES.
WE TURN TO COLORFUL CHARACTERS IN EXCITING COSTUMES, WHO TELL US THAT THEY CAN BRING US SECURITY...
WHEN IN TRUTH THEY BRING NOTHING BUT CHAOS AND DESTRUCTION.
SO, TODAY I WANTED TO MAKE CERTAIN WE HONORED A REAL HERO OF GOTHAM CITY. A MAN WHOSE QUICK THINKING SAVED THE LIVES OF SOME OF THE ONLY SURVIVORS OF THE ARKHAM ATTACK.*
TODAY GOTHAM CITY HONORS SEAN MAHONEY.
CLAP! CLAP! CLAP! CLAP! CLAP! CLAP! CLAP! CLAP! CLAP!
*SEE INFINITE FRONTIER #0
--BEN & DAVE

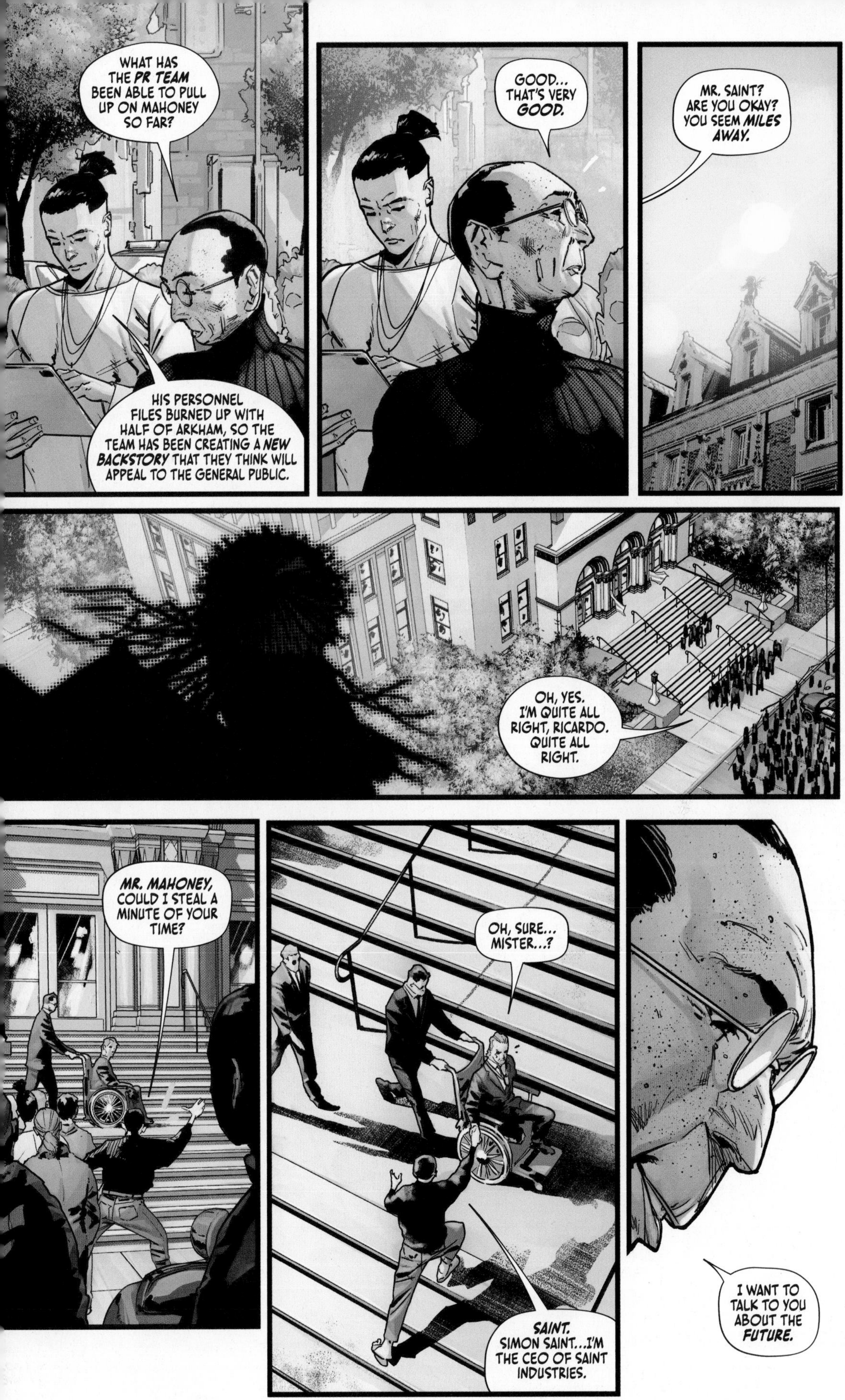
WHAT HAS THE PR TEAM BEEN ABLE TO PULL UP ON MAHONEY SO FAR?
HIS PERSONNEL FILES BURNED UP WITH HALF OF ARKHAM, SO THE TEAM HAS BEEN CREATING A NEW BACKSTORY THAT THEY THINK WILL APPEAL TO THE GENERAL PUBLIC.
GOOD... THAT'S VERY GOOD.
MR. SAINT? ARE YOU OKAY? YOU SEEM MILES AWAY.
OH, YES. I'M QUITE ALL RIGHT, RICARDO. QUITE ALL RIGHT.
MR. MAHONEY, COULD I STEAL A MINUTE OF YOUR TIME?
OH, SURE... MISTER...?
SAINT. SIMON SAINT...I'M THE CEO OF SAINT INDUSTRIES.
I WANT TO TALK TO YOU ABOUT THE FUTURE.

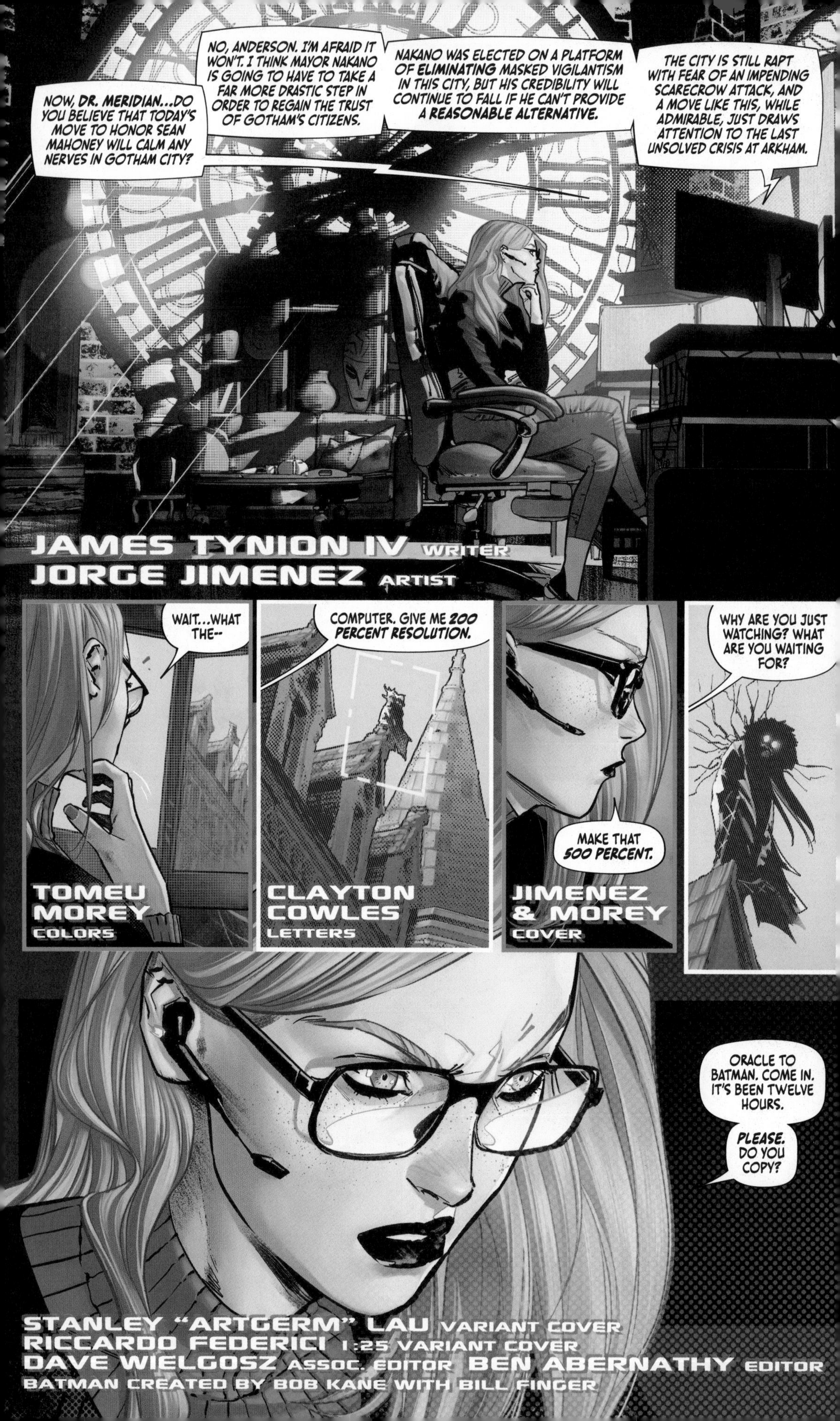
NOW, DR. MERIDIAN...DO YOU BELIEVE THAT TODAY'S MOVE TO HONOR SEAN MAHONEY WILL CALM ANY NERVES IN GOTHAM CITY?
NO, ANDERSON. I'M AFRAID IT WON'T. I THINK MAYOR NAKANO IS GOING TO HAVE TO TAKE A FAR MORE DRASTIC STEP IN ORDER TO REGAIN THE TRUST OF GOTHAM'S CITIZENS.
NAKANO WAS ELECTED ON A PLATFORM OF ELIMINATING MASKED VIGILANTISM IN THIS CITY, BUT HIS CREDIBILITY WILL CONTINUE TO FALL IF HE CAN'T PROVIDE A REASONABLE ALTERNATIVE.
THE CITY IS STILL RAPT WITH FEAR OF AN IMPENDING SCARECROW ATTACK, AND A MOVE LIKE THIS, WHILE ADMIRABLE, JUST DRAWS ATTENTION TO THE LAST UNSOLVED CRISIS AT ARKHAM.
JAMES TYNION IV WRITER
JORGE JIMENEZ ARTIST
WAIT...WHAT THE--
TOMEU MOREY COLORS
COMPUTER. GIVE ME 200 PERCENT RESOLUTION.
CLAYTON COWLES LETTERS
MAKE THAT 500 PERCENT.
JIMENEZ & MOREY COVER
WHY ARE YOU JUST WATCHING? WHAT ARE YOU WAITING FOR?
ORACLE TO BATMAN. COME IN. IT'S BEEN TWELVE HOURS.
PLEASE. DO YOU COPY?
STANLEY "ARTGERM" LAU VARIANT COVER
RICCARDO FEDERICI 1:25 VARIANT COVER
DAVE WIELGOSZ ASSOC. EDITOR BEN ABERNATHY EDITOR
BATMAN CREATED BY BOB KANE WITH BILL FINGER

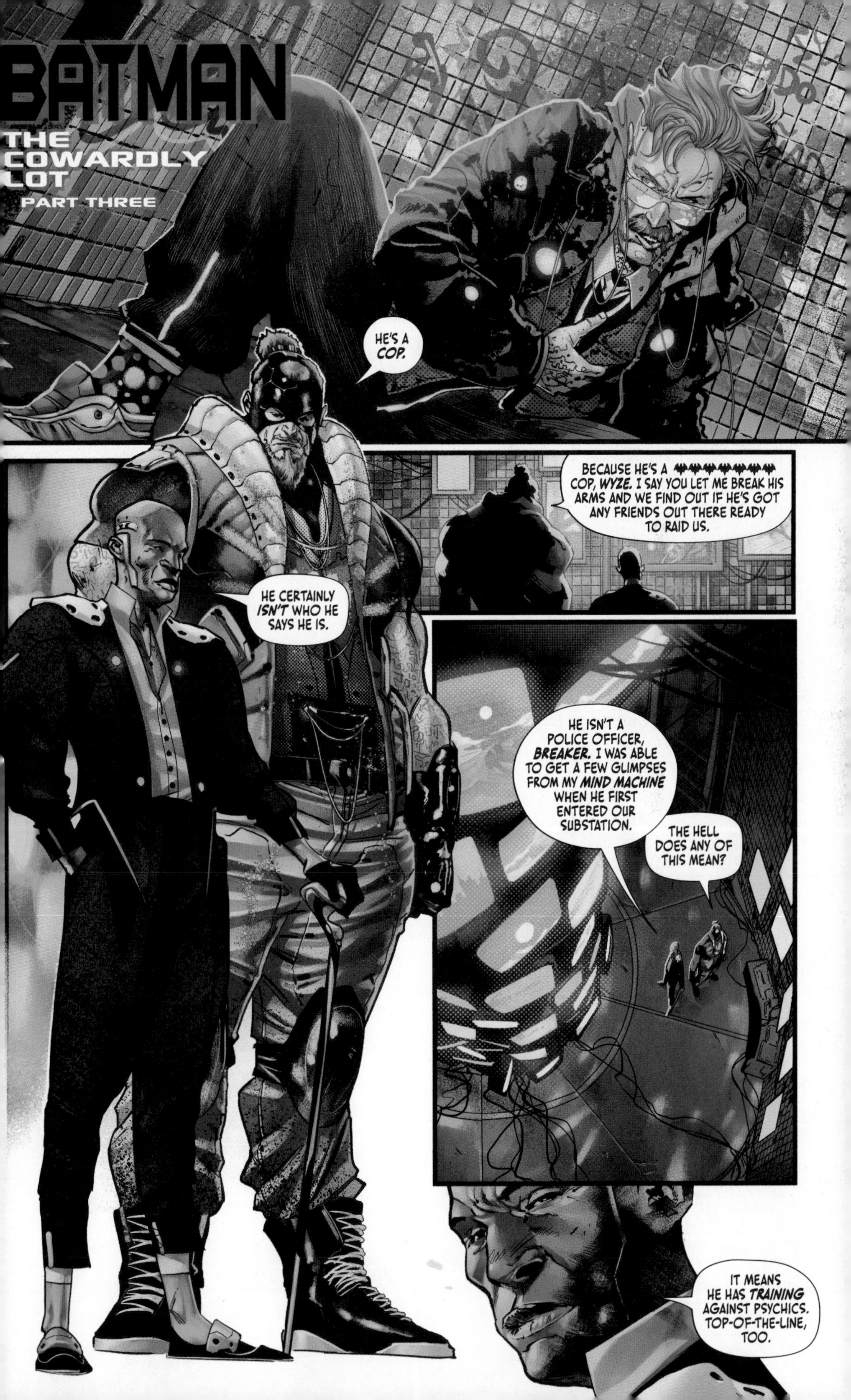
BATMAN
THE COWARDLY LOT
PART THREE
HE'S A *COP.*
BECAUSE HE'S A COP, ***WYZE.*** I SAY YOU LET ME BREAK HIS ARMS AND WE FIND OUT IF HE'S GOT ANY FRIENDS OUT THERE READY TO RAID US.
HE CERTAINLY *ISN'T* WHO HE SAYS HE IS.
HE ISN'T A POLICE OFFICER, ***BREAKER.*** I WAS ABLE TO GET A FEW GLIMPSES FROM MY ***MIND MACHINE*** WHEN HE FIRST ENTERED OUR SUBSTATION.
THE HELL DOES ANY OF THIS MEAN?
IT MEANS HE HAS ***TRAINING*** AGAINST PSYCHICS. TOP-OF-THE-LINE, TOO.

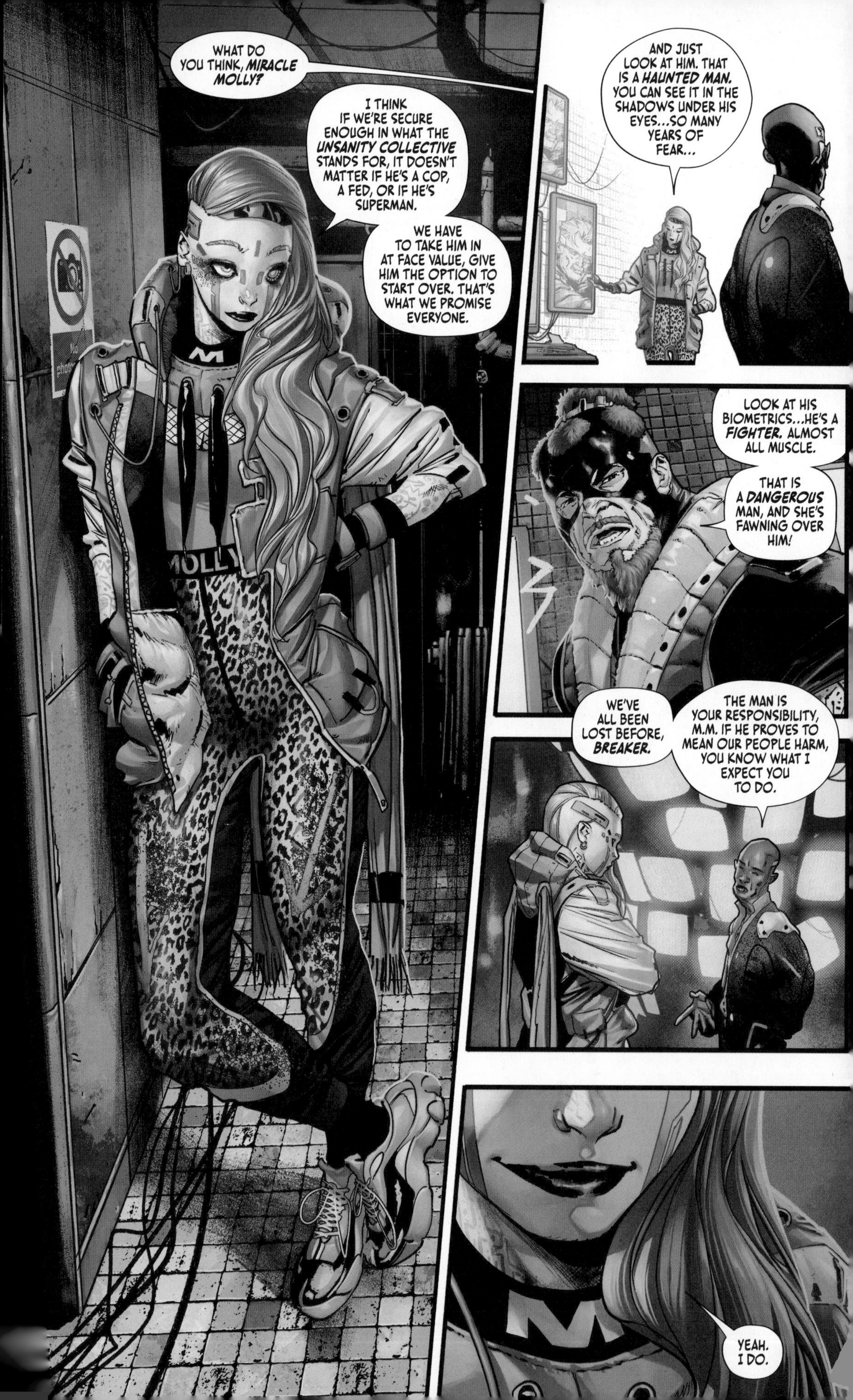
WHAT DO YOU THINK, *MIRACLE MOLLY?*
I THINK IF WE'RE SECURE ENOUGH IN WHAT THE *UNSANITY COLLECTIVE* STANDS FOR, IT DOESN'T MATTER IF HE'S A COP, A FED, OR IF HE'S SUPERMAN.
WE HAVE TO TAKE HIM IN AT FACE VALUE, GIVE HIM THE OPTION TO START OVER. THAT'S WHAT WE PROMISE EVERYONE.
MOLLY
AND JUST LOOK AT HIM. THAT IS A *HAUNTED MAN.* YOU CAN SEE IT IN THE SHADOWS UNDER HIS EYES...SO MANY YEARS OF FEAR...
LOOK AT HIS BIOMETRICS...HE'S A *FIGHTER.* ALMOST ALL MUSCLE.
THAT IS A *DANGEROUS* MAN, AND SHE'S FAWNING OVER HIM!
WE'VE ALL BEEN LOST BEFORE, *BREAKER.*
THE MAN IS YOUR RESPONSIBILITY, M.M. IF HE PROVES TO MEAN OUR PEOPLE HARM, YOU KNOW WHAT I EXPECT YOU TO DO.
YEAH. I DO.

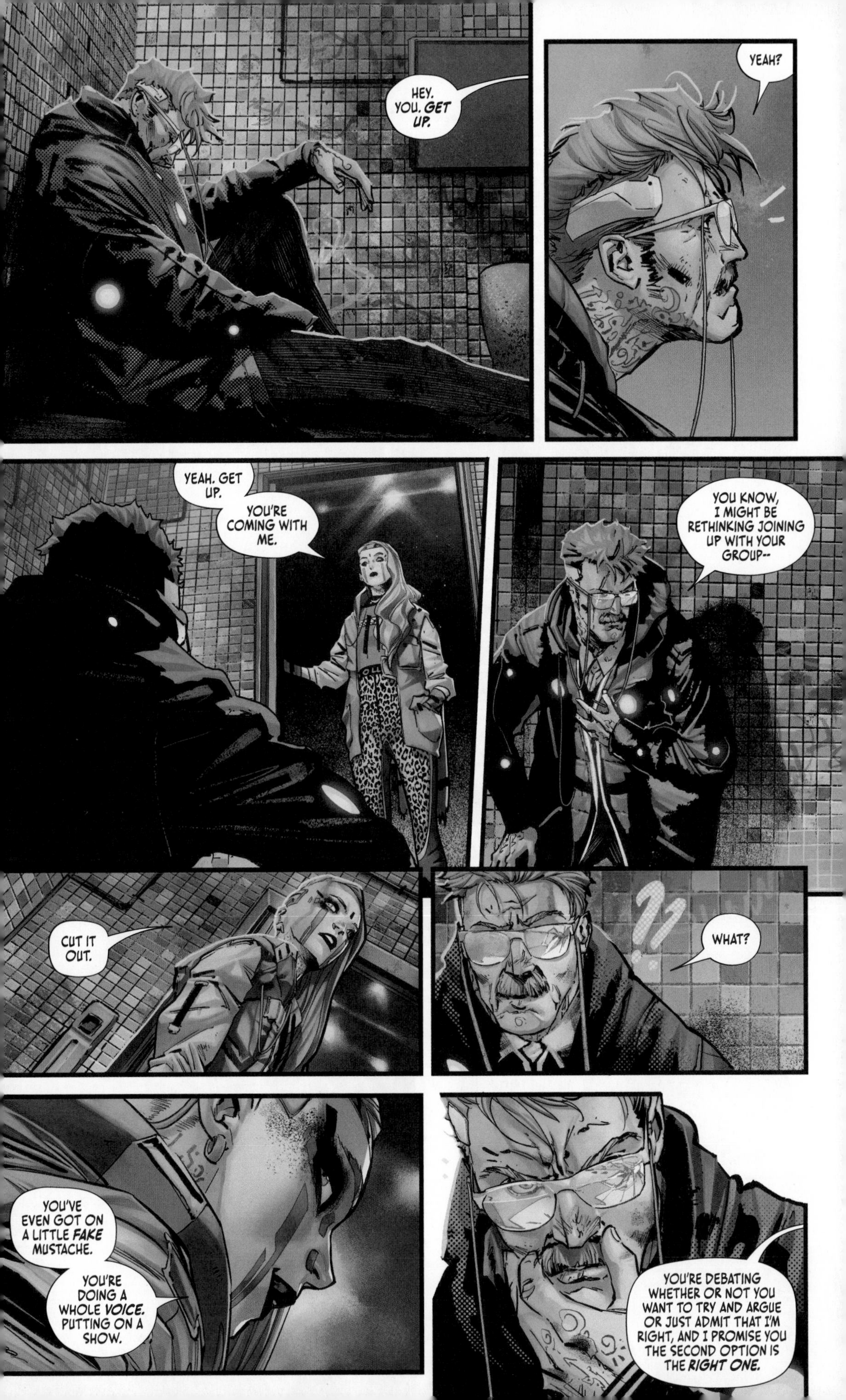
HEY. YOU. GET UP.
YEAH?
YEAH. GET UP.
YOU'RE COMING WITH ME.
YOU KNOW, I MIGHT BE RETHINKING JOINING UP WITH YOUR GROUP--
CUT IT OUT.
WHAT?
YOU'VE EVEN GOT ON A LITTLE FAKE MUSTACHE.
YOU'RE DOING A WHOLE VOICE. PUTTING ON A SHOW.
YOU'RE DEBATING WHETHER OR NOT YOU WANT TO TRY AND ARGUE OR JUST ADMIT THAT I'M RIGHT, AND I PROMISE YOU THE SECOND OPTION IS THE RIGHT ONE.

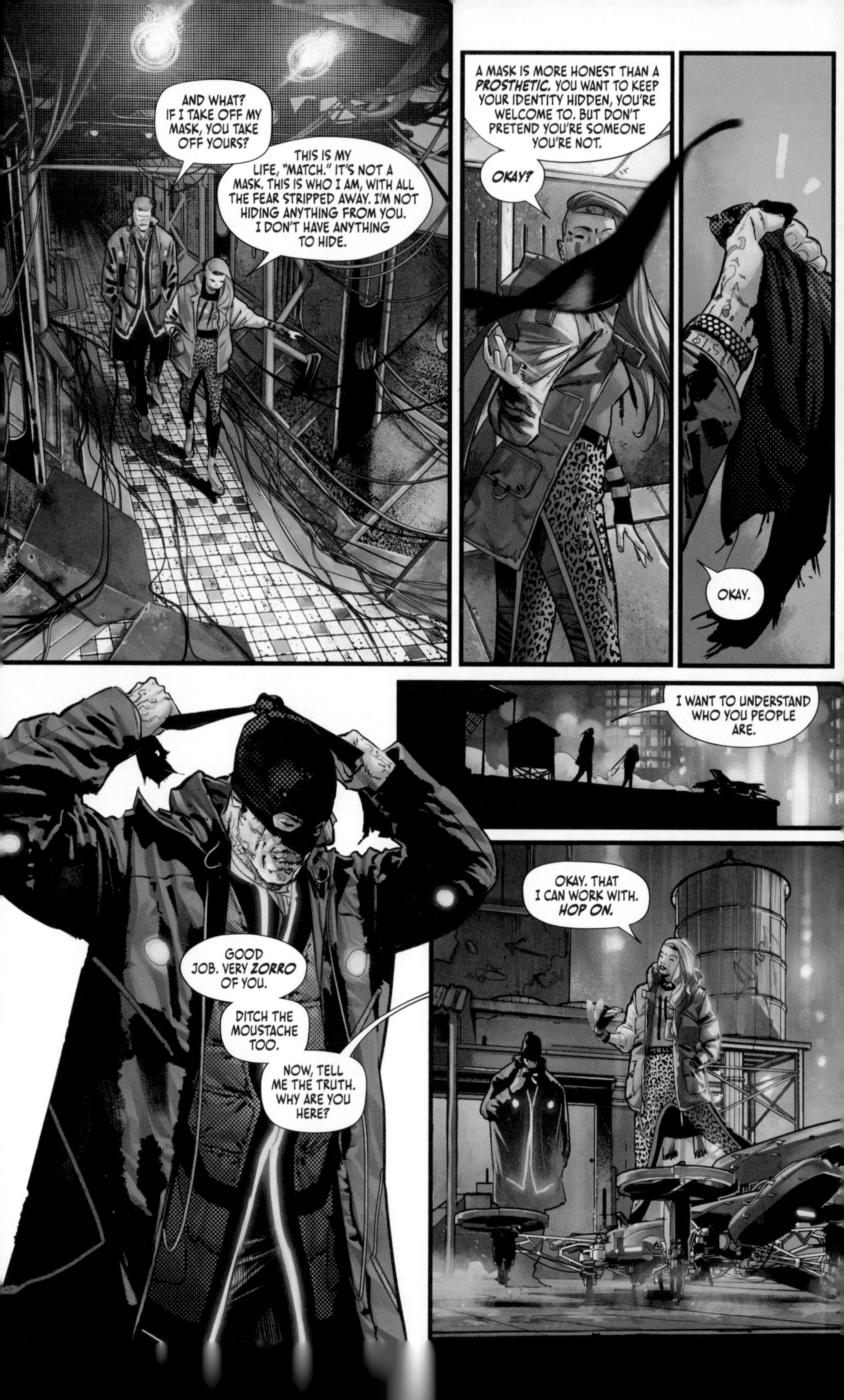
AND WHAT? IF I TAKE OFF MY MASK, YOU TAKE OFF YOURS?
THIS IS MY LIFE, "MATCH." IT'S NOT A MASK. THIS IS WHO I AM, WITH ALL THE FEAR STRIPPED AWAY. I'M NOT HIDING ANYTHING FROM YOU. I DON'T HAVE ANYTHING TO HIDE.
A MASK IS MORE HONEST THAN A *PROSTHETIC.* YOU WANT TO KEEP YOUR IDENTITY HIDDEN, YOU'RE WELCOME TO. BUT DON'T PRETEND YOU'RE SOMEONE YOU'RE NOT.
OKAY?
OKAY.
GOOD JOB. VERY *ZORRO* OF YOU.
DITCH THE MOUSTACHE TOO.
NOW, TELL ME THE TRUTH. WHY ARE YOU HERE?
I WANT TO UNDERSTAND WHO YOU PEOPLE ARE.
OKAY. THAT I CAN WORK WITH. *HOP ON.*

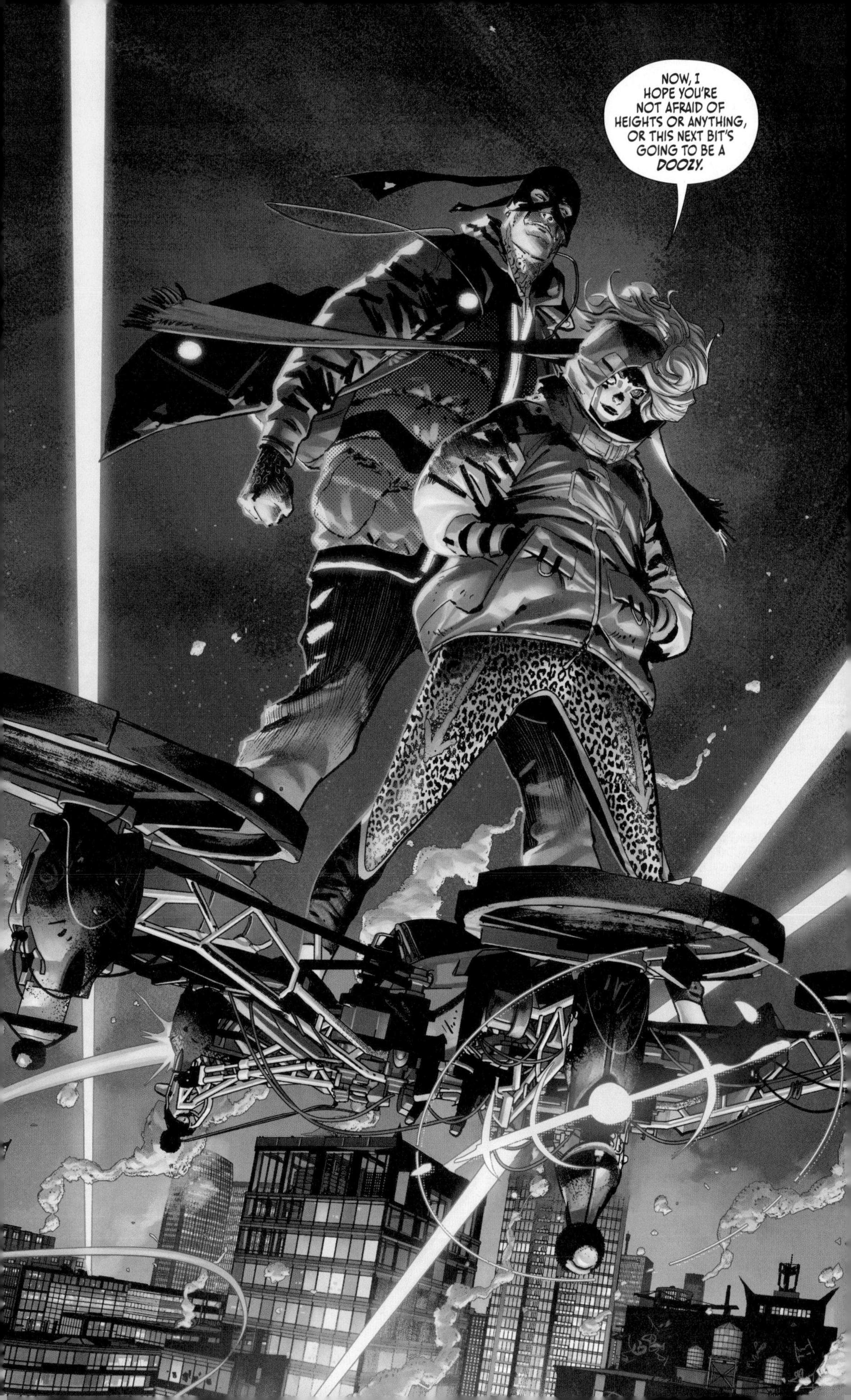
NOW, I HOPE YOU'RE NOT AFRAID OF HEIGHTS OR ANYTHING, OR THIS NEXT BIT'S GOING TO BE A *DOOZY.*

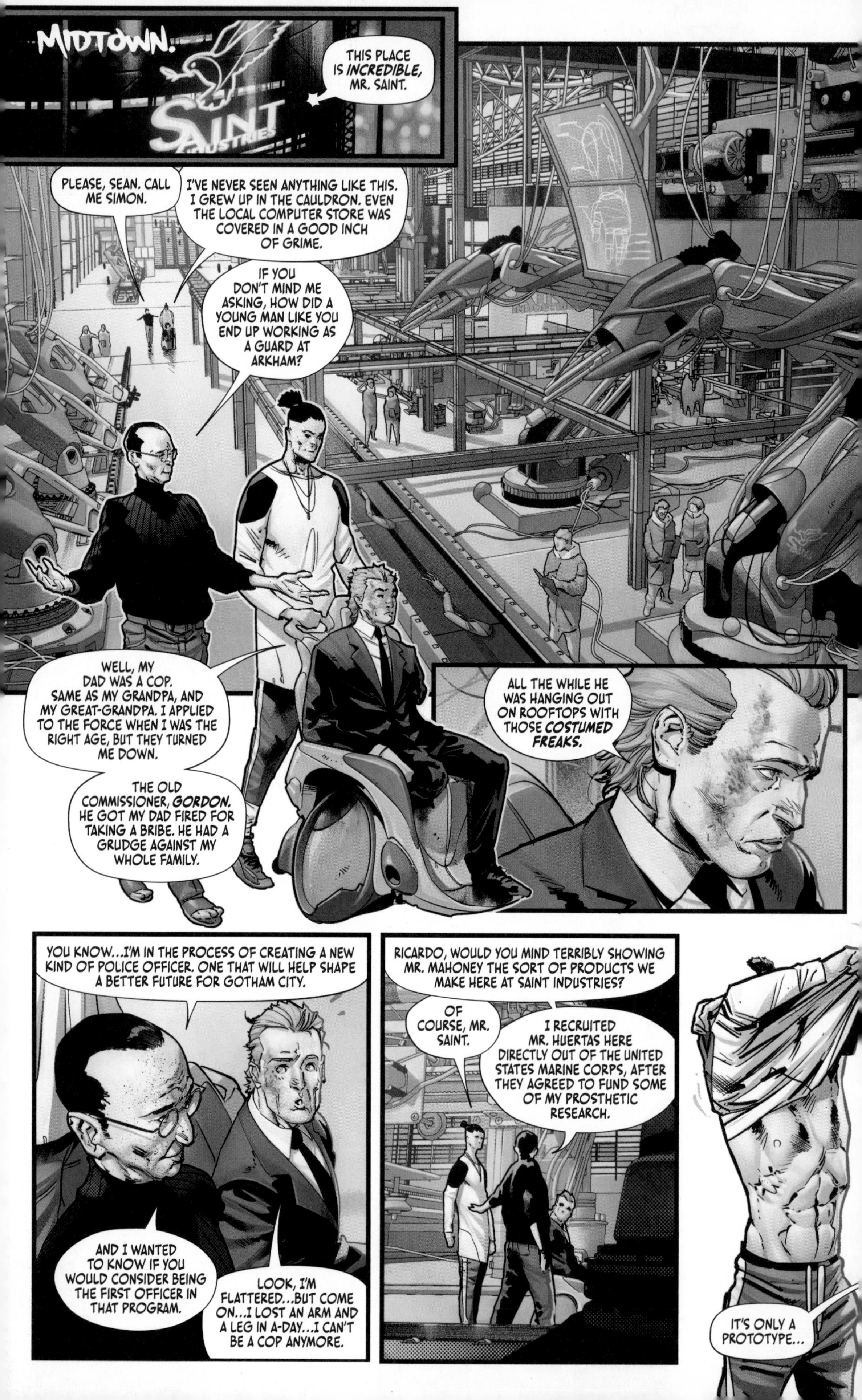
MIDTOWN.
SAINT INDUSTRIES
THIS PLACE IS *INCREDIBLE,* MR. SAINT.
PLEASE, SEAN. CALL ME SIMON.
I'VE NEVER SEEN ANYTHING LIKE THIS. I GREW UP IN THE CAULDRON. EVEN THE LOCAL COMPUTER STORE WAS COVERED IN A GOOD INCH OF GRIME.
IF YOU DON'T MIND ME ASKING, HOW DID A YOUNG MAN LIKE YOU END UP WORKING AS A GUARD AT ARKHAM?
WELL, MY DAD WAS A COP. SAME AS MY GRANDPA, AND MY GREAT-GRANDPA. I APPLIED TO THE FORCE WHEN I WAS THE RIGHT AGE, BUT THEY TURNED ME DOWN.
THE OLD COMMISSIONER, ***GORDON.*** HE GOT MY DAD FIRED FOR TAKING A BRIBE. HE HAD A GRUDGE AGAINST MY WHOLE FAMILY.
ALL THE WHILE HE WAS HANGING OUT ON ROOFTOPS WITH THOSE ***COSTUMED FREAKS.***
YOU KNOW...I'M IN THE PROCESS OF CREATING A NEW KIND OF POLICE OFFICER. ONE THAT WILL HELP SHAPE A BETTER FUTURE FOR GOTHAM CITY.
AND I WANTED TO KNOW IF YOU WOULD CONSIDER BEING THE FIRST OFFICER IN THAT PROGRAM.
LOOK, I'M FLATTERED...BUT COME ON...I LOST AN ARM AND A LEG IN A-DAY...I CAN'T BE A COP ANYMORE.
RICARDO, WOULD YOU MIND TERRIBLY SHOWING MR. MAHONEY THE SORT OF PRODUCTS WE MAKE HERE AT SAINT INDUSTRIES?
OF COURSE, MR. SAINT.
I RECRUITED MR. HUERTAS HERE DIRECTLY OUT OF THE UNITED STATES MARINE CORPS, AFTER THEY AGREED TO FUND SOME OF MY PROSTHETIC RESEARCH.
IT'S ONLY A PROTOTYPE...

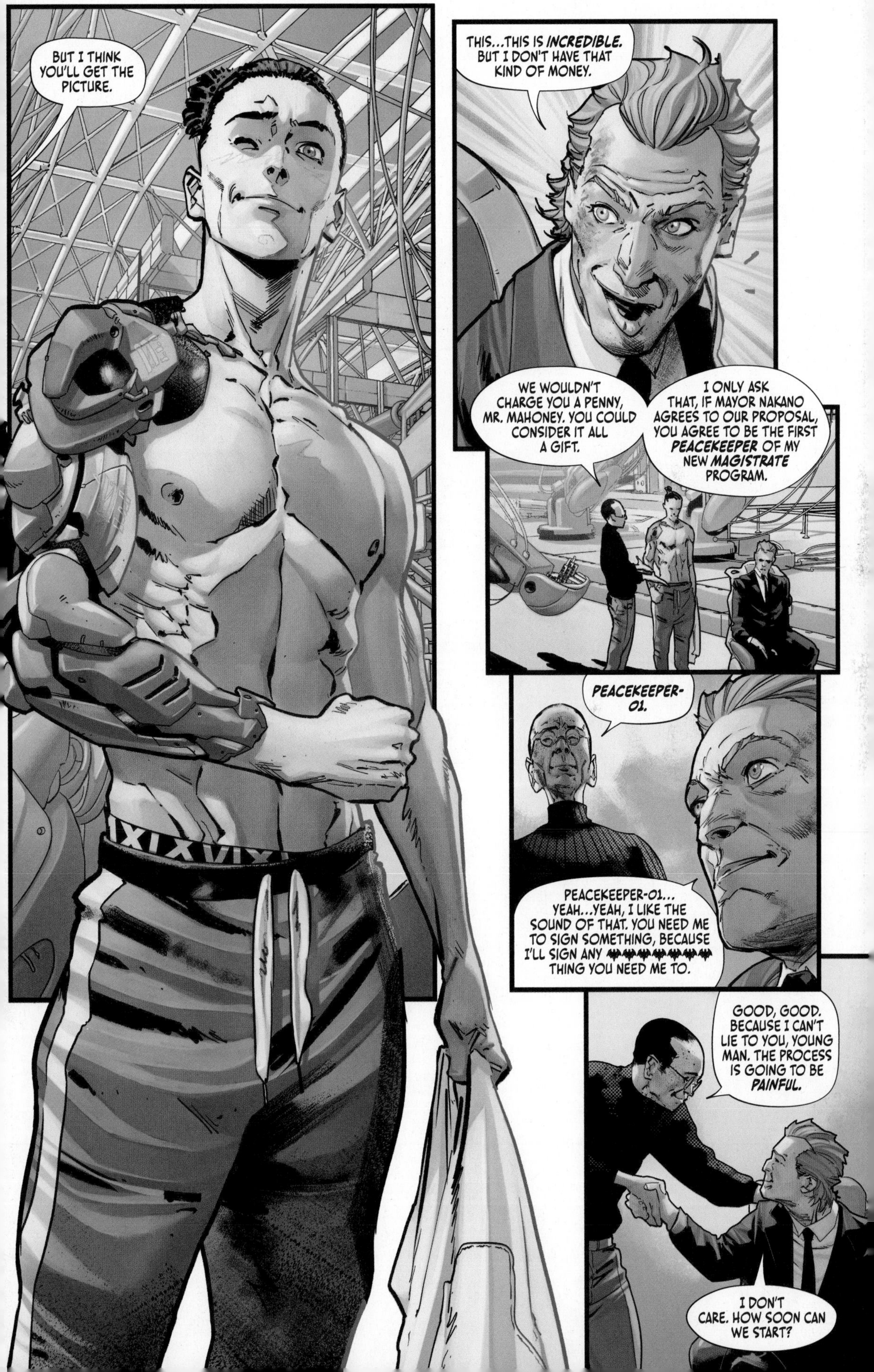
BUT I THINK YOU'LL GET THE PICTURE.
THIS...THIS IS *INCREDIBLE.* BUT I DON'T HAVE THAT KIND OF MONEY.
WE WOULDN'T CHARGE YOU A PENNY, MR. MAHONEY. YOU COULD CONSIDER IT ALL A GIFT.
I ONLY ASK THAT, IF MAYOR NAKANO AGREES TO OUR PROPOSAL, YOU AGREE TO BE THE FIRST ***PEACEKEEPER*** OF MY NEW ***MAGISTRATE*** PROGRAM.
PEACEKEEPER-01.
PEACEKEEPER-01... YEAH...YEAH, I LIKE THE SOUND OF THAT. YOU NEED ME TO SIGN SOMETHING, BECAUSE I'LL SIGN ANY THING YOU NEED ME TO.
GOOD, GOOD. BECAUSE I CAN'T LIE TO YOU, YOUNG MAN. THE PROCESS IS GOING TO BE ***PAINFUL.***
I DON'T CARE. HOW SOON CAN WE START?

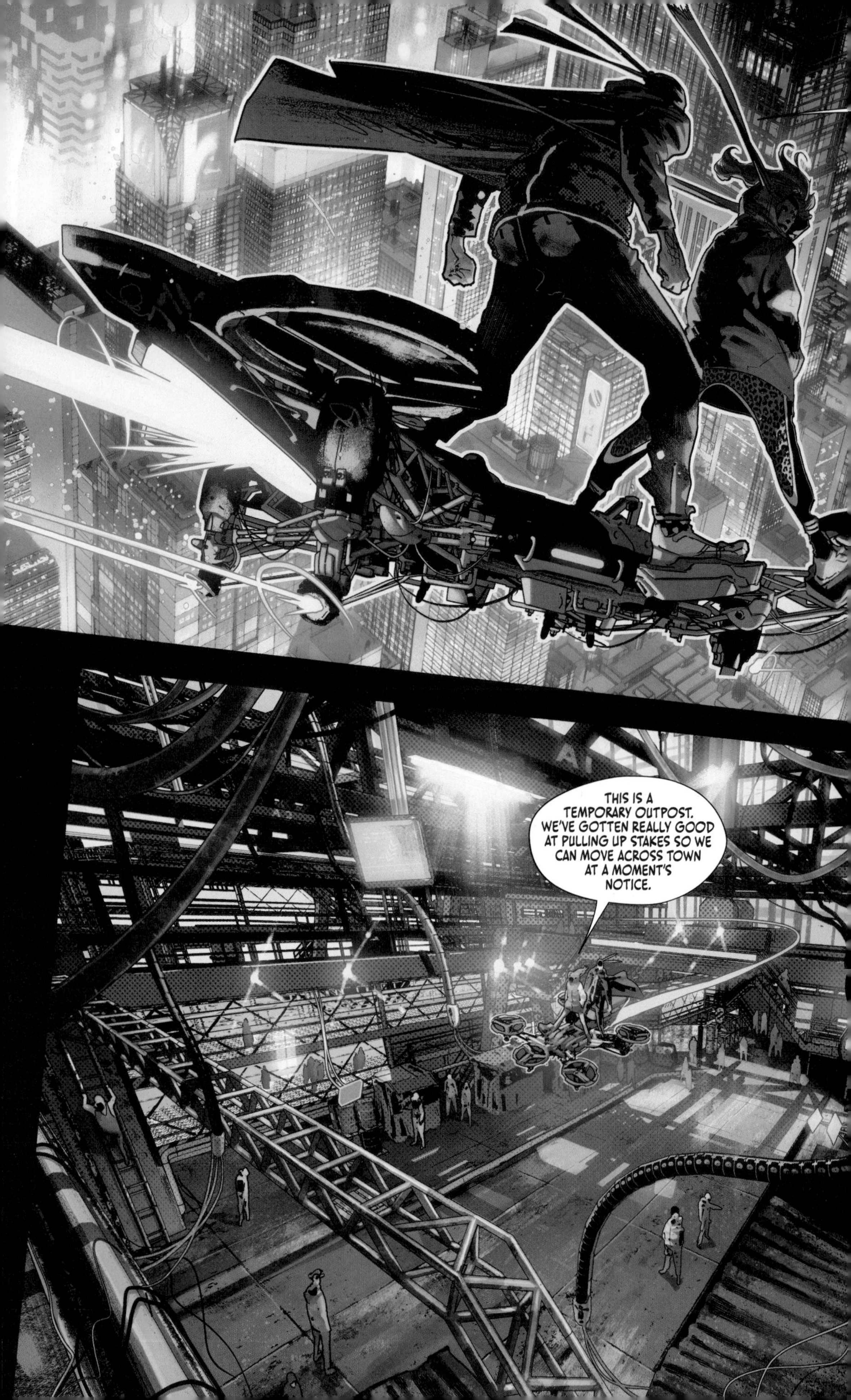
THIS IS A TEMPORARY OUTPOST. WE'VE GOTTEN REALLY GOOD AT PULLING UP STAKES SO WE CAN MOVE ACROSS TOWN AT A MOMENT'S NOTICE.

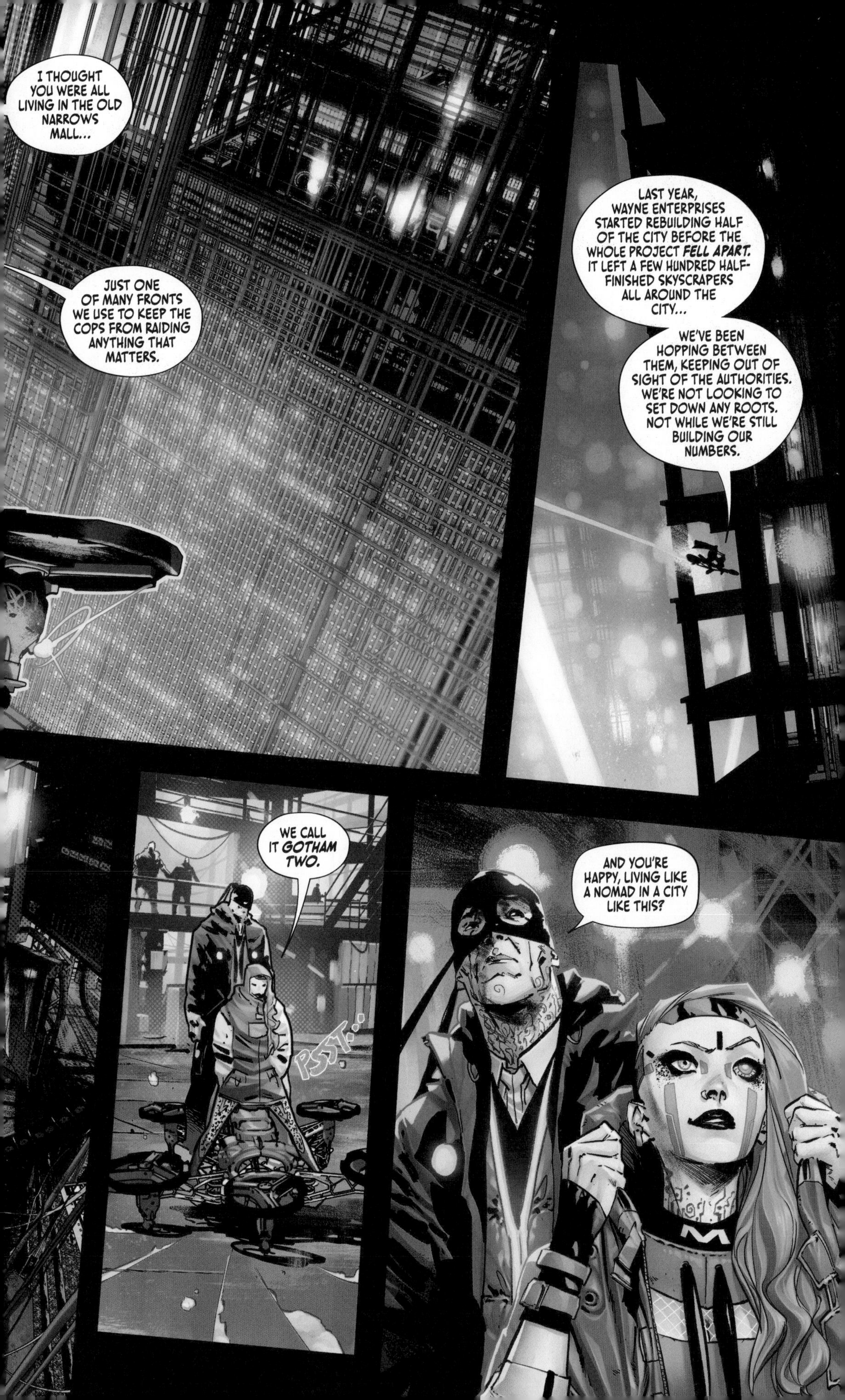
I THOUGHT YOU WERE ALL LIVING IN THE OLD NARROWS MALL...
JUST ONE OF MANY FRONTS WE USE TO KEEP THE COPS FROM RAIDING ANYTHING THAT MATTERS.
LAST YEAR, WAYNE ENTERPRISES STARTED REBUILDING HALF OF THE CITY BEFORE THE WHOLE PROJECT FELL APART. IT LEFT A FEW HUNDRED HALF-FINISHED SKYSCRAPERS ALL AROUND THE CITY...
WE'VE BEEN HOPPING BETWEEN THEM, KEEPING OUT OF SIGHT OF THE AUTHORITIES. WE'RE NOT LOOKING TO SET DOWN ANY ROOTS. NOT WHILE WE'RE STILL BUILDING OUR NUMBERS.
WE CALL IT GOTHAM TWO.
PSST...
AND YOU'RE HAPPY, LIVING LIKE A NOMAD IN A CITY LIKE THIS?

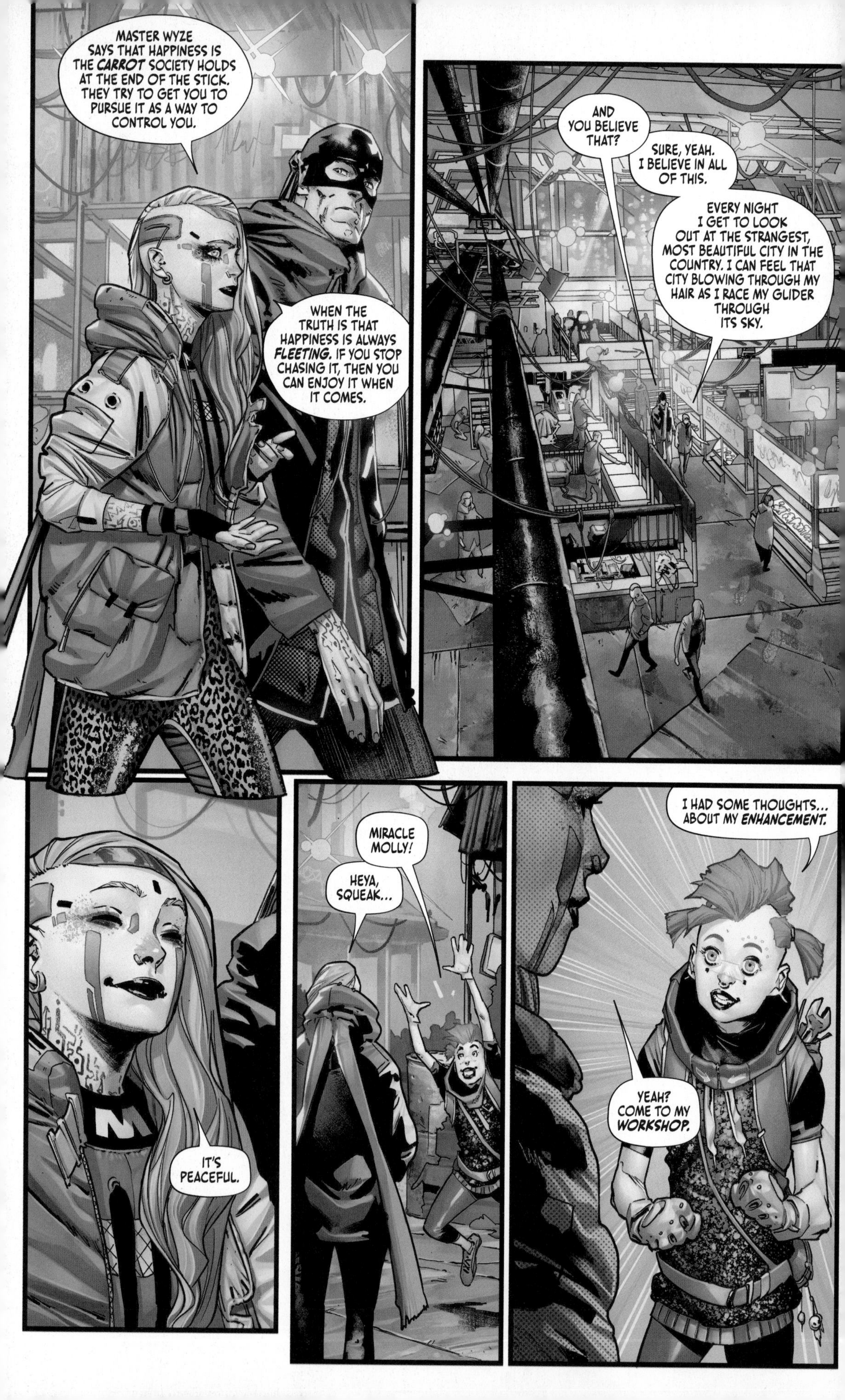
MASTER WYZE SAYS THAT HAPPINESS IS THE CARROT SOCIETY HOLDS AT THE END OF THE STICK. THEY TRY TO GET YOU TO PURSUE IT AS A WAY TO CONTROL YOU.
WHEN THE TRUTH IS THAT HAPPINESS IS ALWAYS FLEETING. IF YOU STOP CHASING IT, THEN YOU CAN ENJOY IT WHEN IT COMES.
AND YOU BELIEVE THAT?
SURE, YEAH. I BELIEVE IN ALL OF THIS.
EVERY NIGHT I GET TO LOOK OUT AT THE STRANGEST, MOST BEAUTIFUL CITY IN THE COUNTRY. I CAN FEEL THAT CITY BLOWING THROUGH MY HAIR AS I RACE MY GLIDER THROUGH ITS SKY.
IT'S PEACEFUL.
MIRACLE MOLLY!
HEYA, SQUEAK...
I HAD SOME THOUGHTS... ABOUT MY ENHANCEMENT.
YEAH? COME TO MY WORKSHOP.

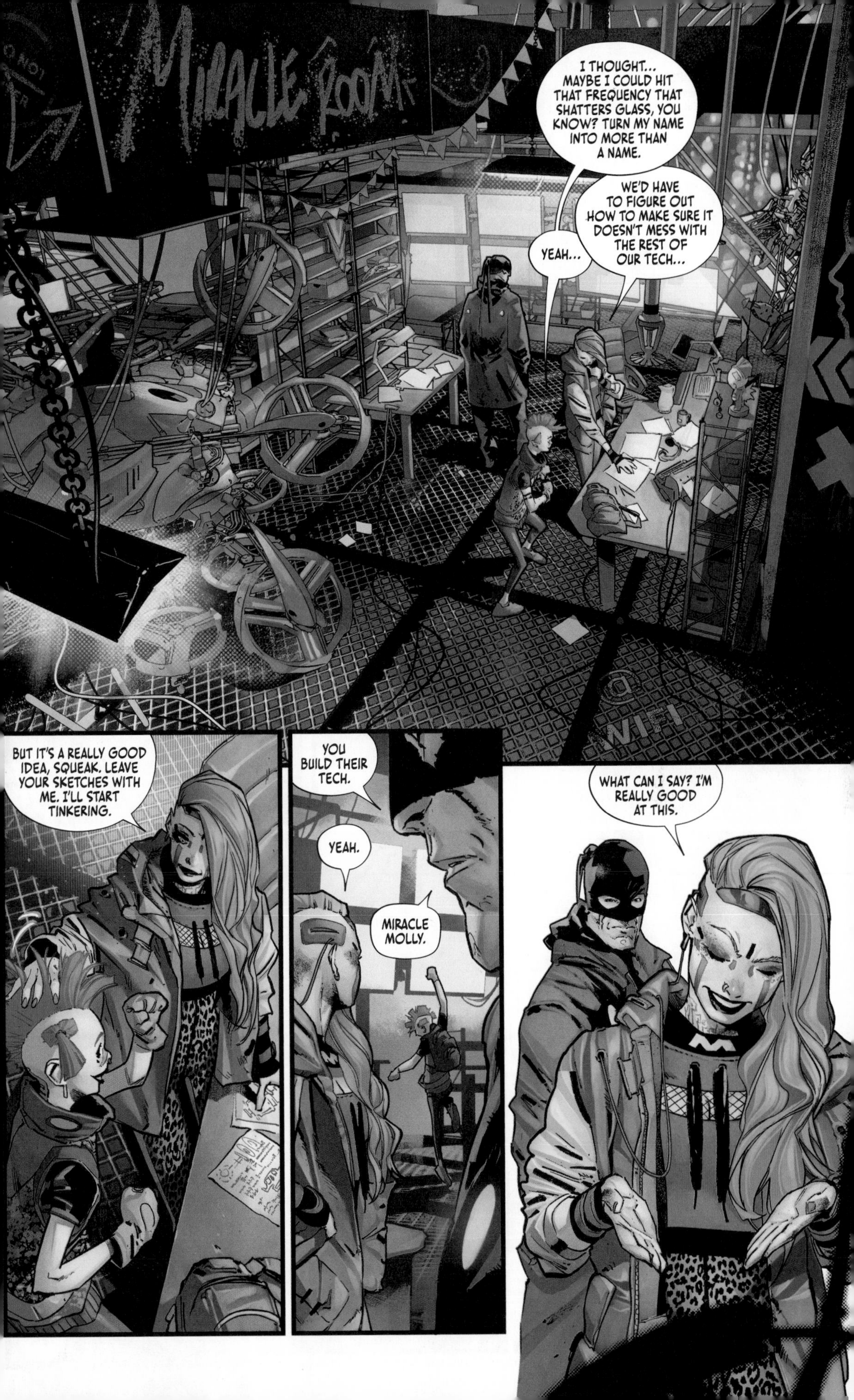
MIRACLE ROOM
I THOUGHT... MAYBE I COULD HIT THAT FREQUENCY THAT SHATTERS GLASS, YOU KNOW? TURN MY NAME INTO MORE THAN A NAME.
YEAH...
WE'D HAVE TO FIGURE OUT HOW TO MAKE SURE IT DOESN'T MESS WITH THE REST OF OUR TECH...
BUT IT'S A REALLY GOOD IDEA, SQUEAK. LEAVE YOUR SKETCHES WITH ME. I'LL START TINKERING.
YOU BUILD THEIR TECH.
YEAH.
MIRACLE MOLLY.
WHAT CAN I SAY? I'M REALLY GOOD AT THIS.

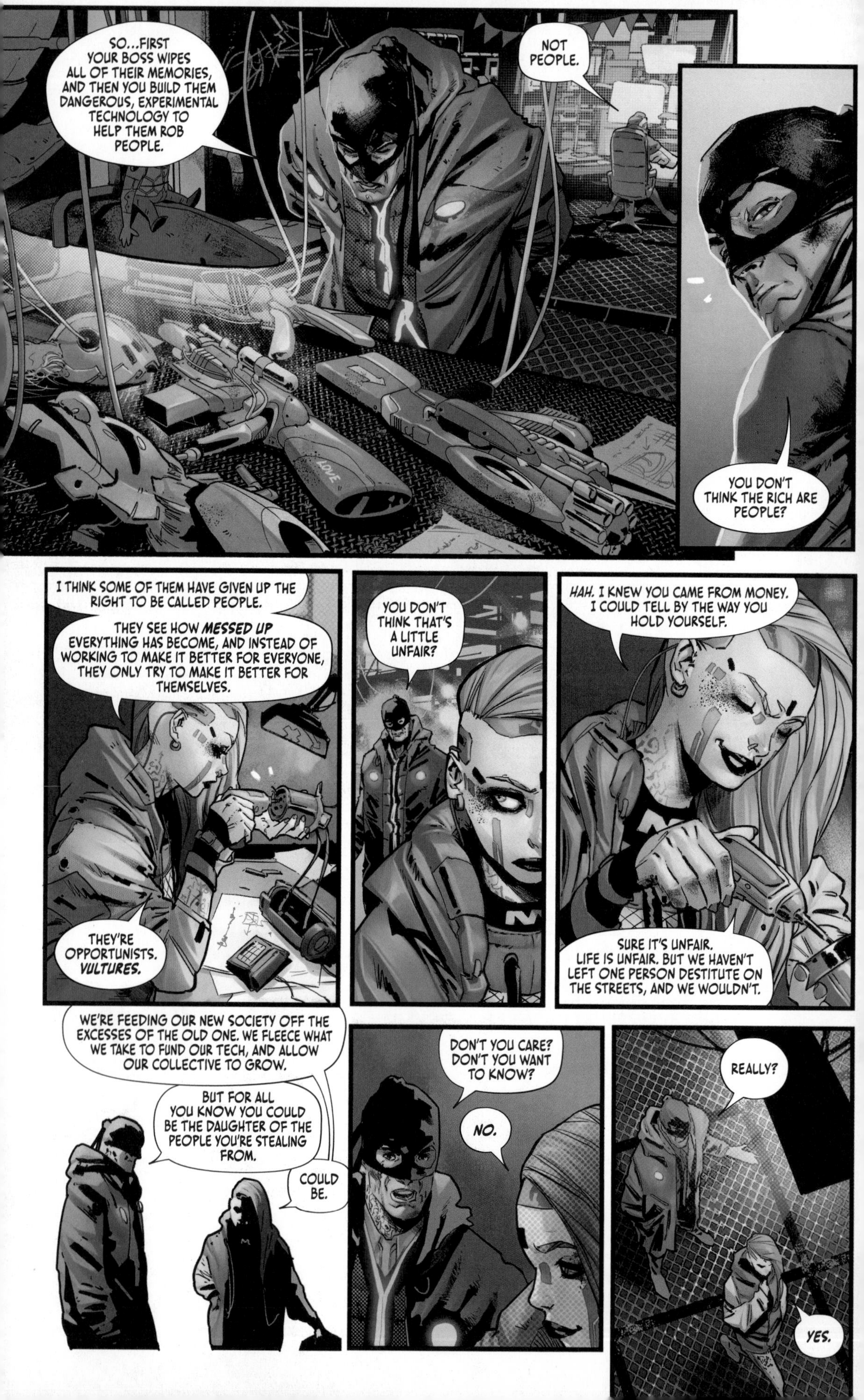
SO...FIRST YOUR BOSS WIPES ALL OF THEIR MEMORIES, AND THEN YOU BUILD THEM DANGEROUS, EXPERIMENTAL TECHNOLOGY TO HELP THEM ROB PEOPLE.
NOT PEOPLE.
YOU DON'T THINK THE RICH ARE PEOPLE?
I THINK SOME OF THEM HAVE GIVEN UP THE RIGHT TO BE CALLED PEOPLE.
THEY SEE HOW MESSED UP EVERYTHING HAS BECOME, AND INSTEAD OF WORKING TO MAKE IT BETTER FOR EVERYONE, THEY ONLY TRY TO MAKE IT BETTER FOR THEMSELVES.
THEY'RE OPPORTUNISTS. VULTURES.
YOU DON'T THINK THAT'S A LITTLE UNFAIR?
HAH. I KNEW YOU CAME FROM MONEY. I COULD TELL BY THE WAY YOU HOLD YOURSELF.
SURE IT'S UNFAIR. LIFE IS UNFAIR. BUT WE HAVEN'T LEFT ONE PERSON DESTITUTE ON THE STREETS, AND WE WOULDN'T.
WE'RE FEEDING OUR NEW SOCIETY OFF THE EXCESSES OF THE OLD ONE. WE FLEECE WHAT WE TAKE TO FUND OUR TECH, AND ALLOW OUR COLLECTIVE TO GROW.
BUT FOR ALL YOU KNOW YOU COULD BE THE DAUGHTER OF THE PEOPLE YOU'RE STEALING FROM.
COULD BE.
DON'T YOU CARE? DON'T YOU WANT TO KNOW?
NO.
REALLY?
YES.

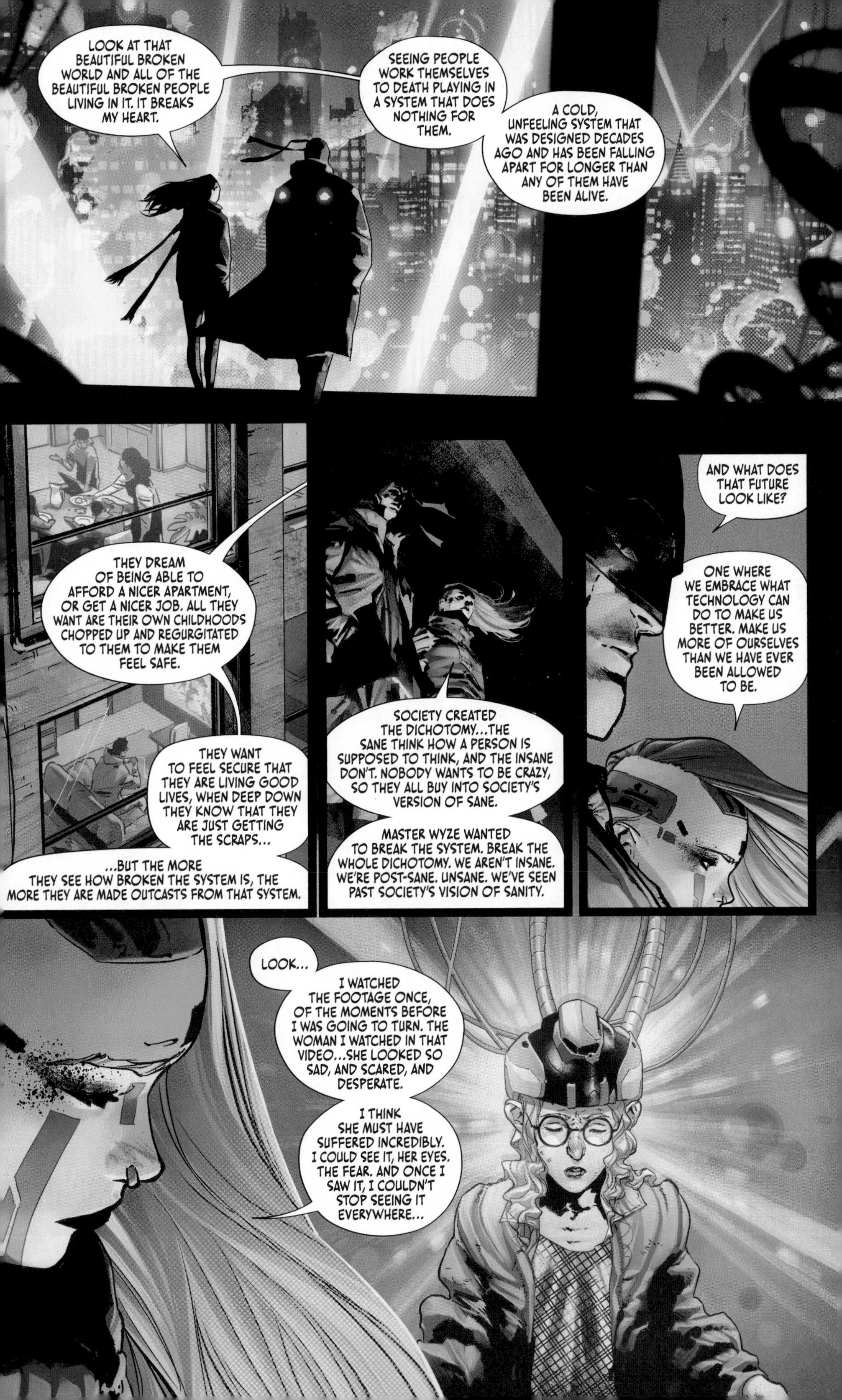
LOOK AT THAT BEAUTIFUL BROKEN WORLD AND ALL OF THE BEAUTIFUL BROKEN PEOPLE LIVING IN IT. IT BREAKS MY HEART.
SEEING PEOPLE WORK THEMSELVES TO DEATH PLAYING IN A SYSTEM THAT DOES NOTHING FOR THEM.
A COLD, UNFEELING SYSTEM THAT WAS DESIGNED DECADES AGO AND HAS BEEN FALLING APART FOR LONGER THAN ANY OF THEM HAVE BEEN ALIVE.
THEY DREAM OF BEING ABLE TO AFFORD A NICER APARTMENT, OR GET A NICER JOB. ALL THEY WANT ARE THEIR OWN CHILDHOODS CHOPPED UP AND REGURGITATED TO THEM TO MAKE THEM FEEL SAFE.
THEY WANT TO FEEL SECURE THAT THEY ARE LIVING GOOD LIVES, WHEN DEEP DOWN THEY KNOW THAT THEY ARE JUST GETTING THE SCRAPS...
...BUT THE MORE THEY SEE HOW BROKEN THE SYSTEM IS, THE MORE THEY ARE MADE OUTCASTS FROM THAT SYSTEM.
SOCIETY CREATED THE DICHOTOMY...THE SANE THINK HOW A PERSON IS SUPPOSED TO THINK, AND THE INSANE DON'T. NOBODY WANTS TO BE CRAZY, SO THEY ALL BUY INTO SOCIETY'S VERSION OF SANE.
MASTER WYZE WANTED TO BREAK THE SYSTEM. BREAK THE WHOLE DICHOTOMY. WE AREN'T INSANE. WE'RE POST-SANE. UNSANE. WE'VE SEEN PAST SOCIETY'S VISION OF SANITY.
AND WHAT DOES THAT FUTURE LOOK LIKE?
ONE WHERE WE EMBRACE WHAT TECHNOLOGY CAN DO TO MAKE US BETTER. MAKE US MORE OF OURSELVES THAN WE HAVE EVER BEEN ALLOWED TO BE.
LOOK...
I WATCHED THE FOOTAGE ONCE, OF THE MOMENTS BEFORE I WAS GOING TO TURN. THE WOMAN I WATCHED IN THAT VIDEO...SHE LOOKED SO SAD, AND SCARED, AND DESPERATE.
I THINK SHE MUST HAVE SUFFERED INCREDIBLY. I COULD SEE IT, HER EYES. THE FEAR. AND ONCE I SAW IT, I COULDN'T STOP SEEING IT EVERYWHERE...

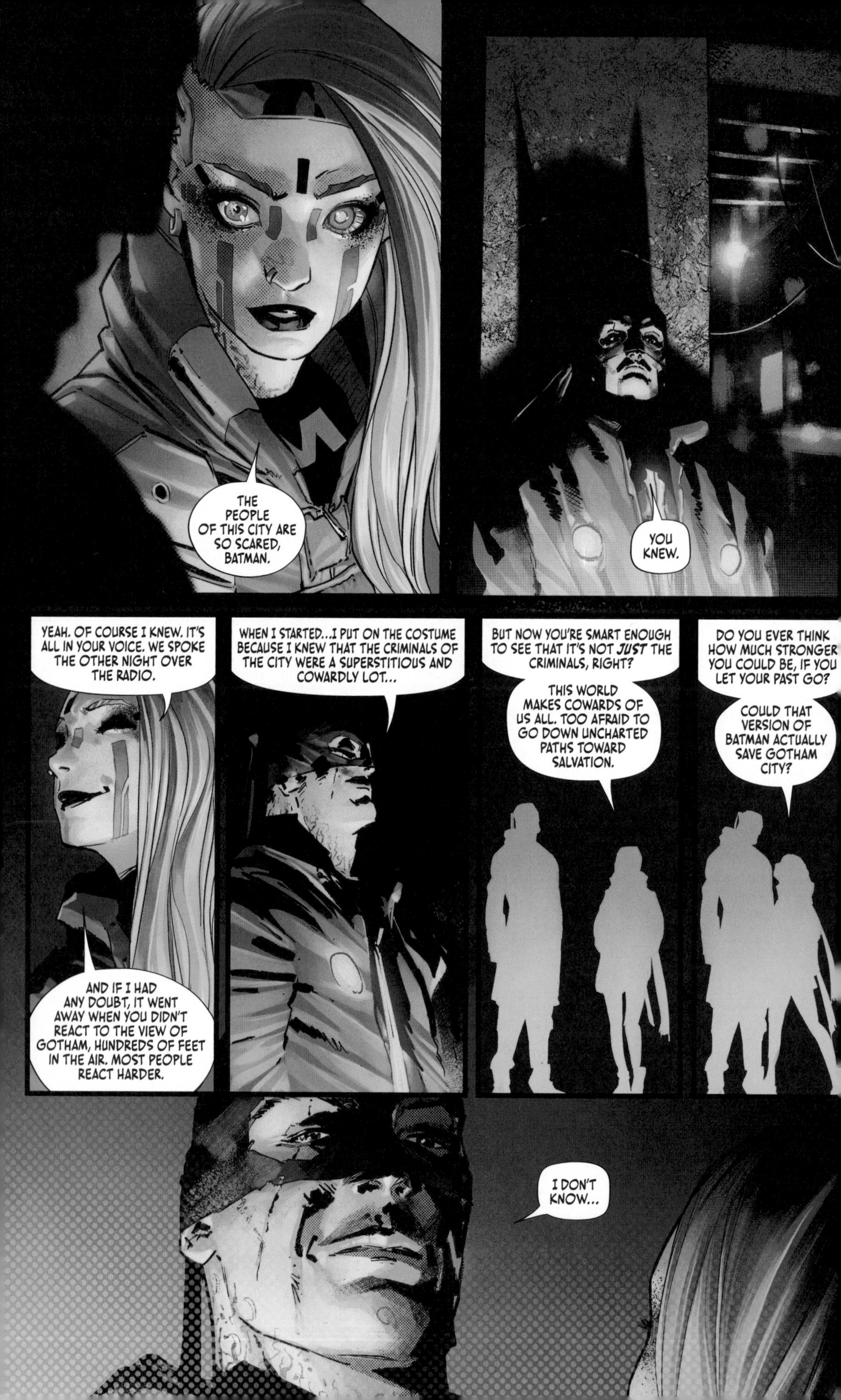
THE PEOPLE OF THIS CITY ARE SO SCARED, BATMAN.
YOU KNEW.
YEAH. OF COURSE I KNEW. IT'S ALL IN YOUR VOICE. WE SPOKE THE OTHER NIGHT OVER THE RADIO.
AND IF I HAD ANY DOUBT, IT WENT AWAY WHEN YOU DIDN'T REACT TO THE VIEW OF GOTHAM, HUNDREDS OF FEET IN THE AIR. MOST PEOPLE REACT HARDER.
WHEN I STARTED...I PUT ON THE COSTUME BECAUSE I KNEW THAT THE CRIMINALS OF THE CITY WERE A SUPERSTITIOUS AND COWARDLY LOT...
BUT NOW YOU'RE SMART ENOUGH TO SEE THAT IT'S NOT *JUST* THE CRIMINALS, RIGHT?
THIS WORLD MAKES COWARDS OF US ALL. TOO AFRAID TO GO DOWN UNCHARTED PATHS TOWARD SALVATION.
DO YOU EVER THINK HOW MUCH STRONGER YOU COULD BE, IF YOU LET YOUR PAST GO?
COULD THAT VERSION OF BATMAN ACTUALLY SAVE GOTHAM CITY?
I DON'T KNOW...

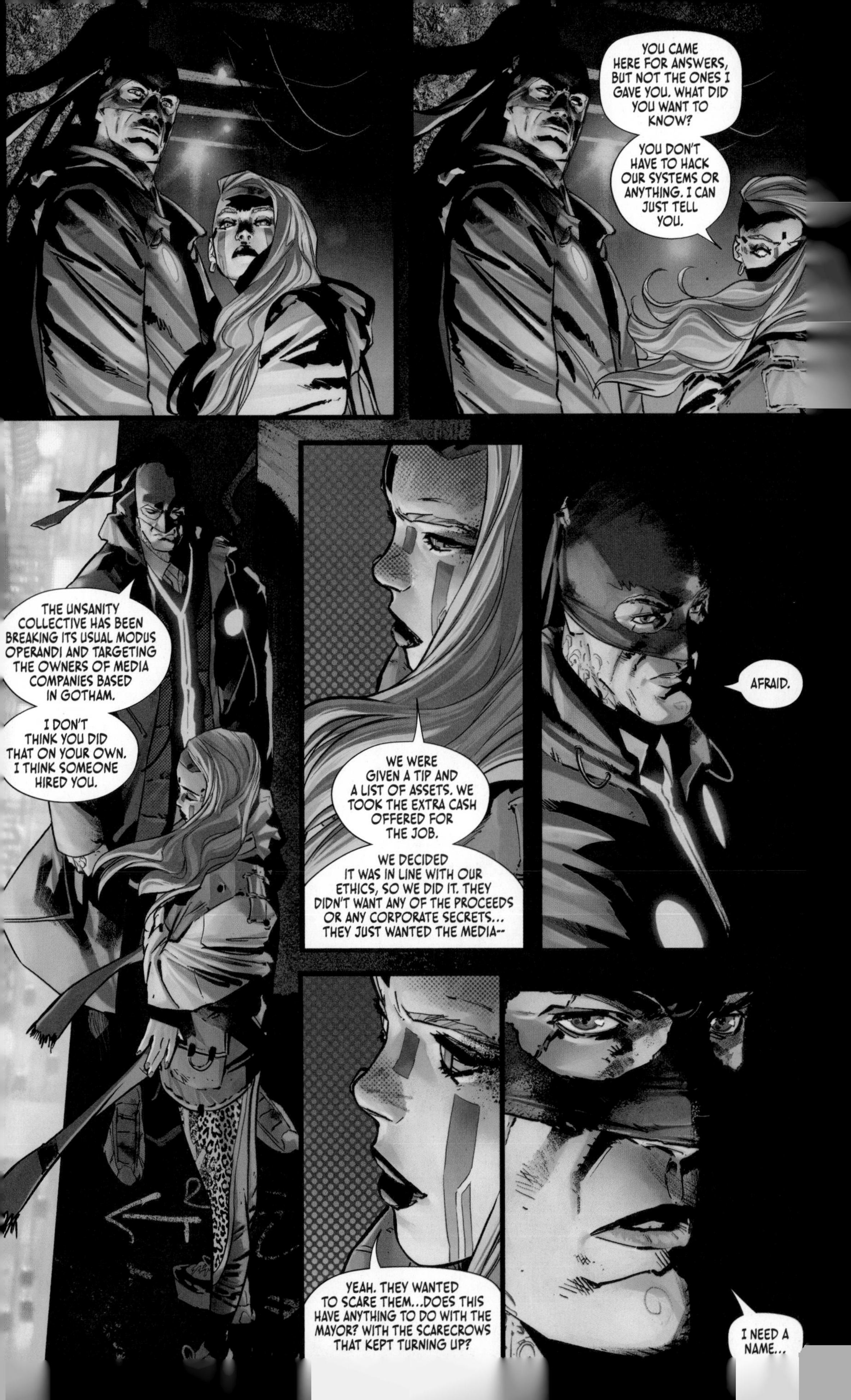
YOU CAME HERE FOR ANSWERS, BUT NOT THE ONES I GAVE YOU. WHAT DID YOU WANT TO KNOW?
YOU DON'T HAVE TO HACK OUR SYSTEMS OR ANYTHING. I CAN JUST TELL YOU.
THE UNSANITY COLLECTIVE HAS BEEN BREAKING ITS USUAL MODUS OPERANDI AND TARGETING THE OWNERS OF MEDIA COMPANIES BASED IN GOTHAM.
I DON'T THINK YOU DID THAT ON YOUR OWN. I THINK SOMEONE HIRED YOU.
WE WERE GIVEN A TIP AND A LIST OF ASSETS. WE TOOK THE EXTRA CASH OFFERED FOR THE JOB.
WE DECIDED IT WAS IN LINE WITH OUR ETHICS, SO WE DID IT. THEY DIDN'T WANT ANY OF THE PROCEEDS OR ANY CORPORATE SECRETS... THEY JUST WANTED THE MEDIA--
AFRAID.
YEAH. THEY WANTED TO SCARE THEM...DOES THIS HAVE ANYTHING TO DO WITH THE MAYOR? WITH THE SCARECROWS THAT KEPT TURNING UP?
I NEED A NAME...

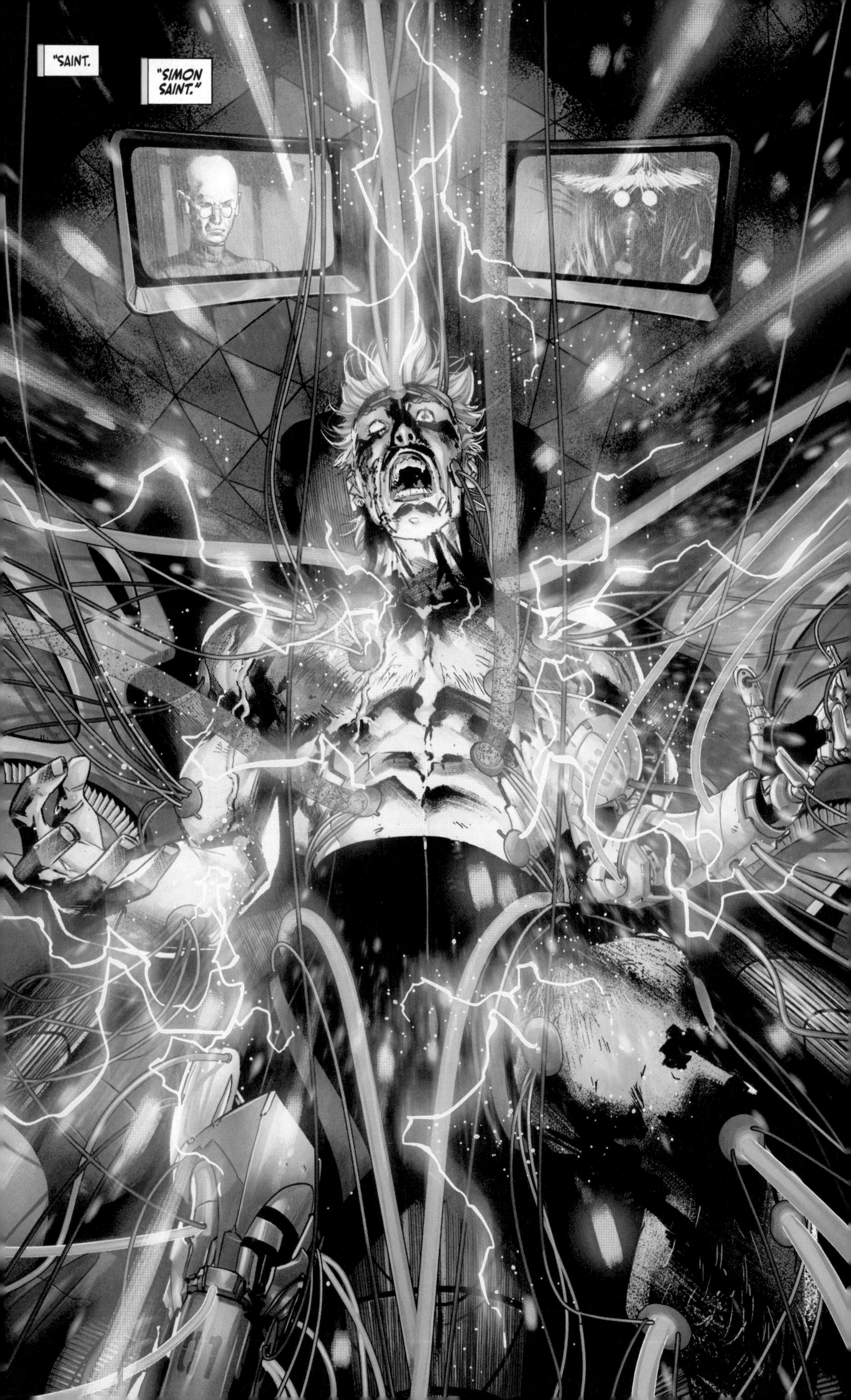
"SAINT.
"SIMON SAINT."

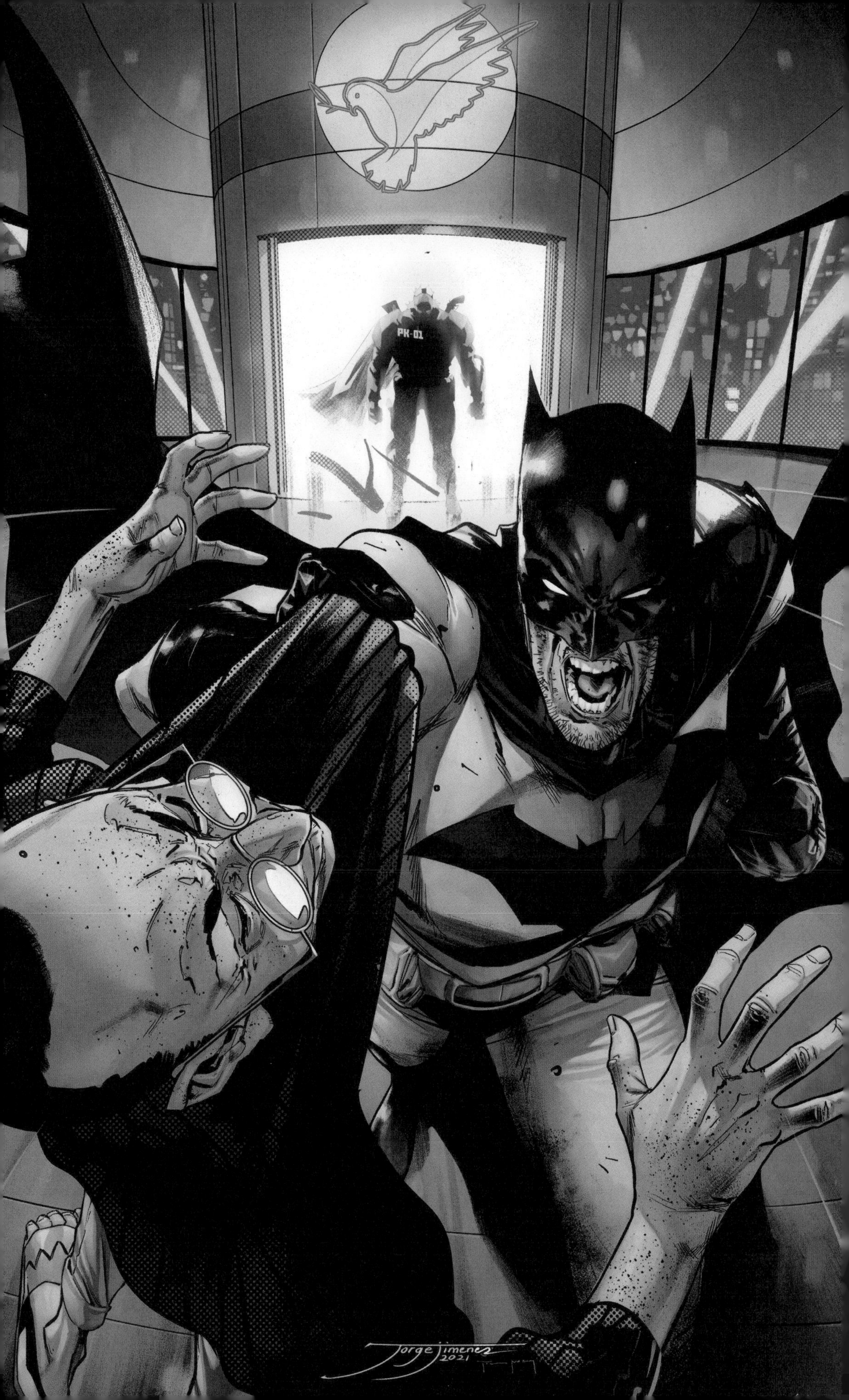
PK-01
Jorge Jimenez
2021

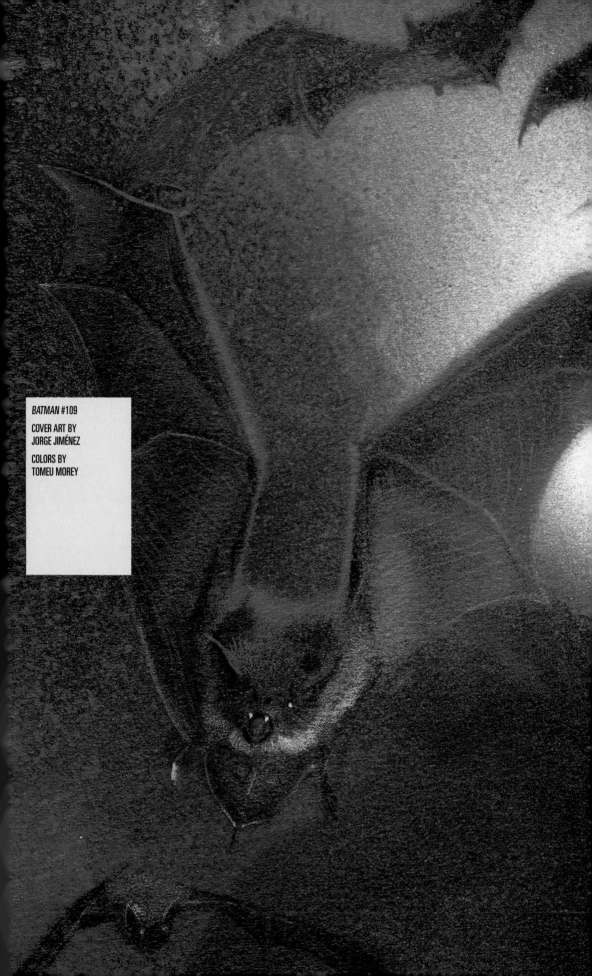

BATMAN #109
COVER ART BY
JORGE JIMÉNEZ

COLORS BY
TOMEU MOREY

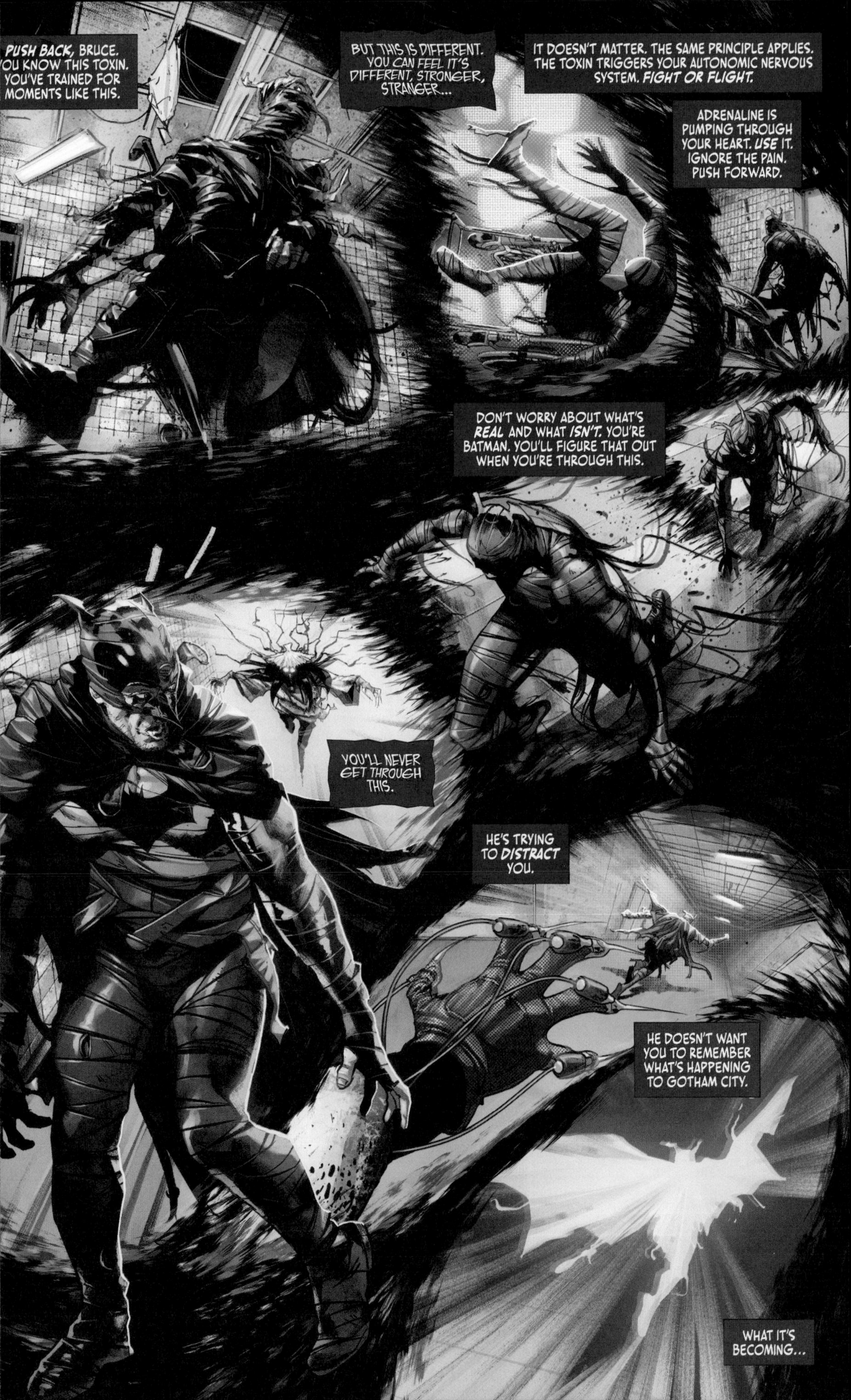
PUSH BACK, BRUCE. YOU KNOW THIS TOXIN. YOU'VE TRAINED FOR MOMENTS LIKE THIS.
BUT THIS IS DIFFERENT. YOU CAN FEEL IT'S DIFFERENT, STRONGER, STRANGER...
IT DOESN'T MATTER. THE SAME PRINCIPLE APPLIES. THE TOXIN TRIGGERS YOUR AUTONOMIC NERVOUS SYSTEM. FIGHT OR FLIGHT.
ADRENALINE IS PUMPING THROUGH YOUR HEART. USE IT. IGNORE THE PAIN. PUSH FORWARD.
DON'T WORRY ABOUT WHAT'S REAL AND WHAT ISN'T. YOU'RE BATMAN. YOU'LL FIGURE THAT OUT WHEN YOU'RE THROUGH THIS.
YOU'LL NEVER GET THROUGH THIS.
HE'S TRYING TO DISTRACT YOU.
HE DOESN'T WANT YOU TO REMEMBER WHAT'S HAPPENING TO GOTHAM CITY.
WHAT IT'S BECOMING...

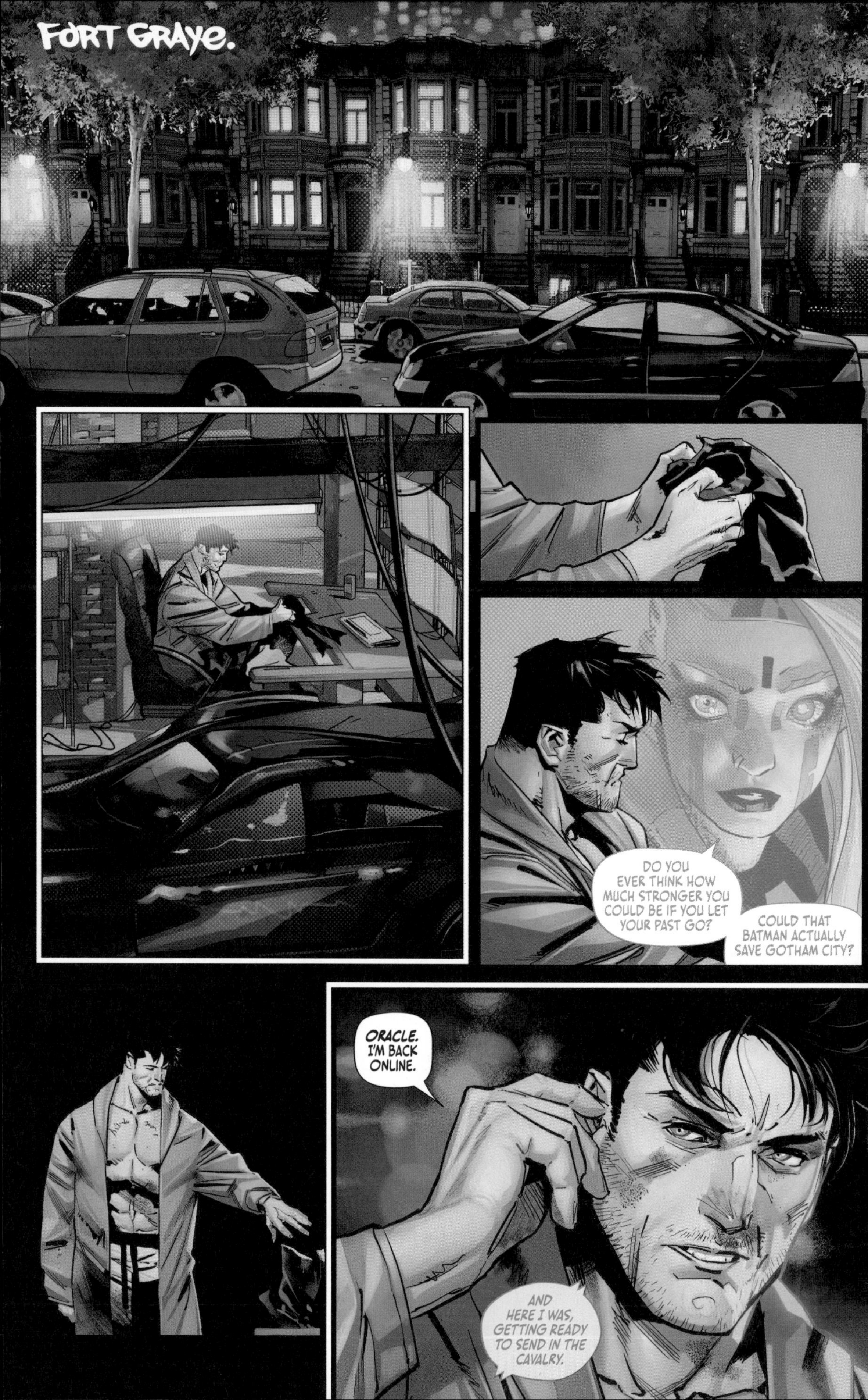
FORT GRAYE.
DO YOU EVER THINK HOW MUCH STRONGER YOU COULD BE IF YOU LET YOUR PAST GO?
COULD THAT BATMAN ACTUALLY SAVE GOTHAM CITY?
ORACLE. I'M BACK ONLINE.
AND HERE I WAS, GETTING READY TO SEND IN THE CAVALRY.

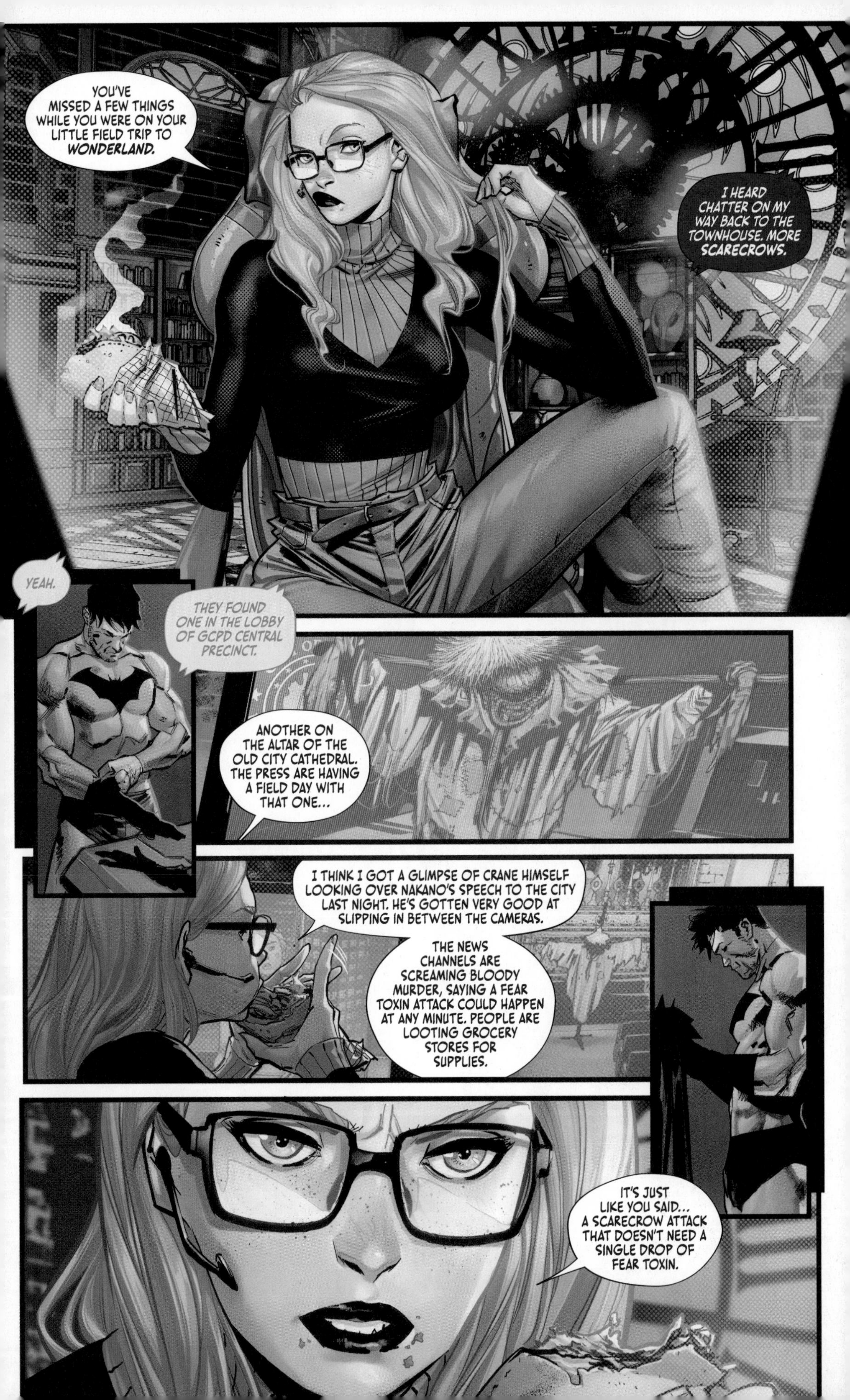
YOU'VE MISSED A FEW THINGS WHILE YOU WERE ON YOUR LITTLE FIELD TRIP TO WONDERLAND.
I HEARD CHATTER ON MY WAY BACK TO THE TOWNHOUSE. MORE SCARECROWS.
YEAH.
THEY FOUND ONE IN THE LOBBY OF GCPD CENTRAL PRECINCT.
ANOTHER ON THE ALTAR OF THE OLD CITY CATHEDRAL. THE PRESS ARE HAVING A FIELD DAY WITH THAT ONE...
I THINK I GOT A GLIMPSE OF CRANE HIMSELF LOOKING OVER NAKANO'S SPEECH TO THE CITY LAST NIGHT. HE'S GOTTEN VERY GOOD AT SLIPPING IN BETWEEN THE CAMERAS.
THE NEWS CHANNELS ARE SCREAMING BLOODY MURDER, SAYING A FEAR TOXIN ATTACK COULD HAPPEN AT ANY MINUTE. PEOPLE ARE LOOTING GROCERY STORES FOR SUPPLIES.
IT'S JUST LIKE YOU SAID... A SCARECROW ATTACK THAT DOESN'T NEED A SINGLE DROP OF FEAR TOXIN.

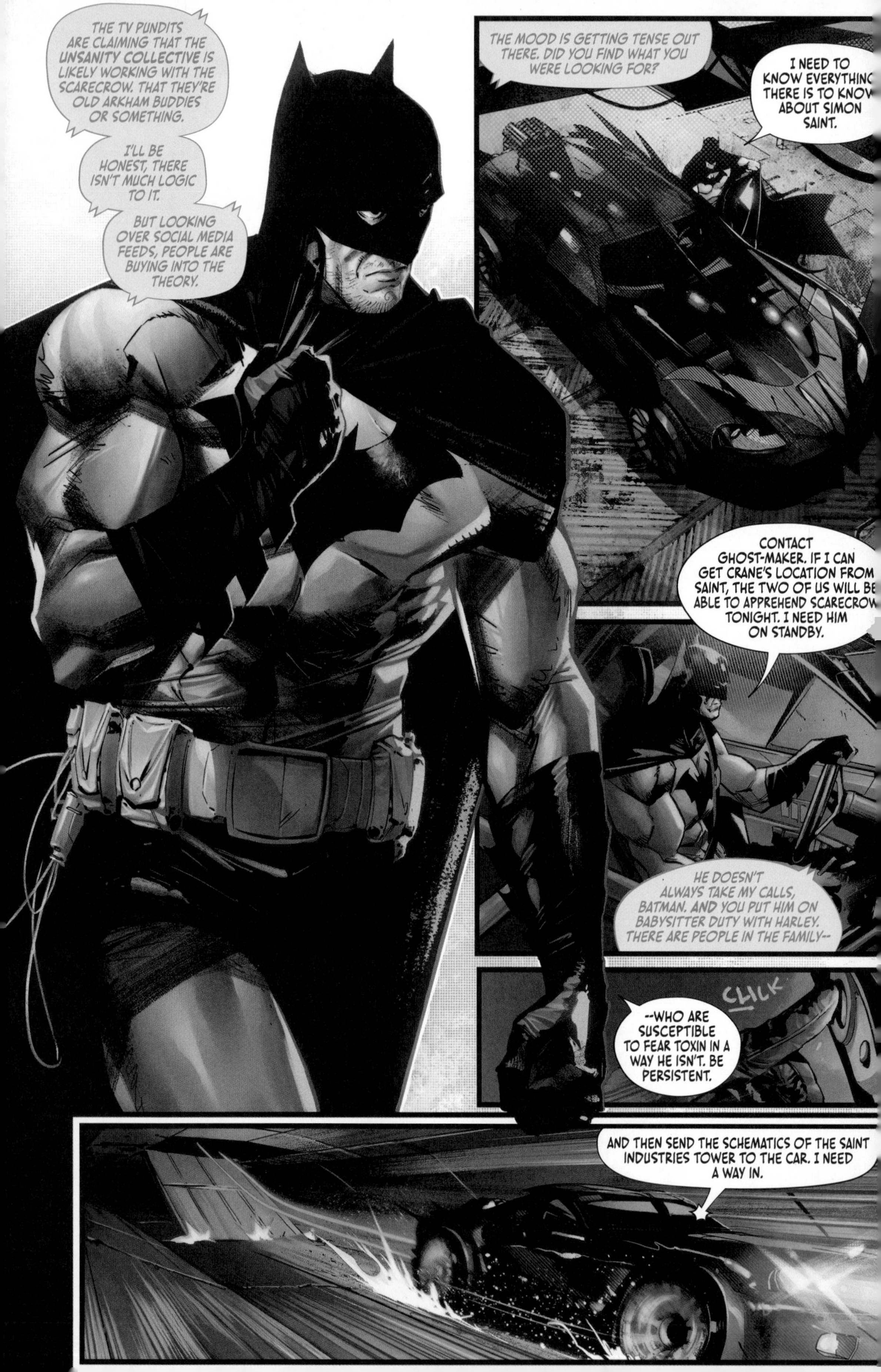
THE TV PUNDITS ARE CLAIMING THAT THE UNSANITY COLLECTIVE IS LIKELY WORKING WITH THE SCARECROW. THAT THEY'RE OLD ARKHAM BUDDIES OR SOMETHING.
I'LL BE HONEST, THERE ISN'T MUCH LOGIC TO IT.
BUT LOOKING OVER SOCIAL MEDIA FEEDS, PEOPLE ARE BUYING INTO THE THEORY.
THE MOOD IS GETTING TENSE OUT THERE. DID YOU FIND WHAT YOU WERE LOOKING FOR?
I NEED TO KNOW EVERYTHING THERE IS TO KNOW ABOUT SIMON SAINT.
CONTACT GHOST-MAKER. IF I CAN GET CRANE'S LOCATION FROM SAINT, THE TWO OF US WILL BE ABLE TO APPREHEND SCARECROW TONIGHT. I NEED HIM ON STANDBY.
HE DOESN'T ALWAYS TAKE MY CALLS, BATMAN. AND YOU PUT HIM ON BABYSITTER DUTY WITH HARLEY. THERE ARE PEOPLE IN THE FAMILY--
CLICK
--WHO ARE SUSCEPTIBLE TO FEAR TOXIN IN A WAY HE ISN'T. BE PERSISTENT.
AND THEN SEND THE SCHEMATICS OF THE SAINT INDUSTRIES TOWER TO THE CAR. I NEED A WAY IN.

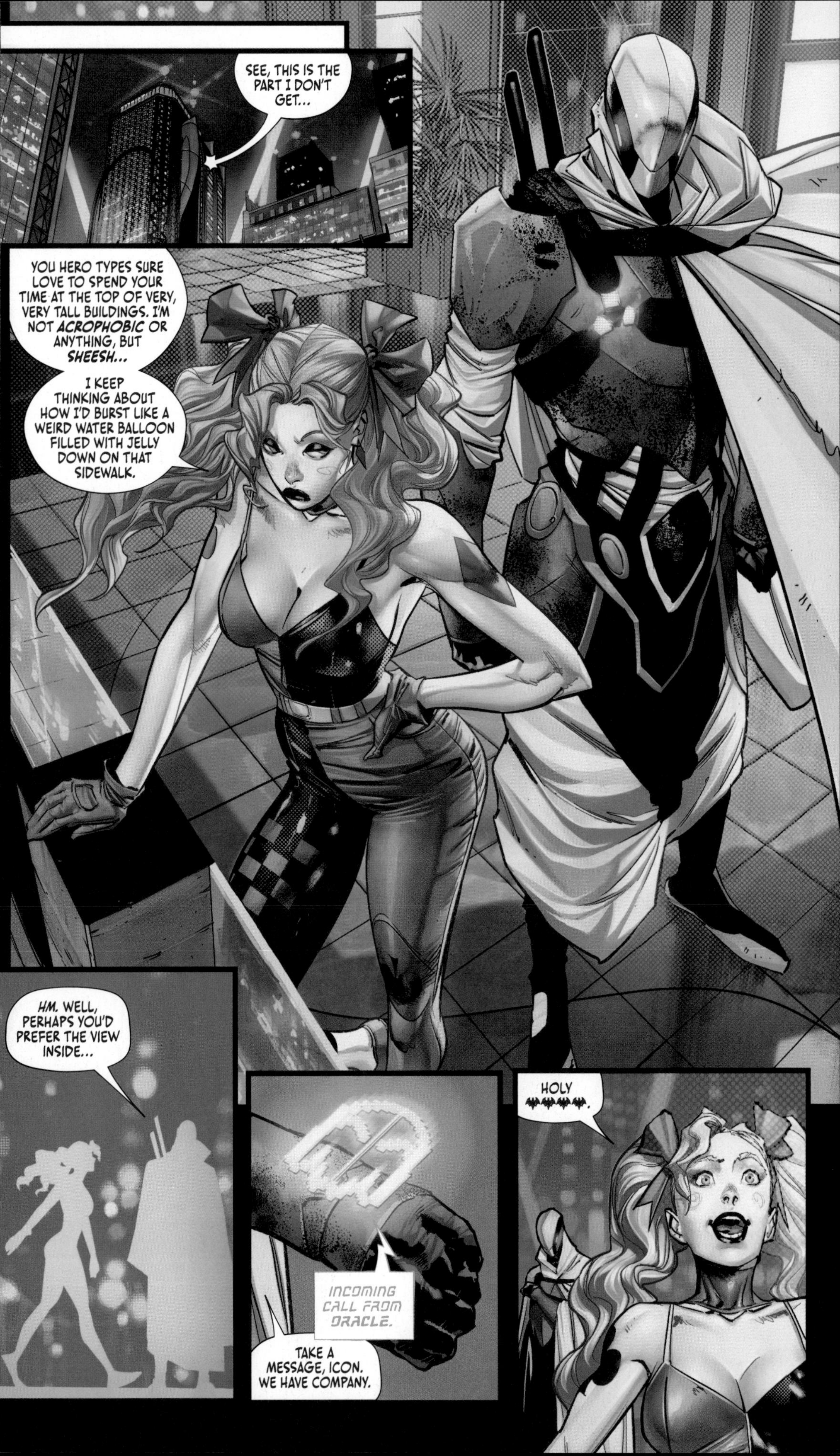
SEE, THIS IS THE PART I DON'T GET...
YOU HERO TYPES SURE LOVE TO SPEND YOUR TIME AT THE TOP OF VERY, VERY TALL BUILDINGS. I'M NOT ACROPHOBIC OR ANYTHING, BUT SHEESH...
I KEEP THINKING ABOUT HOW I'D BURST LIKE A WEIRD WATER BALLOON FILLED WITH JELLY DOWN ON THAT SIDEWALK.
HM. WELL, PERHAPS YOU'D PREFER THE VIEW INSIDE...
INCOMING CALL FROM ORACLE.
TAKE A MESSAGE, ICON. WE HAVE COMPANY.
HOLY

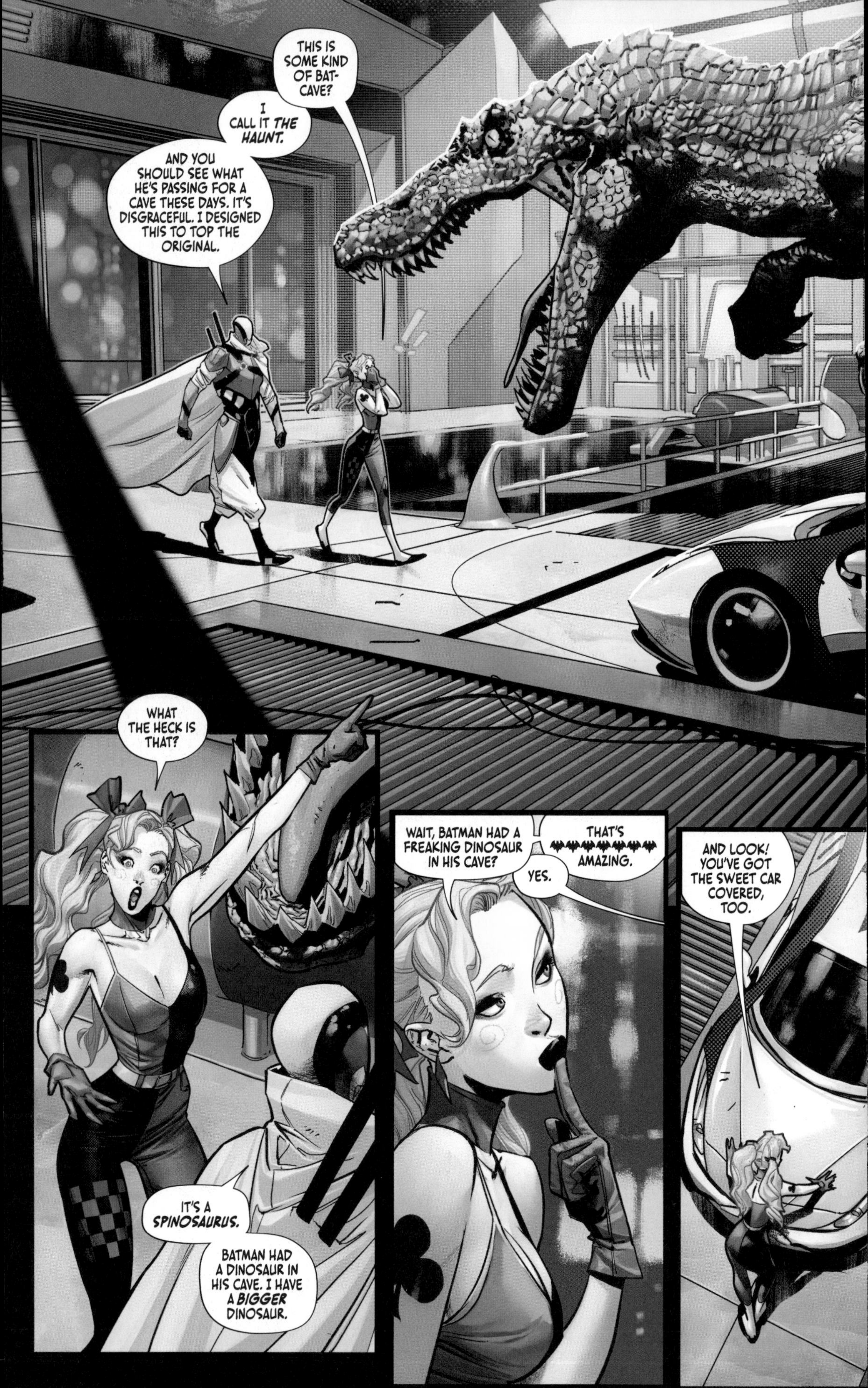

THIS IS SOME KIND OF BAT-CAVE?
I CALL IT *THE HAUNT.*
AND YOU SHOULD SEE WHAT HE'S PASSING FOR A CAVE THESE DAYS. IT'S DISGRACEFUL. I DESIGNED THIS TO TOP THE ORIGINAL.
WHAT THE HECK IS THAT?
IT'S A *SPINOSAURUS.*
BATMAN HAD A DINOSAUR IN HIS CAVE. I HAVE A *BIGGER* DINOSAUR.
WAIT, BATMAN HAD A FREAKING DINOSAUR IN HIS CAVE?
YES.
THAT'S AMAZING.
AND LOOK! YOU'VE GOT THE SWEET CAR COVERED, TOO.

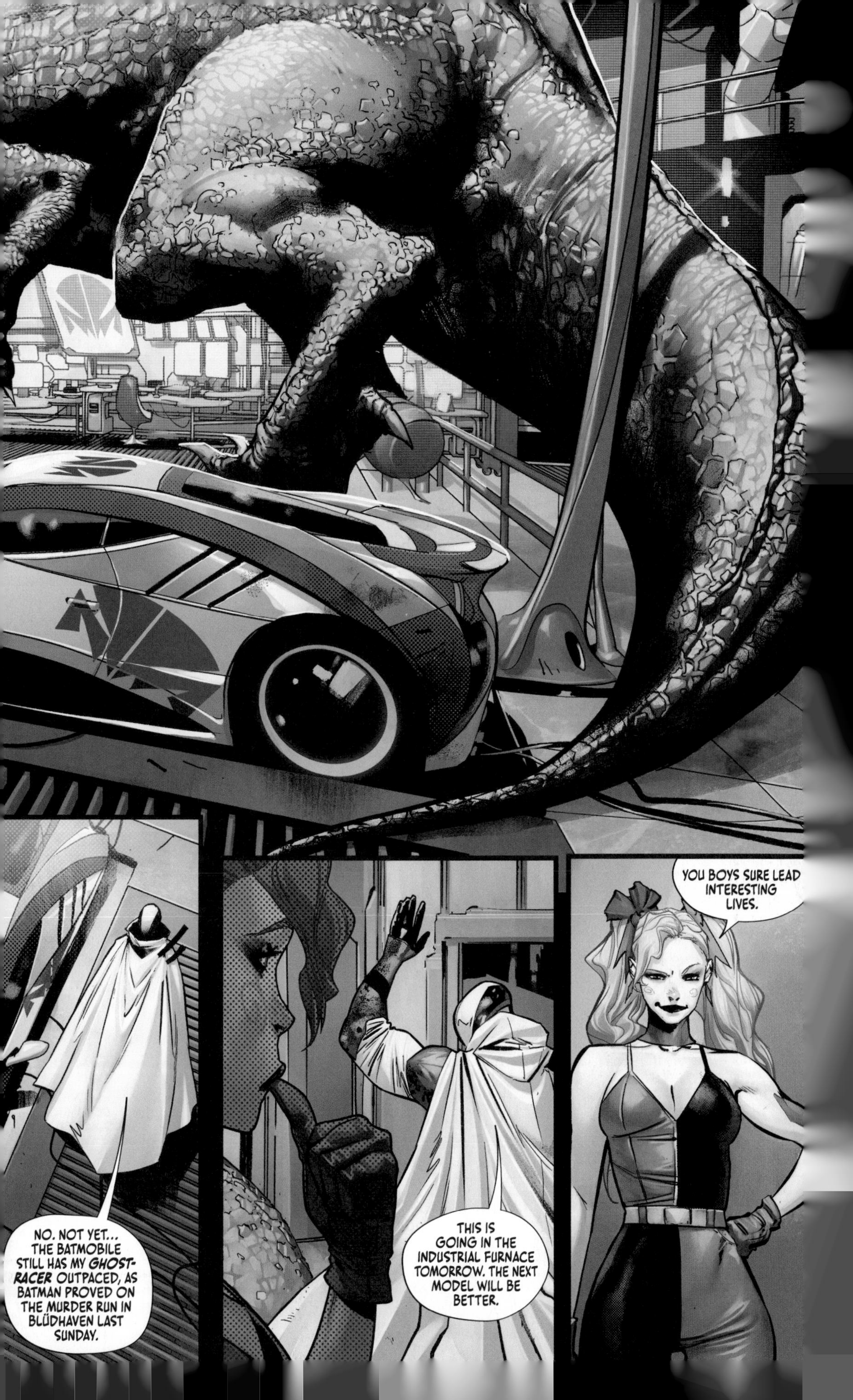
NO. NOT YET... THE BATMOBILE STILL HAS MY *GHOST-RACER* OUTPACED, AS BATMAN PROVED ON THE MURDER RUN IN BLÜDHAVEN LAST SUNDAY.
THIS IS GOING IN THE INDUSTRIAL FURNACE TOMORROW. THE NEXT MODEL WILL BE BETTER.
YOU BOYS SURE LEAD INTERESTING LIVES.

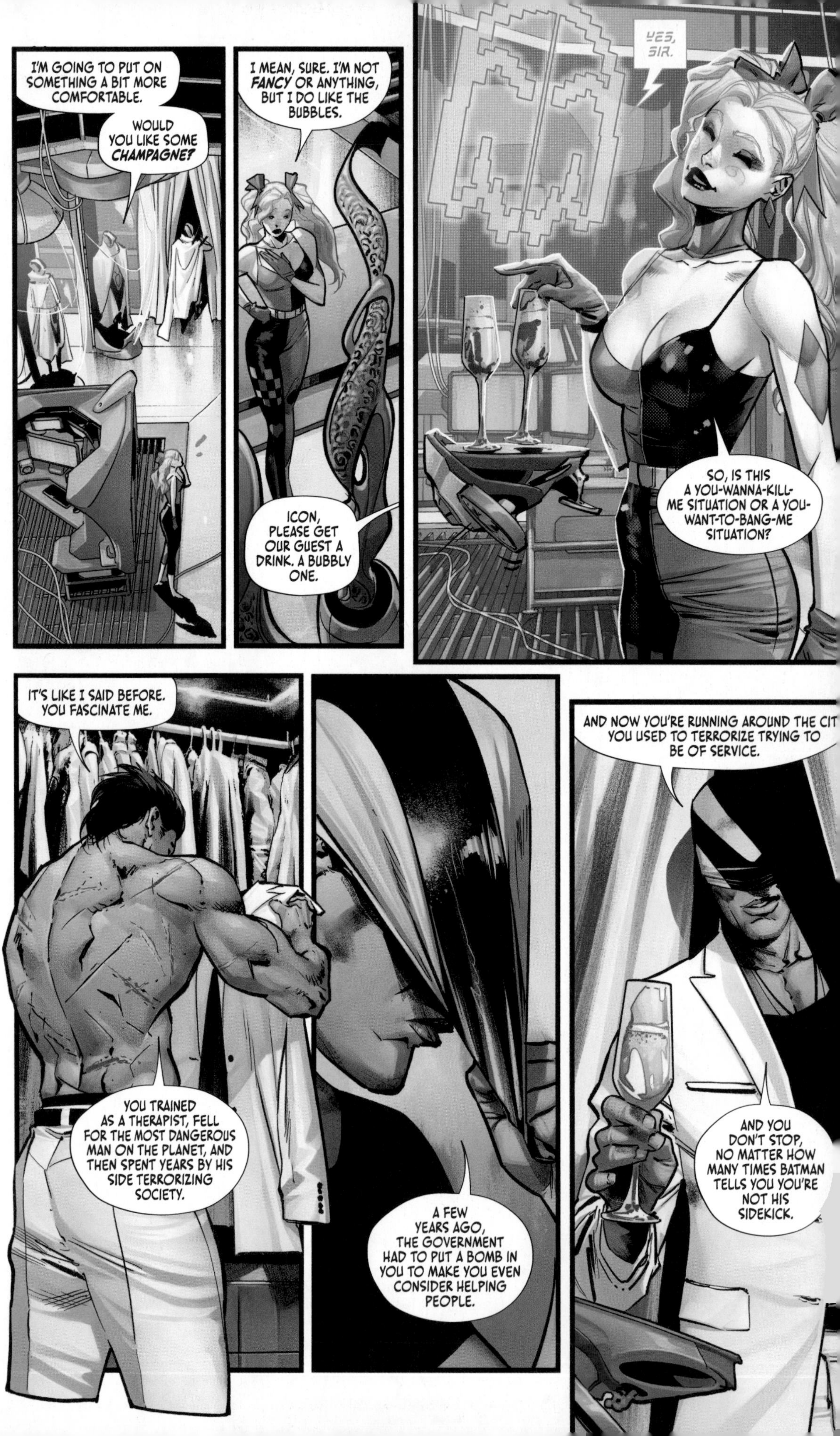
I'M GOING TO PUT ON SOMETHING A BIT MORE COMFORTABLE.
WOULD YOU LIKE SOME CHAMPAGNE?
I MEAN, SURE. I'M NOT FANCY OR ANYTHING, BUT I DO LIKE THE BUBBLES.
ICON, PLEASE GET OUR GUEST A DRINK. A BUBBLY ONE.
YES, SIR.
SO, IS THIS A YOU-WANNA-KILL-ME SITUATION OR A YOU-WANT-TO-BANG-ME SITUATION?
IT'S LIKE I SAID BEFORE. YOU FASCINATE ME.
YOU TRAINED AS A THERAPIST, FELL FOR THE MOST DANGEROUS MAN ON THE PLANET, AND THEN SPENT YEARS BY HIS SIDE TERRORIZING SOCIETY.
A FEW YEARS AGO, THE GOVERNMENT HAD TO PUT A BOMB IN YOU TO MAKE YOU EVEN CONSIDER HELPING PEOPLE.
AND NOW YOU'RE RUNNING AROUND THE CIT
YOU USED TO TERRORIZE TRYING TO BE OF SERVICE.
AND YOU DON'T STOP, NO MATTER HOW MANY TIMES BATMAN TELLS YOU YOU'RE NOT HIS SIDEKICK.

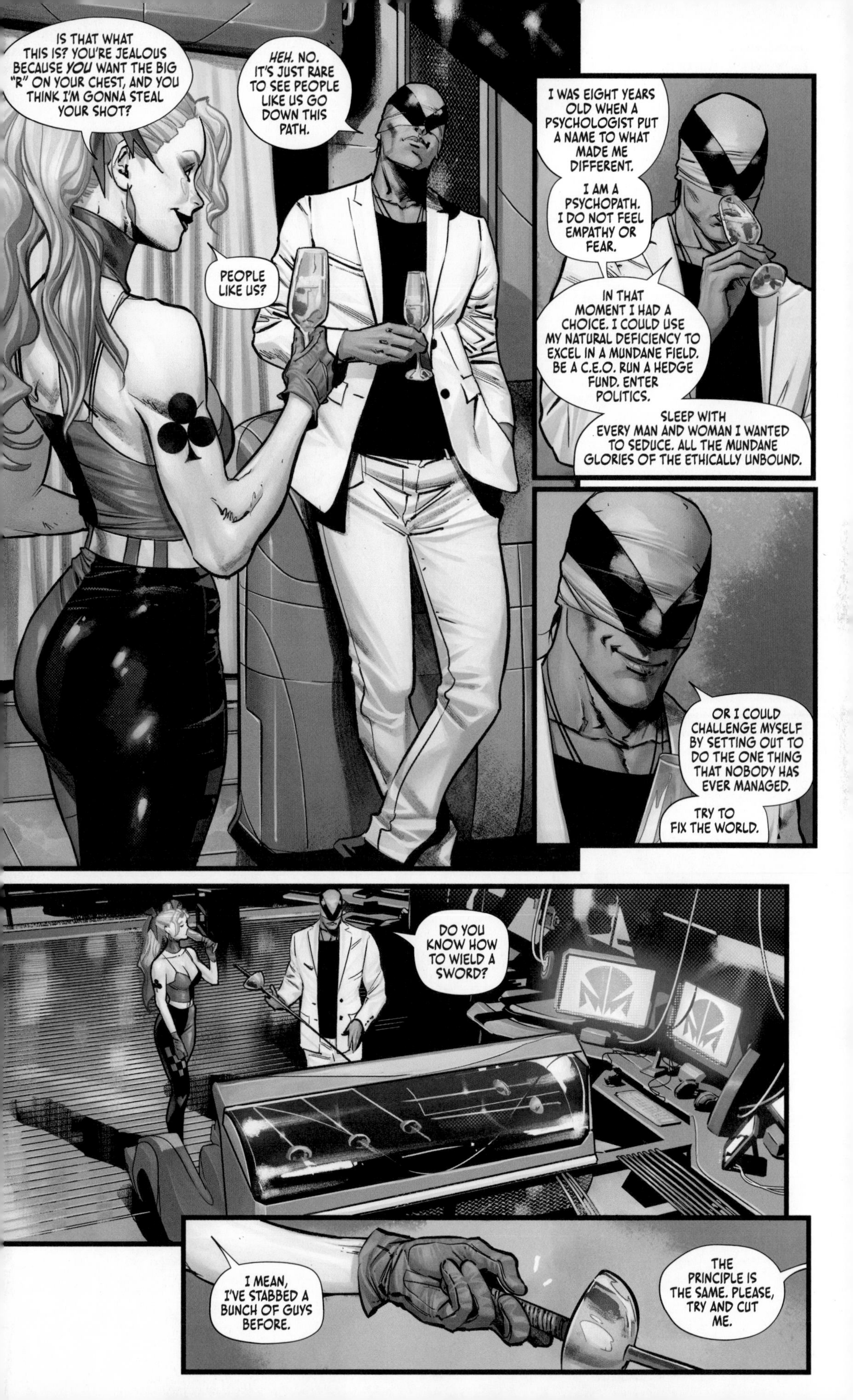
IS THAT WHAT THIS IS? YOU'RE JEALOUS BECAUSE *YOU* WANT THE BIG "R" ON YOUR CHEST, AND YOU THINK I'M GONNA STEAL YOUR SHOT?
HEH. NO. IT'S JUST RARE TO SEE PEOPLE LIKE US GO DOWN THIS PATH.
PEOPLE LIKE US?
I WAS EIGHT YEARS OLD WHEN A PSYCHOLOGIST PUT A NAME TO WHAT MADE ME DIFFERENT.
I AM A PSYCHOPATH. I DO NOT FEEL EMPATHY OR FEAR.
IN THAT MOMENT I HAD A CHOICE. I COULD USE MY NATURAL DEFICIENCY TO EXCEL IN A MUNDANE FIELD. BE A C.E.O. RUN A HEDGE FUND. ENTER POLITICS.
SLEEP WITH EVERY MAN AND WOMAN I WANTED TO SEDUCE. ALL THE MUNDANE GLORIES OF THE ETHICALLY UNBOUND.
OR I COULD CHALLENGE MYSELF BY SETTING OUT TO DO THE ONE THING THAT NOBODY HAS EVER MANAGED.
TRY TO FIX THE WORLD.
DO YOU KNOW HOW TO WIELD A SWORD?
I MEAN, I'VE STABBED A BUNCH OF GUYS BEFORE.
THE PRINCIPLE IS THE SAME. PLEASE, TRY AND CUT ME.

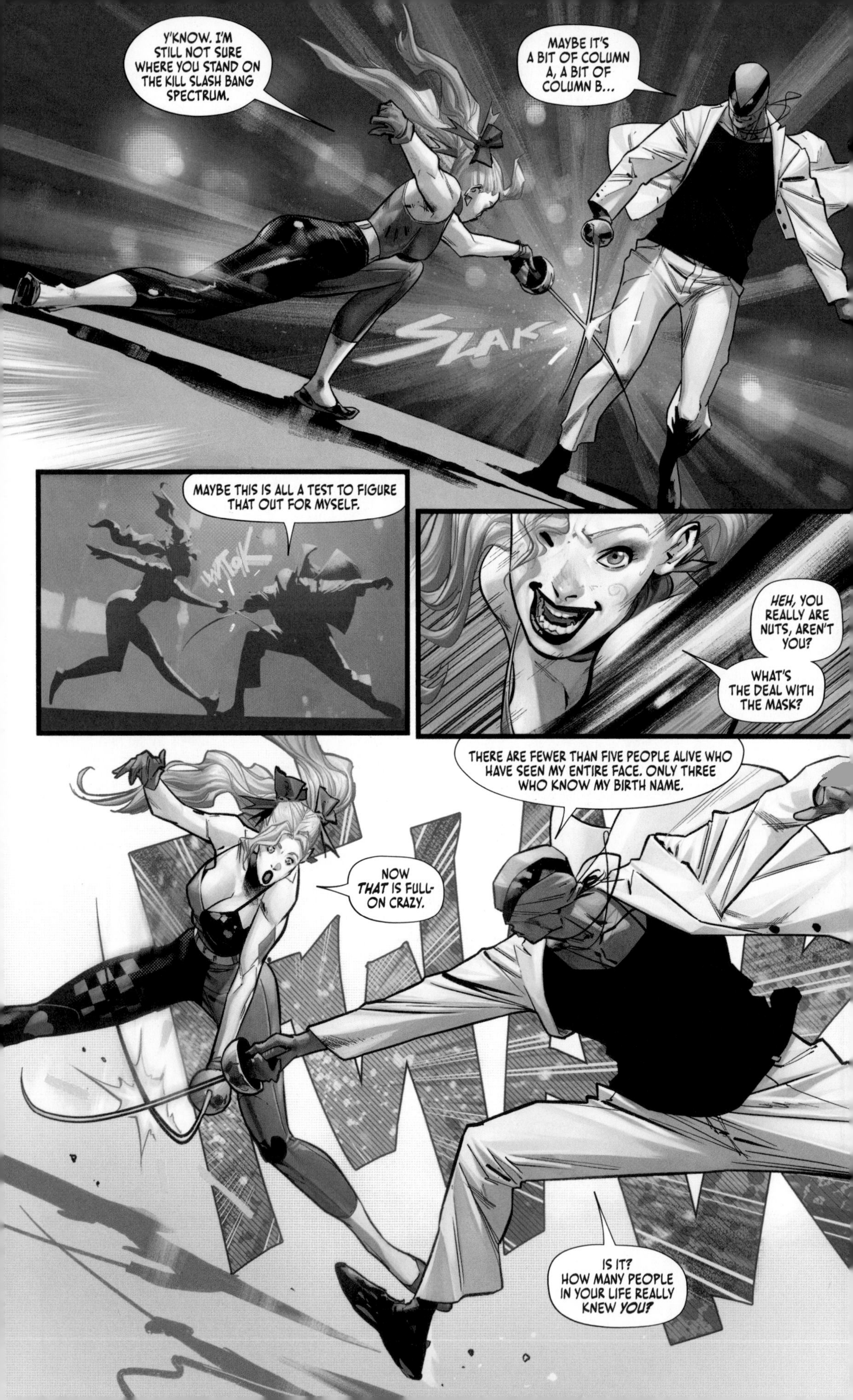
Y'KNOW. I'M STILL NOT SURE WHERE YOU STAND ON THE KILL SLASH BANG SPECTRUM.
MAYBE IT'S A BIT OF COLUMN A, A BIT OF COLUMN B...
SLAK
MAYBE THIS IS ALL A TEST TO FIGURE THAT OUT FOR MYSELF.
HEH, YOU REALLY ARE NUTS, AREN'T YOU?
WHAT'S THE DEAL WITH THE MASK?
THERE ARE FEWER THAN FIVE PEOPLE ALIVE WHO HAVE SEEN MY ENTIRE FACE. ONLY THREE WHO KNOW MY BIRTH NAME.
NOW *THAT* IS FULL-ON CRAZY.
IS IT? HOW MANY PEOPLE IN YOUR LIFE REALLY KNEW *YOU?*

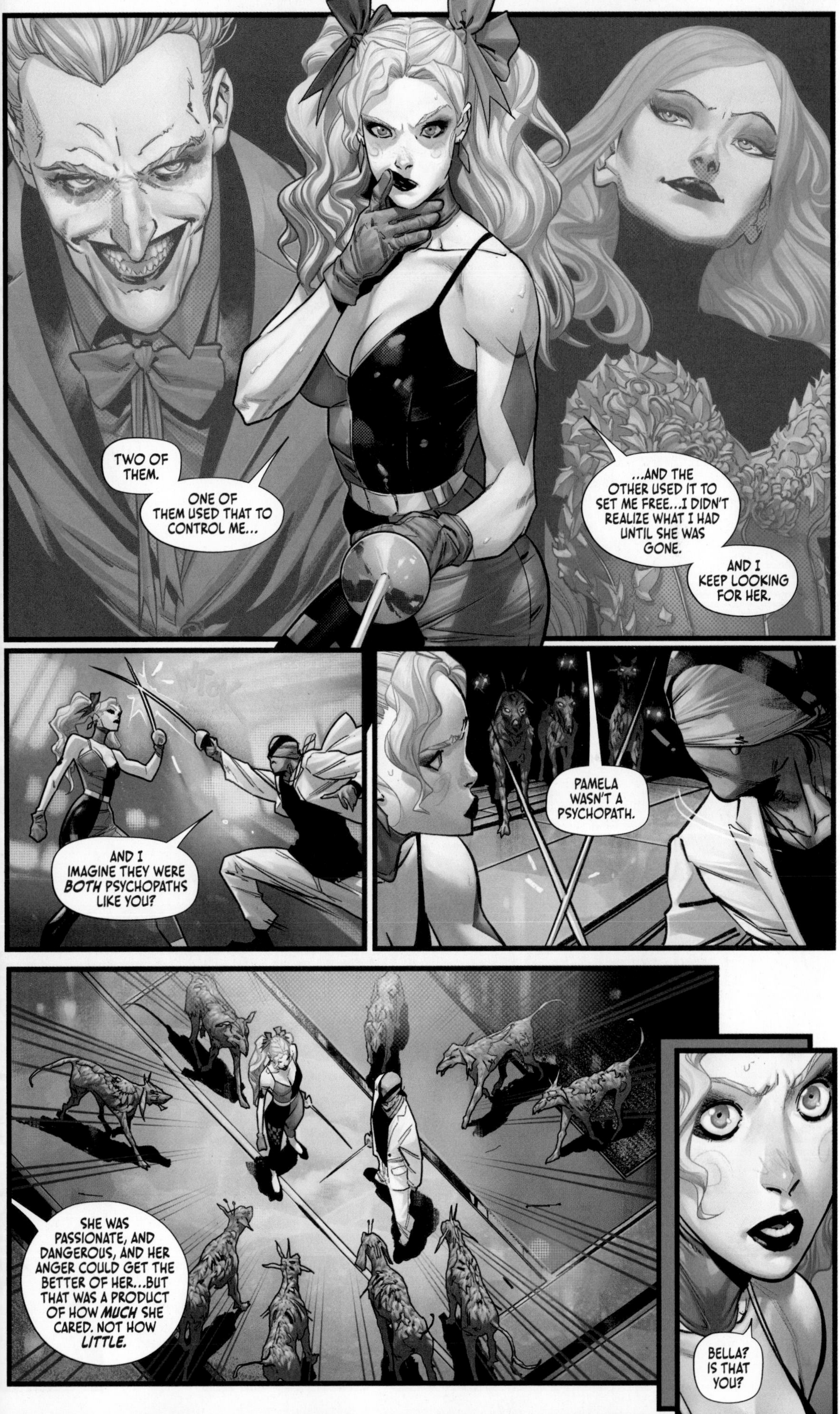
TWO OF THEM.
ONE OF THEM USED THAT TO CONTROL ME...
...AND THE OTHER USED IT TO SET ME FREE...I DIDN'T REALIZE WHAT I HAD UNTIL SHE WAS GONE.
AND I KEEP LOOKING FOR HER.
AND I IMAGINE THEY WERE *BOTH* PSYCHOPATHS LIKE YOU?
PAMELA WASN'T A PSYCHOPATH.
SHE WAS PASSIONATE, AND DANGEROUS, AND HER ANGER COULD GET THE BETTER OF HER...BUT THAT WAS A PRODUCT OF HOW *MUCH* SHE CARED. NOT HOW *LITTLE*.
BELLA? IS THAT YOU?

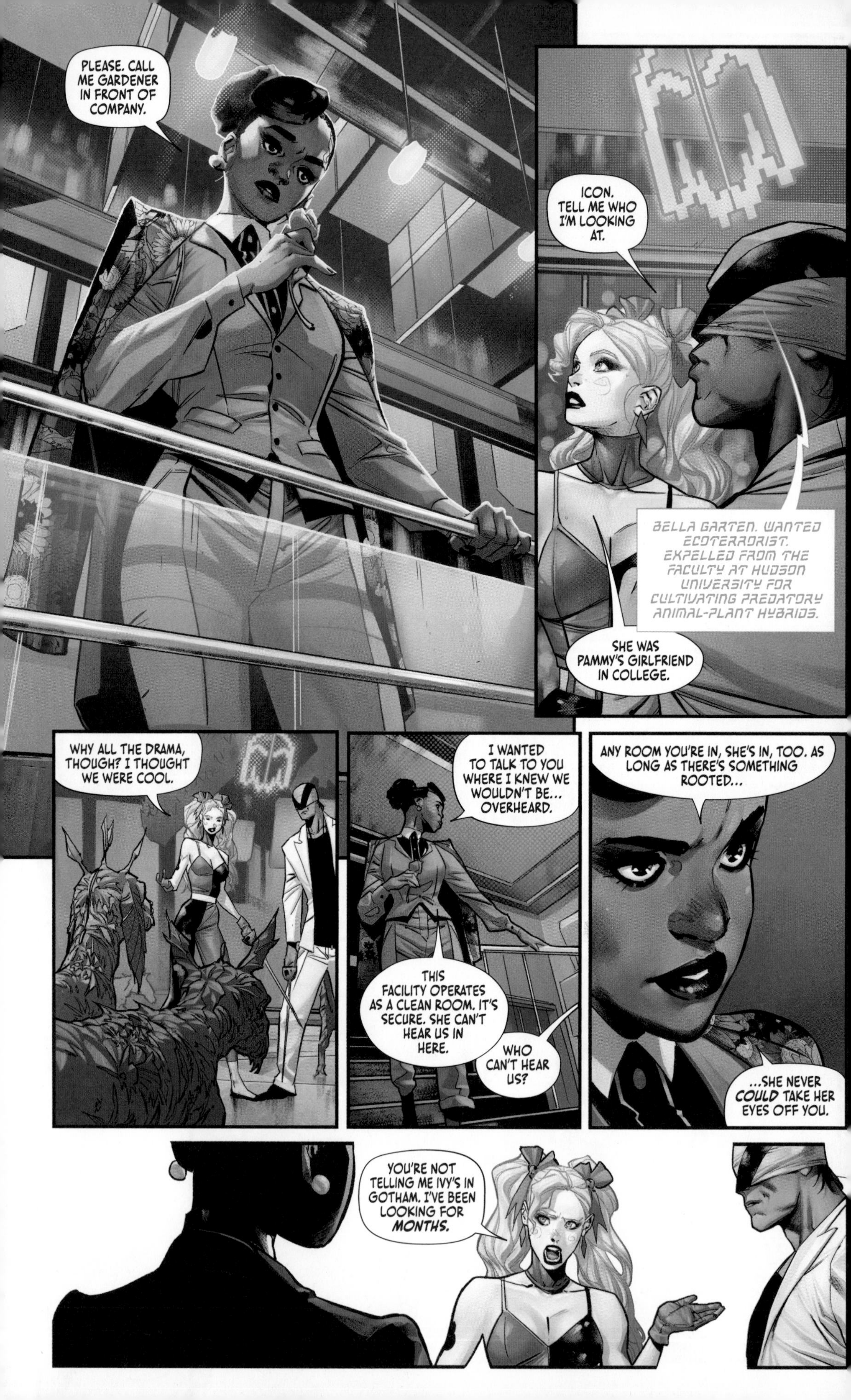
PLEASE. CALL ME GARDENER IN FRONT OF COMPANY.
ICON. TELL ME WHO I'M LOOKING AT.
BELLA GARTEN. WANTED ECOTERRORIST. EXPELLED FROM THE FACULTY AT HUDSON UNIVERSITY FOR CULTIVATING PREDATORY ANIMAL-PLANT HYBRIDS.
SHE WAS PAMMY'S GIRLFRIEND IN COLLEGE.
WHY ALL THE DRAMA, THOUGH? I THOUGHT WE WERE COOL.
I WANTED TO TALK TO YOU WHERE I KNEW WE WOULDN'T BE... OVERHEARD.
THIS FACILITY OPERATES AS A CLEAN ROOM. IT'S SECURE. SHE CAN'T HEAR US IN HERE.
WHO CAN'T HEAR US?
ANY ROOM YOU'RE IN, SHE'S IN, TOO. AS LONG AS THERE'S SOMETHING ROOTED...
...SHE NEVER *COULD* TAKE HER EYES OFF YOU.
YOU'RE NOT TELLING ME IVY'S IN GOTHAM. I'VE BEEN LOOKING FOR *MONTHS.*

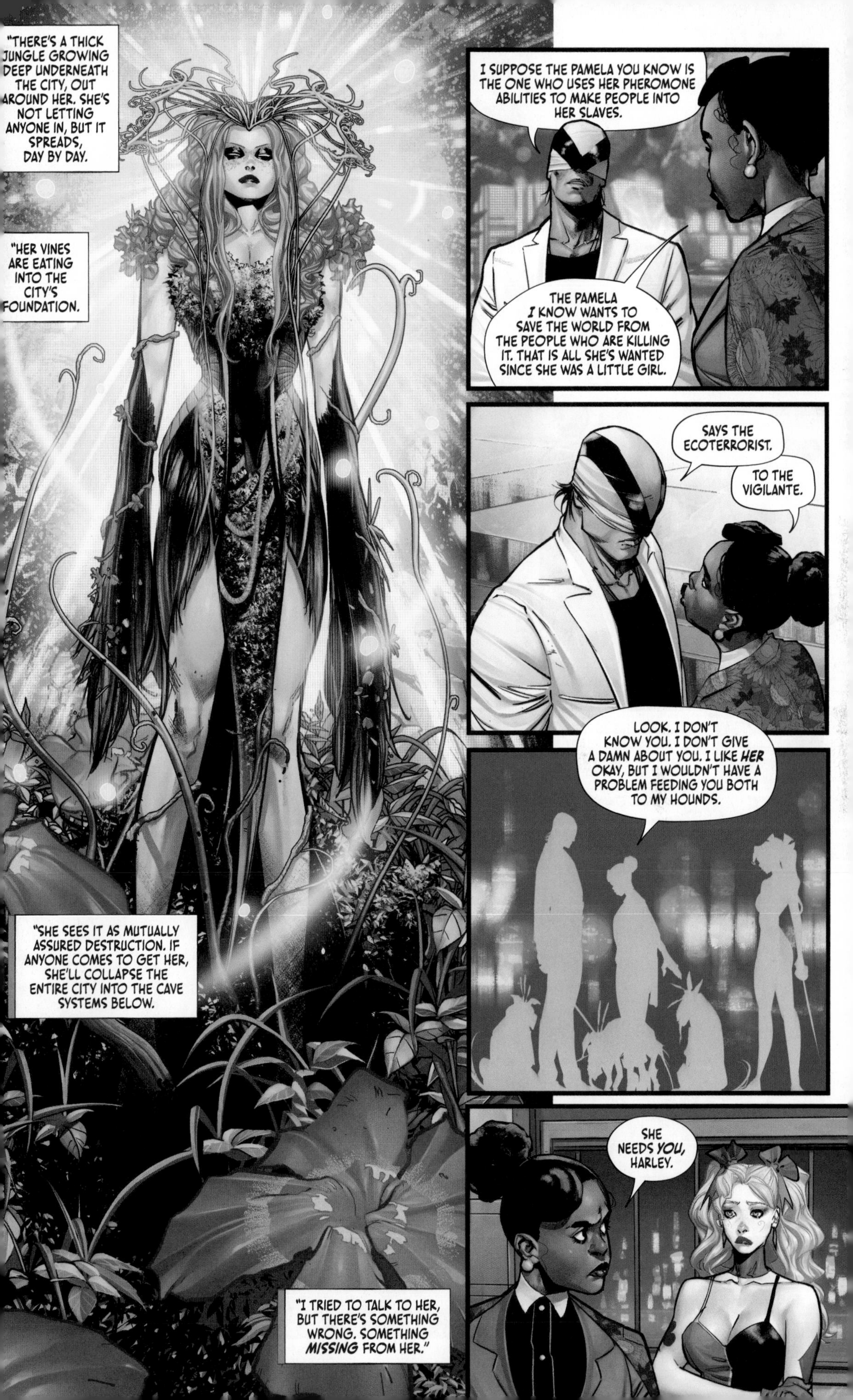
"THERE'S A THICK JUNGLE GROWING DEEP UNDERNEATH THE CITY, OUT AROUND HER. SHE'S NOT LETTING ANYONE IN, BUT IT SPREADS, DAY BY DAY.
"HER VINES ARE EATING INTO THE CITY'S FOUNDATION.
"SHE SEES IT AS MUTUALLY ASSURED DESTRUCTION. IF ANYONE COMES TO GET HER, SHE'LL COLLAPSE THE ENTIRE CITY INTO THE CAVE SYSTEMS BELOW.
"I TRIED TO TALK TO HER, BUT THERE'S SOMETHING WRONG. SOMETHING *MISSING* FROM HER."
I SUPPOSE THE PAMELA YOU KNOW IS THE ONE WHO USES HER PHEROMONE ABILITIES TO MAKE PEOPLE INTO HER SLAVES.
THE PAMELA *I* KNOW WANTS TO SAVE THE WORLD FROM THE PEOPLE WHO ARE KILLING IT. THAT IS ALL SHE'S WANTED SINCE SHE WAS A LITTLE GIRL.
SAYS THE ECOTERRORIST.
TO THE VIGILANTE.
LOOK. I DON'T KNOW YOU. I DON'T GIVE A DAMN ABOUT YOU. I LIKE *HER* OKAY, BUT I WOULDN'T HAVE A PROBLEM FEEDING YOU BOTH TO MY HOUNDS.
SHE NEEDS *YOU*, HARLEY.

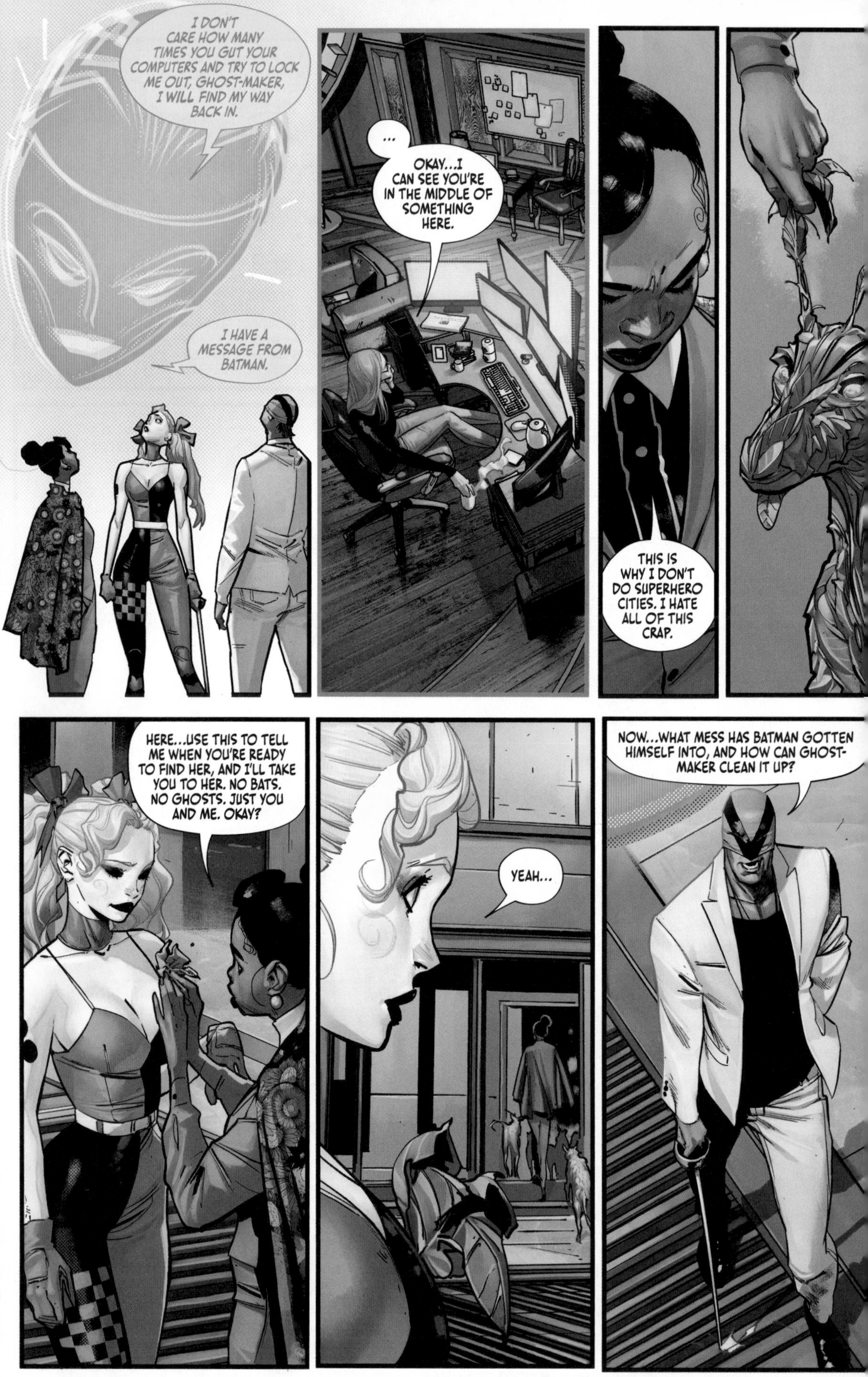
I DON'T CARE HOW MANY TIMES YOU GUT YOUR COMPUTERS AND TRY TO LOCK ME OUT, GHOST-MAKER, I WILL FIND MY WAY BACK IN.
I HAVE A MESSAGE FROM BATMAN.
...
OKAY...I CAN SEE YOU'RE IN THE MIDDLE OF SOMETHING HERE.
THIS IS WHY I DON'T DO SUPERHERO CITIES. I HATE ALL OF THIS CRAP.
HERE...USE THIS TO TELL ME WHEN YOU'RE READY TO FIND HER, AND I'LL TAKE YOU TO HER. NO BATS. NO GHOSTS. JUST YOU AND ME. OKAY?
YEAH...
NOW...WHAT MESS HAS BATMAN GOTTEN HIMSELF INTO, AND HOW CAN GHOST-MAKER CLEAN IT UP?

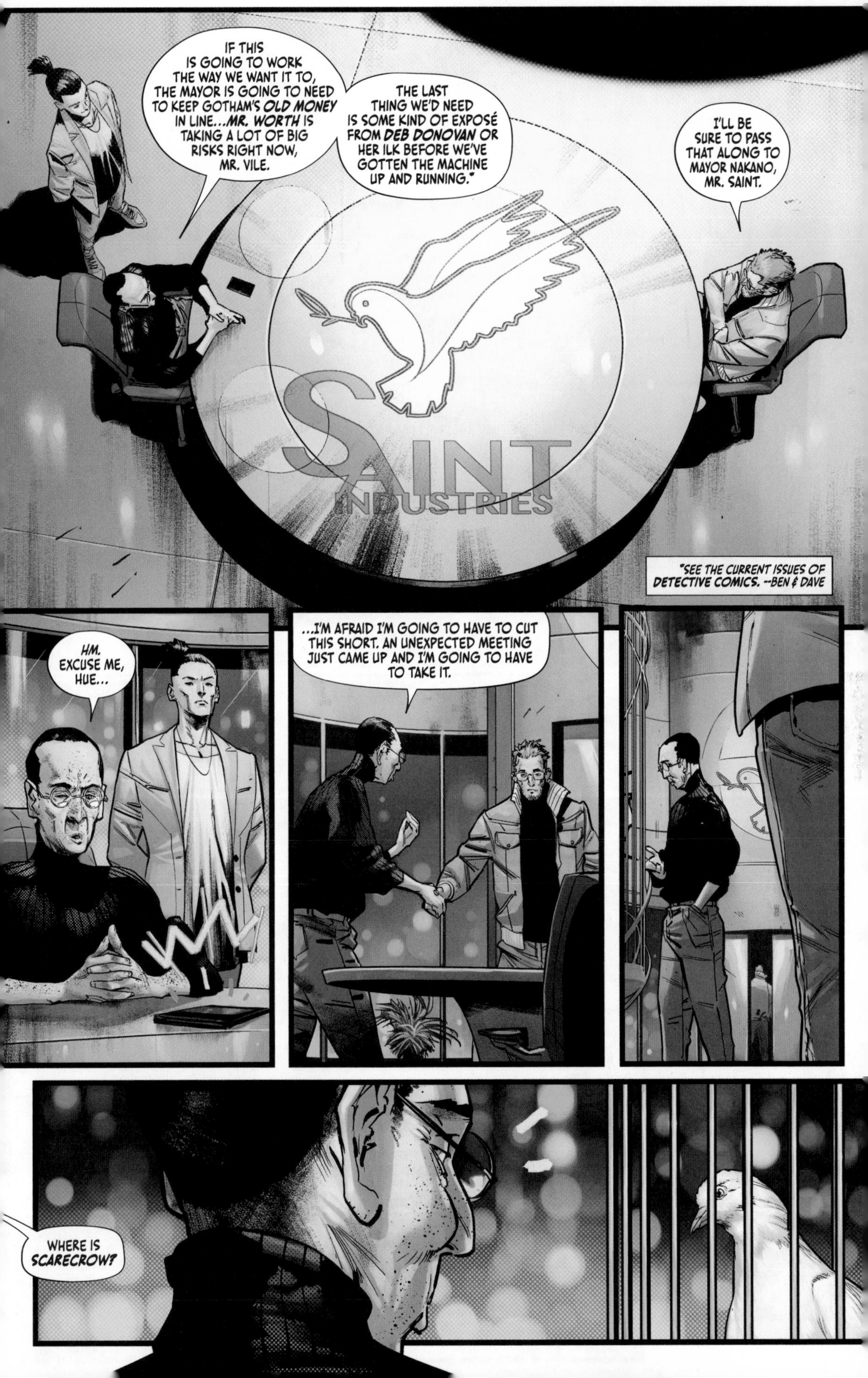

IF THIS IS GOING TO WORK THE WAY WE WANT IT TO, THE MAYOR IS GOING TO NEED TO KEEP GOTHAM'S OLD MONEY IN LINE...MR. WORTH IS TAKING A LOT OF BIG RISKS RIGHT NOW, MR. VILE.
THE LAST THING WE'D NEED IS SOME KIND OF EXPOSÉ FROM DEB DONOVAN OR HER ILK BEFORE WE'VE GOTTEN THE MACHINE UP AND RUNNING.*
I'LL BE SURE TO PASS THAT ALONG TO MAYOR NAKANO, MR. SAINT.
SAINT INDUSTRIES
*SEE THE CURRENT ISSUES OF DETECTIVE COMICS. --BEN & DAVE
HM. EXCUSE ME, HUE...
...I'M AFRAID I'M GOING TO HAVE TO CUT THIS SHORT. AN UNEXPECTED MEETING JUST CAME UP AND I'M GOING TO HAVE TO TAKE IT.
WHERE IS SCARECROW?

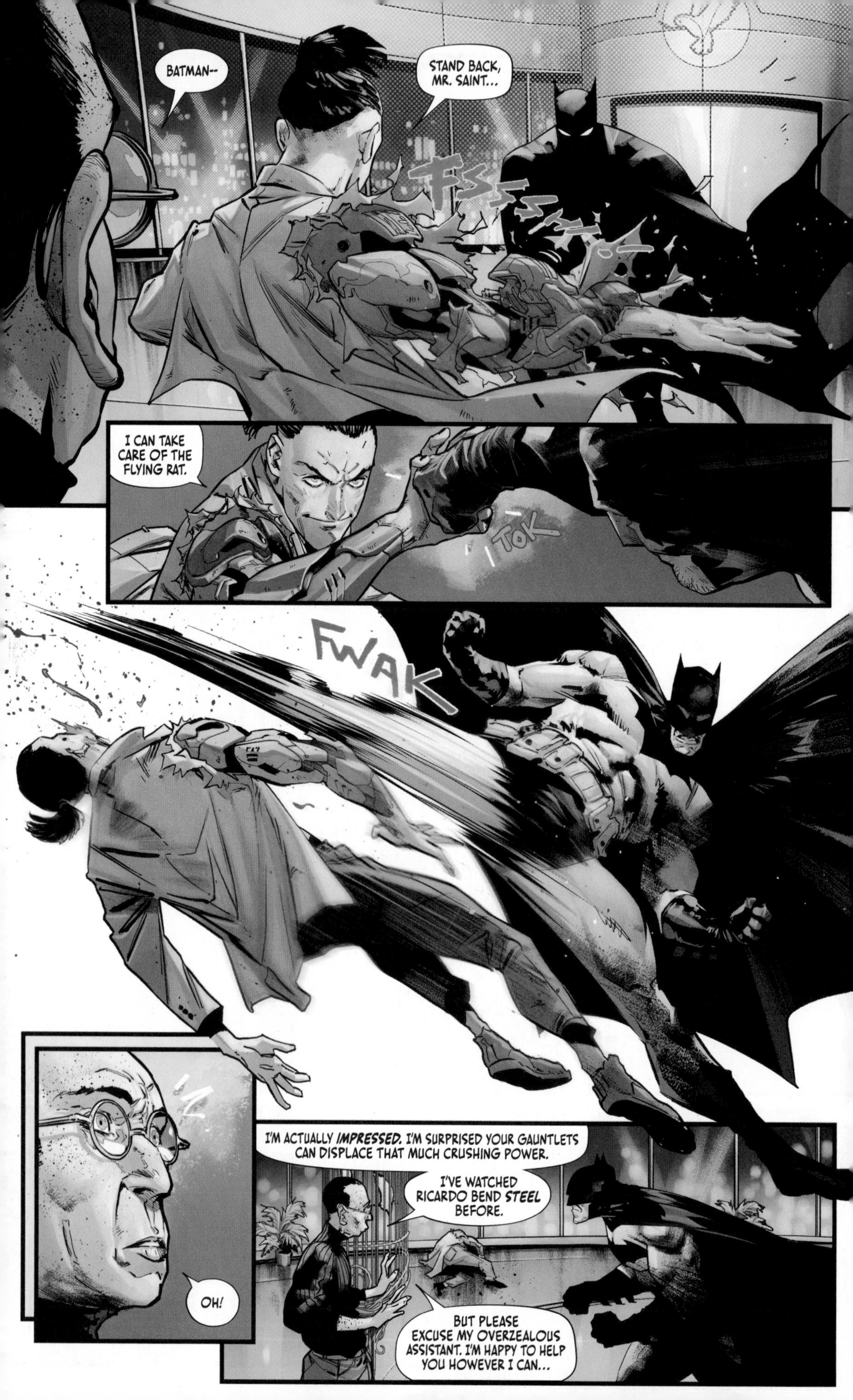
BATMAN--
STAND BACK, MR. SAINT...
FSSSHH
I CAN TAKE CARE OF THE FLYING RAT.
TOK
FWAK
OH!
I'M ACTUALLY IMPRESSED. I'M SURPRISED YOUR GAUNTLETS CAN DISPLACE THAT MUCH CRUSHING POWER.
I'VE WATCHED RICARDO BEND STEEL BEFORE.
BUT PLEASE EXCUSE MY OVERZEALOUS ASSISTANT. I'M HAPPY TO HELP YOU HOWEVER I CAN...

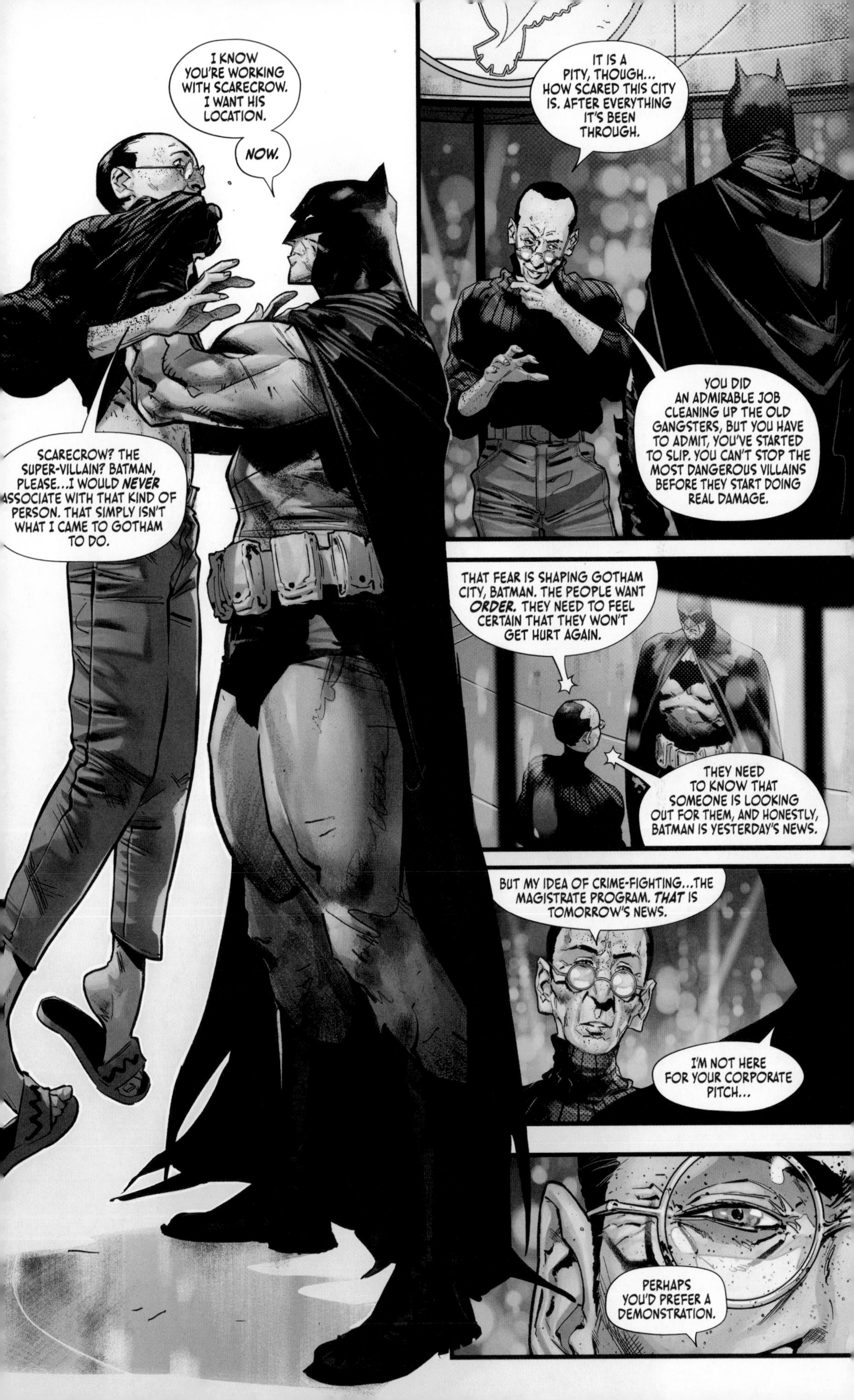
I KNOW YOU'RE WORKING WITH SCARECROW. I WANT HIS LOCATION.
NOW.
SCARECROW? THE SUPER-VILLAIN? BATMAN, PLEASE...I WOULD NEVER ASSOCIATE WITH THAT KIND OF PERSON. THAT SIMPLY ISN'T WHAT I CAME TO GOTHAM TO DO.
IT IS A PITY, THOUGH... HOW SCARED THIS CITY IS. AFTER EVERYTHING IT'S BEEN THROUGH.
YOU DID AN ADMIRABLE JOB CLEANING UP THE OLD GANGSTERS, BUT YOU HAVE TO ADMIT, YOU'VE STARTED TO SLIP. YOU CAN'T STOP THE MOST DANGEROUS VILLAINS BEFORE THEY START DOING REAL DAMAGE.
THAT FEAR IS SHAPING GOTHAM CITY, BATMAN. THE PEOPLE WANT ORDER. THEY NEED TO FEEL CERTAIN THAT THEY WON'T GET HURT AGAIN.
THEY NEED TO KNOW THAT SOMEONE IS LOOKING OUT FOR THEM, AND HONESTLY, BATMAN IS YESTERDAY'S NEWS.
BUT MY IDEA OF CRIME-FIGHTING...THE MAGISTRATE PROGRAM. THAT IS TOMORROW'S NEWS.
I'M NOT HERE FOR YOUR CORPORATE PITCH...
PERHAPS YOU'D PREFER A DEMONSTRATION.

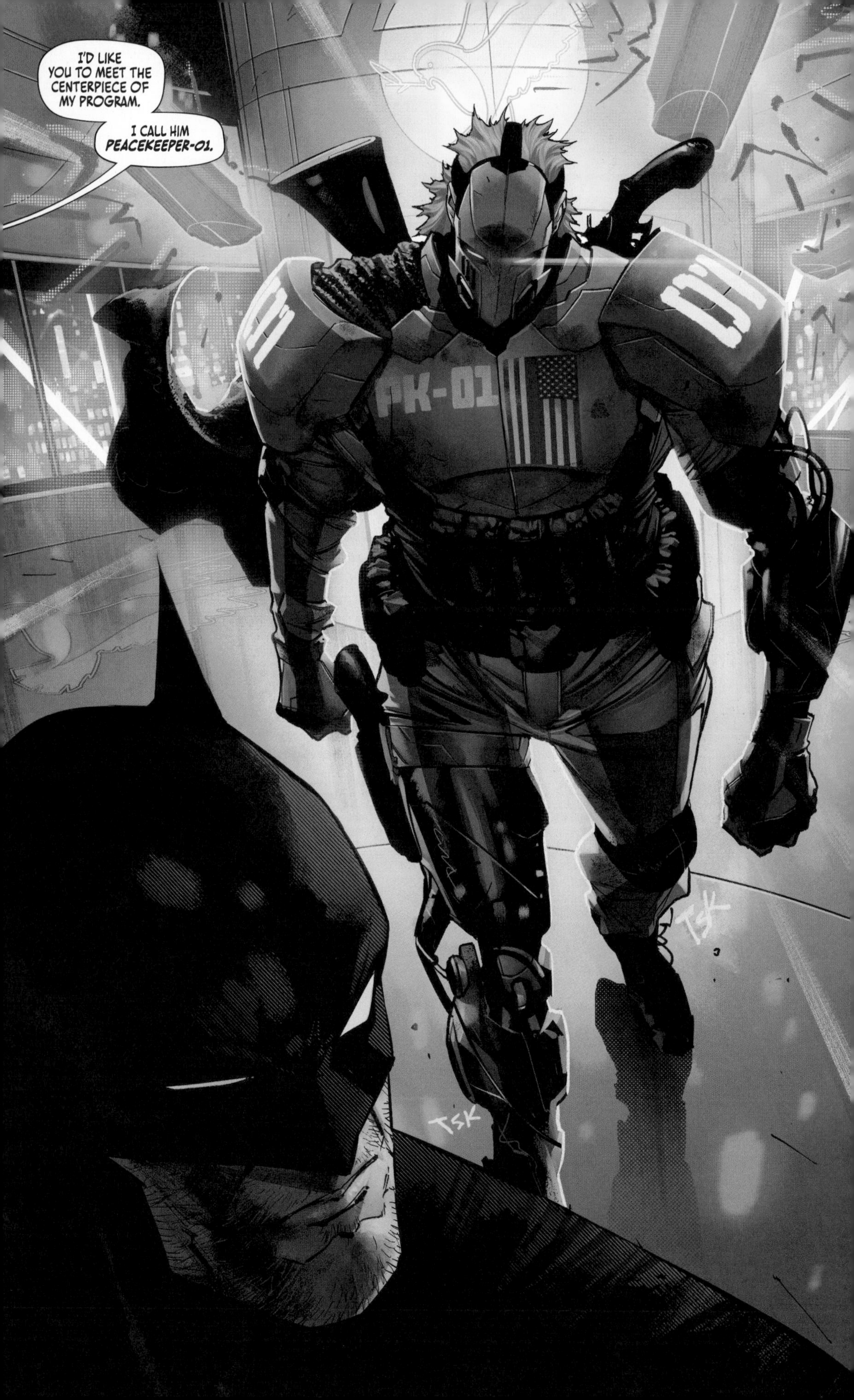
I'D LIKE YOU TO MEET THE CENTERPIECE OF MY PROGRAM.
I CALL HIM *PEACEKEEPER-01.*
PK-01
TSK
TSK

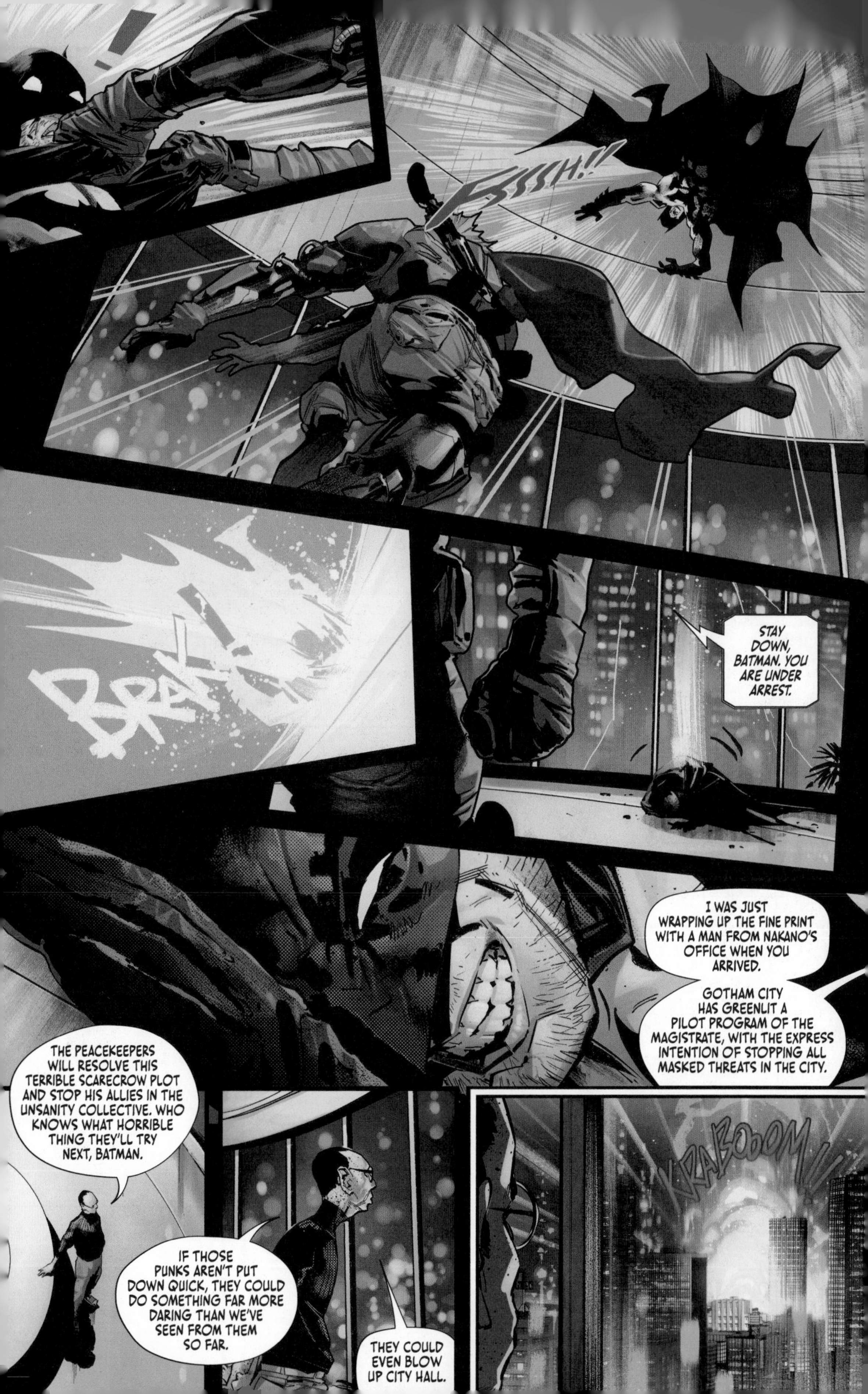
STAY DOWN, BATMAN. YOU ARE UNDER ARREST.
I WAS JUST WRAPPING UP THE FINE PRINT WITH A MAN FROM NAKANO'S OFFICE WHEN YOU ARRIVED.
GOTHAM CITY HAS GREENLIT A PILOT PROGRAM OF THE MAGISTRATE, WITH THE EXPRESS INTENTION OF STOPPING ALL MASKED THREATS IN THE CITY.
THE PEACEKEEPERS WILL RESOLVE THIS TERRIBLE SCARECROW PLOT AND STOP HIS ALLIES IN THE UNSANITY COLLECTIVE. WHO KNOWS WHAT HORRIBLE THING THEY'LL TRY NEXT, BATMAN.
IF THOSE PUNKS AREN'T PUT DOWN QUICK, THEY COULD DO SOMETHING FAR MORE DARING THAN WE'VE SEEN FROM THEM SO FAR.
THEY COULD EVEN BLOW UP CITY HALL.

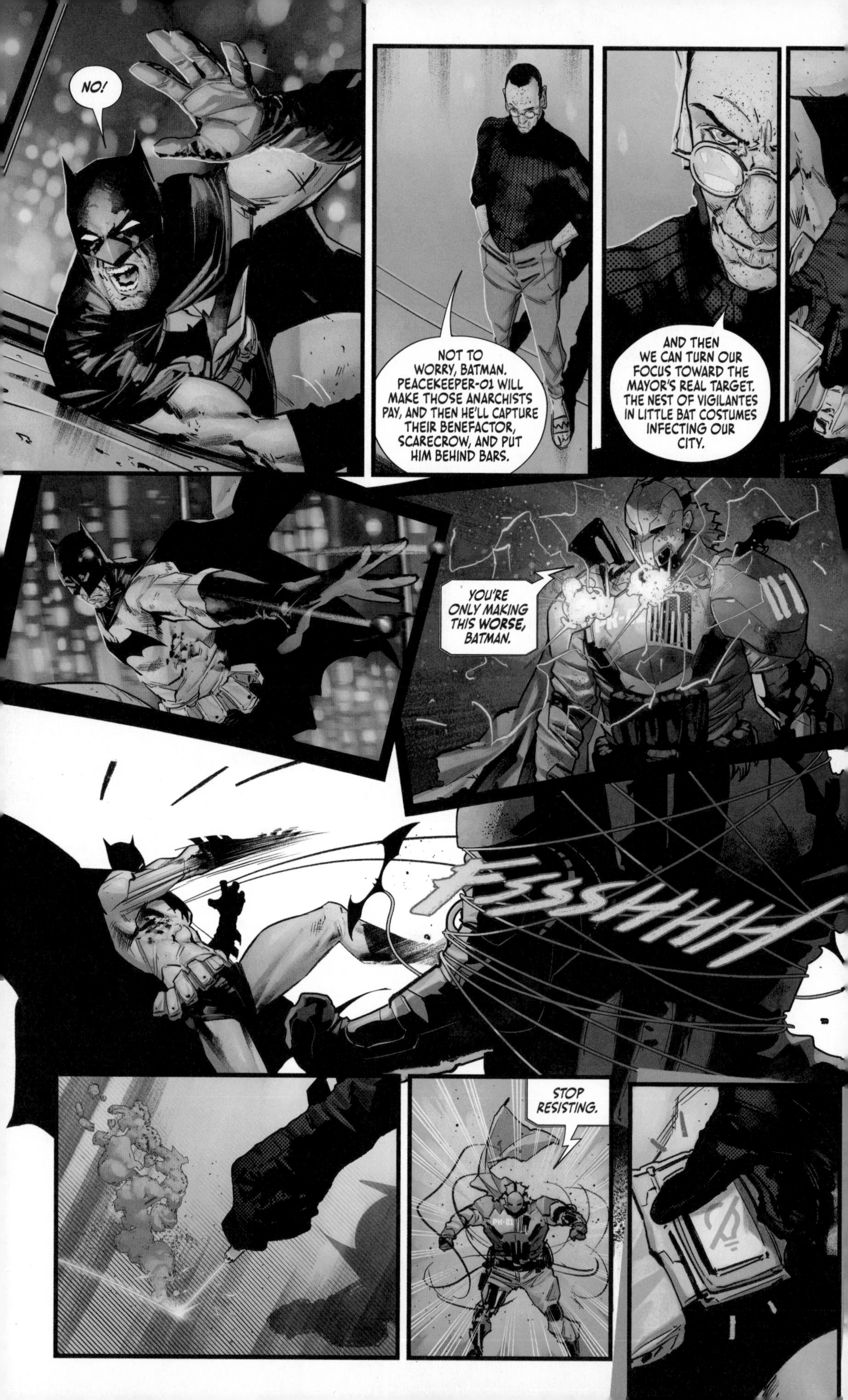
NO!
NOT TO WORRY, BATMAN. PEACEKEEPER-01 WILL MAKE THOSE ANARCHISTS PAY, AND THEN HE'LL CAPTURE THEIR BENEFACTOR, SCARECROW, AND PUT HIM BEHIND BARS.
AND THEN WE CAN TURN OUR FOCUS TOWARD THE MAYOR'S REAL TARGET. THE NEST OF VIGILANTES IN LITTLE BAT COSTUMES INFECTING OUR CITY.
YOU'RE ONLY MAKING THIS WORSE, BATMAN.
FSSSHHH
STOP RESISTING.

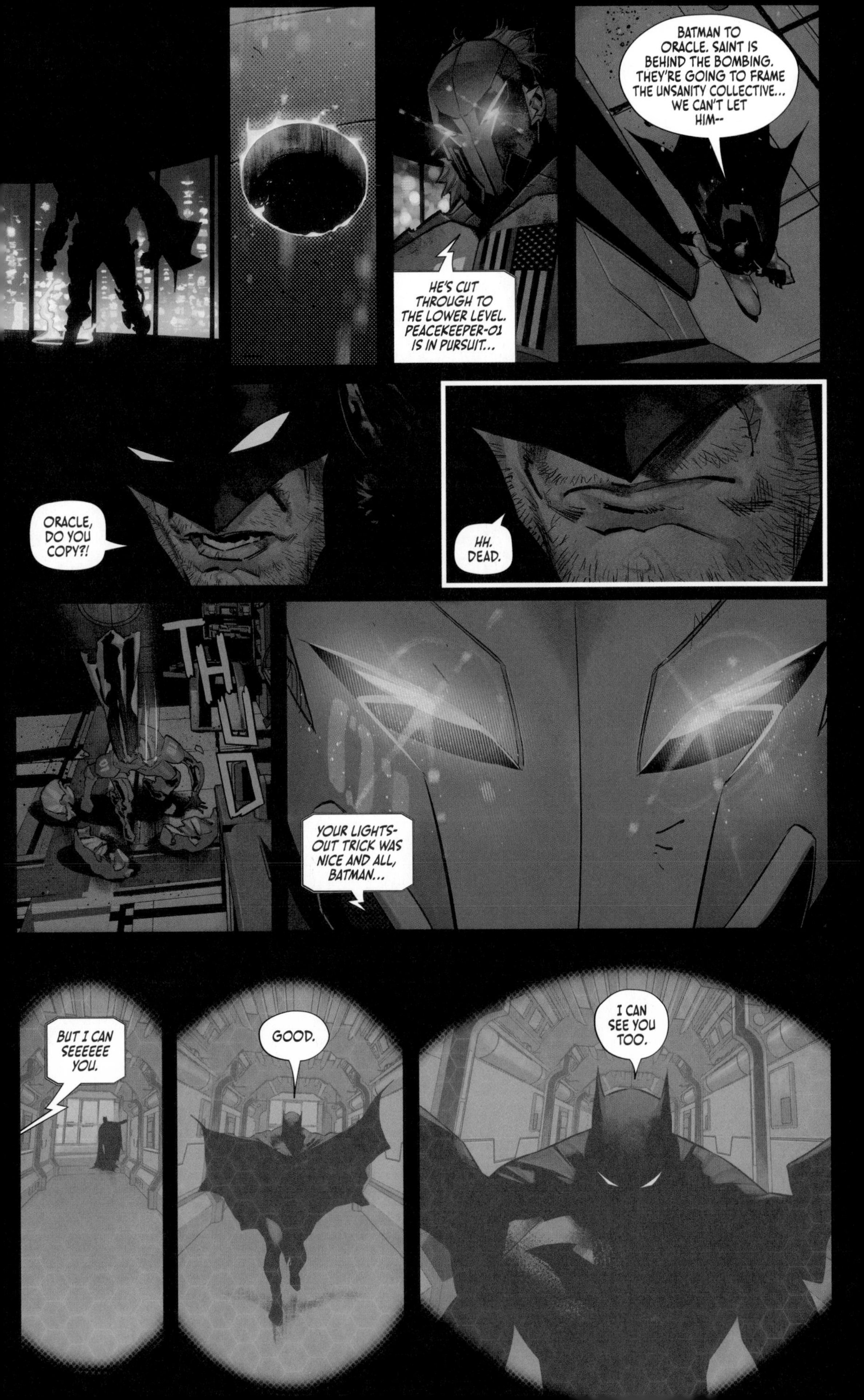
HE'S CUT THROUGH TO THE LOWER LEVEL. PEACEKEEPER-01 IS IN PURSUIT...
BATMAN TO ORACLE. SAINT IS BEHIND THE BOMBING. THEY'RE GOING TO FRAME THE UNSANITY COLLECTIVE... WE CAN'T LET HIM--
ORACLE, DO YOU COPY?!
HH. DEAD.
THUD
YOUR LIGHTS-OUT TRICK WAS NICE AND ALL, BATMAN...
BUT I CAN SEEEEEE YOU.
GOOD.
I CAN SEE YOU TOO.

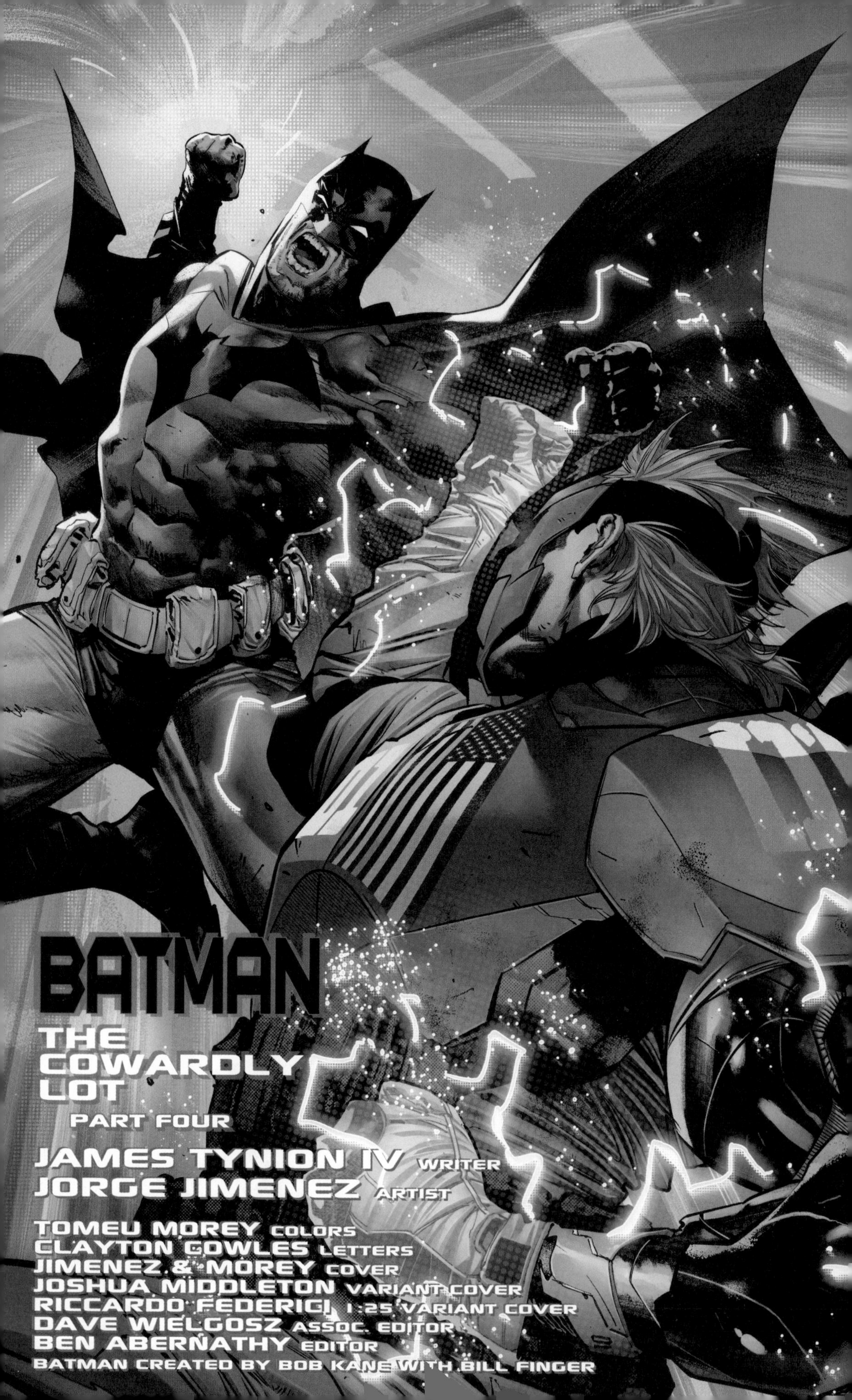
BATMAN
THE COWARDLY LOT
PART FOUR
JAMES TYNION IV WRITER
JORGE JIMENEZ ARTIST
TOMEU MOREY COLORS
CLAYTON COWLES LETTERS
JIMENEZ & MOREY COVER
JOSHUA MIDDLETON VARIANT COVER
RICCARDO FEDERICI 1:25 VARIANT COVER
DAVE WIELGOSZ ASSOC. EDITOR
BEN ABERNATHY EDITOR
BATMAN CREATED BY BOB KANE WITH BILL FINGER

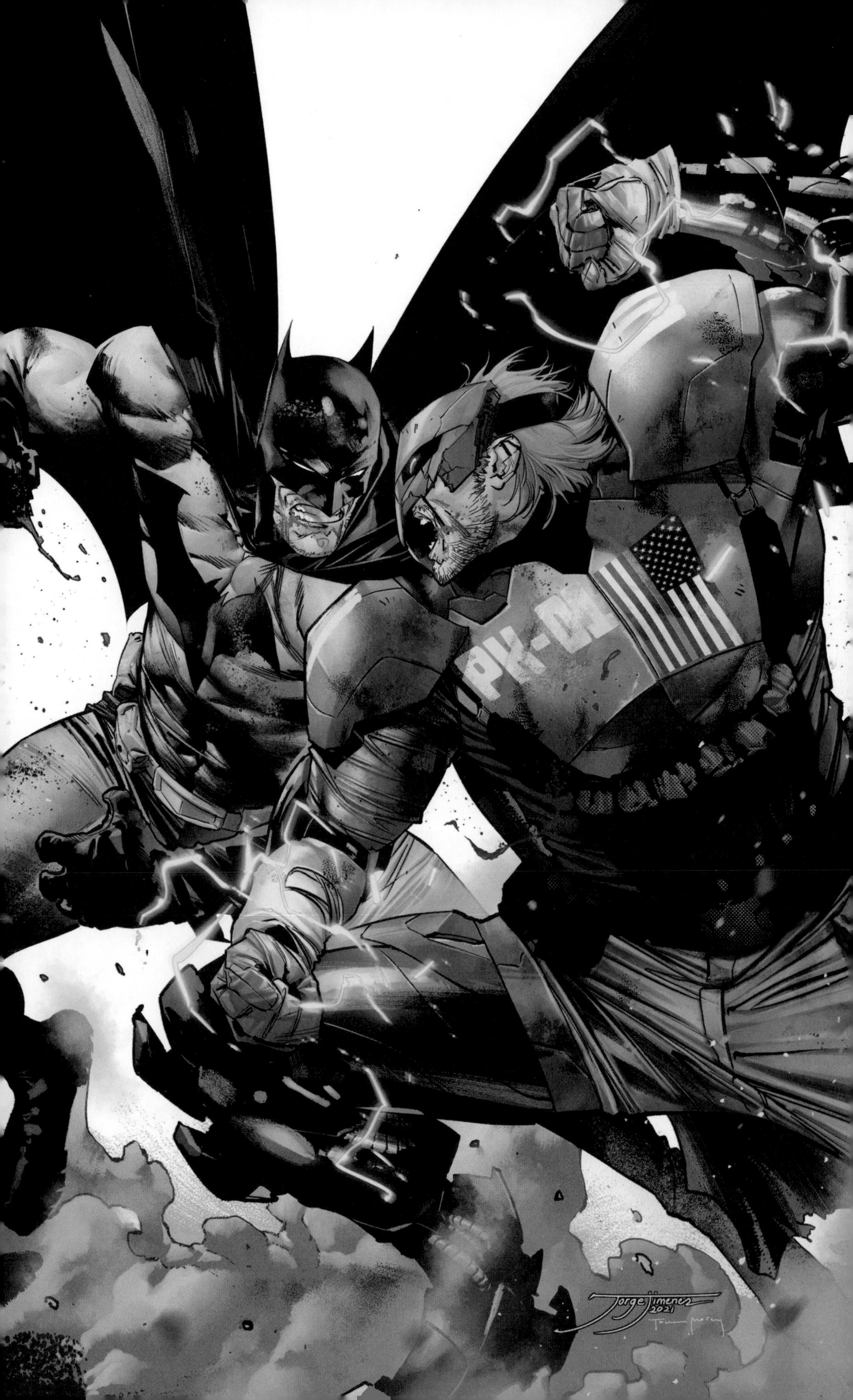
Jorge Jimenez 2021

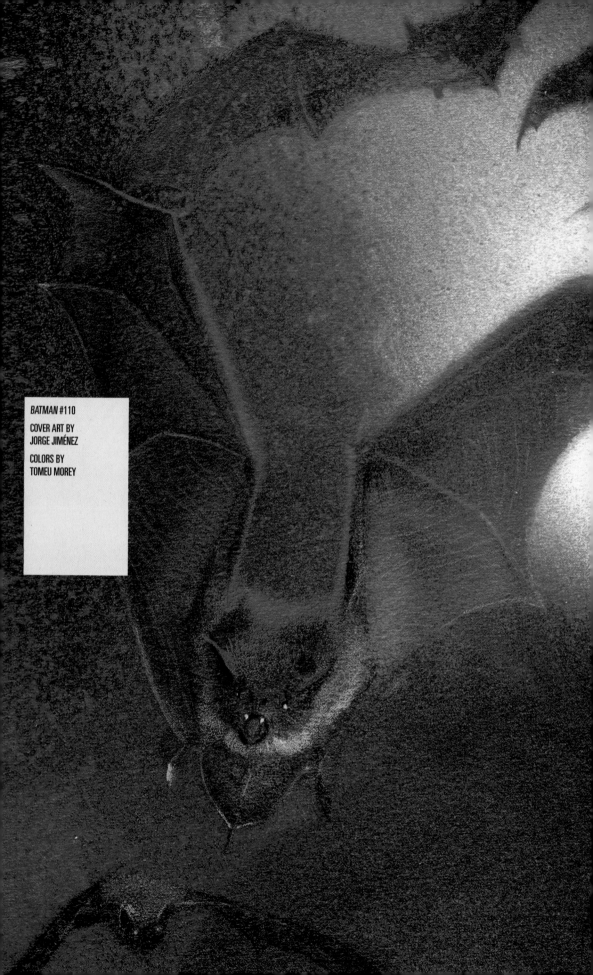

BATMAN #110
COVER ART BY
JORGE JIMÉNEZ
COLORS BY
TOMEU MOREY

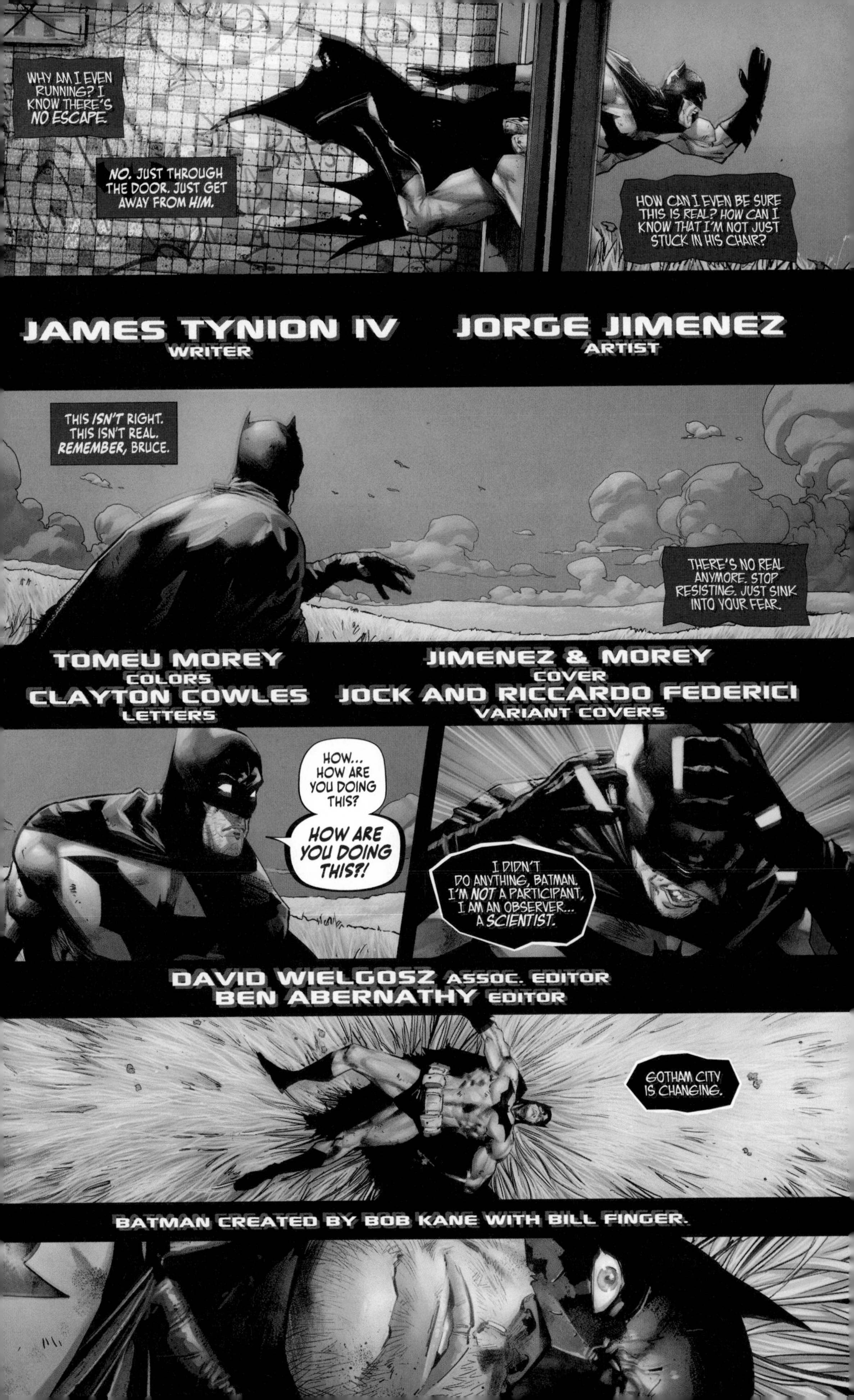
WHY AM I EVEN RUNNING? I KNOW THERE'S NO ESCAPE.
NO. JUST THROUGH THE DOOR. JUST GET AWAY FROM HIM.
HOW CAN I EVEN BE SURE THIS IS REAL? HOW CAN I KNOW THAT I'M NOT JUST STUCK IN HIS CHAIR?
JAMES TYNION IV WRITER
JORGE JIMENEZ ARTIST
THIS ISN'T RIGHT. THIS ISN'T REAL. REMEMBER, BRUCE.
THERE'S NO REAL ANYMORE. STOP RESISTING. JUST SINK INTO YOUR FEAR.
TOMEU MOREY COLORS
CLAYTON COWLES LETTERS
JIMENEZ & MOREY COVER
JOCK AND RICCARDO FEDERICI VARIANT COVERS
HOW... HOW ARE YOU DOING THIS?
HOW ARE YOU DOING THIS?!
I DIDN'T DO ANYTHING, BATMAN. I'M NOT A PARTICIPANT, I AM AN OBSERVER... A SCIENTIST.
DAVID WIELGOSZ ASSOC. EDITOR
BEN ABERNATHY EDITOR
GOTHAM CITY IS CHANGING.
BATMAN CREATED BY BOB KANE WITH BILL FINGER.

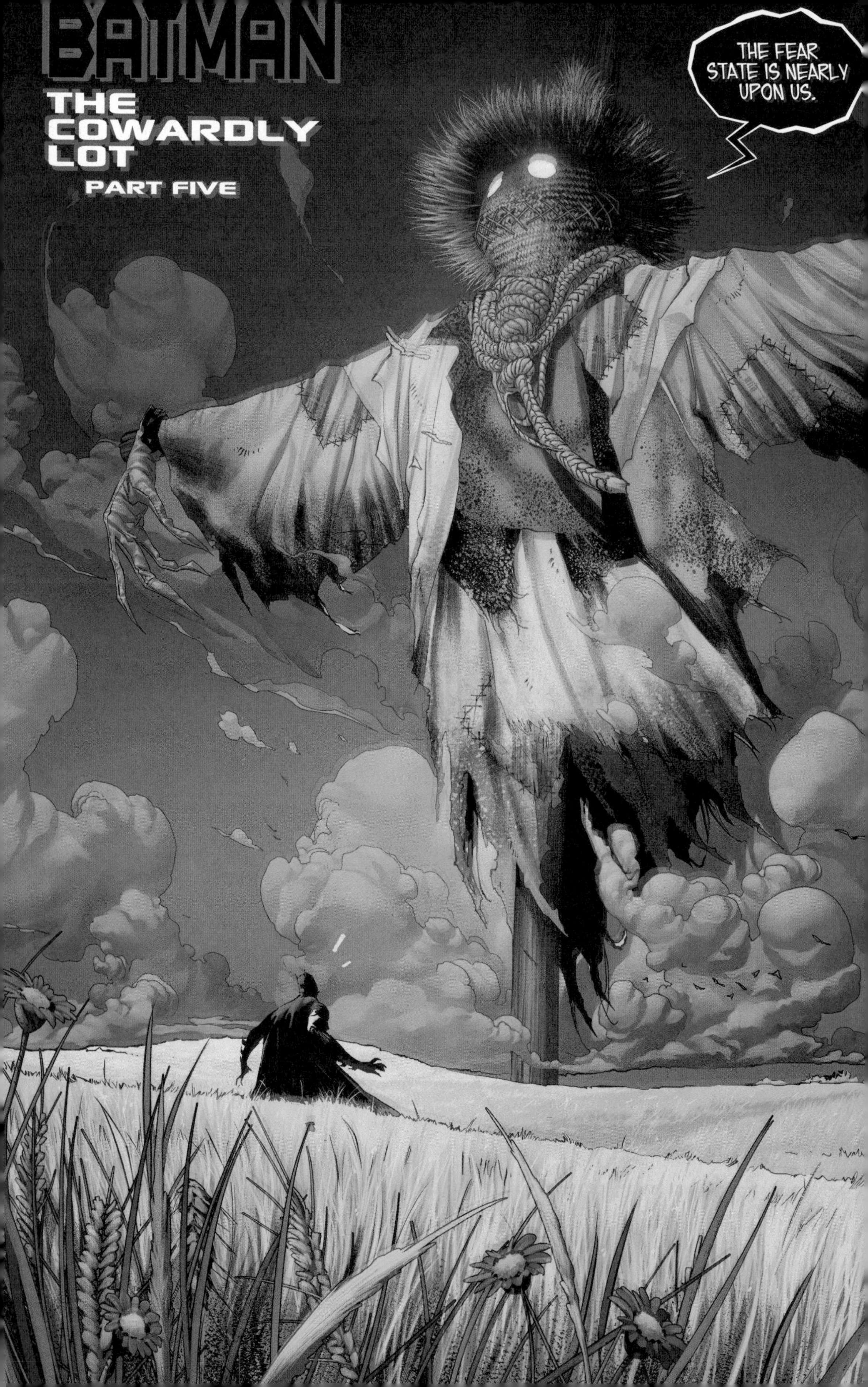
BATMAN
THE COWARDLY LOT
PART FIVE
THE FEAR STATE IS NEARLY UPON US.

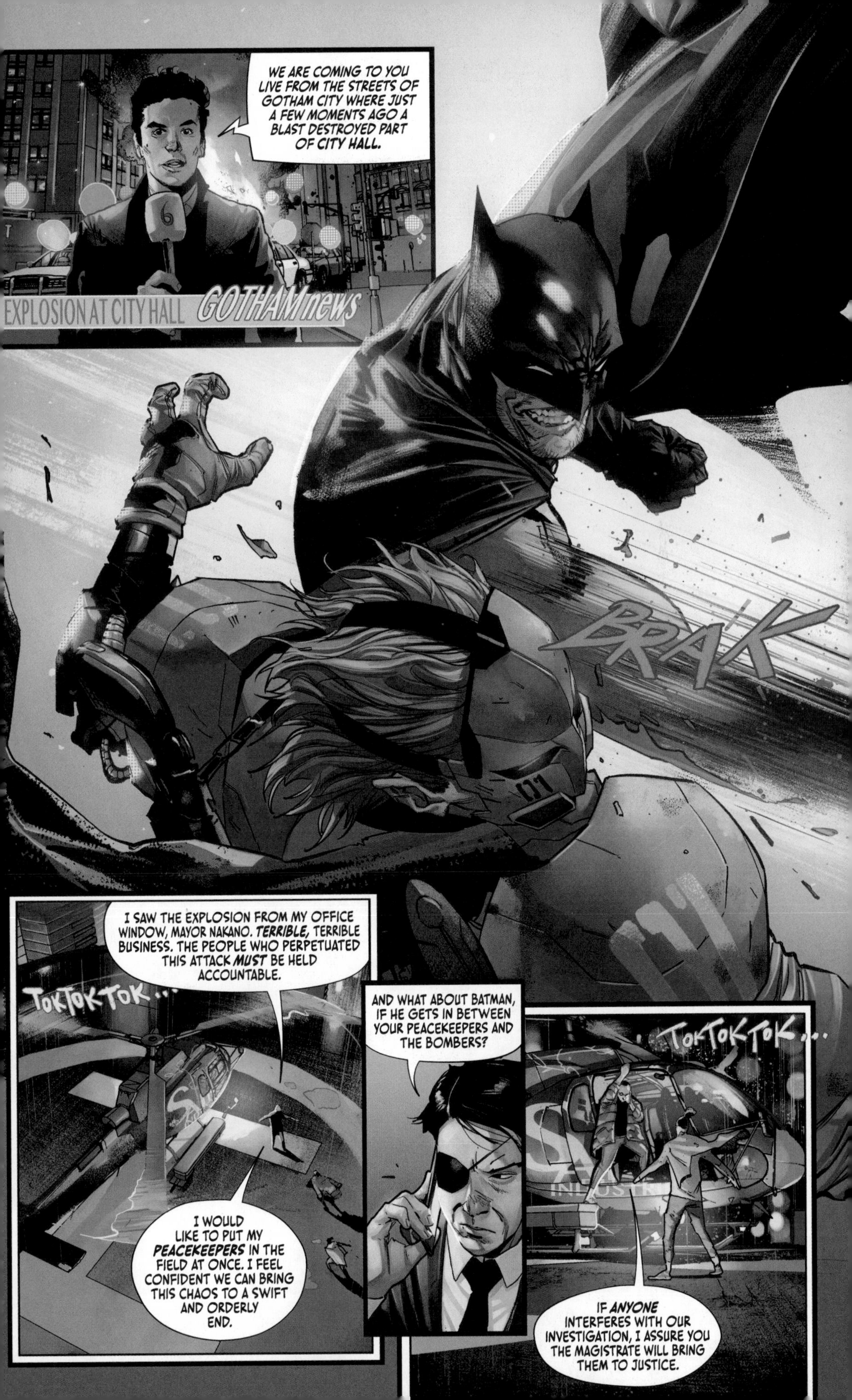
WE ARE COMING TO YOU LIVE FROM THE STREETS OF GOTHAM CITY WHERE JUST A FEW MOMENTS AGO A BLAST DESTROYED PART OF CITY HALL.
EXPLOSION AT CITY HALL
GOTHAM news
BRAK
I SAW THE EXPLOSION FROM MY OFFICE WINDOW, MAYOR NAKANO. TERRIBLE, TERRIBLE BUSINESS. THE PEOPLE WHO PERPETUATED THIS ATTACK MUST BE HELD ACCOUNTABLE.
TOKTOKTOK...
I WOULD LIKE TO PUT MY PEACEKEEPERS IN THE FIELD AT ONCE. I FEEL CONFIDENT WE CAN BRING THIS CHAOS TO A SWIFT AND ORDERLY END.
AND WHAT ABOUT BATMAN, IF HE GETS IN BETWEEN YOUR PEACEKEEPERS AND THE BOMBERS?
TOKTOKTOK...
IF ANYONE INTERFERES WITH OUR INVESTIGATION, I ASSURE YOU THE MAGISTRATE WILL BRING THEM TO JUSTICE.

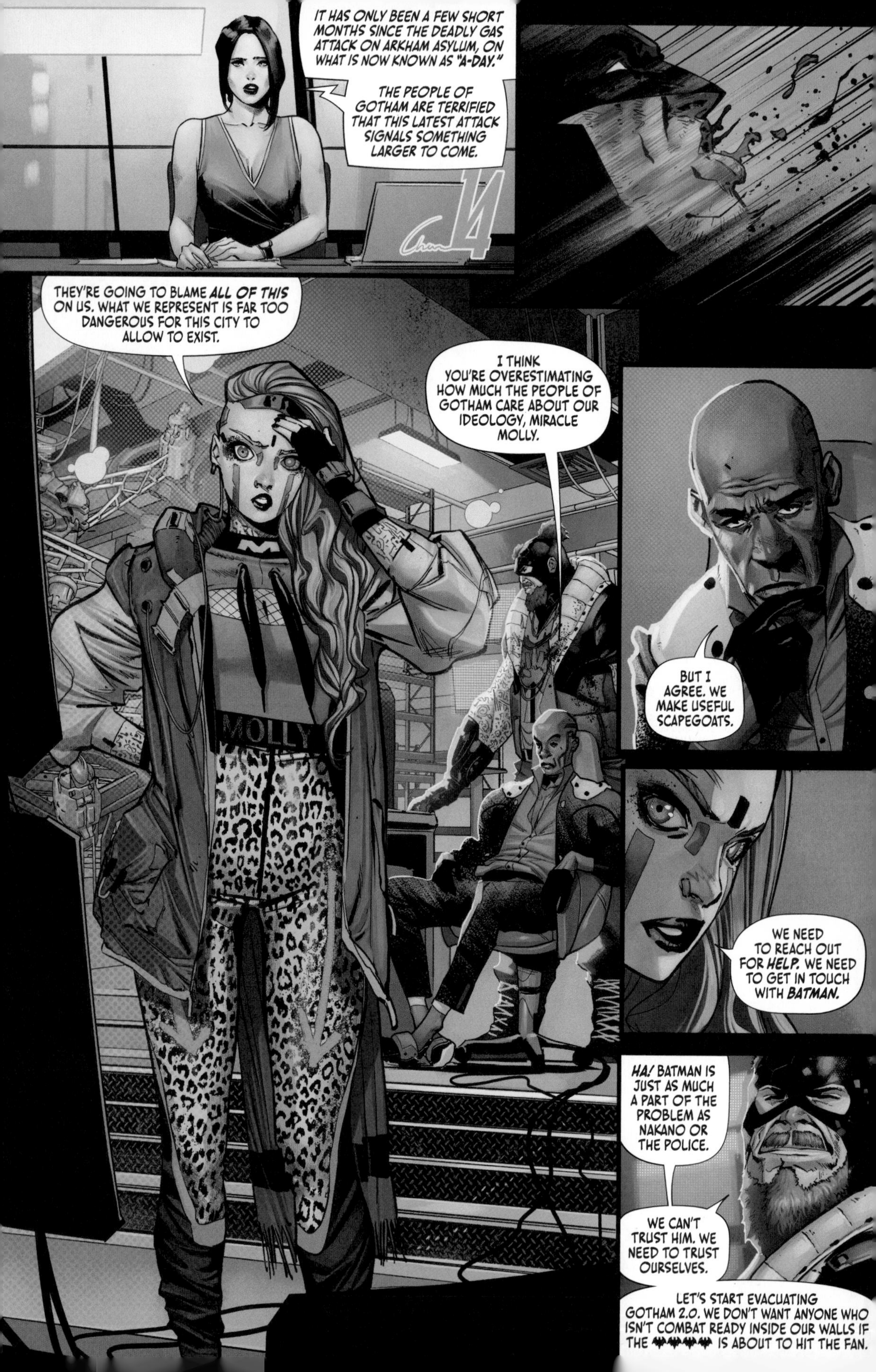
IT HAS ONLY BEEN A FEW SHORT MONTHS SINCE THE DEADLY GAS ATTACK ON ARKHAM ASYLUM, ON WHAT IS NOW KNOWN AS "A-DAY."
THE PEOPLE OF GOTHAM ARE TERRIFIED THAT THIS LATEST ATTACK SIGNALS SOMETHING LARGER TO COME.
THEY'RE GOING TO BLAME ALL OF THIS ON US. WHAT WE REPRESENT IS FAR TOO DANGEROUS FOR THIS CITY TO ALLOW TO EXIST.
I THINK YOU'RE OVERESTIMATING HOW MUCH THE PEOPLE OF GOTHAM CARE ABOUT OUR IDEOLOGY, MIRACLE MOLLY.
BUT I AGREE. WE MAKE USEFUL SCAPEGOATS.
WE NEED TO REACH OUT FOR HELP. WE NEED TO GET IN TOUCH WITH BATMAN.
HA! BATMAN IS JUST AS MUCH A PART OF THE PROBLEM AS NAKANO OR THE POLICE.
WE CAN'T TRUST HIM. WE NEED TO TRUST OURSELVES.
LET'S START EVACUATING GOTHAM 2.0. WE DON'T WANT ANYONE WHO ISN'T COMBAT READY INSIDE OUR WALLS IF THE IS ABOUT TO HIT THE FAN.
MOLLY

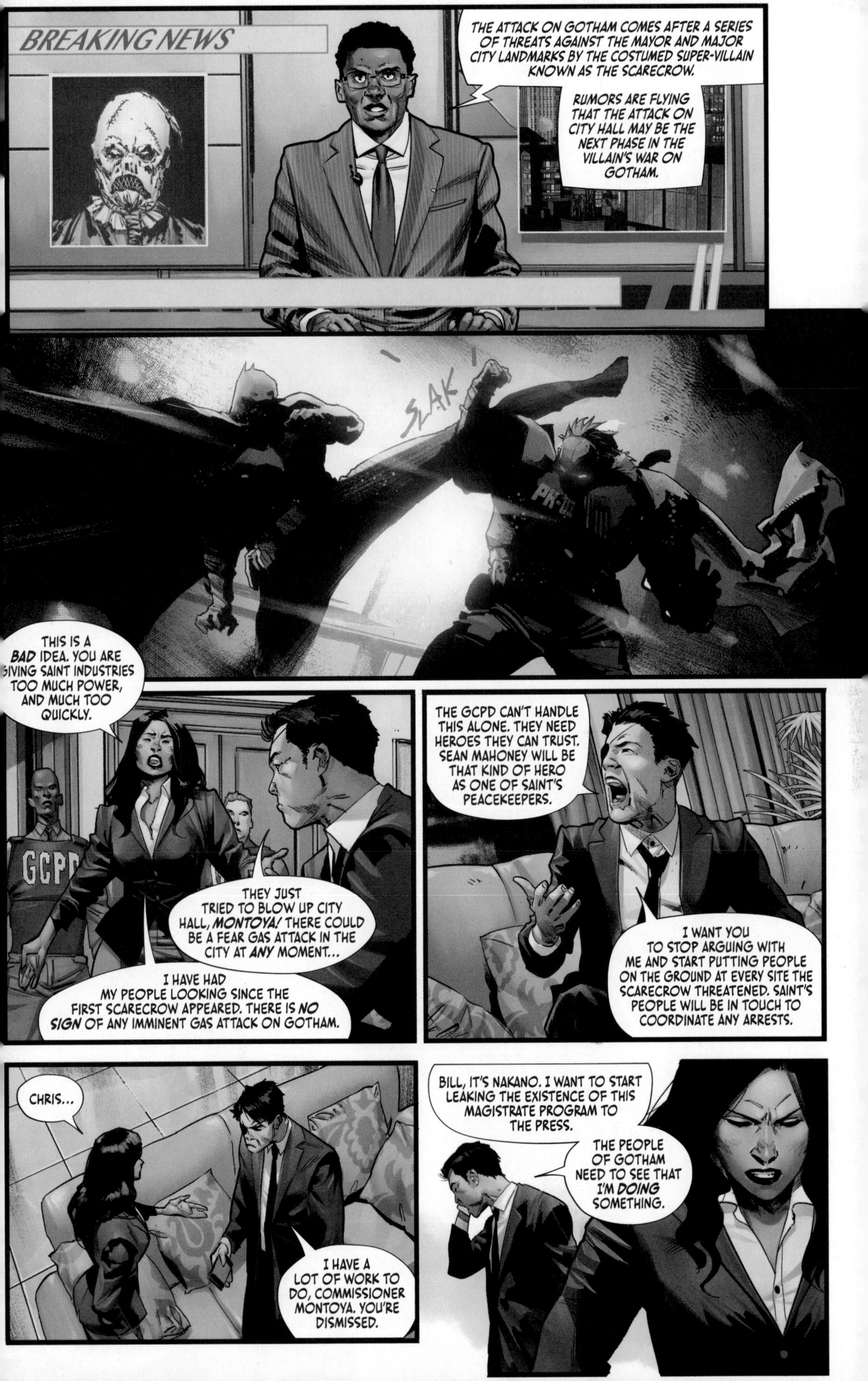
BREAKING NEWS
THE ATTACK ON GOTHAM COMES AFTER A SERIES OF THREATS AGAINST THE MAYOR AND MAJOR CITY LANDMARKS BY THE COSTUMED SUPER-VILLAIN KNOWN AS THE SCARECROW.
RUMORS ARE FLYING THAT THE ATTACK ON CITY HALL MAY BE THE NEXT PHASE IN THE VILLAIN'S WAR ON GOTHAM.
SLAK
THIS IS A BAD IDEA. YOU ARE GIVING SAINT INDUSTRIES TOO MUCH POWER, AND MUCH TOO QUICKLY.
THEY JUST TRIED TO BLOW UP CITY HALL, MONTOYA! THERE COULD BE A FEAR GAS ATTACK IN THE CITY AT ANY MOMENT...
I HAVE HAD MY PEOPLE LOOKING SINCE THE FIRST SCARECROW APPEARED. THERE IS NO SIGN OF ANY IMMINENT GAS ATTACK ON GOTHAM.
THE GCPD CAN'T HANDLE THIS ALONE. THEY NEED HEROES THEY CAN TRUST. SEAN MAHONEY WILL BE THAT KIND OF HERO AS ONE OF SAINT'S PEACEKEEPERS.
I WANT YOU TO STOP ARGUING WITH ME AND START PUTTING PEOPLE ON THE GROUND AT EVERY SITE THE SCARECROW THREATENED. SAINT'S PEOPLE WILL BE IN TOUCH TO COORDINATE ANY ARRESTS.
CHRIS...
I HAVE A LOT OF WORK TO DO, COMMISSIONER MONTOYA. YOU'RE DISMISSED.
BILL, IT'S NAKANO. I WANT TO START LEAKING THE EXISTENCE OF THIS MAGISTRATE PROGRAM TO THE PRESS.
THE PEOPLE OF GOTHAM NEED TO SEE THAT I'M DOING SOMETHING.

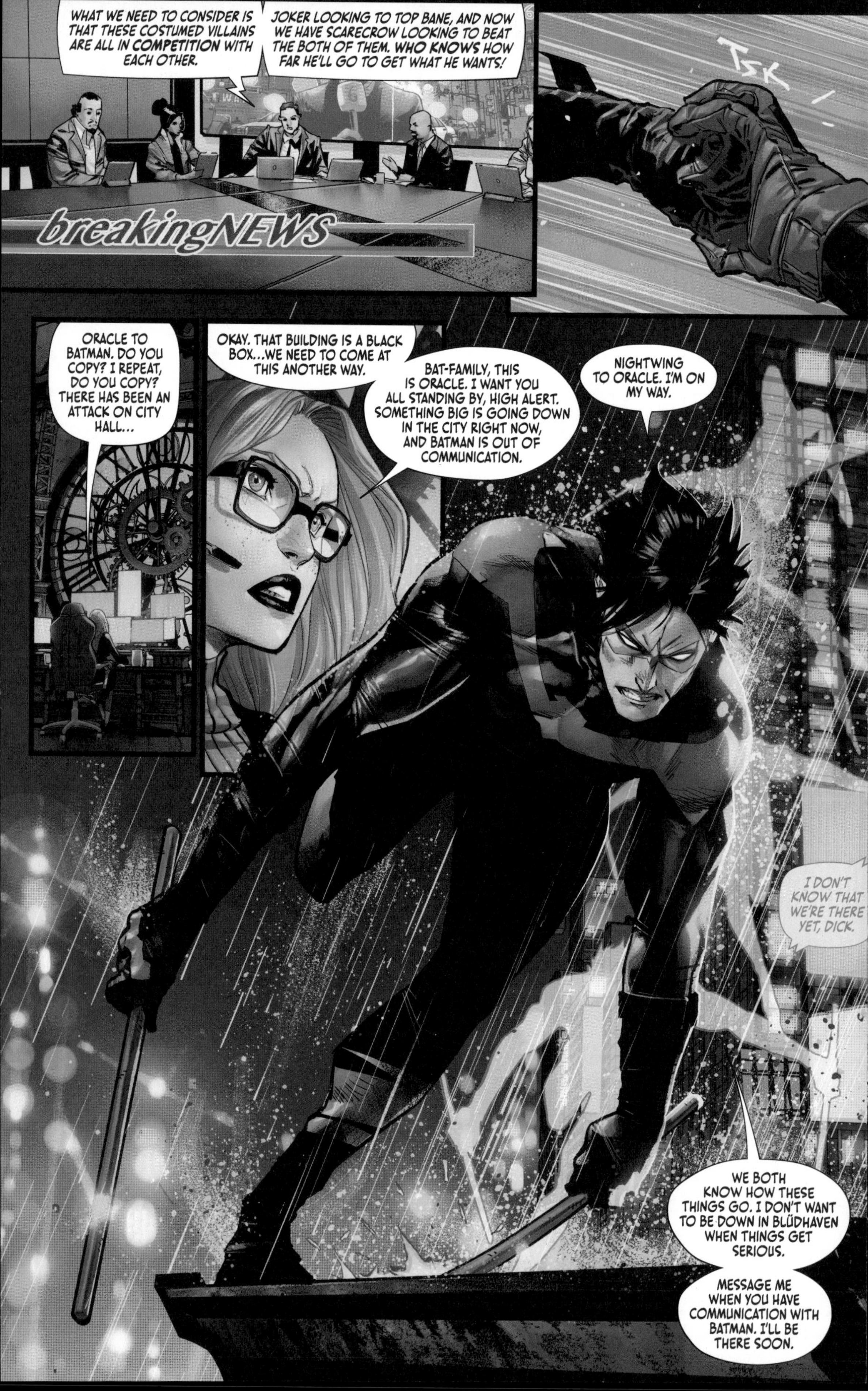
WHAT WE NEED TO CONSIDER IS THAT THESE COSTUMED VILLAINS ARE ALL IN COMPETITION WITH EACH OTHER.
JOKER LOOKING TO TOP BANE, AND NOW WE HAVE SCARECROW LOOKING TO BEAT THE BOTH OF THEM. WHO KNOWS HOW FAR HE'LL GO TO GET WHAT HE WANTS!
breakingNEWS
TSK
ORACLE TO BATMAN. DO YOU COPY? I REPEAT, DO YOU COPY? THERE HAS BEEN AN ATTACK ON CITY HALL...
OKAY. THAT BUILDING IS A BLACK BOX...WE NEED TO COME AT THIS ANOTHER WAY.
BAT-FAMILY, THIS IS ORACLE. I WANT YOU ALL STANDING BY, HIGH ALERT. SOMETHING BIG IS GOING DOWN IN THE CITY RIGHT NOW, AND BATMAN IS OUT OF COMMUNICATION.
NIGHTWING TO ORACLE. I'M ON MY WAY.
I DON'T KNOW THAT WE'RE THERE YET, DICK.
WE BOTH KNOW HOW THESE THINGS GO. I DON'T WANT TO BE DOWN IN BLÜDHAVEN WHEN THINGS GET SERIOUS.
MESSAGE ME WHEN YOU HAVE COMMUNICATION WITH BATMAN. I'LL BE THERE SOON.

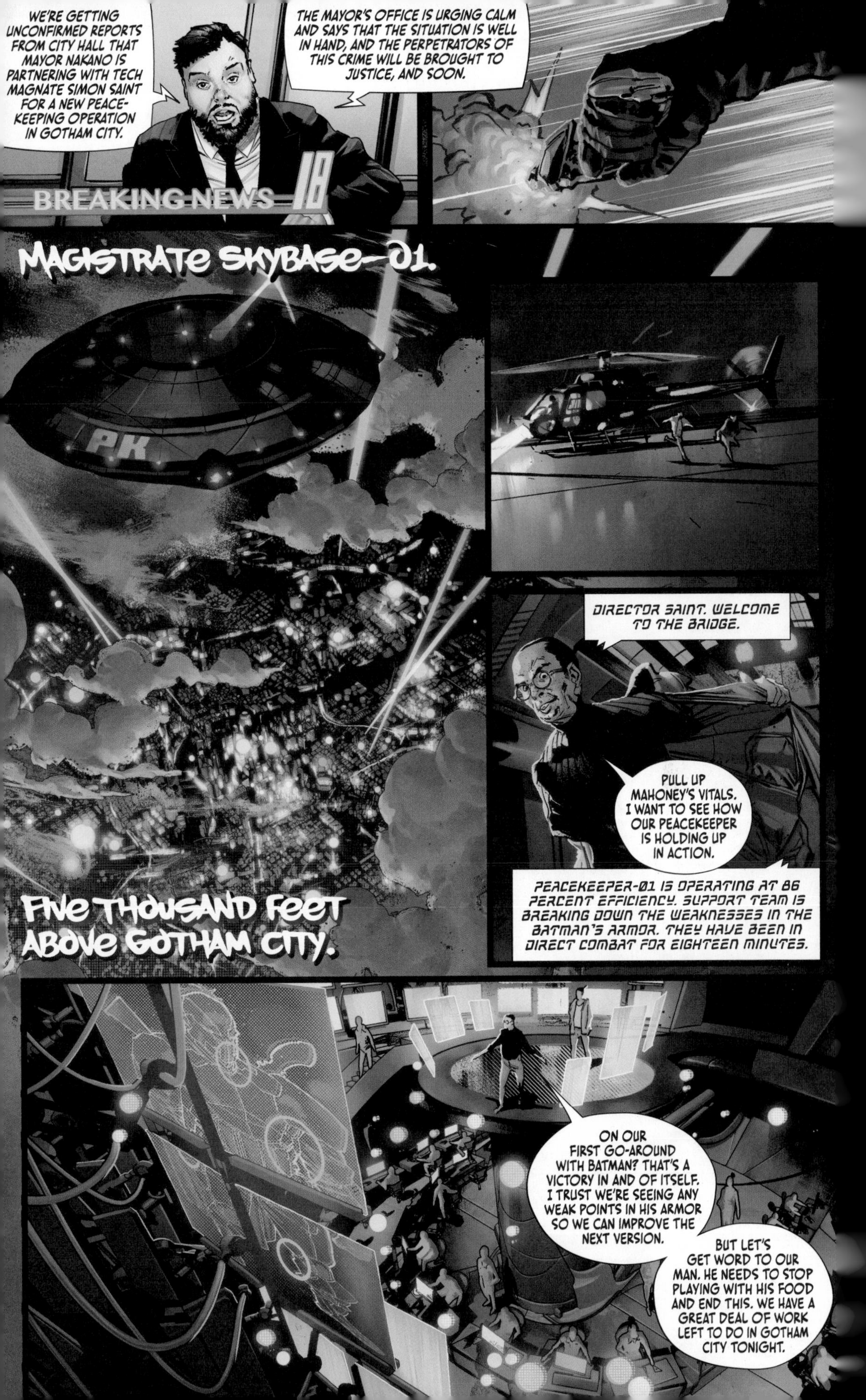
WE'RE GETTING UNCONFIRMED REPORTS FROM CITY HALL THAT MAYOR NAKANO IS PARTNERING WITH TECH MAGNATE SIMON SAINT FOR A NEW PEACE-KEEPING OPERATION IN GOTHAM CITY.
THE MAYOR'S OFFICE IS URGING CALM AND SAYS THAT THE SITUATION IS WELL IN HAND, AND THE PERPETRATORS OF THIS CRIME WILL BE BROUGHT TO JUSTICE, AND SOON.
BREAKING NEWS
18
MAGISTRATE SKYBASE-01.
PK
FIVE THOUSAND FEET ABOVE GOTHAM CITY.
DIRECTOR SAINT. WELCOME TO THE BRIDGE.
PULL UP MAHONEY'S VITALS. I WANT TO SEE HOW OUR PEACEKEEPER IS HOLDING UP IN ACTION.
PEACEKEEPER-01 IS OPERATING AT 86 PERCENT EFFICIENCY. SUPPORT TEAM IS BREAKING DOWN THE WEAKNESSES IN THE BATMAN'S ARMOR. THEY HAVE BEEN IN DIRECT COMBAT FOR EIGHTEEN MINUTES.
ON OUR FIRST GO-AROUND WITH BATMAN? THAT'S A VICTORY IN AND OF ITSELF. I TRUST WE'RE SEEING ANY WEAK POINTS IN HIS ARMOR SO WE CAN IMPROVE THE NEXT VERSION.
BUT LET'S GET WORD TO OUR MAN. HE NEEDS TO STOP PLAYING WITH HIS FOOD AND END THIS. WE HAVE A GREAT DEAL OF WORK LEFT TO DO IN GOTHAM CITY TONIGHT.

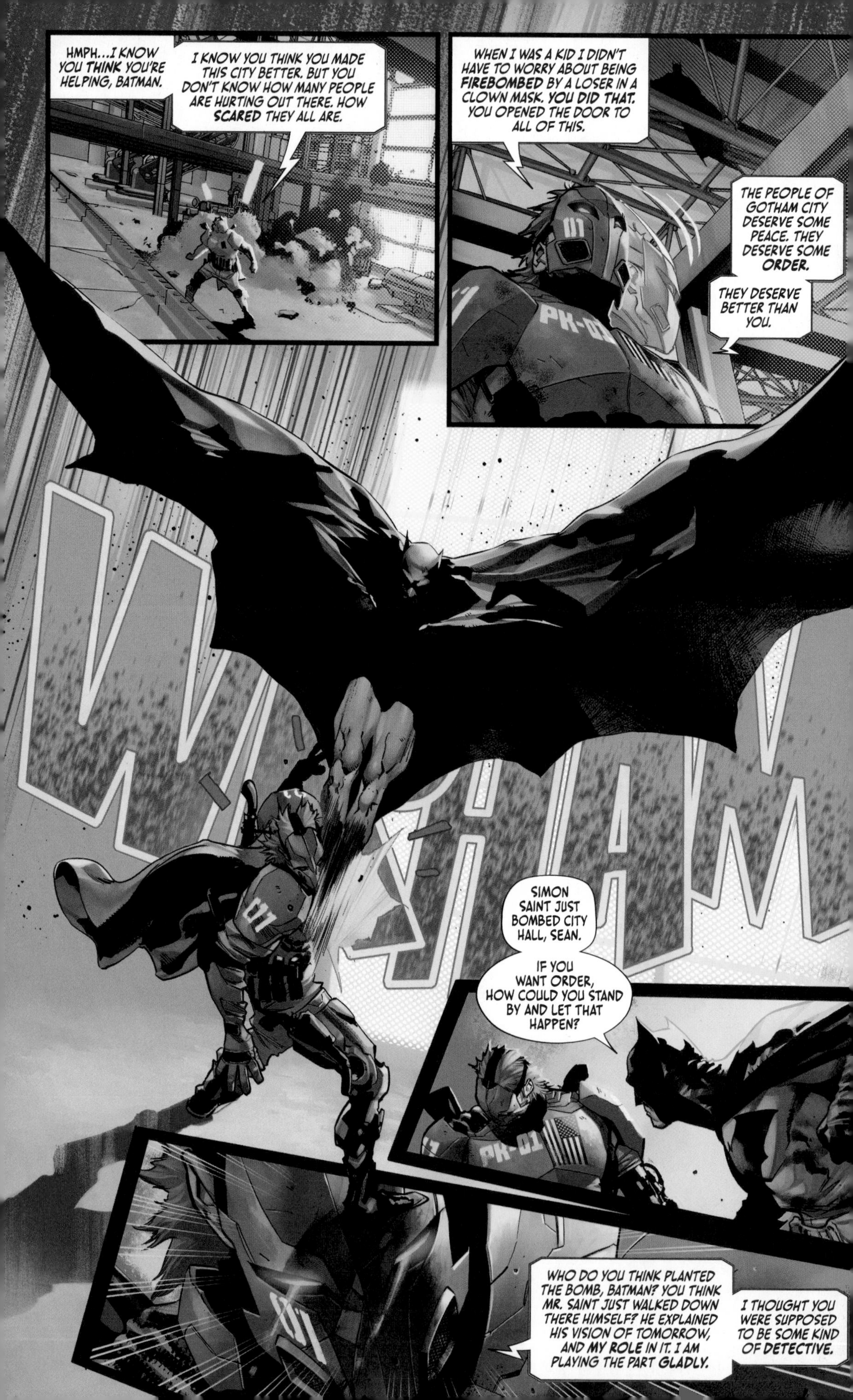
HMPH...I KNOW YOU THINK YOU'RE HELPING, BATMAN.
I KNOW YOU THINK YOU MADE THIS CITY BETTER. BUT YOU DON'T KNOW HOW MANY PEOPLE ARE HURTING OUT THERE. HOW SCARED THEY ALL ARE.
WHEN I WAS A KID I DIDN'T HAVE TO WORRY ABOUT BEING FIREBOMBED BY A LOSER IN A CLOWN MASK. YOU DID THAT. YOU OPENED THE DOOR TO ALL OF THIS.
THE PEOPLE OF GOTHAM CITY DESERVE SOME PEACE. THEY DESERVE SOME ORDER.
THEY DESERVE BETTER THAN YOU.
PK-01
SIMON SAINT JUST BOMBED CITY HALL, SEAN.
IF YOU WANT ORDER, HOW COULD YOU STAND BY AND LET THAT HAPPEN?
PK-01
WHO DO YOU THINK PLANTED THE BOMB, BATMAN? YOU THINK MR. SAINT JUST WALKED DOWN THERE HIMSELF? HE EXPLAINED HIS VISION OF TOMORROW, AND MY ROLE IN IT. I AM PLAYING THE PART GLADLY.
I THOUGHT YOU WERE SUPPOSED TO BE SOME KIND OF DETECTIVE.

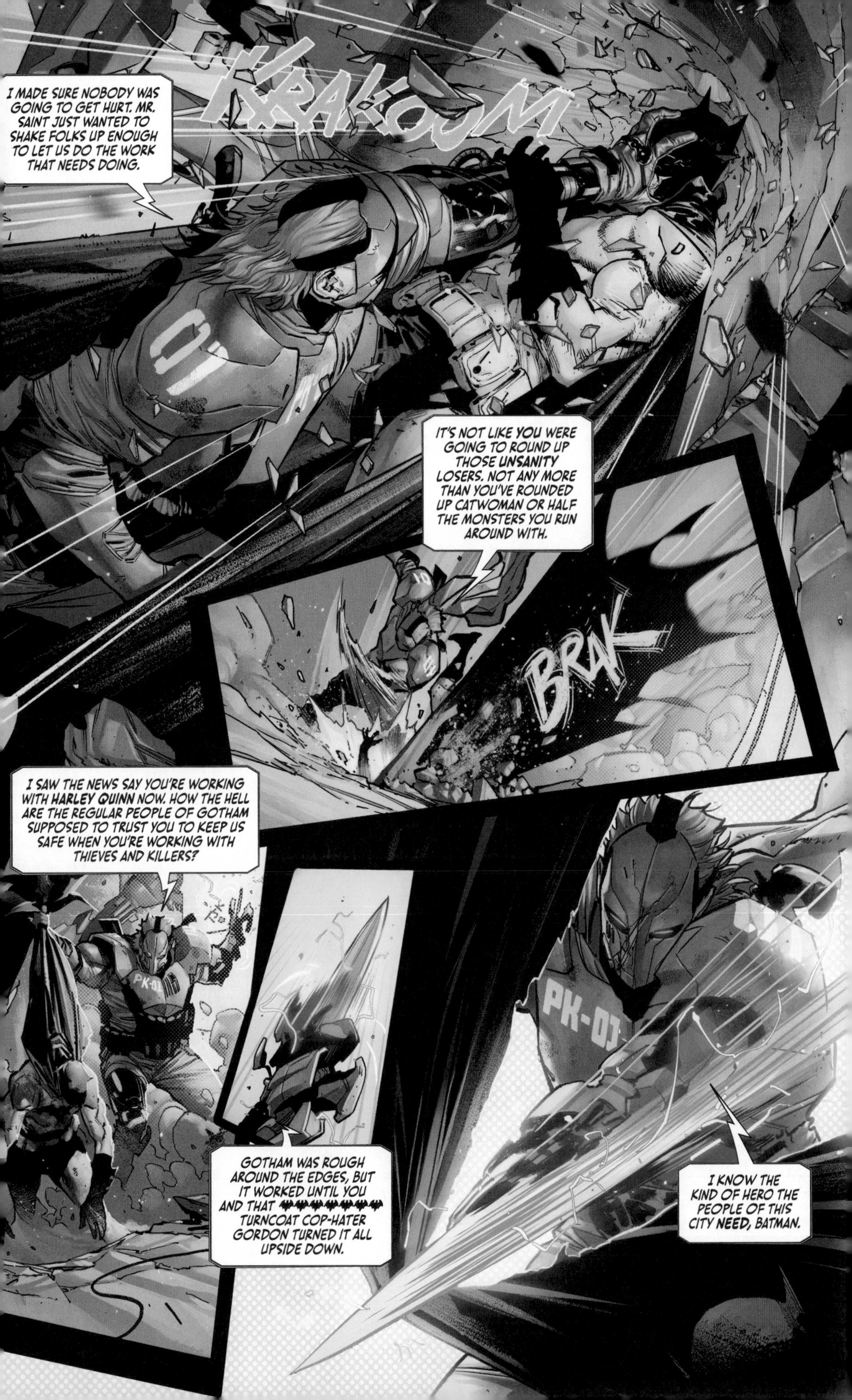
KRAKOOM
I MADE SURE NOBODY WAS GOING TO GET HURT. MR. SAINT JUST WANTED TO SHAKE FOLKS UP ENOUGH TO LET US DO THE WORK THAT NEEDS DOING.
IT'S NOT LIKE YOU WERE GOING TO ROUND UP THOSE UNSANITY LOSERS. NOT ANY MORE THAN YOU'VE ROUNDED UP CATWOMAN OR HALF THE MONSTERS YOU RUN AROUND WITH.
BRAK
I SAW THE NEWS SAY YOU'RE WORKING WITH HARLEY QUINN NOW. HOW THE HELL ARE THE REGULAR PEOPLE OF GOTHAM SUPPOSED TO TRUST YOU TO KEEP US SAFE WHEN YOU'RE WORKING WITH THIEVES AND KILLERS?
GOTHAM WAS ROUGH AROUND THE EDGES, BUT IT WORKED UNTIL YOU AND THAT TURNCOAT COP-HATER GORDON TURNED IT ALL UPSIDE DOWN.
I KNOW THE KIND OF HERO THE PEOPLE OF THIS CITY NEED, BATMAN.

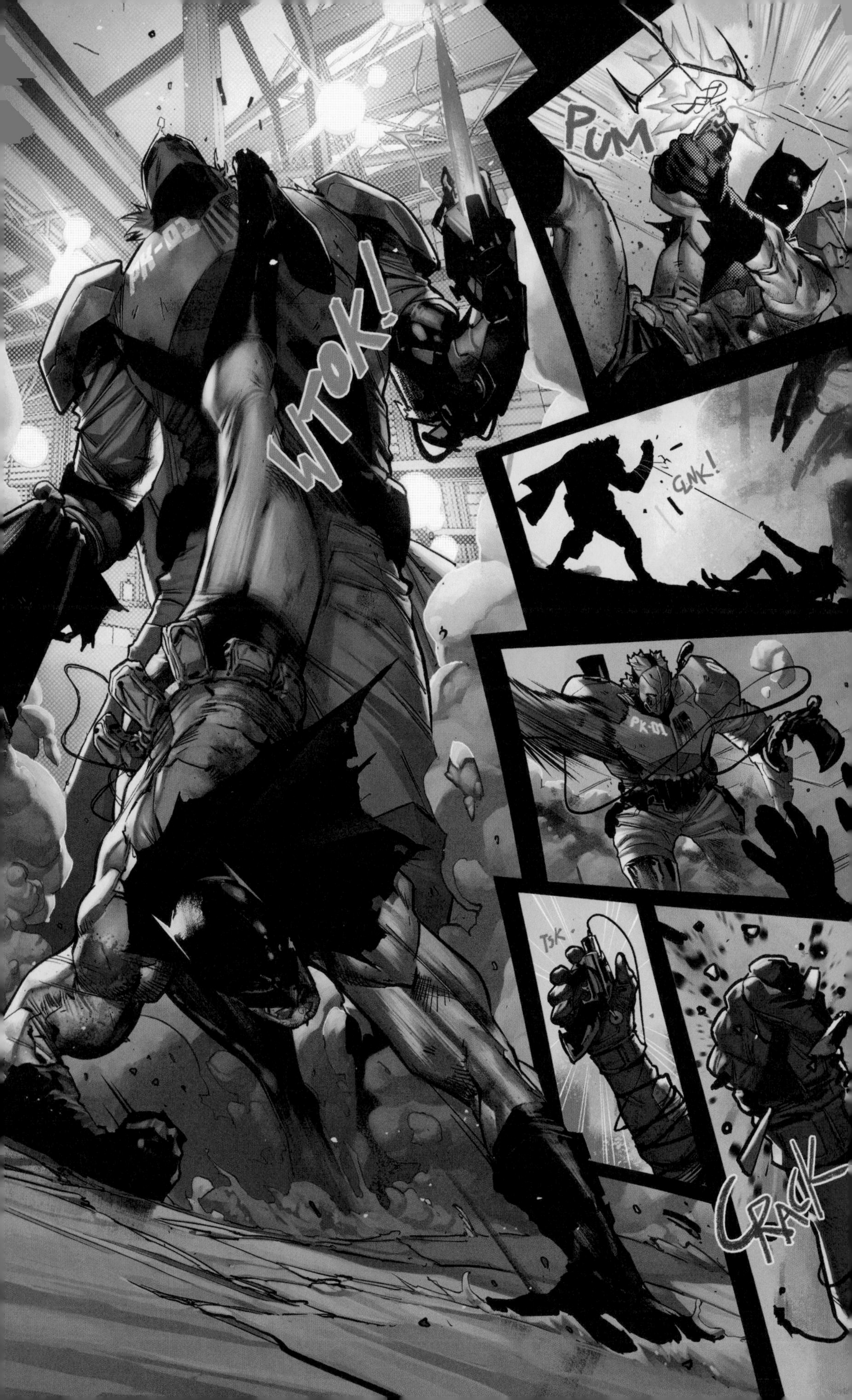
WTOK!
PUM
CLNK!
PK-01
TSK
CRACK

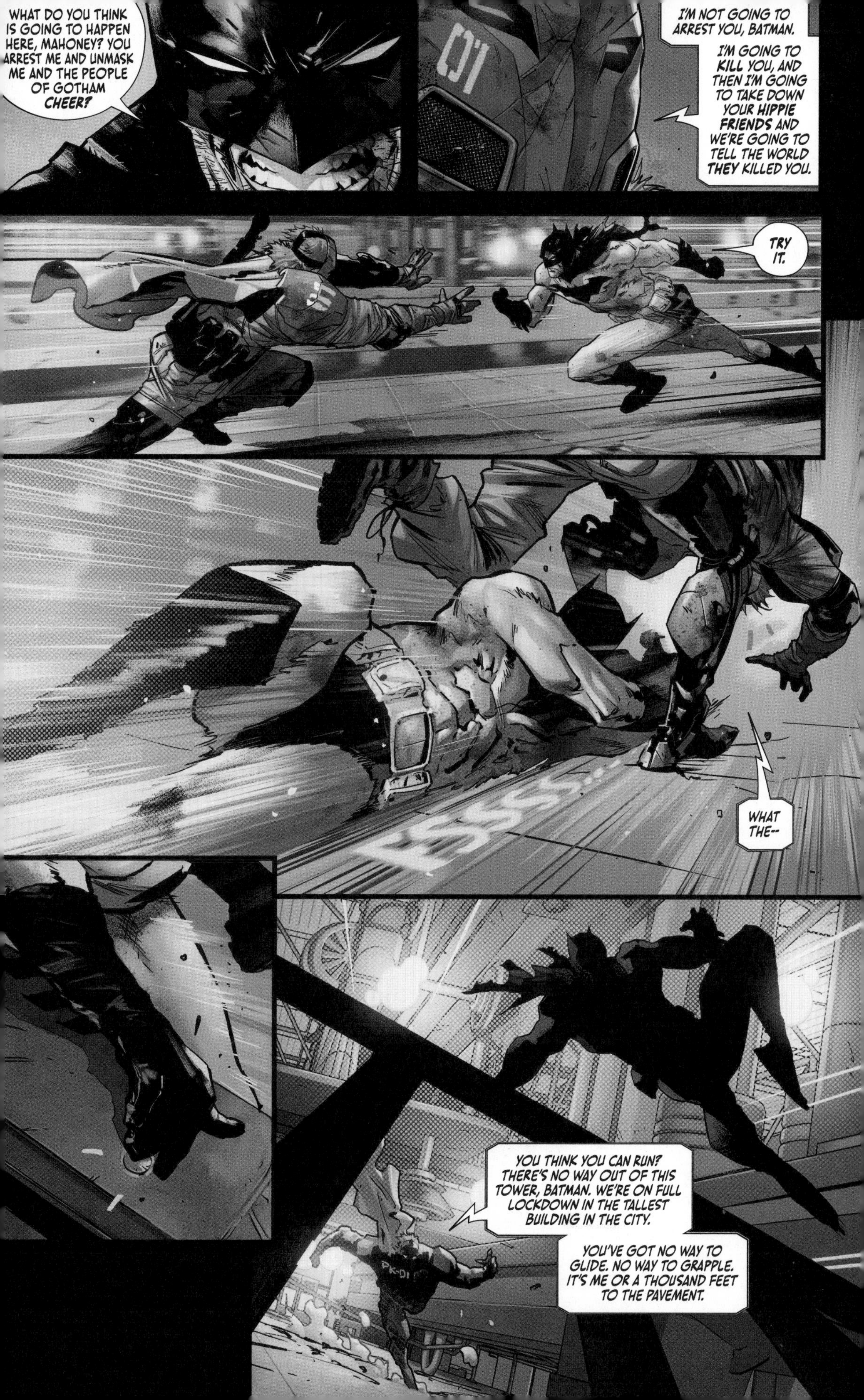
WHAT DO YOU THINK IS GOING TO HAPPEN HERE, MAHONEY? YOU ARREST ME AND UNMASK ME AND THE PEOPLE OF GOTHAM CHEER?
I'M NOT GOING TO ARREST YOU, BATMAN.
I'M GOING TO KILL YOU, AND THEN I'M GOING TO TAKE DOWN YOUR HIPPIE FRIENDS AND WE'RE GOING TO TELL THE WORLD THEY KILLED YOU.
TRY IT.
FSSSS...
WHAT THE--
YOU THINK YOU CAN RUN? THERE'S NO WAY OUT OF THIS TOWER, BATMAN. WE'RE ON FULL LOCKDOWN IN THE TALLEST BUILDING IN THE CITY.
YOU'VE GOT NO WAY TO GLIDE. NO WAY TO GRAPPLE. IT'S ME OR A THOUSAND FEET TO THE PAVEMENT.

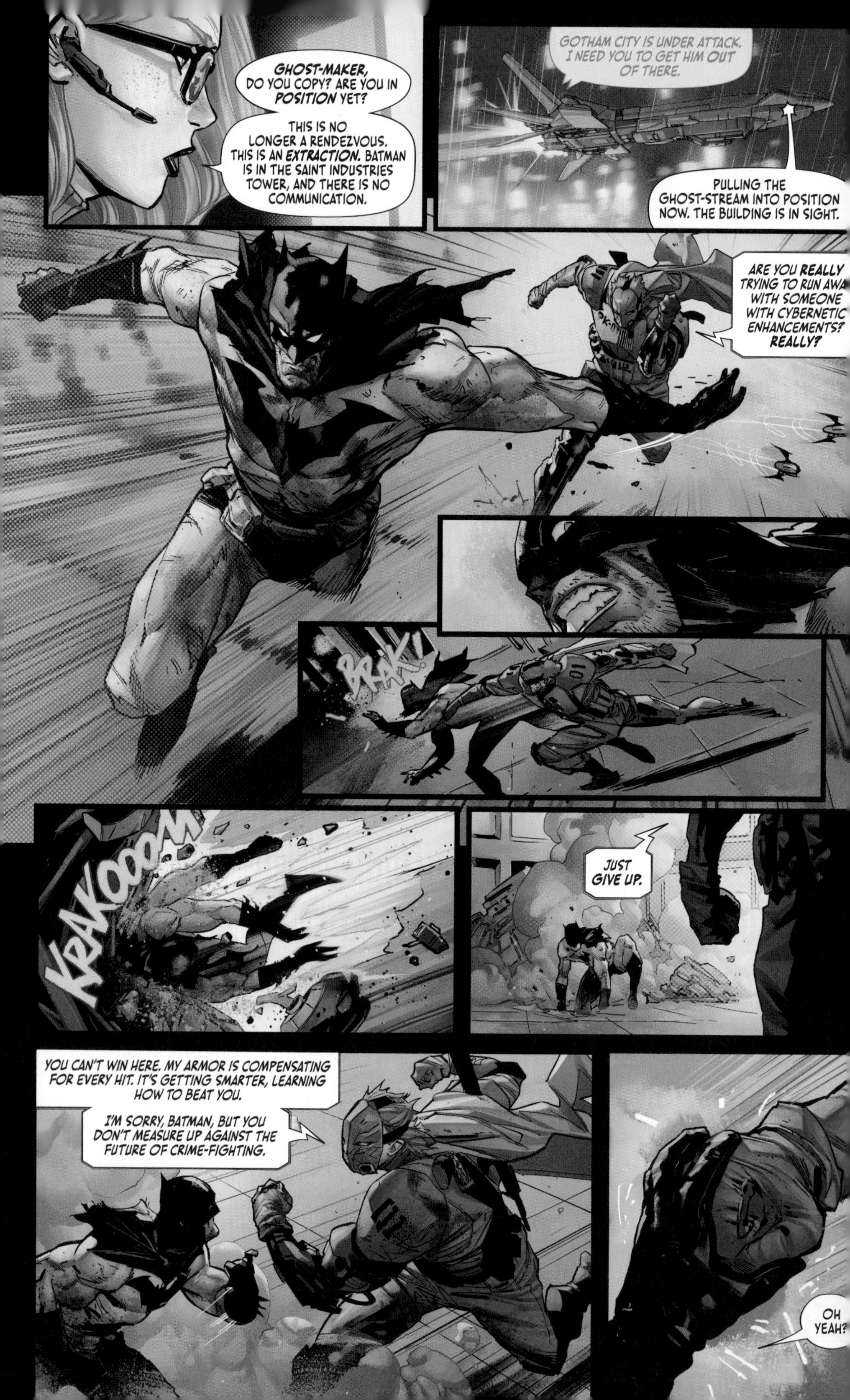

GHOST-MAKER, DO YOU COPY? ARE YOU IN POSITION YET?
THIS IS NO LONGER A RENDEZVOUS. THIS IS AN EXTRACTION. BATMAN IS IN THE SAINT INDUSTRIES TOWER, AND THERE IS NO COMMUNICATION.
GOTHAM CITY IS UNDER ATTACK. I NEED YOU TO GET HIM OUT OF THERE.
PULLING THE GHOST-STREAM INTO POSITION NOW. THE BUILDING IS IN SIGHT.
ARE YOU REALLY TRYING TO RUN AWA WITH SOMEONE WITH CYBERNETIC ENHANCEMENTS? REALLY?
BRAK!
KRAKOOOM
JUST GIVE UP.
YOU CAN'T WIN HERE. MY ARMOR IS COMPENSATING FOR EVERY HIT. IT'S GETTING SMARTER, LEARNING HOW TO BEAT YOU.
I'M SORRY, BATMAN, BUT YOU DON'T MEASURE UP AGAINST THE FUTURE OF CRIME-FIGHTING.
OH YEAH?

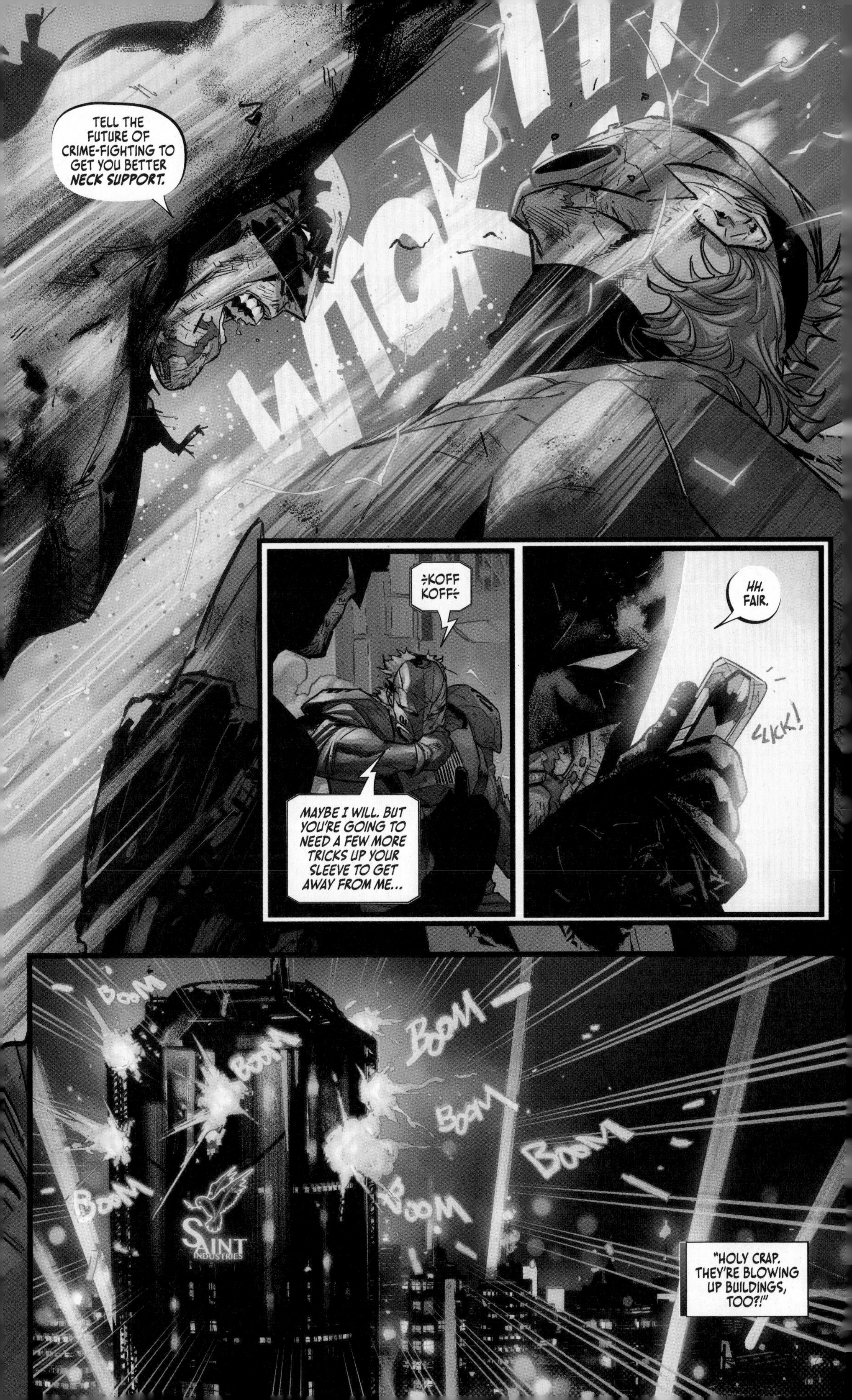
TELL THE FUTURE OF CRIME-FIGHTING TO GET YOU BETTER NECK SUPPORT.
WHCK!!!
=KOFF KOFF=
MAYBE I WILL. BUT YOU'RE GOING TO NEED A FEW MORE TRICKS UP YOUR SLEEVE TO GET AWAY FROM ME...
HH. FAIR.
CLICK!
BOOM
BOOM
BOOM
BOOM
BOOM
BOOM
BOOM
BOOM
SAINT INDUSTRIES
"HOLY CRAP. THEY'RE BLOWING UP BUILDINGS, TOO?!"

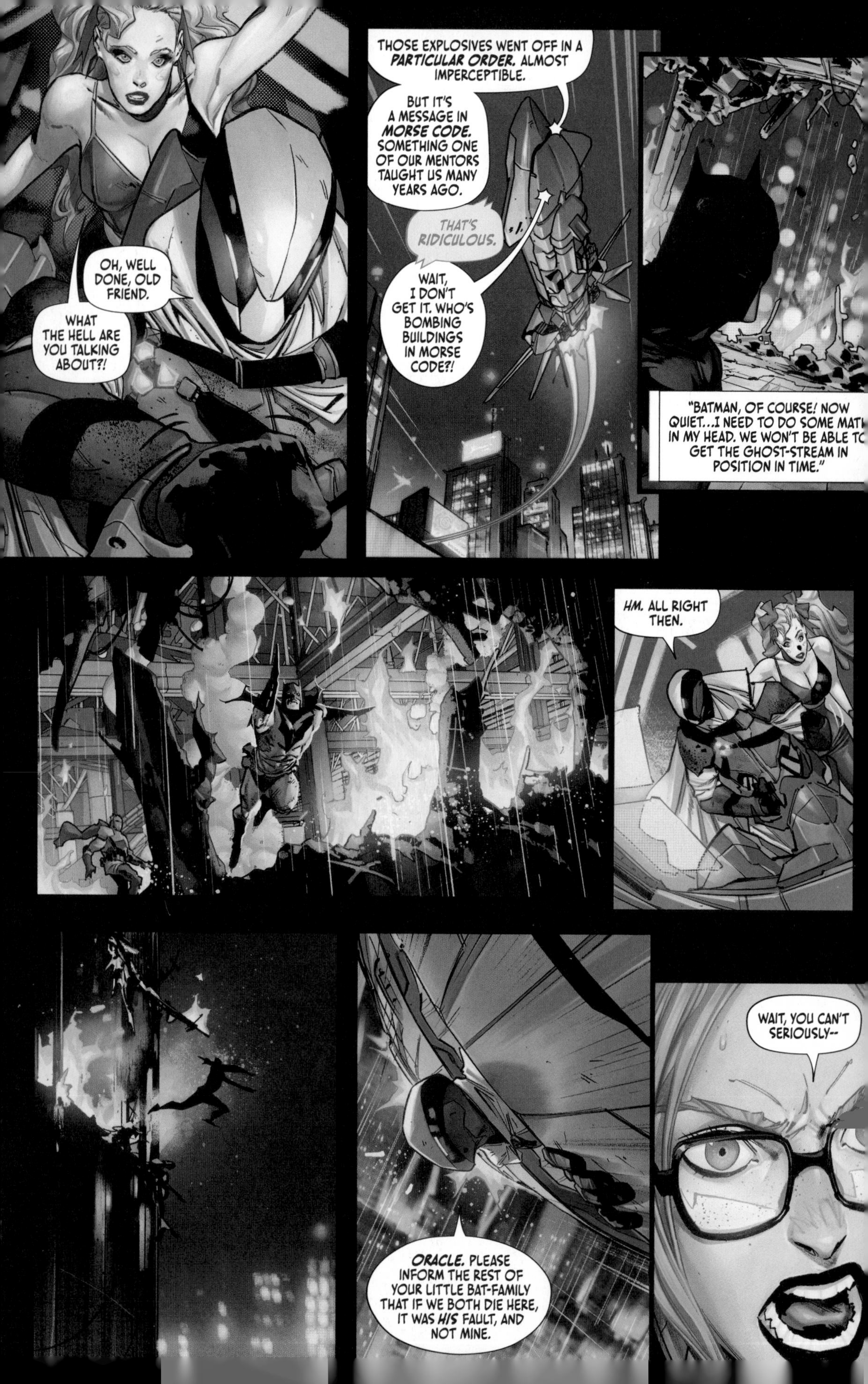
OH, WELL DONE, OLD FRIEND.
WHAT THE HELL ARE YOU TALKING ABOUT?!
THOSE EXPLOSIVES WENT OFF IN A PARTICULAR ORDER. ALMOST IMPERCEPTIBLE.
BUT IT'S A MESSAGE IN MORSE CODE. SOMETHING ONE OF OUR MENTORS TAUGHT US MANY YEARS AGO.
THAT'S RIDICULOUS.
WAIT, I DON'T GET IT. WHO'S BOMBING BUILDINGS IN MORSE CODE?!
"BATMAN, OF COURSE! NOW QUIET...I NEED TO DO SOME MATH IN MY HEAD. WE WON'T BE ABLE TO GET THE GHOST-STREAM IN POSITION IN TIME."
HM. ALL RIGHT THEN.
ORACLE. PLEASE INFORM THE REST OF YOUR LITTLE BAT-FAMILY THAT IF WE BOTH DIE HERE, IT WAS HIS FAULT, AND NOT MINE.
WAIT, YOU CAN'T SERIOUSLY--

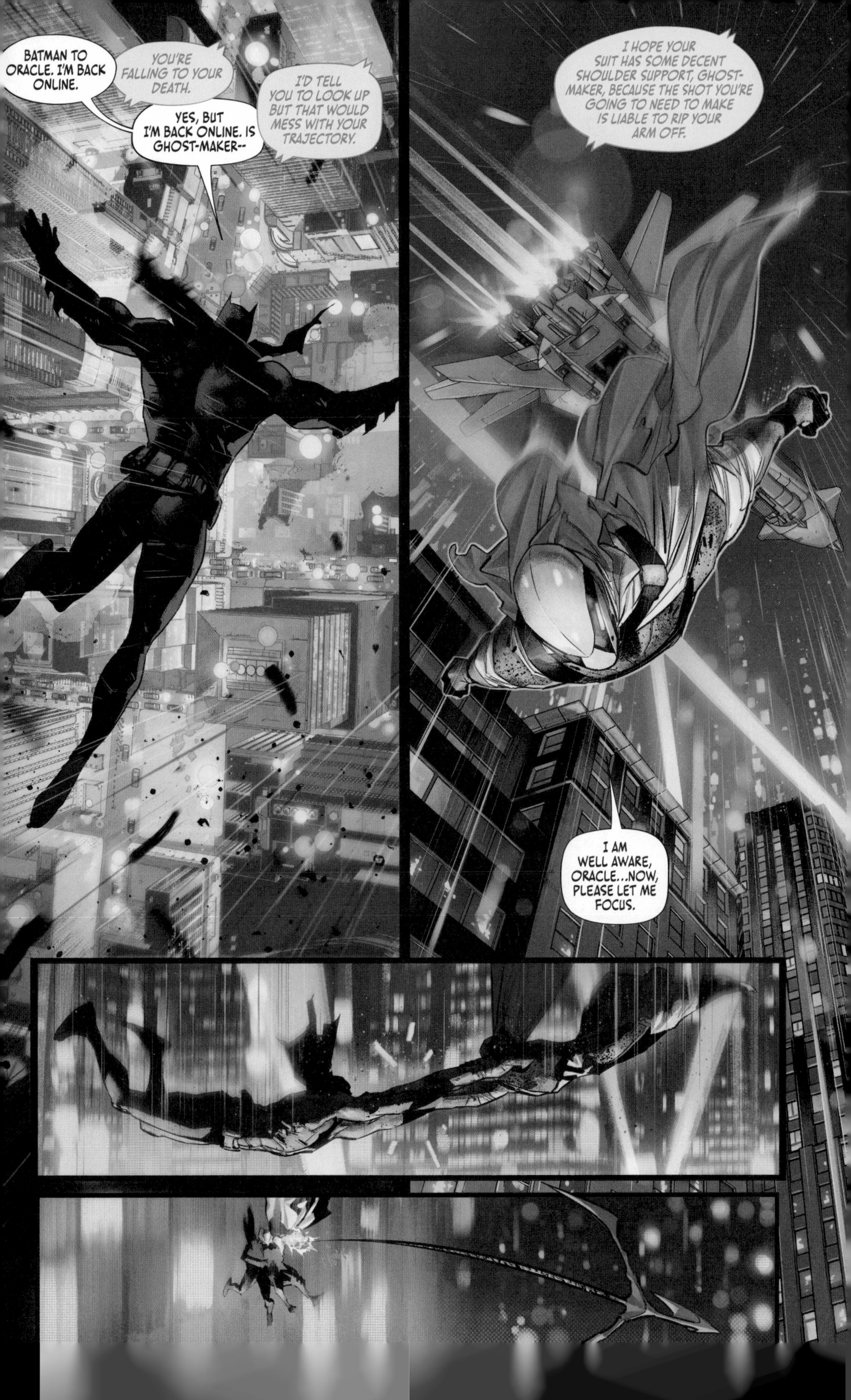
BATMAN TO ORACLE. I'M BACK ONLINE.
YOU'RE FALLING TO YOUR DEATH.
YES, BUT I'M BACK ONLINE. IS GHOST-MAKER--
I'D TELL YOU TO LOOK UP BUT THAT WOULD MESS WITH YOUR TRAJECTORY.
I HOPE YOUR SUIT HAS SOME DECENT SHOULDER SUPPORT, GHOST-MAKER, BECAUSE THE SHOT YOU'RE GOING TO NEED TO MAKE IS LIABLE TO RIP YOUR ARM OFF.
I AM WELL AWARE, ORACLE...NOW, PLEASE LET ME FOCUS.

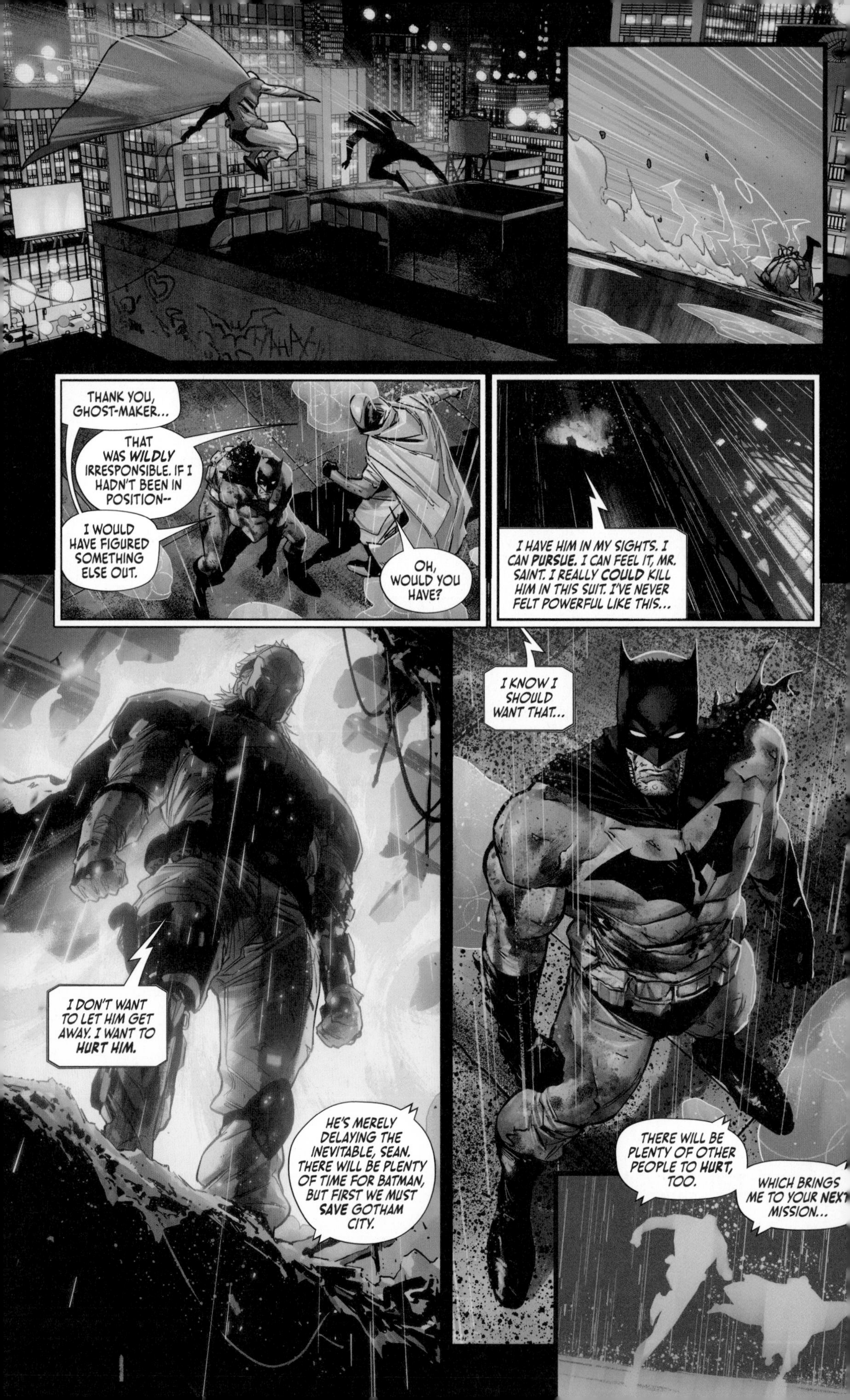
THANK YOU, GHOST-MAKER...
THAT WAS WILDLY IRRESPONSIBLE. IF I HADN'T BEEN IN POSITION--
I WOULD HAVE FIGURED SOMETHING ELSE OUT.
OH, WOULD YOU HAVE?
I HAVE HIM IN MY SIGHTS. I CAN PURSUE. I CAN FEEL IT, MR. SAINT. I REALLY COULD KILL HIM IN THIS SUIT. I'VE NEVER FELT POWERFUL LIKE THIS...
I KNOW I SHOULD WANT THAT...
I DON'T WANT TO LET HIM GET AWAY. I WANT TO HURT HIM.
HE'S MERELY DELAYING THE INEVITABLE, SEAN. THERE WILL BE PLENTY OF TIME FOR BATMAN, BUT FIRST WE MUST SAVE GOTHAM CITY.
THERE WILL BE PLENTY OF OTHER PEOPLE TO HURT, TOO.
WHICH BRINGS ME TO YOUR NEXT MISSION...

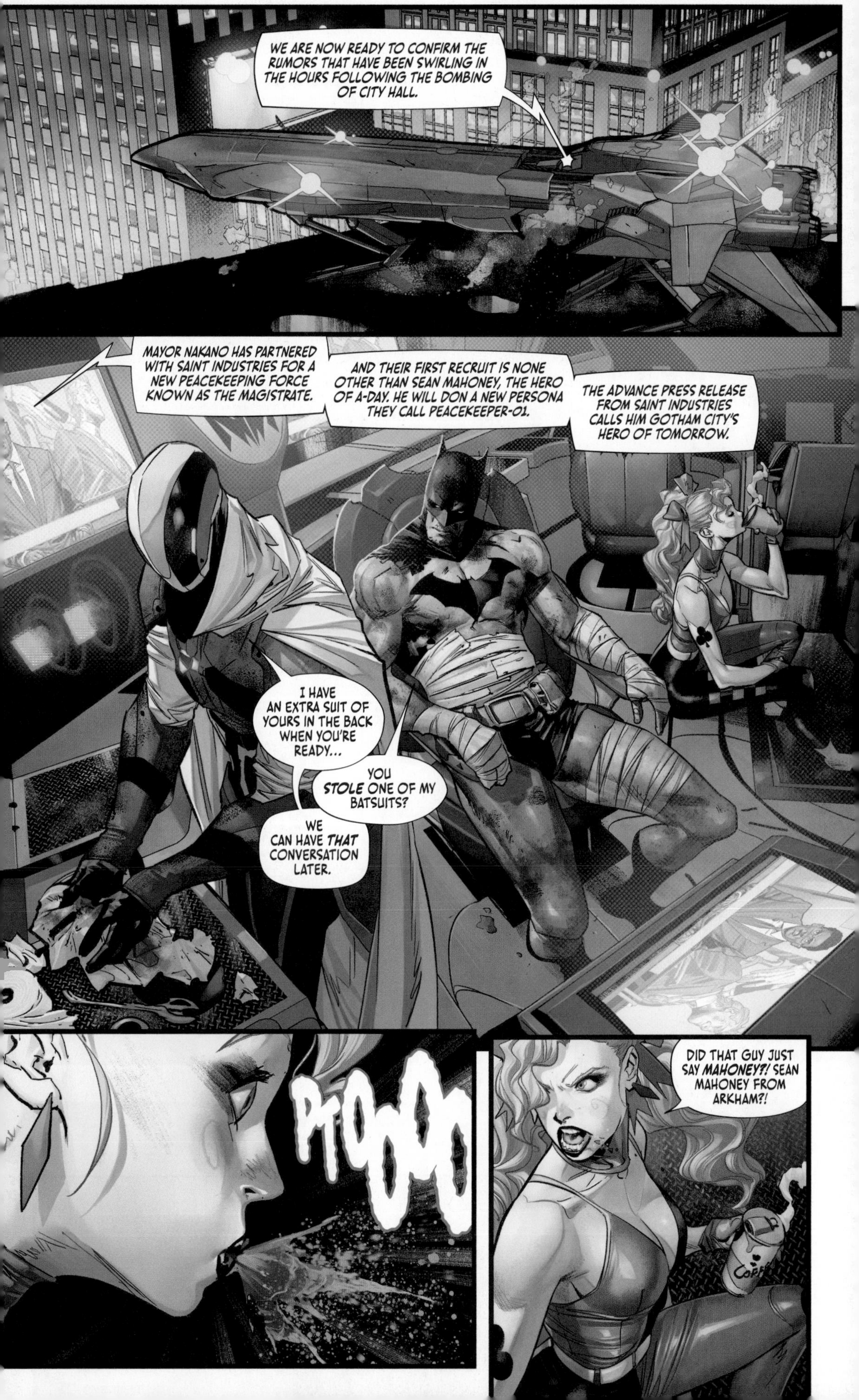
WE ARE NOW READY TO CONFIRM THE RUMORS THAT HAVE BEEN SWIRLING IN THE HOURS FOLLOWING THE BOMBING OF CITY HALL.
MAYOR NAKANO HAS PARTNERED WITH SAINT INDUSTRIES FOR A NEW PEACEKEEPING FORCE KNOWN AS THE MAGISTRATE.
AND THEIR FIRST RECRUIT IS NONE OTHER THAN SEAN MAHONEY, THE HERO OF A-DAY. HE WILL DON A NEW PERSONA THEY CALL PEACEKEEPER-01.
THE ADVANCE PRESS RELEASE FROM SAINT INDUSTRIES CALLS HIM GOTHAM CITY'S HERO OF TOMORROW.
I HAVE AN EXTRA SUIT OF YOURS IN THE BACK WHEN YOU'RE READY...
YOU *STOLE* ONE OF MY BATSUITS?
WE CAN HAVE *THAT* CONVERSATION LATER.
PTOOOO
DID THAT GUY JUST SAY *MAHONEY?!* SEAN MAHONEY FROM ARKHAM?!

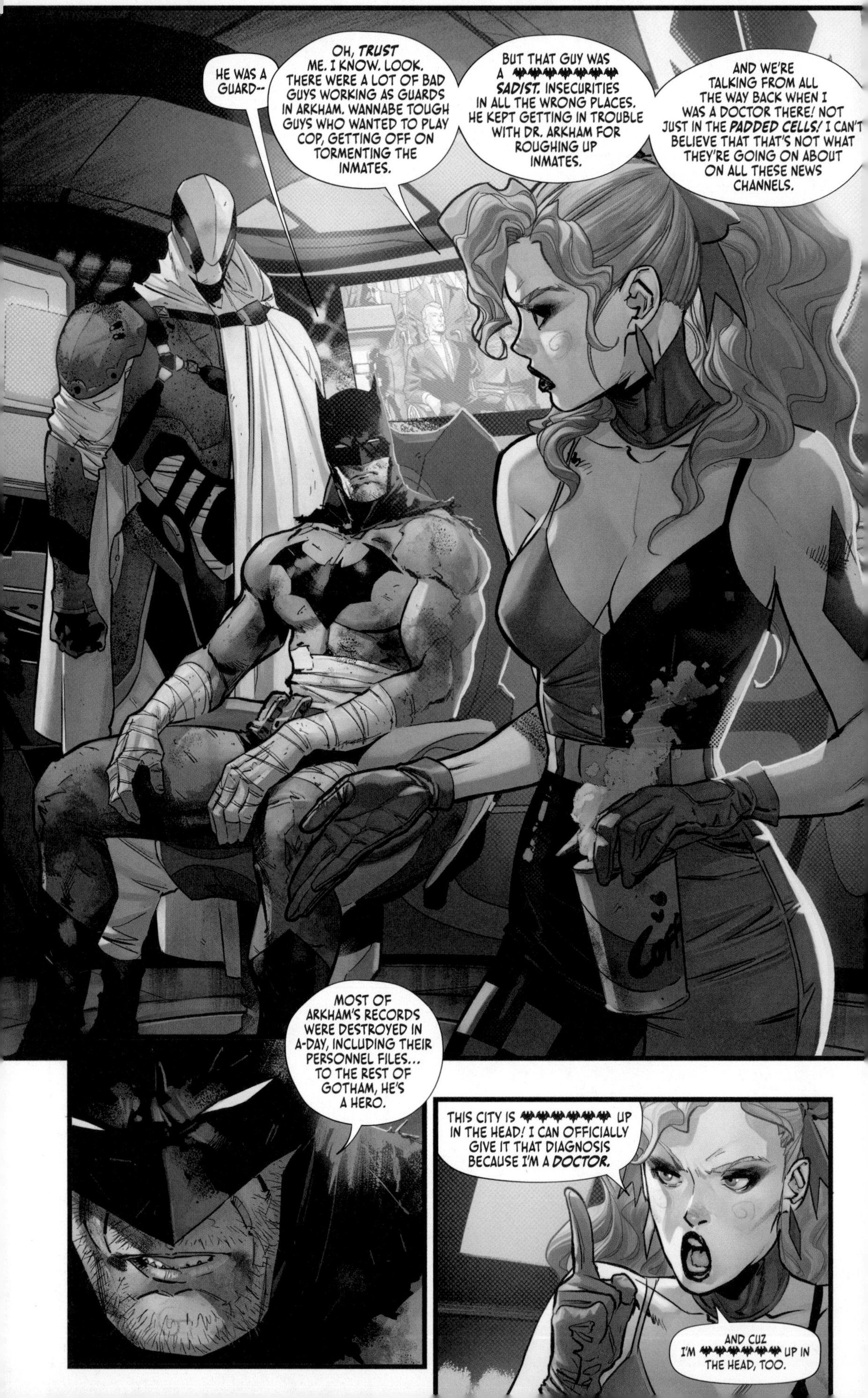
HE WAS A GUARD--
OH, TRUST ME. I KNOW. LOOK. THERE WERE A LOT OF BAD GUYS WORKING AS GUARDS IN ARKHAM. WANNABE TOUGH GUYS WHO WANTED TO PLAY COP, GETTING OFF ON TORMENTING THE INMATES.
BUT THAT GUY WAS A SADIST. INSECURITIES IN ALL THE WRONG PLACES. HE KEPT GETTING IN TROUBLE WITH DR. ARKHAM FOR ROUGHING UP INMATES.
AND WE'RE TALKING FROM ALL THE WAY BACK WHEN I WAS A DOCTOR THERE! NOT JUST IN THE PADDED CELLS! I CAN'T BELIEVE THAT THAT'S NOT WHAT THEY'RE GOING ON ABOUT ON ALL THESE NEWS CHANNELS.
MOST OF ARKHAM'S RECORDS WERE DESTROYED IN A-DAY, INCLUDING THEIR PERSONNEL FILES... TO THE REST OF GOTHAM, HE'S A HERO.
THIS CITY IS UP IN THE HEAD! I CAN OFFICIALLY GIVE IT THAT DIAGNOSIS BECAUSE I'M A DOCTOR.
AND CUZ I'M UP IN THE HEAD, TOO.

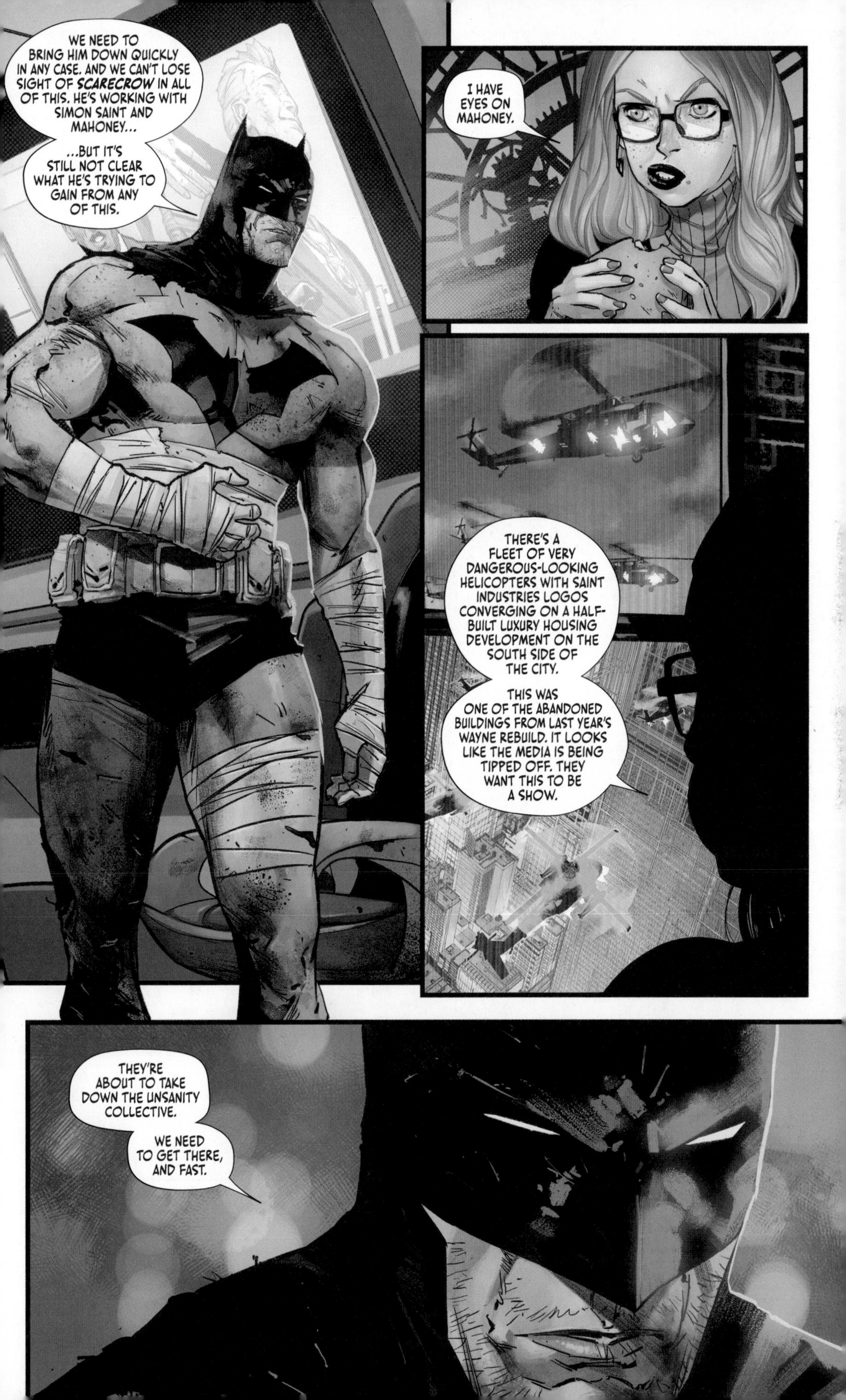
WE NEED TO BRING HIM DOWN QUICKLY IN ANY CASE. AND WE CAN'T LOSE SIGHT OF *SCARECROW* IN ALL OF THIS. HE'S WORKING WITH SIMON SAINT AND MAHONEY...
...BUT IT'S STILL NOT CLEAR WHAT HE'S TRYING TO GAIN FROM ANY OF THIS.
I HAVE EYES ON MAHONEY.
THERE'S A FLEET OF VERY DANGEROUS-LOOKING HELICOPTERS WITH SAINT INDUSTRIES LOGOS CONVERGING ON A HALF-BUILT LUXURY HOUSING DEVELOPMENT ON THE SOUTH SIDE OF THE CITY.
THIS WAS ONE OF THE ABANDONED BUILDINGS FROM LAST YEAR'S WAYNE REBUILD. IT LOOKS LIKE THE MEDIA IS BEING TIPPED OFF. THEY WANT THIS TO BE A SHOW.
THEY'RE ABOUT TO TAKE DOWN THE UNSANITY COLLECTIVE.
WE NEED TO GET THERE, AND FAST.

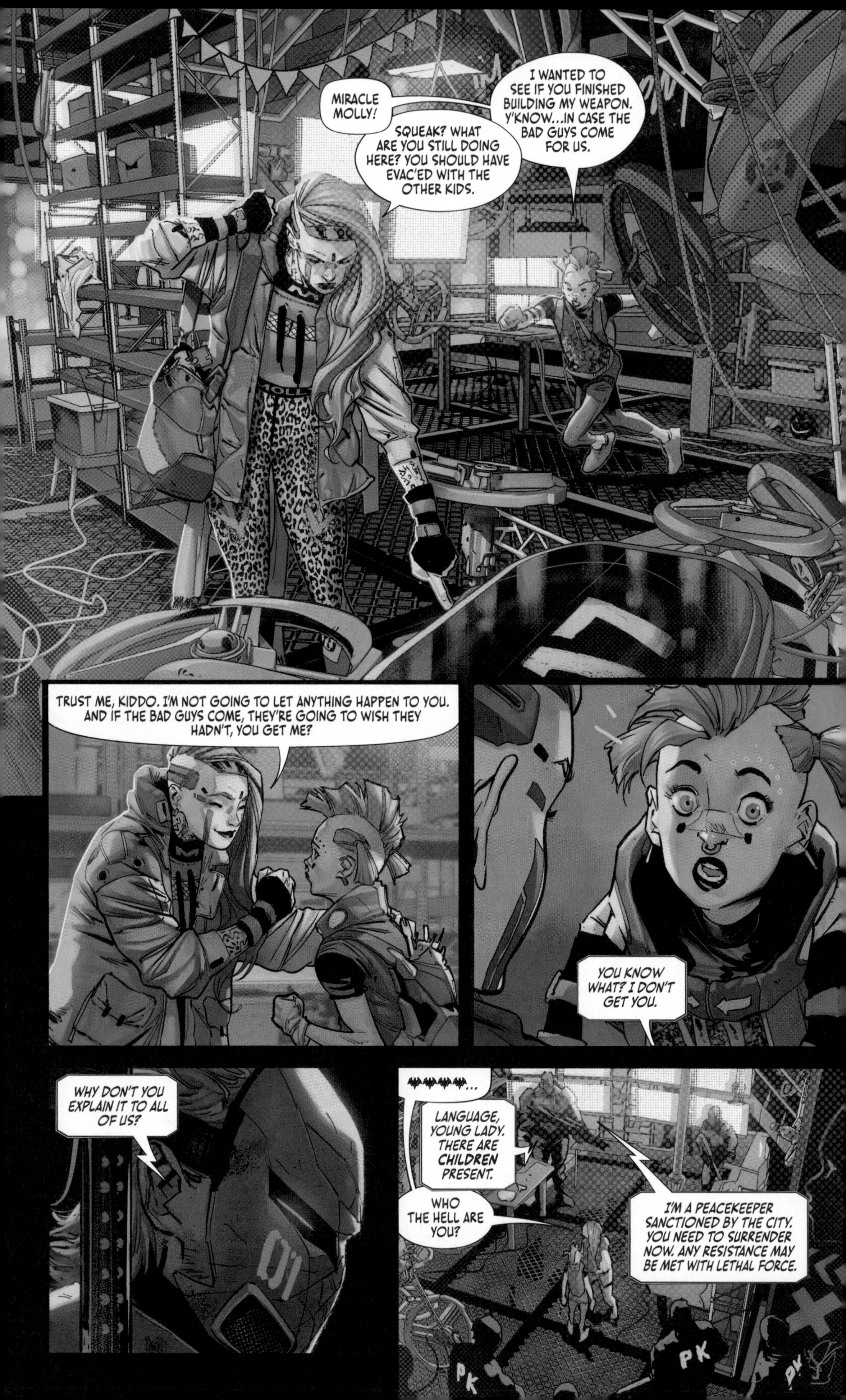
MIRACLE MOLLY!
I WANTED TO SEE IF YOU FINISHED BUILDING MY WEAPON. Y'KNOW...IN CASE THE BAD GUYS COME FOR US.
SQUEAK? WHAT ARE YOU STILL DOING HERE? YOU SHOULD HAVE EVAC'ED WITH THE OTHER KIDS.
TRUST ME, KIDDO. I'M NOT GOING TO LET ANYTHING HAPPEN TO YOU. AND IF THE BAD GUYS COME, THEY'RE GOING TO WISH THEY HADN'T, YOU GET ME?
YOU KNOW WHAT? I DON'T GET YOU.
WHY DON'T YOU EXPLAIN IT TO ALL OF US?
LANGUAGE, YOUNG LADY. THERE ARE CHILDREN PRESENT.
WHO THE HELL ARE YOU?
I'M A PEACEKEEPER SANCTIONED BY THE CITY. YOU NEED TO SURRENDER NOW. ANY RESISTANCE MAY BE MET WITH LETHAL FORCE.
PK
PK

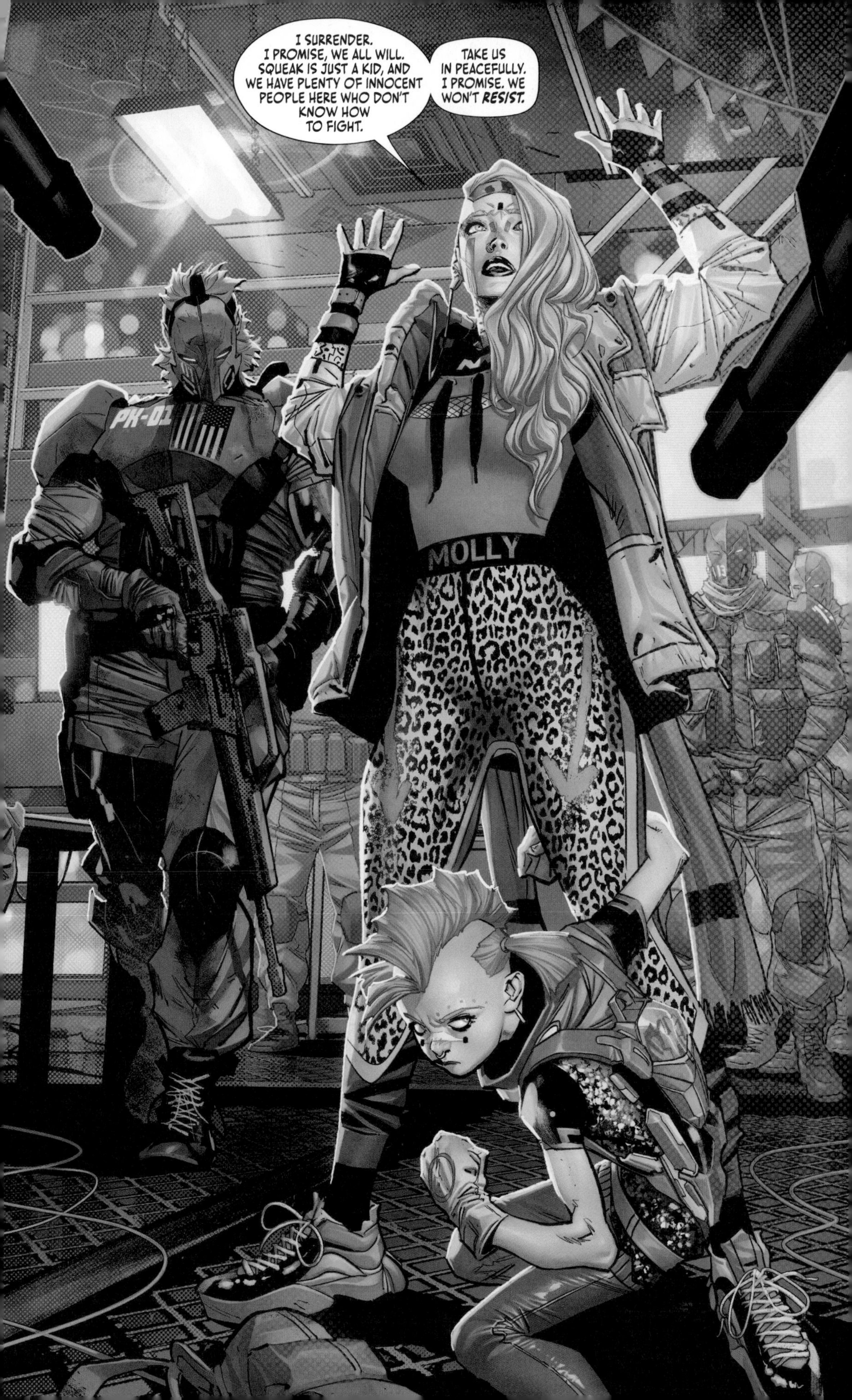
I SURRENDER. I PROMISE, WE ALL WILL. SQUEAK IS JUST A KID, AND WE HAVE PLENTY OF INNOCENT PEOPLE HERE WHO DON'T KNOW HOW TO FIGHT.
TAKE US IN PEACEFULLY. I PROMISE. WE WON'T *RESIST.*
PK-01
MOLLY

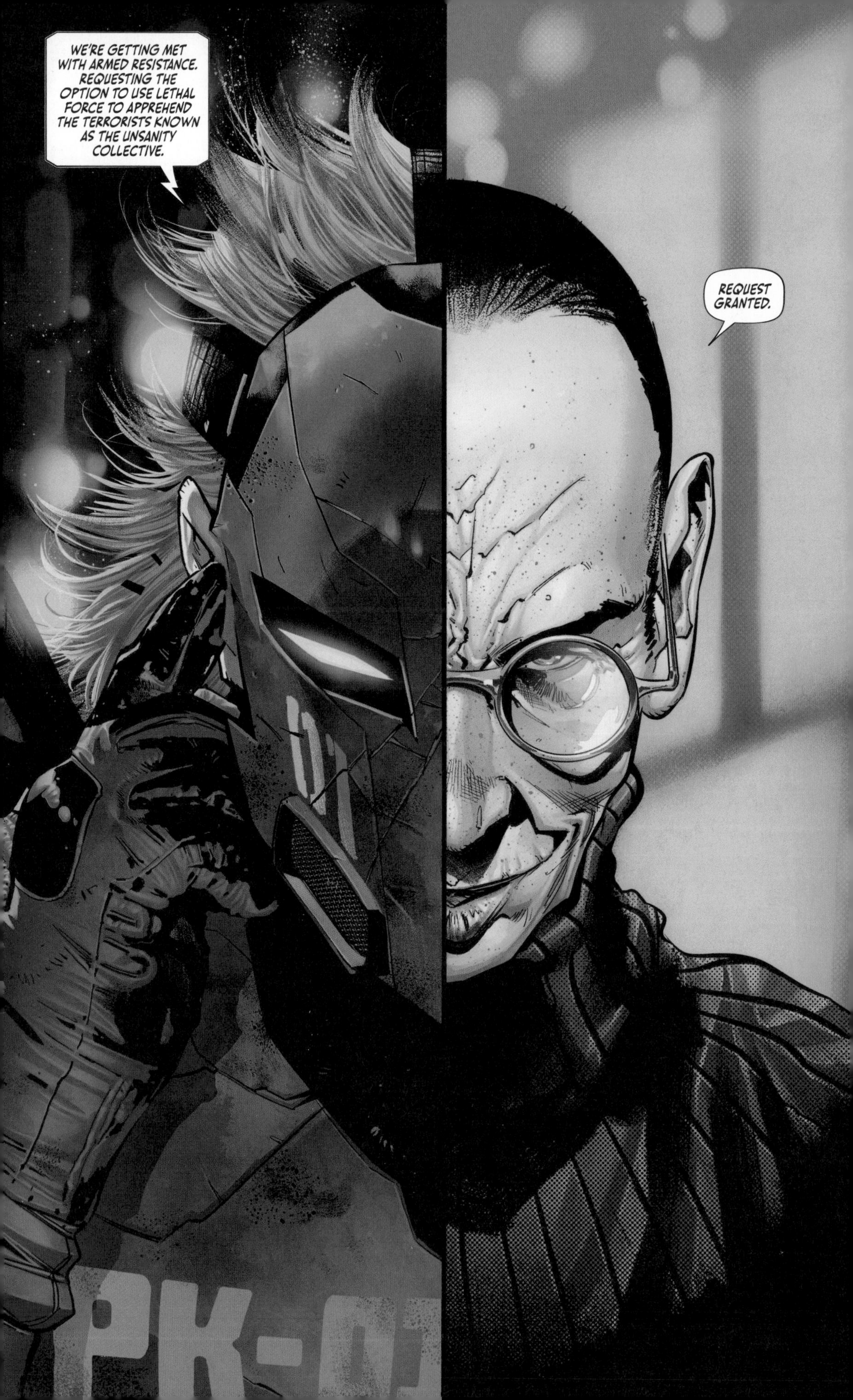
WE'RE GETTING MET WITH ARMED RESISTANCE. REQUESTING THE OPTION TO USE LETHAL FORCE TO APPREHEND THE TERRORISTS KNOWN AS THE UNSANITY COLLECTIVE.
REQUEST GRANTED.
PK-0

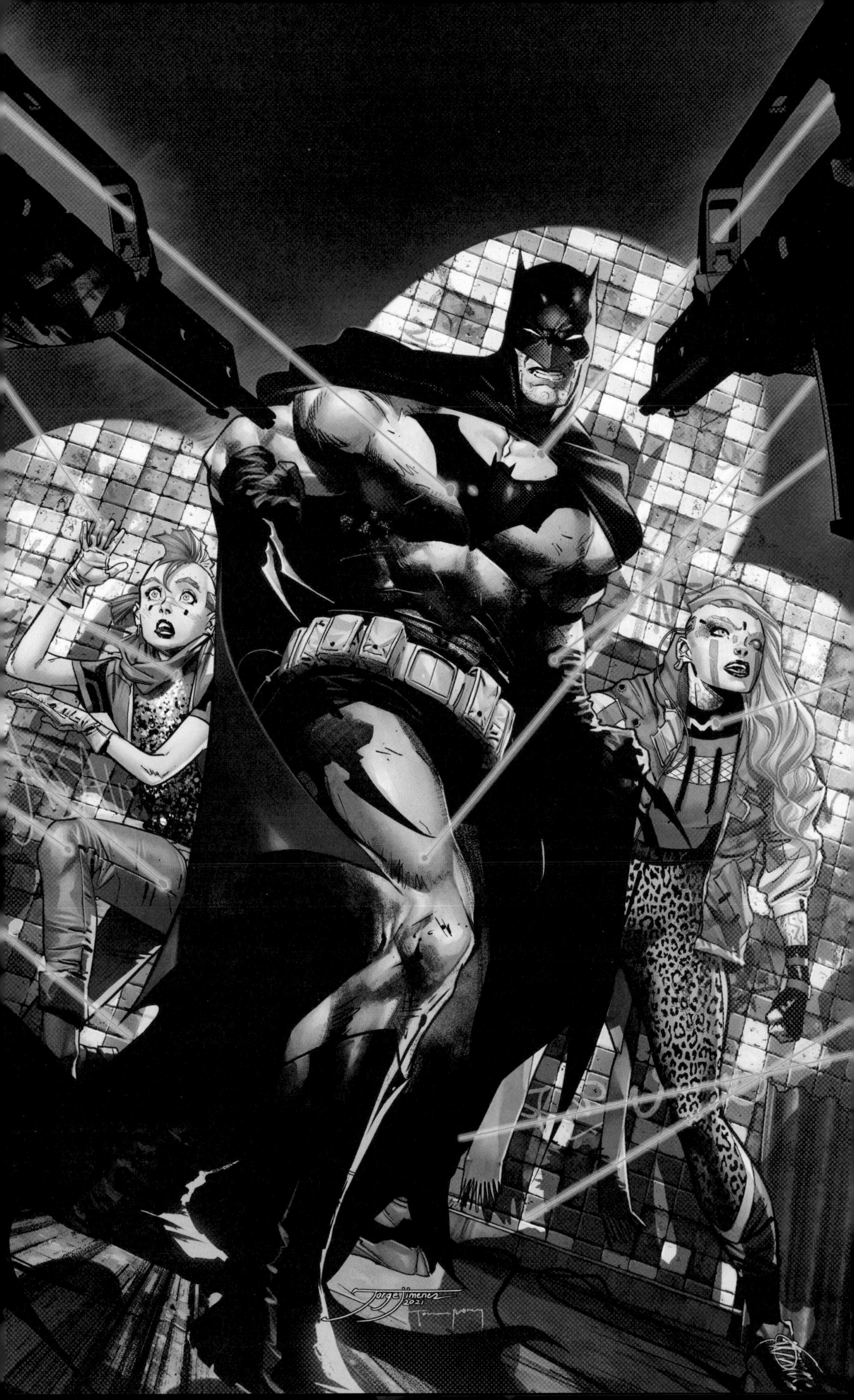
Jorge Jimenez
2021

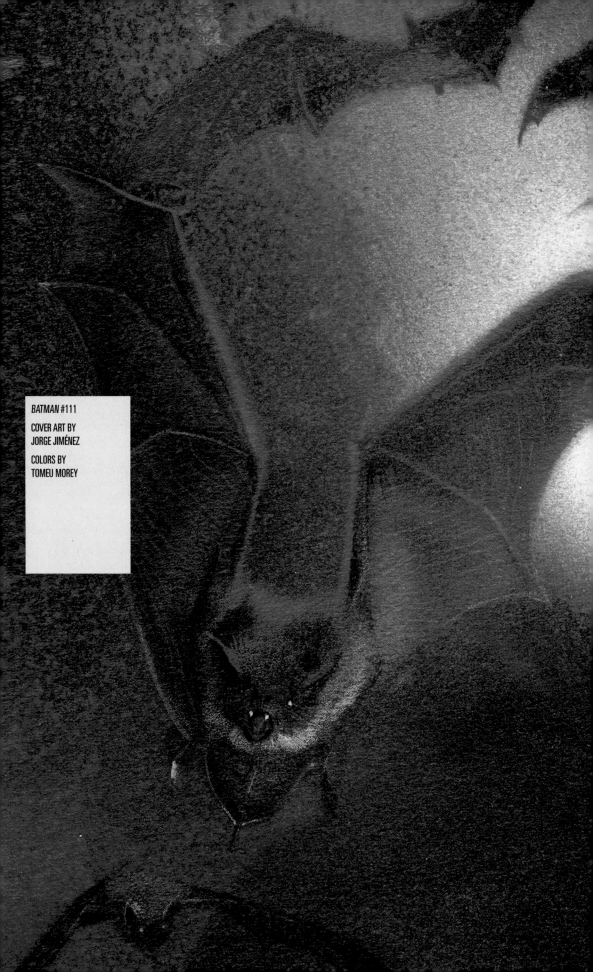

BATMAN #111
COVER ART BY
JORGE JIMÉNEZ

COLORS BY
TOMEU MOREY

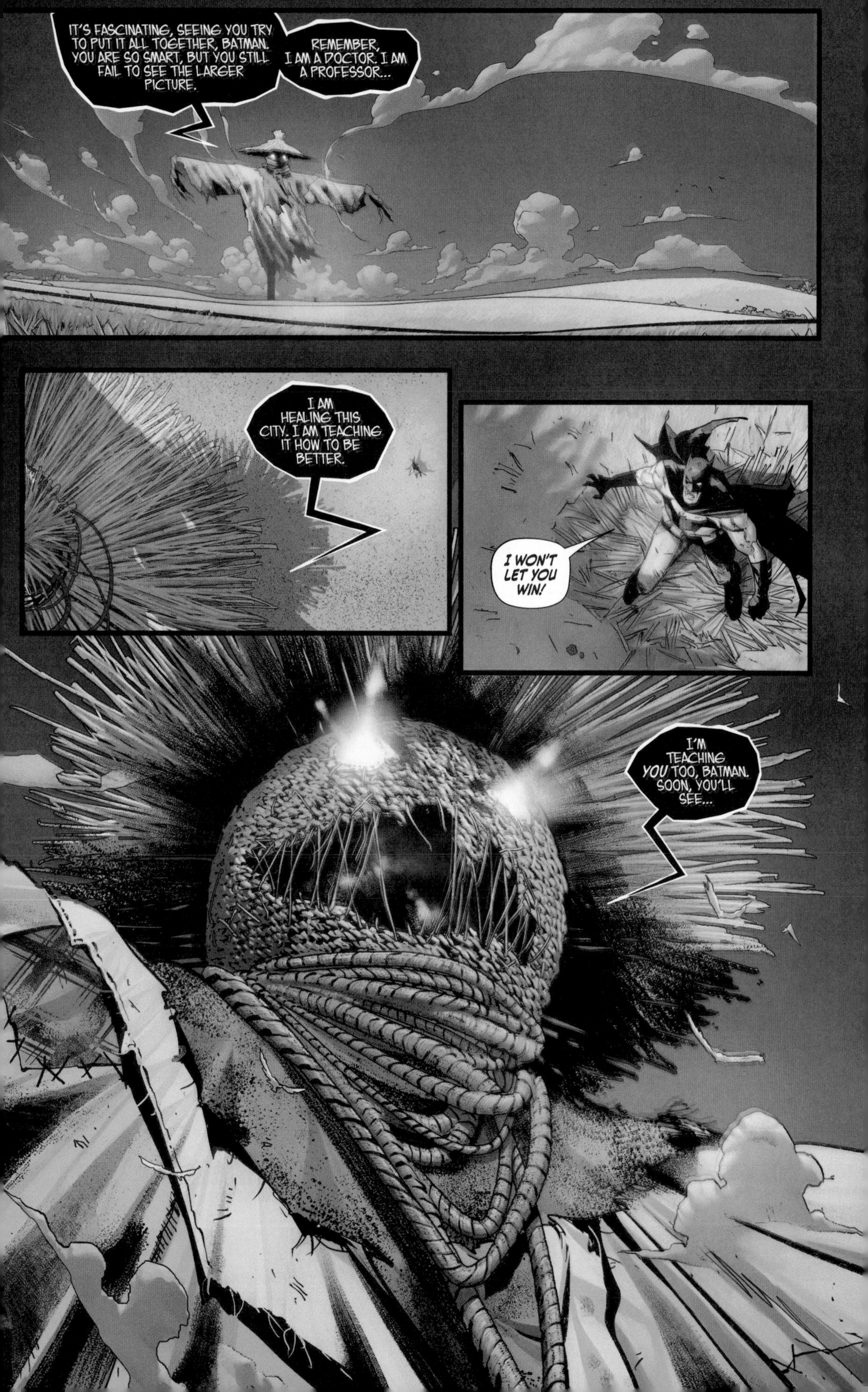
IT'S FASCINATING, SEEING YOU TRY TO PUT IT ALL TOGETHER, BATMAN. YOU ARE SO SMART, BUT YOU STILL FAIL TO SEE THE LARGER PICTURE.
REMEMBER, I AM A DOCTOR. I AM A PROFESSOR...
I AM HEALING THIS CITY. I AM TEACHING IT HOW TO BE BETTER.
I WON'T LET YOU WIN!
I'M TEACHING YOU TOO, BATMAN. SOON, YOU'LL SEE...

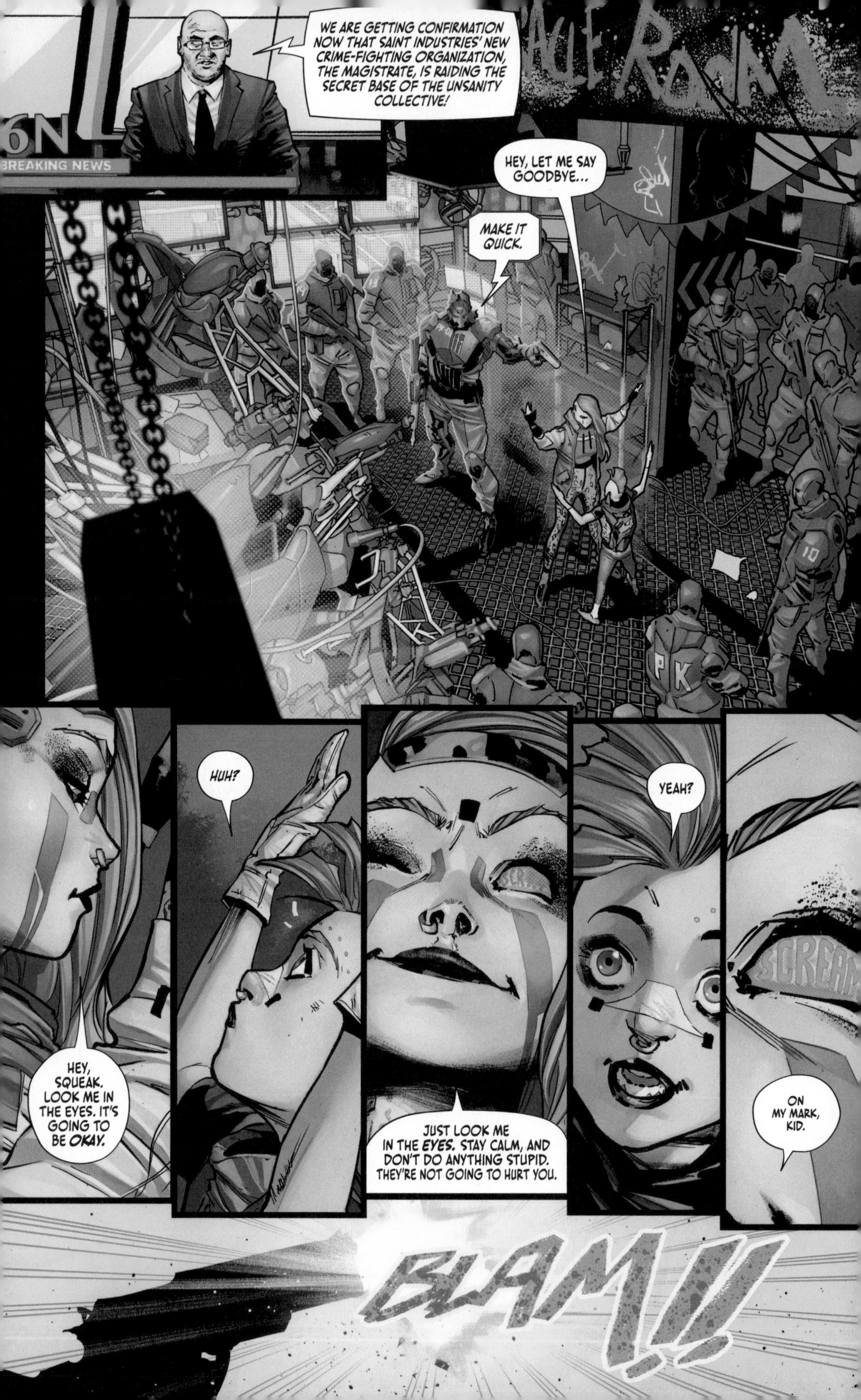
WE ARE GETTING CONFIRMATION NOW THAT SAINT INDUSTRIES' NEW CRIME-FIGHTING ORGANIZATION, THE MAGISTRATE, IS RAIDING THE SECRET BASE OF THE UNSANITY COLLECTIVE!
6N
BREAKING NEWS
HEY, LET ME SAY GOODBYE...
MAKE IT QUICK.
HEY, SQUEAK. LOOK ME IN THE EYES. IT'S GOING TO BE OKAY.
HUH?
JUST LOOK ME IN THE EYES. STAY CALM, AND DON'T DO ANYTHING STUPID. THEY'RE NOT GOING TO HURT YOU.
YEAH?
ON MY MARK, KID.
BLAM!!

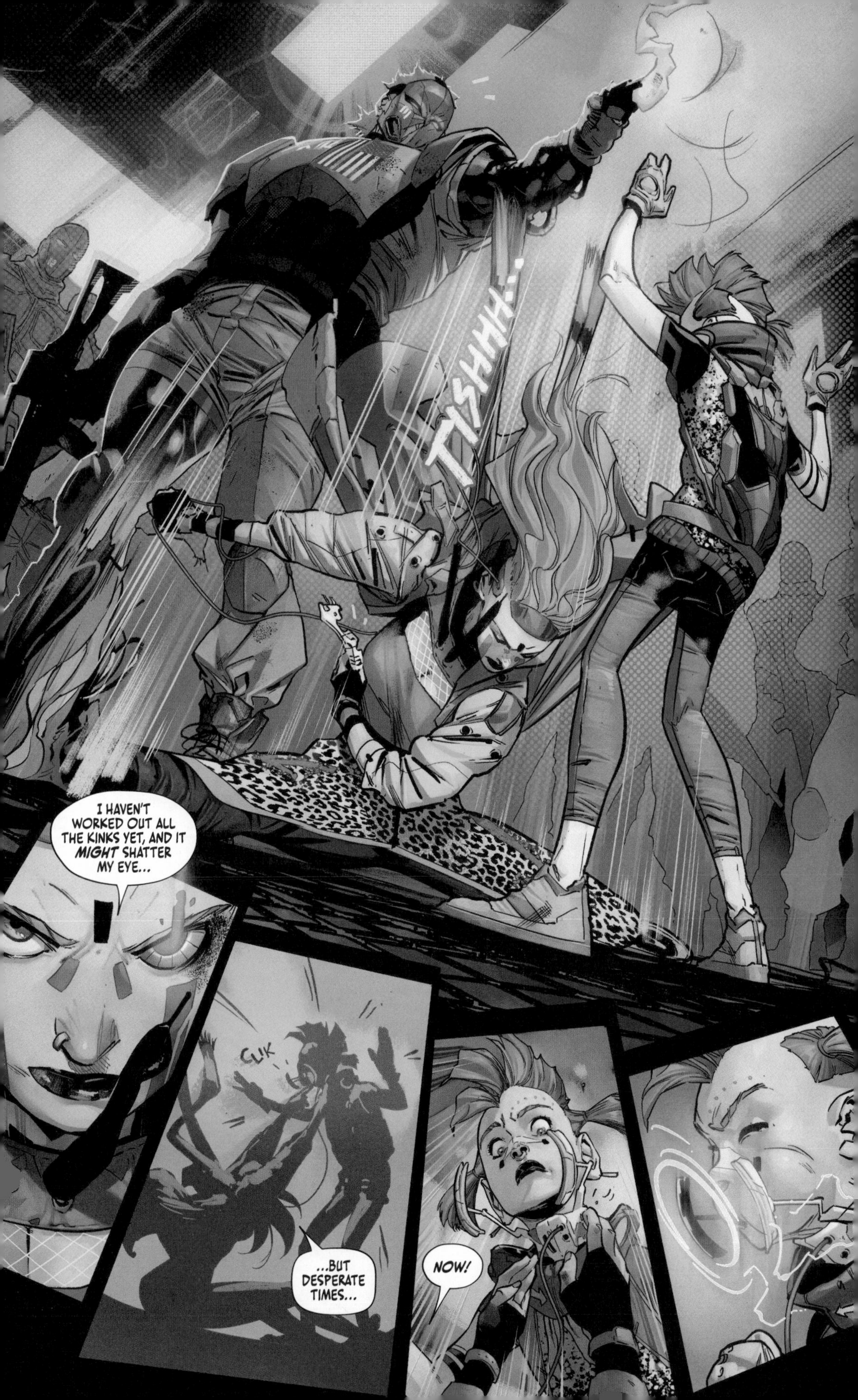
TISHHH...
I HAVEN'T WORKED OUT ALL THE KINKS YET, AND IT *MIGHT* SHATTER MY EYE...
CLIK
...BUT DESPERATE TIMES...
NOW!

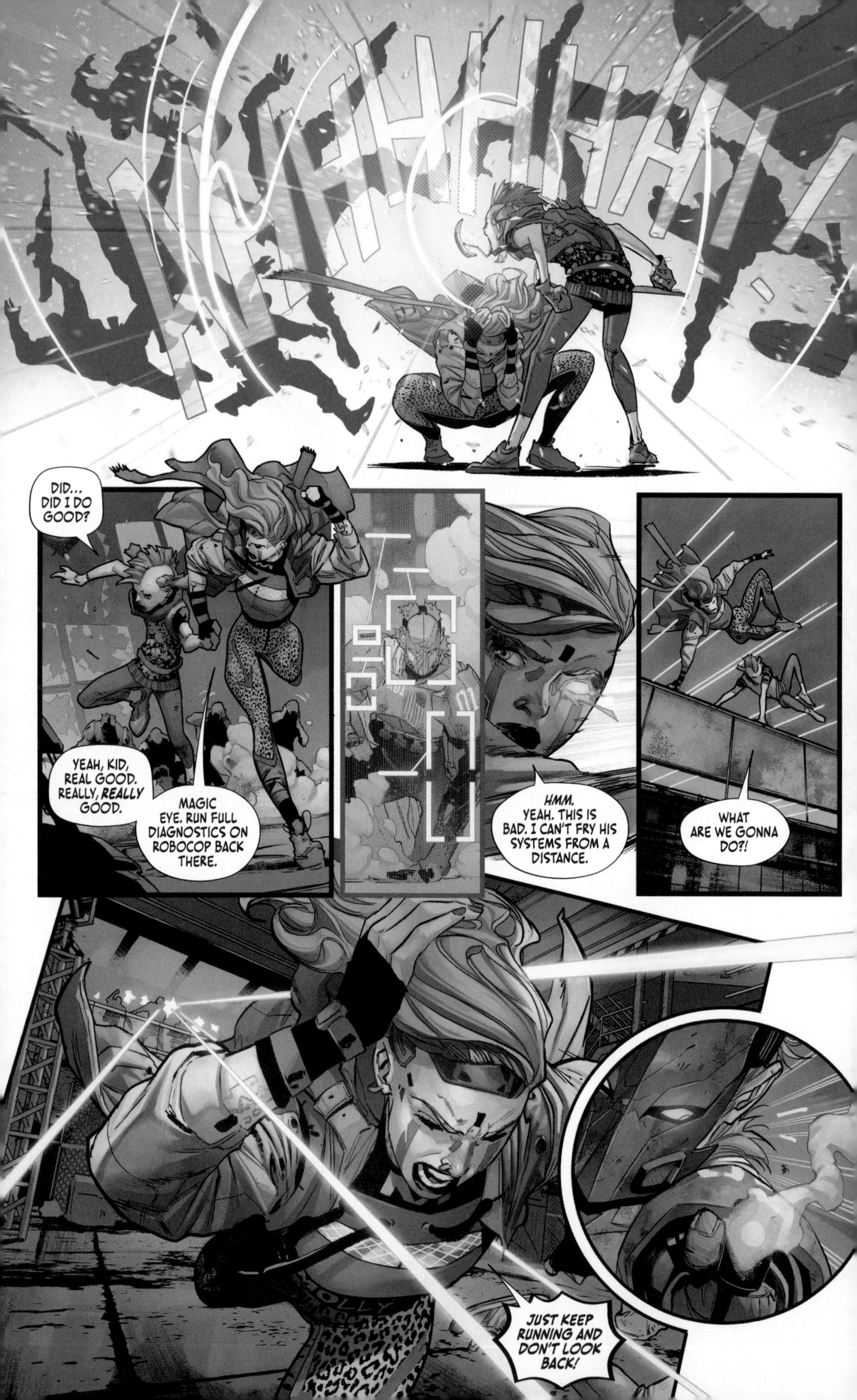
DID... DID I DO GOOD?
YEAH, KID, REAL GOOD. REALLY, *REALLY* GOOD.
MAGIC EYE. RUN FULL DIAGNOSTICS ON ROBOCOP BACK THERE.
HMM. YEAH. THIS IS BAD. I CAN'T FRY HIS SYSTEMS FROM A DISTANCE.
WHAT ARE WE GONNA DO?!
JUST KEEP RUNNING AND DON'T LOOK BACK!

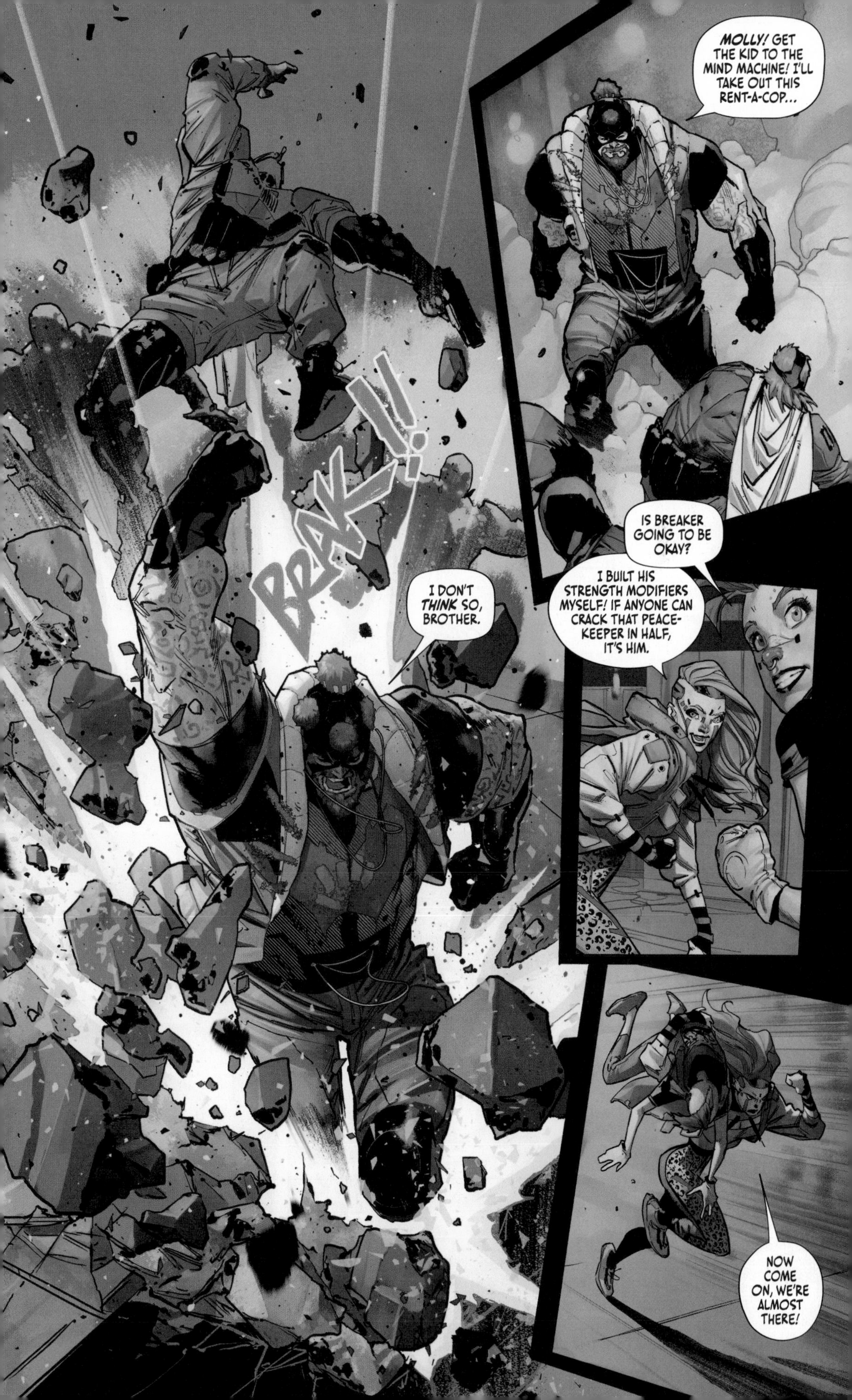
MOLLY! GET THE KID TO THE MIND MACHINE! I'LL TAKE OUT THIS RENT-A-COP...
BRAK!!
I DON'T THINK SO, BROTHER.
IS BREAKER GOING TO BE OKAY?
I BUILT HIS STRENGTH MODIFIERS MYSELF! IF ANYONE CAN CRACK THAT PEACE-KEEPER IN HALF, IT'S HIM.
NOW COME ON, WE'RE ALMOST THERE!

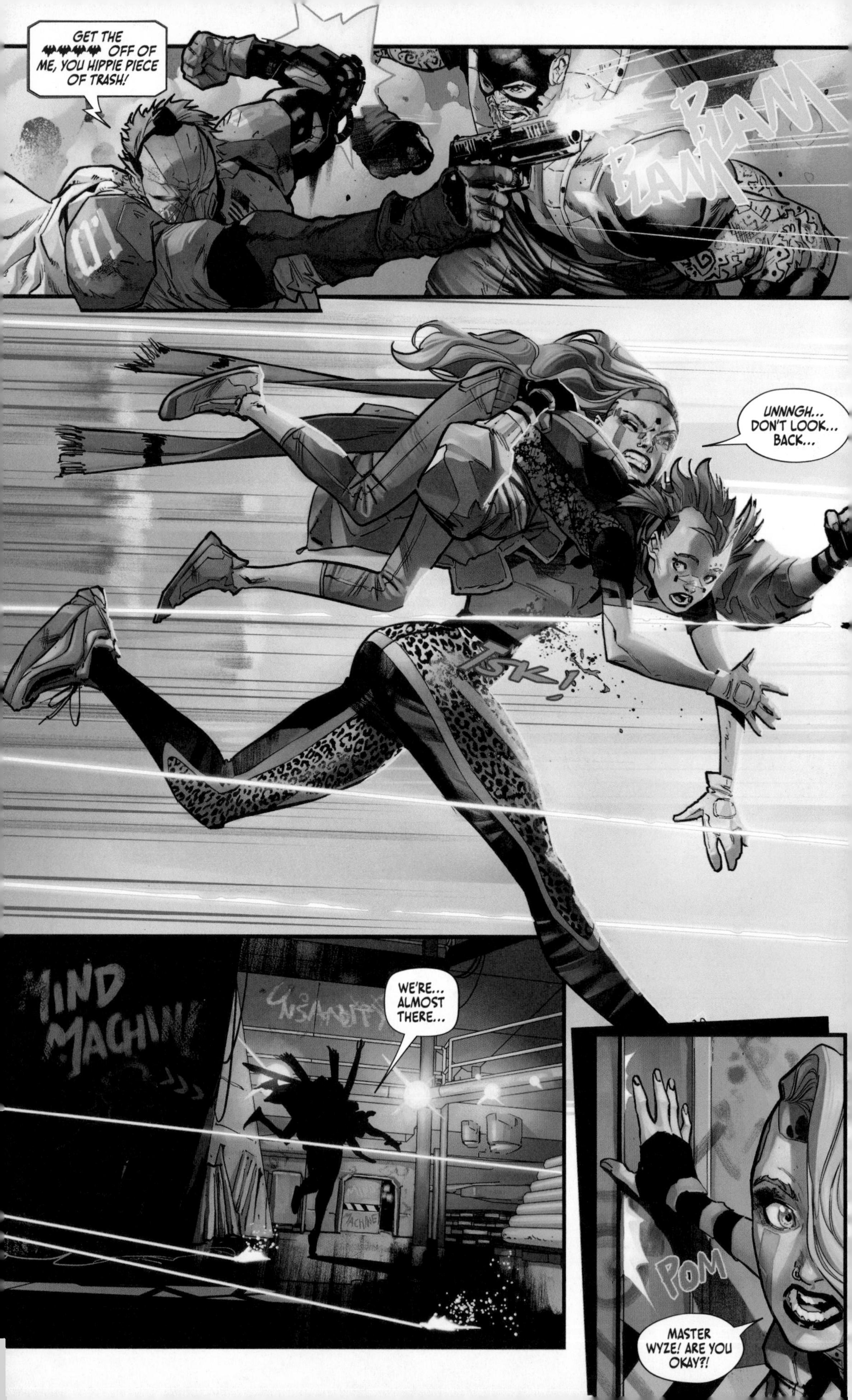
GET THE ✦✦✦✦ OFF OF ME, YOU HIPPIE PIECE OF TRASH!
BLAM BLAM
UNNNGH... DON'T LOOK... BACK...
TSK!
WE'RE... ALMOST THERE...
POM
MASTER WYZE! ARE YOU OKAY?!

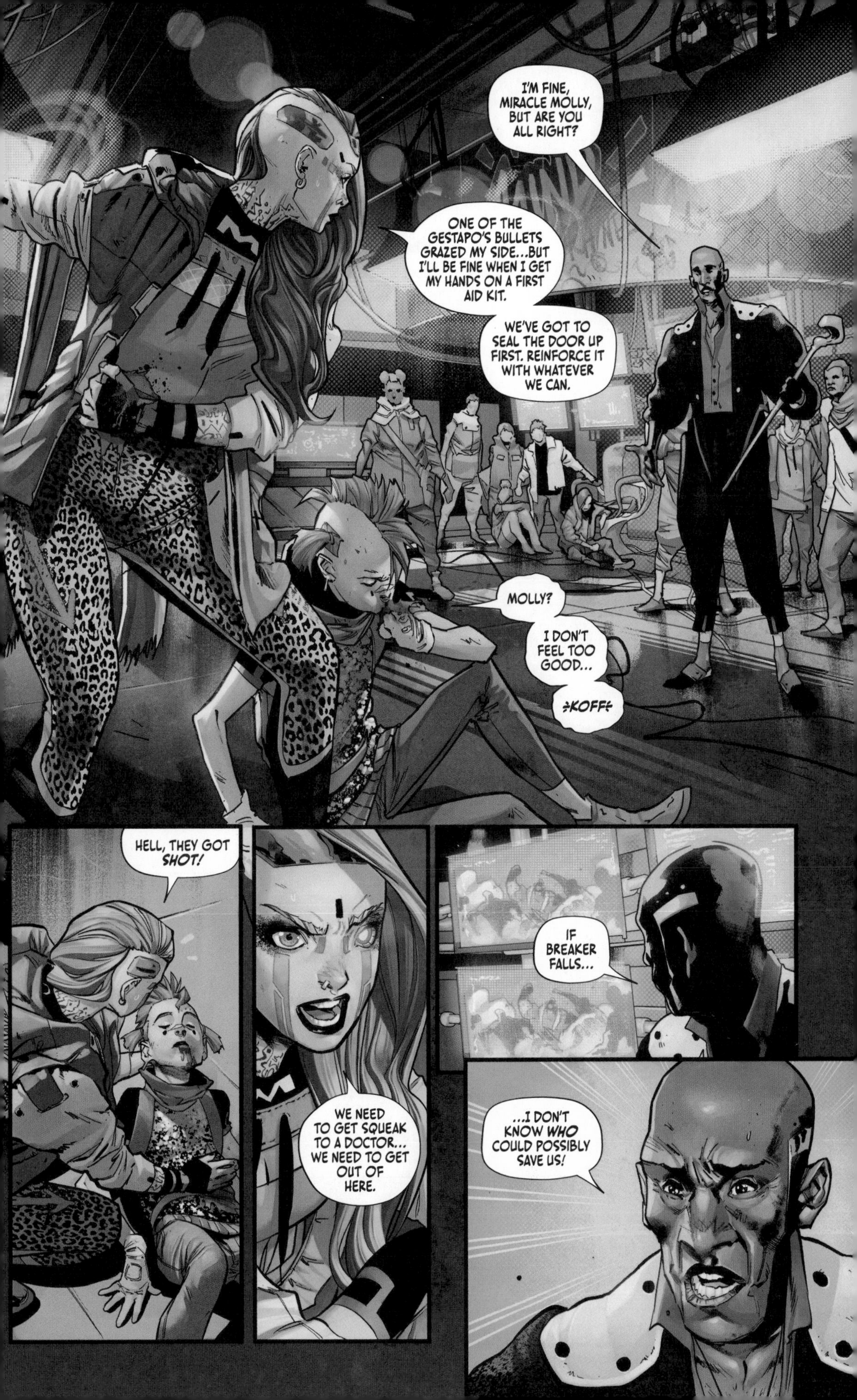
I'M FINE, MIRACLE MOLLY, BUT ARE YOU ALL RIGHT?
ONE OF THE GESTAPO'S BULLETS GRAZED MY SIDE...BUT I'LL BE FINE WHEN I GET MY HANDS ON A FIRST AID KIT.
WE'VE GOT TO SEAL THE DOOR UP FIRST. REINFORCE IT WITH WHATEVER WE CAN.
MOLLY?
I DON'T FEEL TOO GOOD...
KOFF
HELL, THEY GOT SHOT!
WE NEED TO GET SQUEAK TO A DOCTOR... WE NEED TO GET OUT OF HERE.
IF BREAKER FALLS...
...I DON'T KNOW WHO COULD POSSIBLY SAVE US!

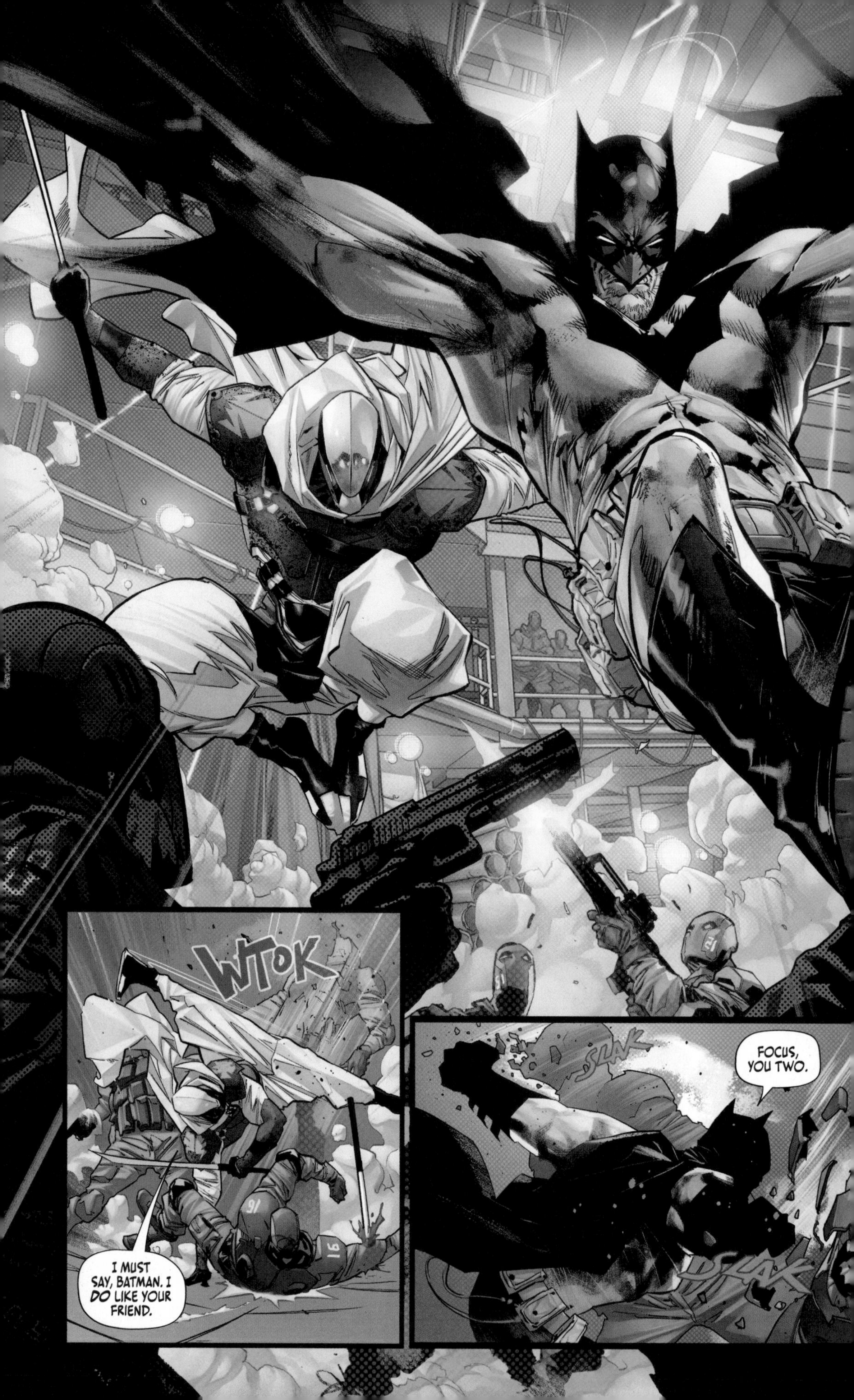
WTOK
I MUST SAY, BATMAN. I *DO* LIKE YOUR FRIEND.
SLAK
FOCUS, YOU TWO.
SLAK

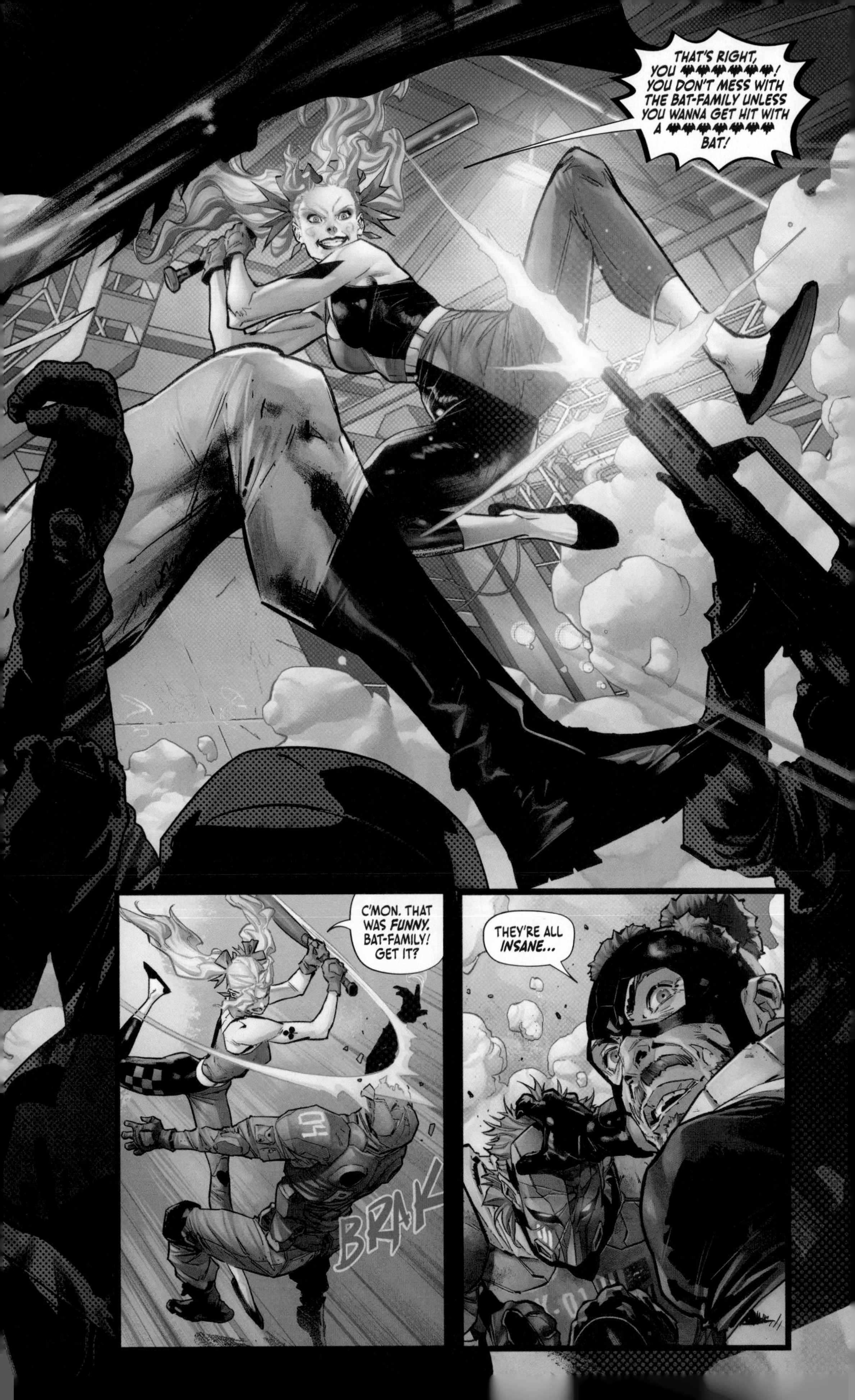

THAT'S RIGHT, YOU ! YOU DON'T MESS WITH THE BAT-FAMILY UNLESS YOU WANNA GET HIT WITH A BAT!
C'MON. THAT WAS *FUNNY.* BAT-FAMILY! GET IT?
BRAK
THEY'RE ALL *INSANE...*

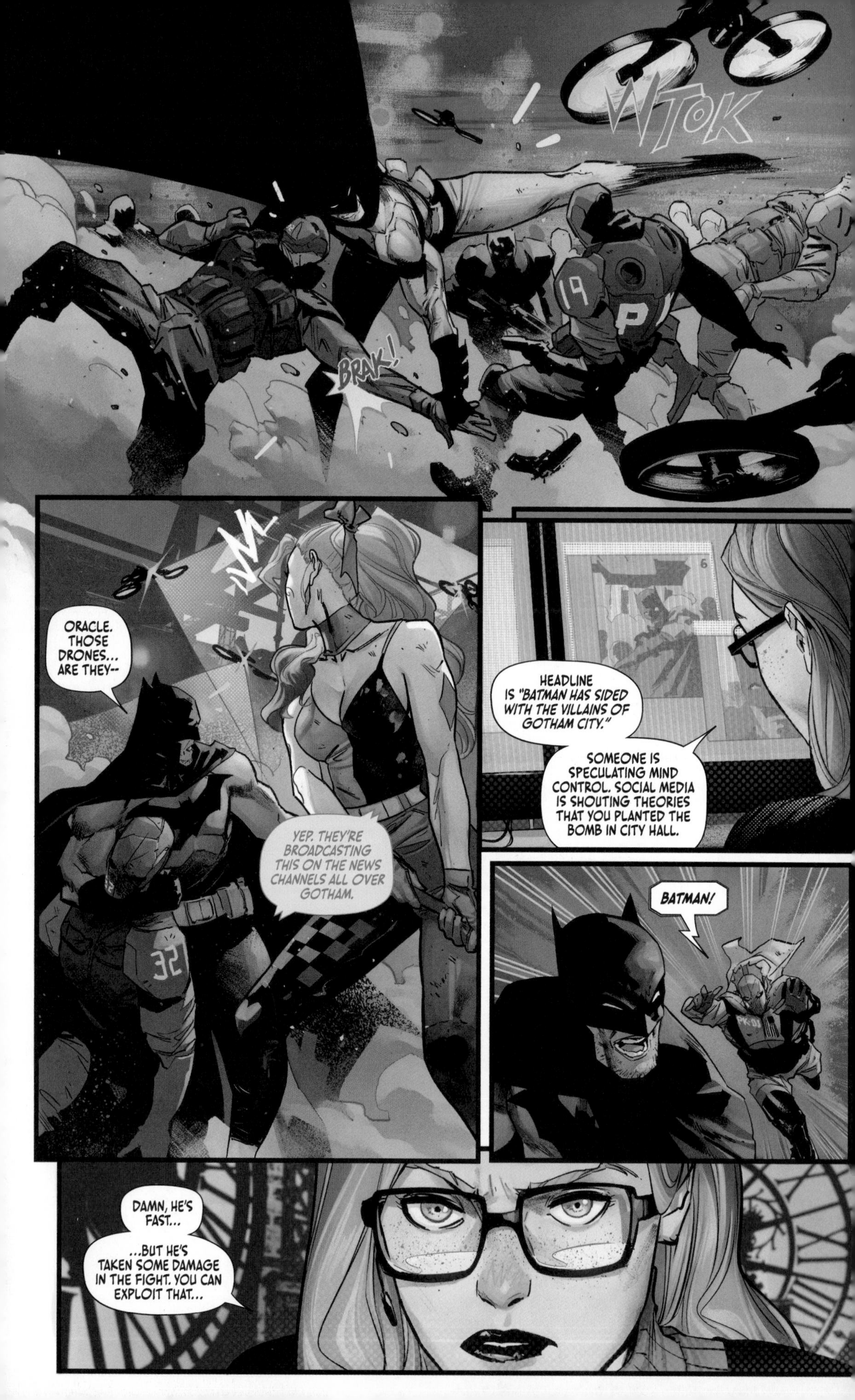

WTOK
BRAK!
ORACLE. THOSE DRONES... ARE THEY--
YEP. THEY'RE BROADCASTING THIS ON THE NEWS CHANNELS ALL OVER GOTHAM.
HEADLINE IS "BATMAN HAS SIDED WITH THE VILLAINS OF GOTHAM CITY."
SOMEONE IS SPECULATING MIND CONTROL. SOCIAL MEDIA IS SHOUTING THEORIES THAT YOU PLANTED THE BOMB IN CITY HALL.
BATMAN!
DAMN, HE'S FAST...
...BUT HE'S TAKEN SOME DAMAGE IN THE FIGHT. YOU CAN EXPLOIT THAT...

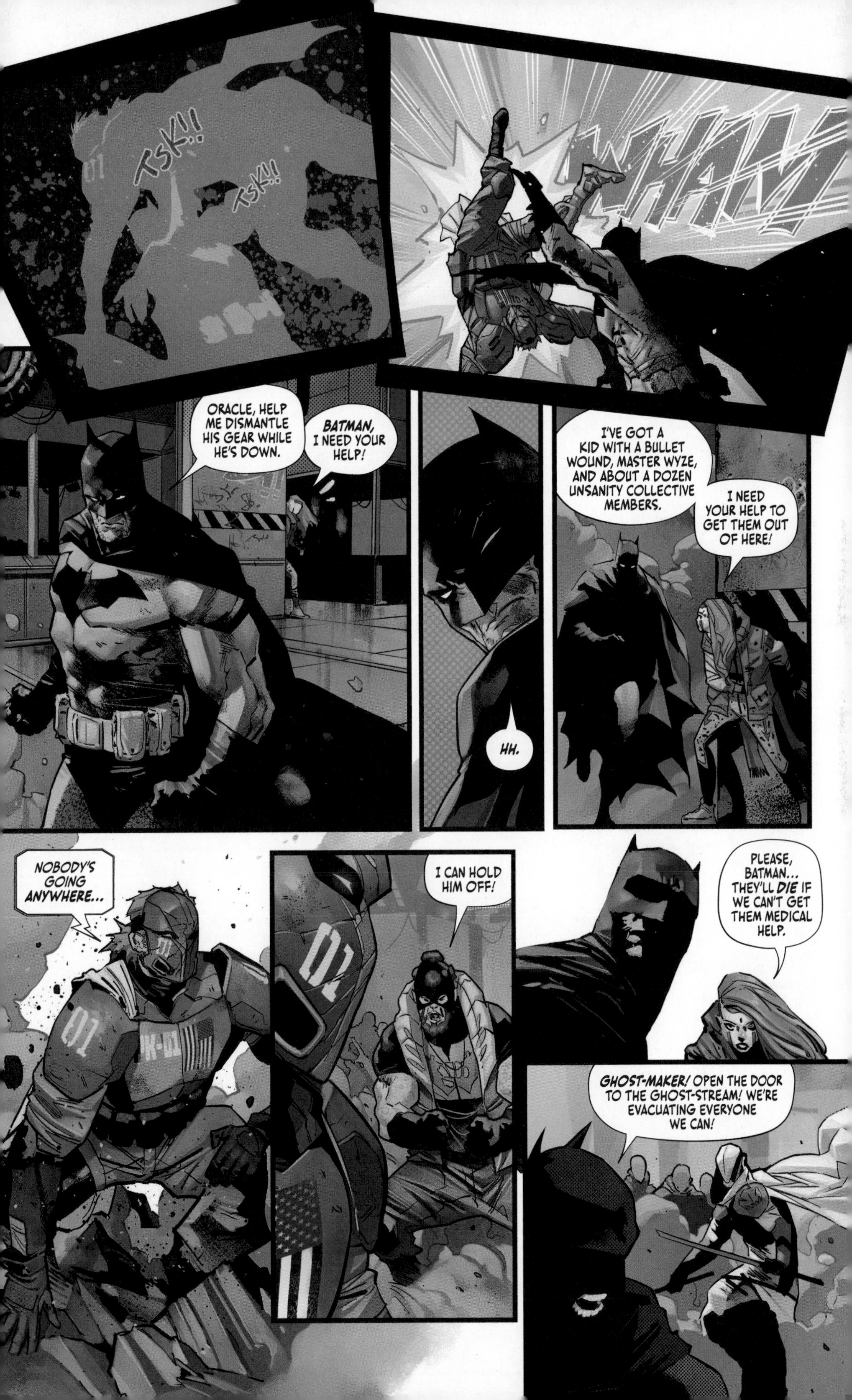
TSK!!
TSK!!
WHAM!
ORACLE, HELP ME DISMANTLE HIS GEAR WHILE HE'S DOWN.
BATMAN, I NEED YOUR HELP!
HH.
I'VE GOT A KID WITH A BULLET WOUND, MASTER WYZE, AND ABOUT A DOZEN UNSANITY COLLECTIVE MEMBERS.
I NEED YOUR HELP TO GET THEM OUT OF HERE!
NOBODY'S GOING ANYWHERE...
I CAN HOLD HIM OFF!
PLEASE, BATMAN... THEY'LL DIE IF WE CAN'T GET THEM MEDICAL HELP.
GHOST-MAKER! OPEN THE DOOR TO THE GHOST-STREAM! WE'RE EVACUATING EVERYONE WE CAN!

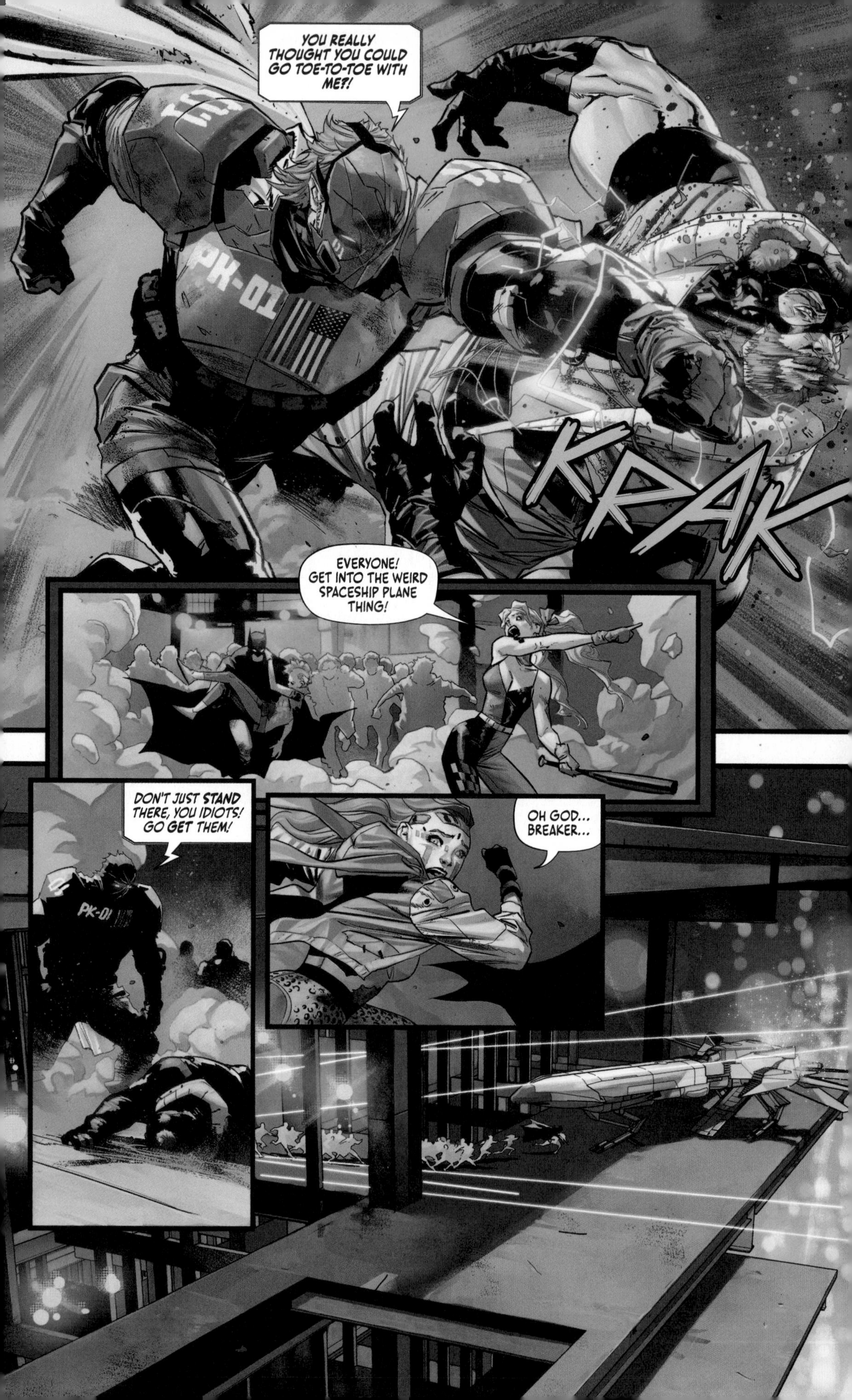
YOU REALLY THOUGHT YOU COULD GO TOE-TO-TOE WITH ME?!
KRAK
EVERYONE! GET INTO THE WEIRD SPACESHIP PLANE THING!
DON'T JUST STAND THERE, YOU IDIOTS! GO GET THEM!
OH GOD... BREAKER...
PK-01

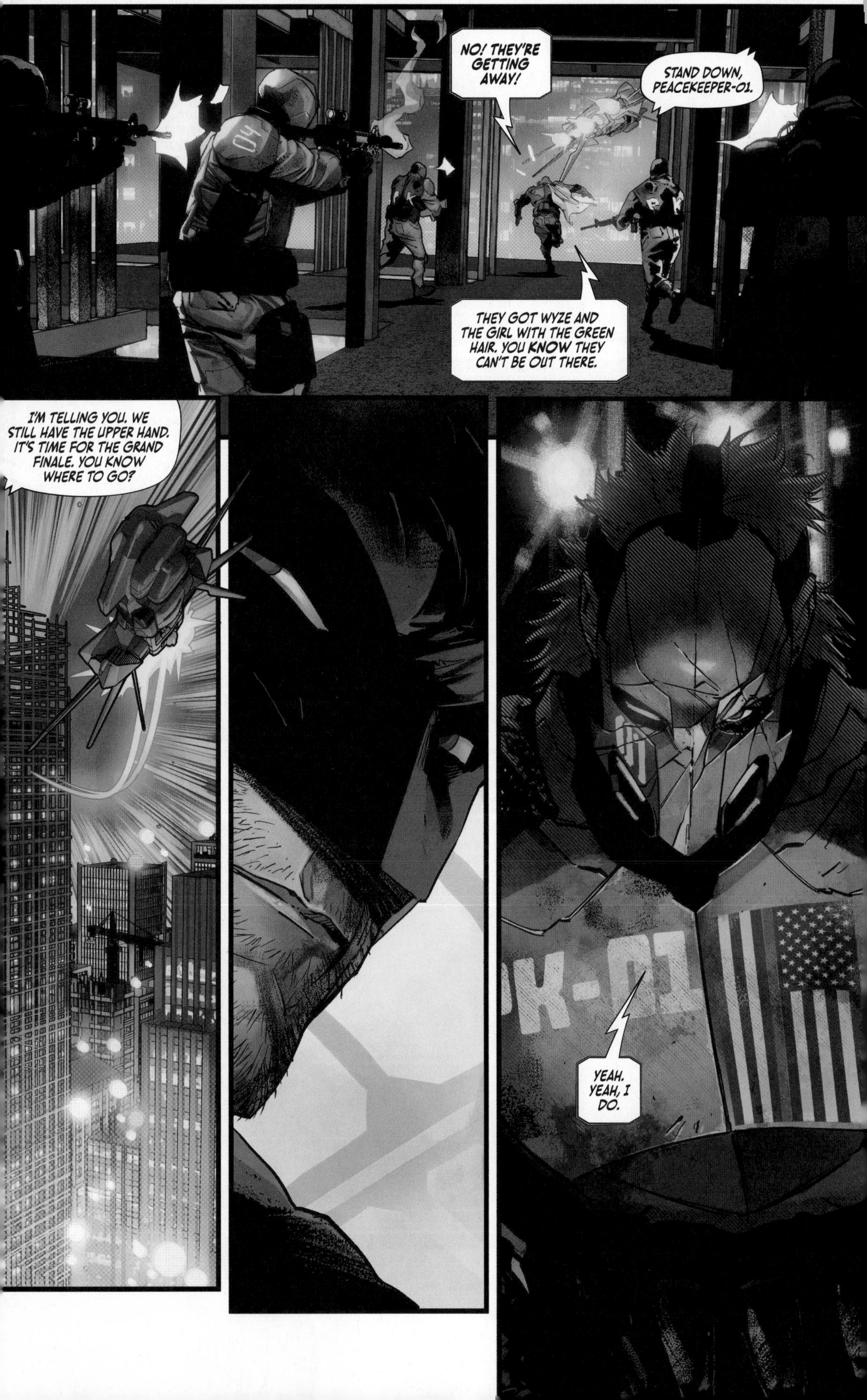
NO! THEY'RE GETTING AWAY!
STAND DOWN, PEACEKEEPER-01.
THEY GOT WYZE AND THE GIRL WITH THE GREEN HAIR. YOU KNOW THEY CAN'T BE OUT THERE.
I'M TELLING YOU. WE STILL HAVE THE UPPER HAND. IT'S TIME FOR THE GRAND FINALE. YOU KNOW WHERE TO GO?
YEAH. YEAH, I DO.

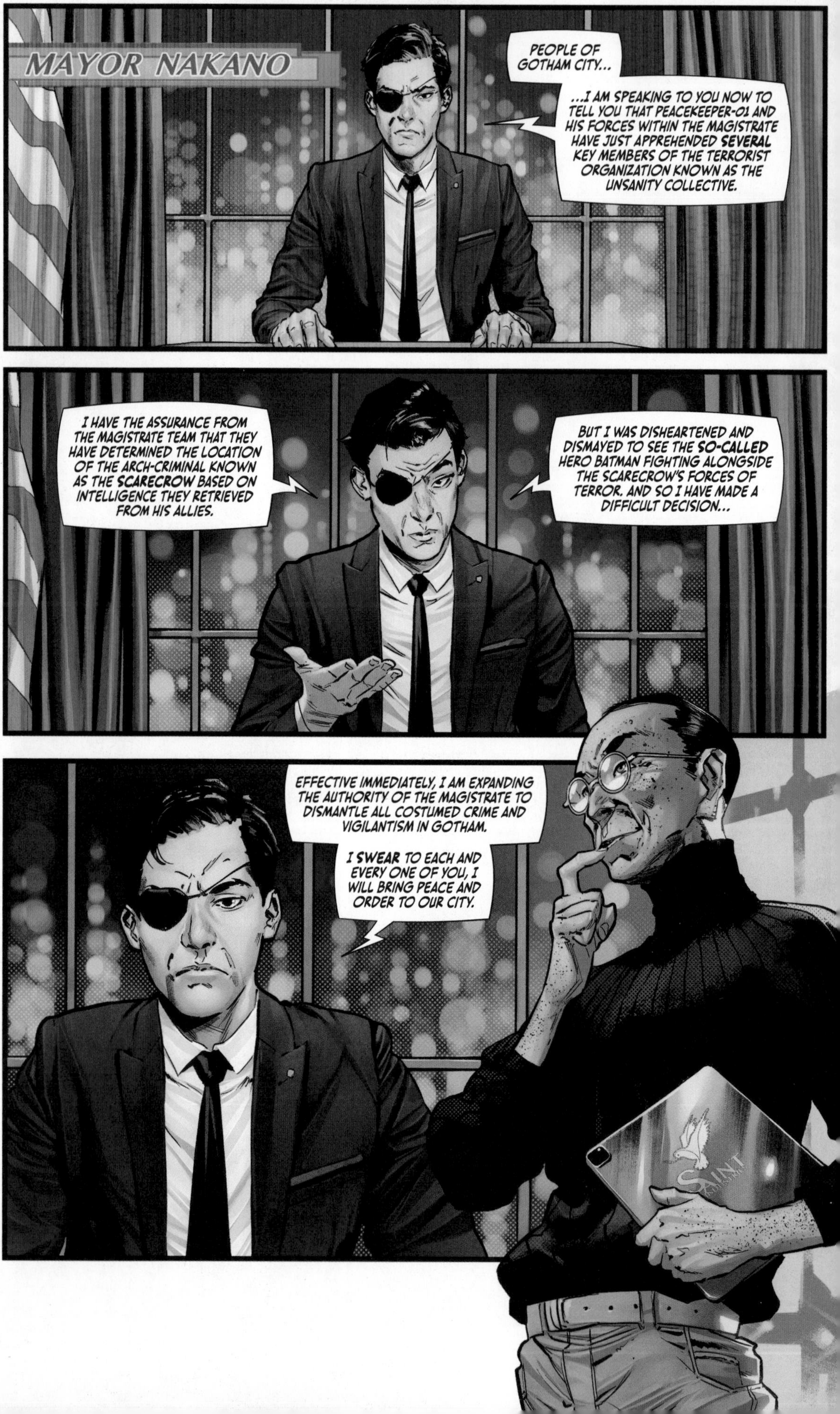
MAYOR NAKANO
PEOPLE OF GOTHAM CITY...
...I AM SPEAKING TO YOU NOW TO TELL YOU THAT PEACEKEEPER-01 AND HIS FORCES WITHIN THE MAGISTRATE HAVE JUST APPREHENDED SEVERAL KEY MEMBERS OF THE TERRORIST ORGANIZATION KNOWN AS THE UNSANITY COLLECTIVE.
I HAVE THE ASSURANCE FROM THE MAGISTRATE TEAM THAT THEY HAVE DETERMINED THE LOCATION OF THE ARCH-CRIMINAL KNOWN AS THE SCARECROW BASED ON INTELLIGENCE THEY RETRIEVED FROM HIS ALLIES.
BUT I WAS DISHEARTENED AND DISMAYED TO SEE THE SO-CALLED HERO BATMAN FIGHTING ALONGSIDE THE SCARECROW'S FORCES OF TERROR. AND SO I HAVE MADE A DIFFICULT DECISION...
EFFECTIVE IMMEDIATELY, I AM EXPANDING THE AUTHORITY OF THE MAGISTRATE TO DISMANTLE ALL COSTUMED CRIME AND VIGILANTISM IN GOTHAM.
I SWEAR TO EACH AND EVERY ONE OF YOU, I WILL BRING PEACE AND ORDER TO OUR CITY.
SAINT

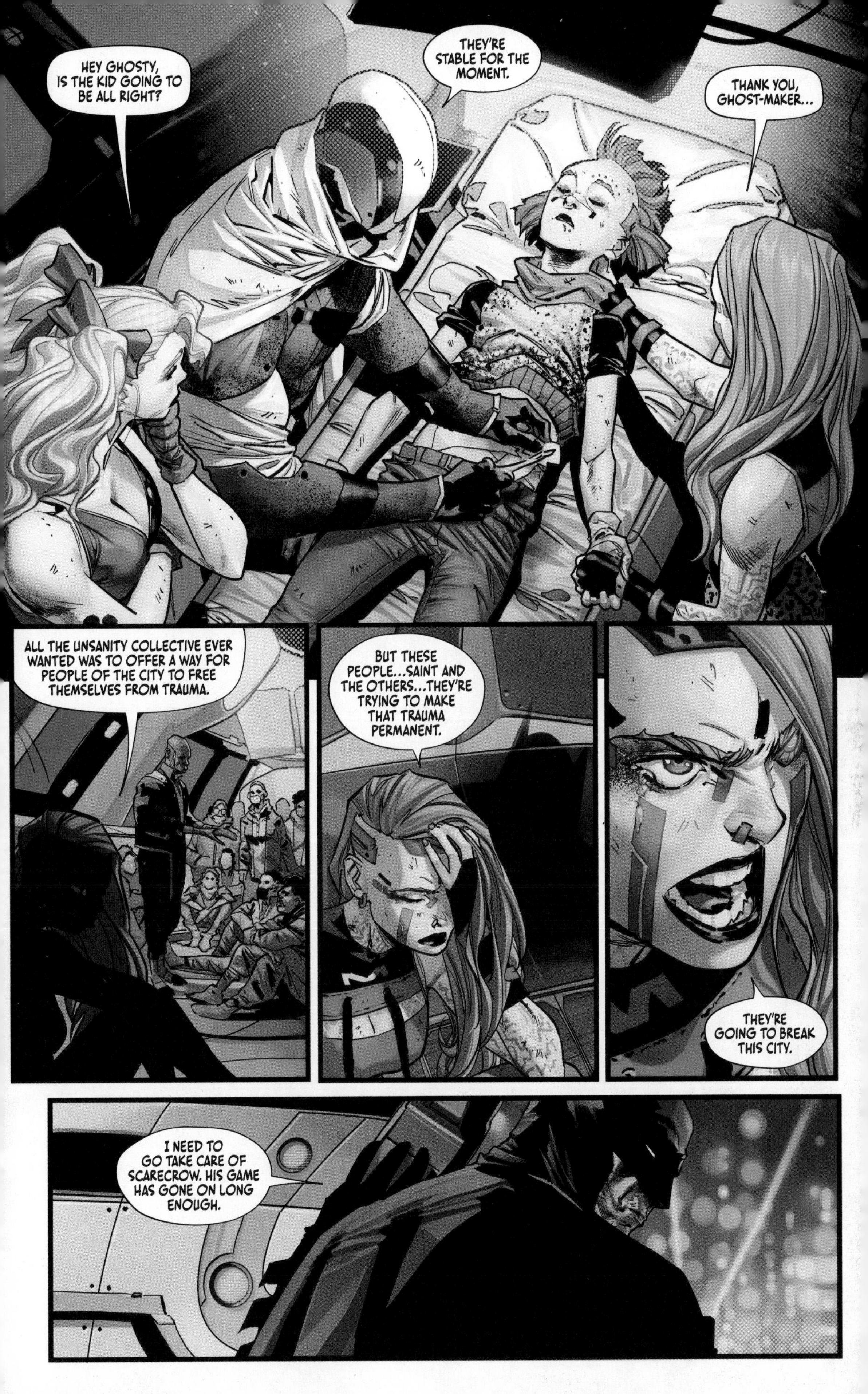
HEY GHOSTY, IS THE KID GOING TO BE ALL RIGHT?
THEY'RE STABLE FOR THE MOMENT.
THANK YOU, GHOST-MAKER...
ALL THE UNSANITY COLLECTIVE EVER WANTED WAS TO OFFER A WAY FOR PEOPLE OF THE CITY TO FREE THEMSELVES FROM TRAUMA.
BUT THESE PEOPLE...SAINT AND THE OTHERS...THEY'RE TRYING TO MAKE THAT TRAUMA PERMANENT.
THEY'RE GOING TO BREAK THIS CITY.
I NEED TO GO TAKE CARE OF SCARECROW. HIS GAME HAS GONE ON LONG ENOUGH.

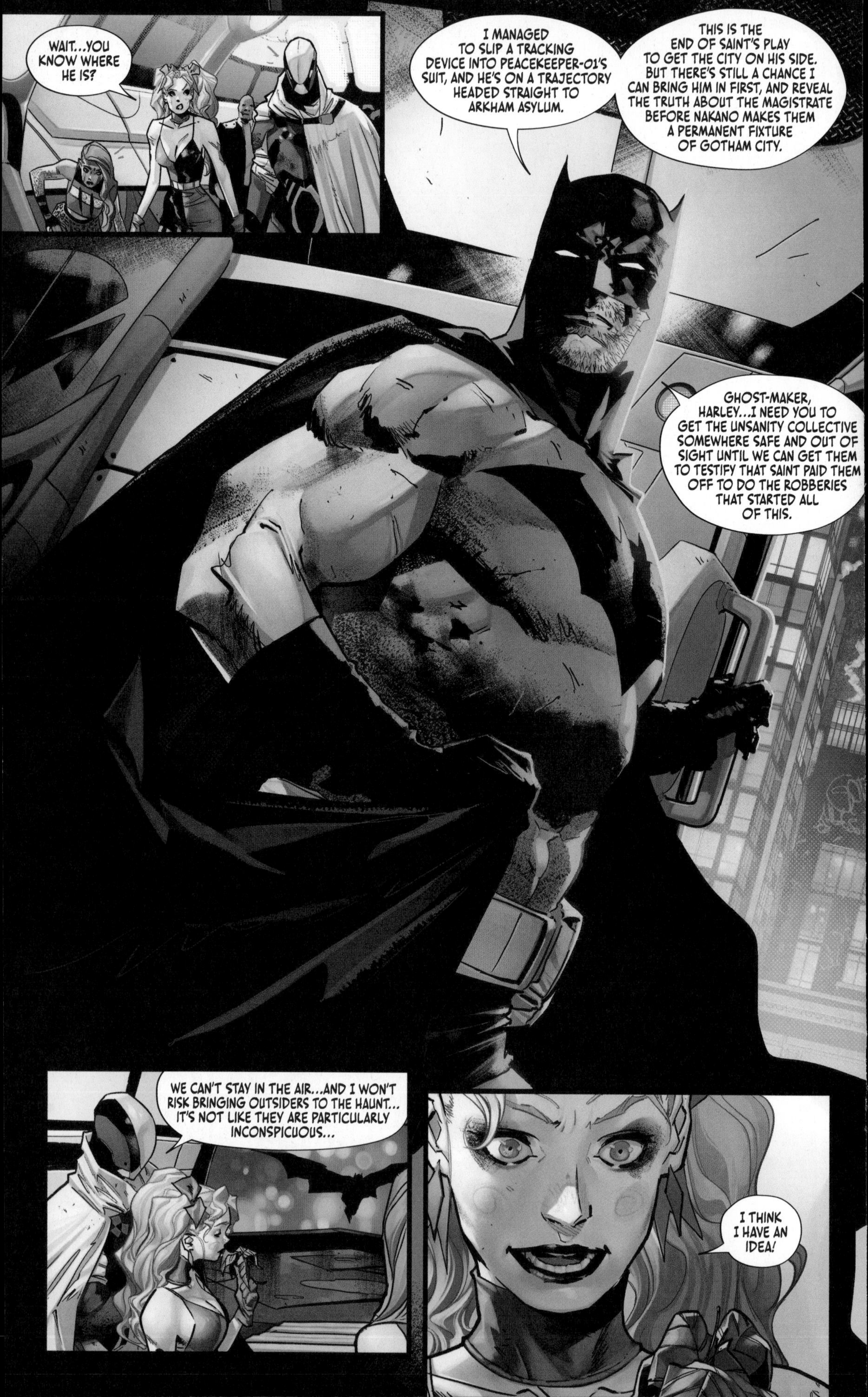
WAIT...YOU KNOW WHERE HE IS?
I MANAGED TO SLIP A TRACKING DEVICE INTO PEACEKEEPER-01'S SUIT, AND HE'S ON A TRAJECTORY HEADED STRAIGHT TO ARKHAM ASYLUM.
THIS IS THE END OF SAINT'S PLAY TO GET THE CITY ON HIS SIDE. BUT THERE'S STILL A CHANCE I CAN BRING HIM IN FIRST, AND REVEAL THE TRUTH ABOUT THE MAGISTRATE BEFORE NAKANO MAKES THEM A PERMANENT FIXTURE OF GOTHAM CITY.
GHOST-MAKER, HARLEY...I NEED YOU TO GET THE UNSANITY COLLECTIVE SOMEWHERE SAFE AND OUT OF SIGHT UNTIL WE CAN GET THEM TO TESTIFY THAT SAINT PAID THEM OFF TO DO THE ROBBERIES THAT STARTED ALL OF THIS.
WE CAN'T STAY IN THE AIR...AND I WON'T RISK BRINGING OUTSIDERS TO THE HAUNT... IT'S NOT LIKE THEY ARE PARTICULARLY INCONSPICUOUS...
I THINK I HAVE AN IDEA!

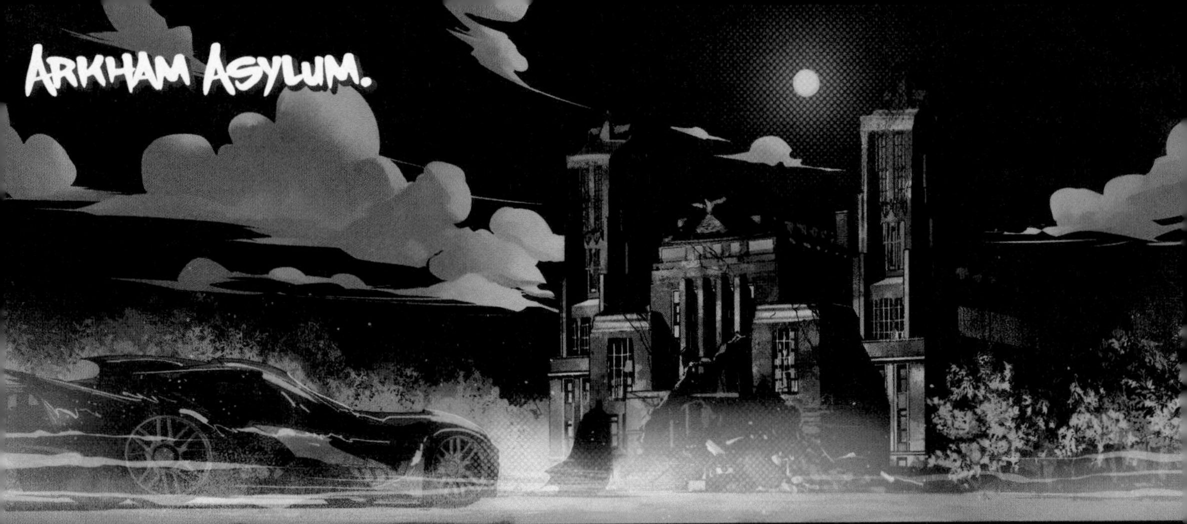
ARKHAM ASYLUM.

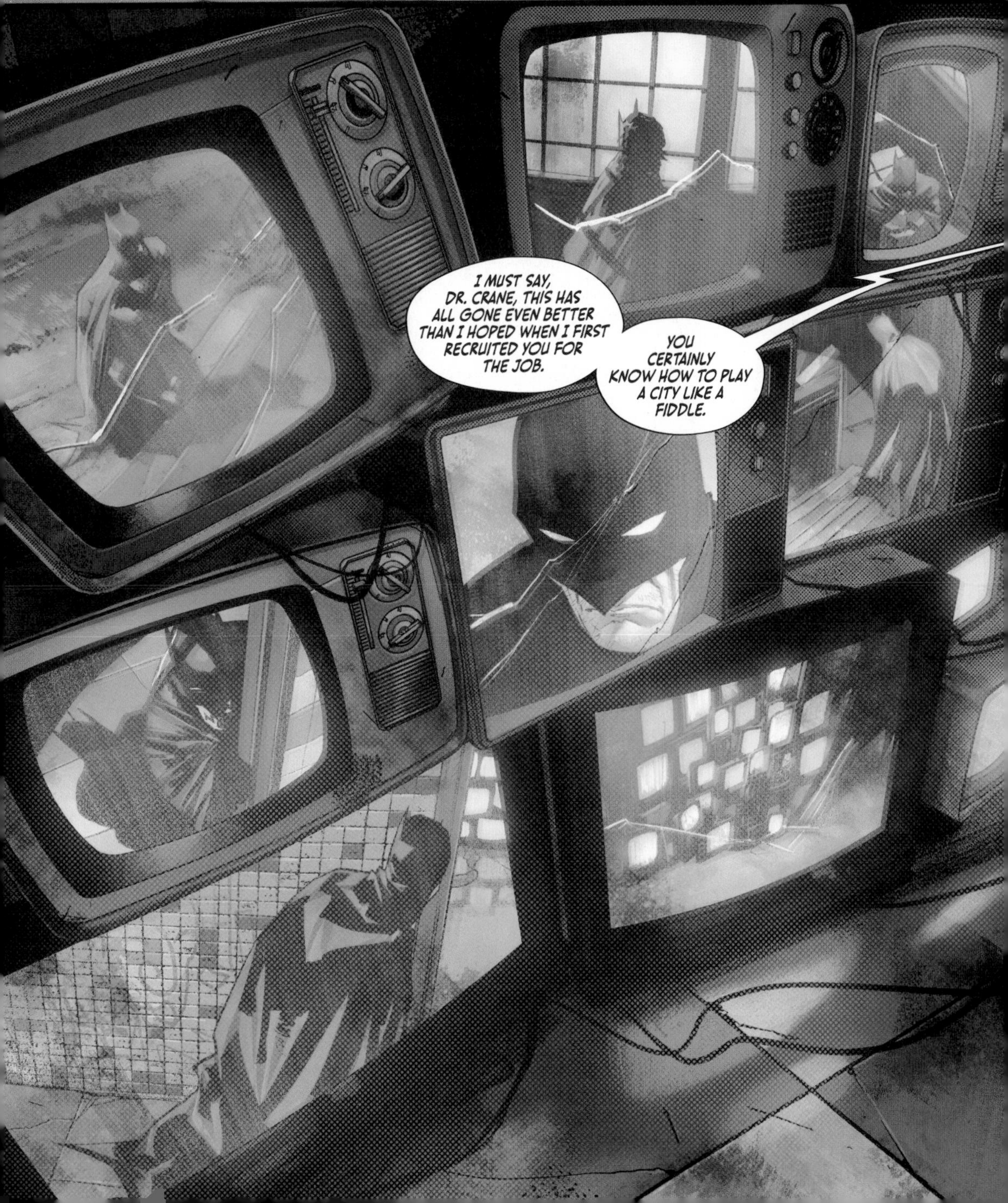
I MUST SAY, DR. CRANE, THIS HAS ALL GONE EVEN BETTER THAN I HOPED WHEN I FIRST RECRUITED YOU FOR THE JOB.
YOU CERTAINLY KNOW HOW TO PLAY A CITY LIKE A FIDDLE.

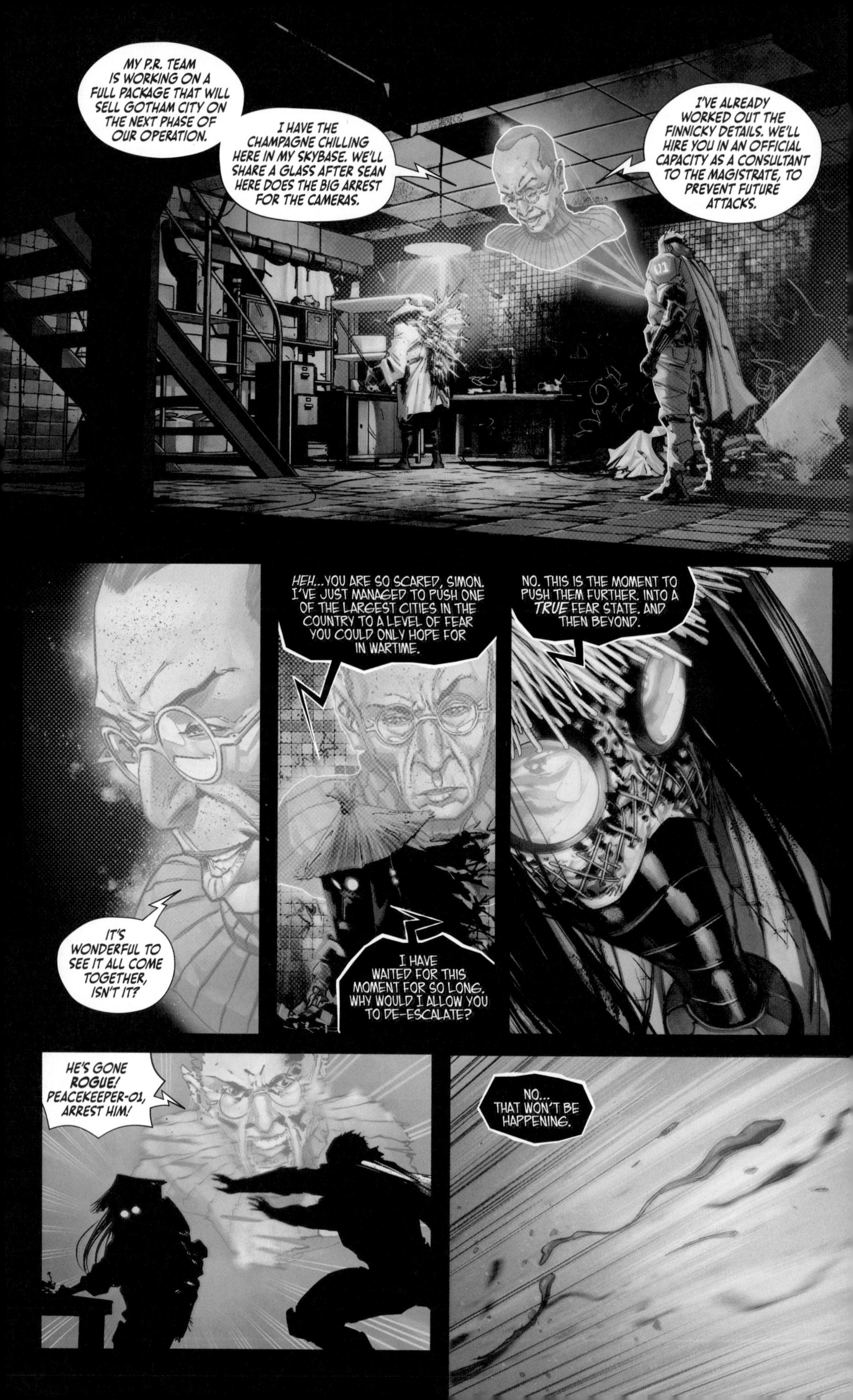
MY P.R. TEAM IS WORKING ON A FULL PACKAGE THAT WILL SELL GOTHAM CITY ON THE NEXT PHASE OF OUR OPERATION.
I HAVE THE CHAMPAGNE CHILLING HERE IN MY SKYBASE. WE'LL SHARE A GLASS AFTER SEAN HERE DOES THE BIG ARREST FOR THE CAMERAS.
I'VE ALREADY WORKED OUT THE FINNICKY DETAILS. WE'LL HIRE YOU IN AN OFFICIAL CAPACITY AS A CONSULTANT TO THE MAGISTRATE, TO PREVENT FUTURE ATTACKS.
IT'S WONDERFUL TO SEE IT ALL COME TOGETHER, ISN'T IT?
HEH...YOU ARE SO SCARED, SIMON. I'VE JUST MANAGED TO PUSH ONE OF THE LARGEST CITIES IN THE COUNTRY TO A LEVEL OF FEAR YOU COULD ONLY HOPE FOR IN WARTIME.
I HAVE WAITED FOR THIS MOMENT FOR SO LONG. WHY WOULD I ALLOW YOU TO DE-ESCALATE?
NO. THIS IS THE MOMENT TO PUSH THEM FURTHER. INTO A TRUE FEAR STATE. AND THEN BEYOND.
HE'S GONE ROGUE! PEACEKEEPER-01, ARREST HIM!
NO... THAT WON'T BE HAPPENING.

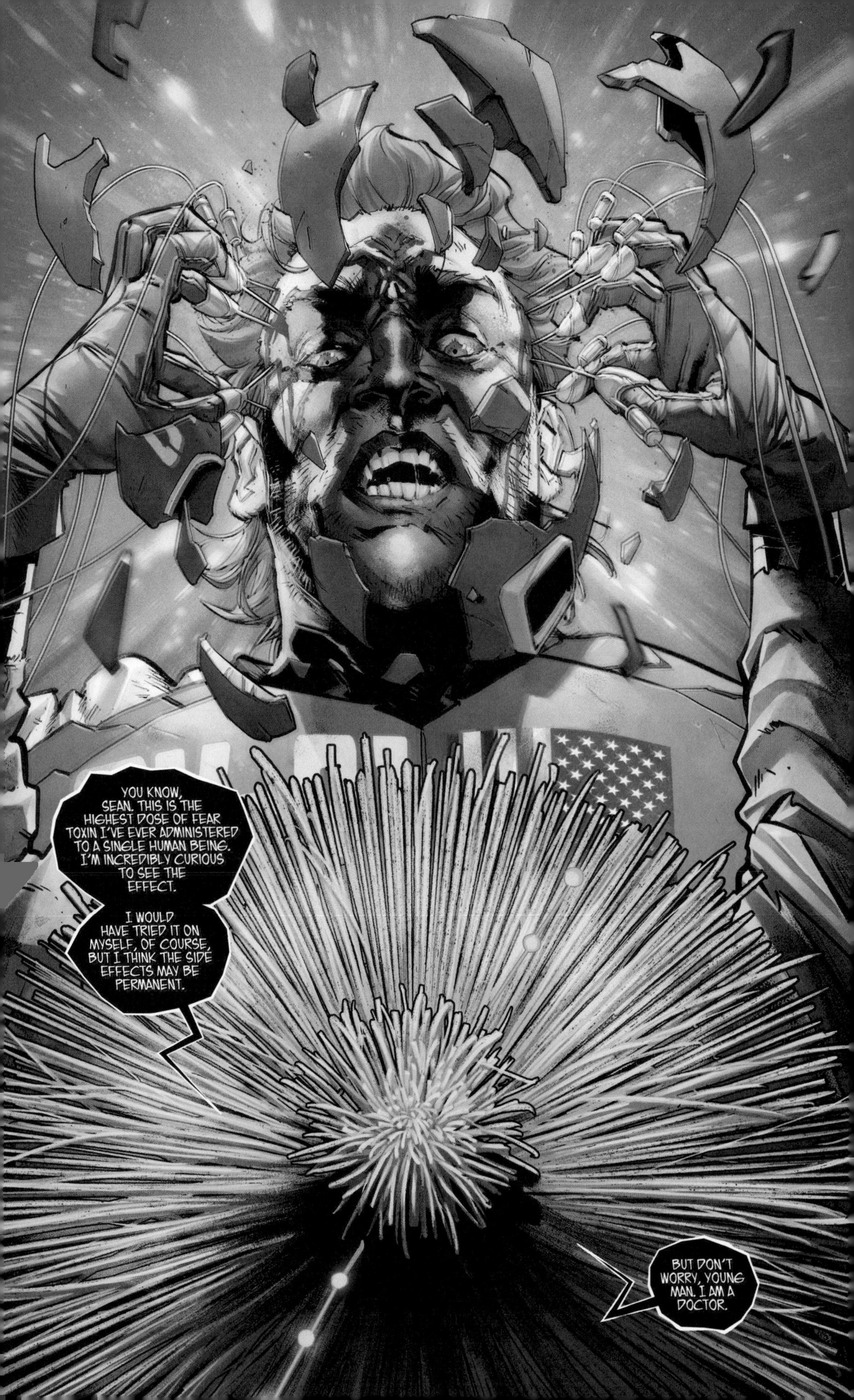
YOU KNOW, SEAN. THIS IS THE HIGHEST DOSE OF FEAR TOXIN I'VE EVER ADMINISTERED TO A SINGLE HUMAN BEING. I'M INCREDIBLY CURIOUS TO SEE THE EFFECT.
I WOULD HAVE TRIED IT ON MYSELF, OF COURSE, BUT I THINK THE SIDE EFFECTS MAY BE PERMANENT.
BUT DON'T WORRY, YOUNG MAN. I AM A DOCTOR.

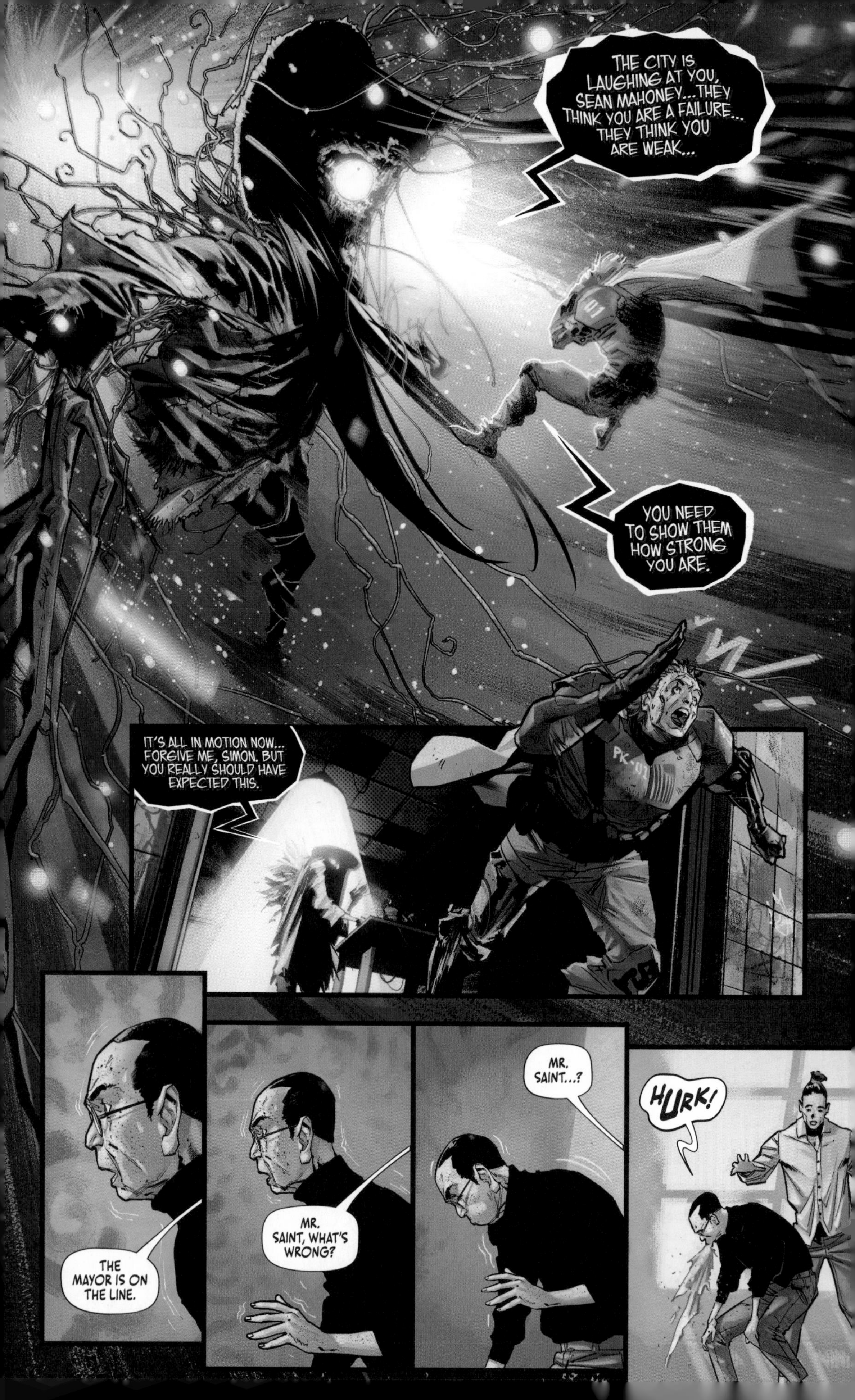
THE CITY IS LAUGHING AT YOU, SEAN MAHONEY...THEY THINK YOU ARE A FAILURE... THEY THINK YOU ARE WEAK...
YOU NEED TO SHOW THEM HOW STRONG YOU ARE.
IT'S ALL IN MOTION NOW... FORGIVE ME, SIMON. BUT YOU REALLY SHOULD HAVE EXPECTED THIS.
THE MAYOR IS ON THE LINE.
MR. SAINT, WHAT'S WRONG?
MR. SAINT...?
HURK!

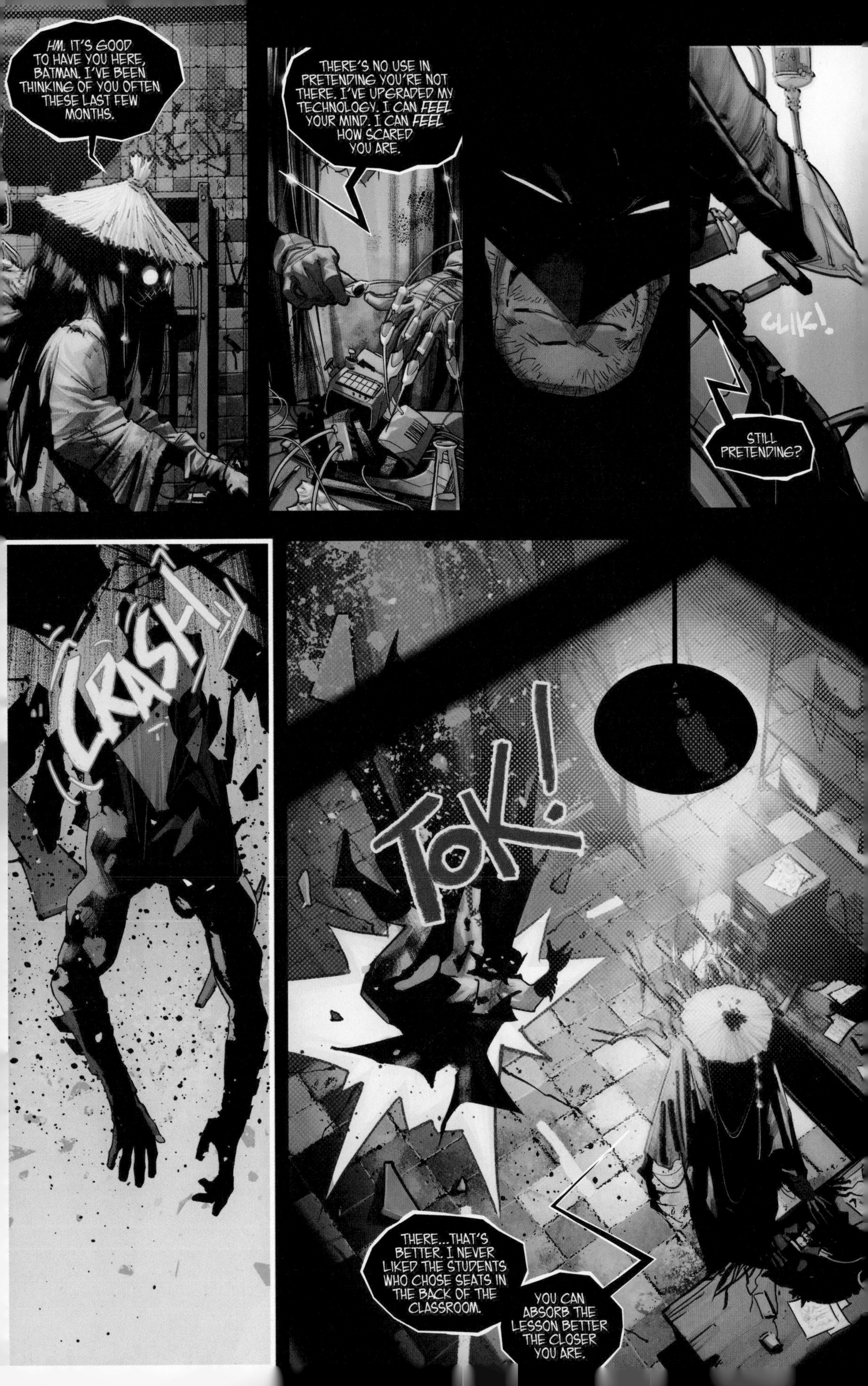
HM. IT'S GOOD TO HAVE YOU HERE, BATMAN. I'VE BEEN THINKING OF YOU OFTEN THESE LAST FEW MONTHS.
THERE'S NO USE IN PRETENDING YOU'RE NOT THERE. I'VE UPGRADED MY TECHNOLOGY. I CAN FEEL YOUR MIND. I CAN FEEL HOW SCARED YOU ARE.
CLIK!
STILL PRETENDING?
CRASH
TOK!
THERE...THAT'S BETTER. I NEVER LIKED THE STUDENTS WHO CHOSE SEATS IN THE BACK OF THE CLASSROOM.
YOU CAN ABSORB THE LESSON BETTER THE CLOSER YOU ARE.

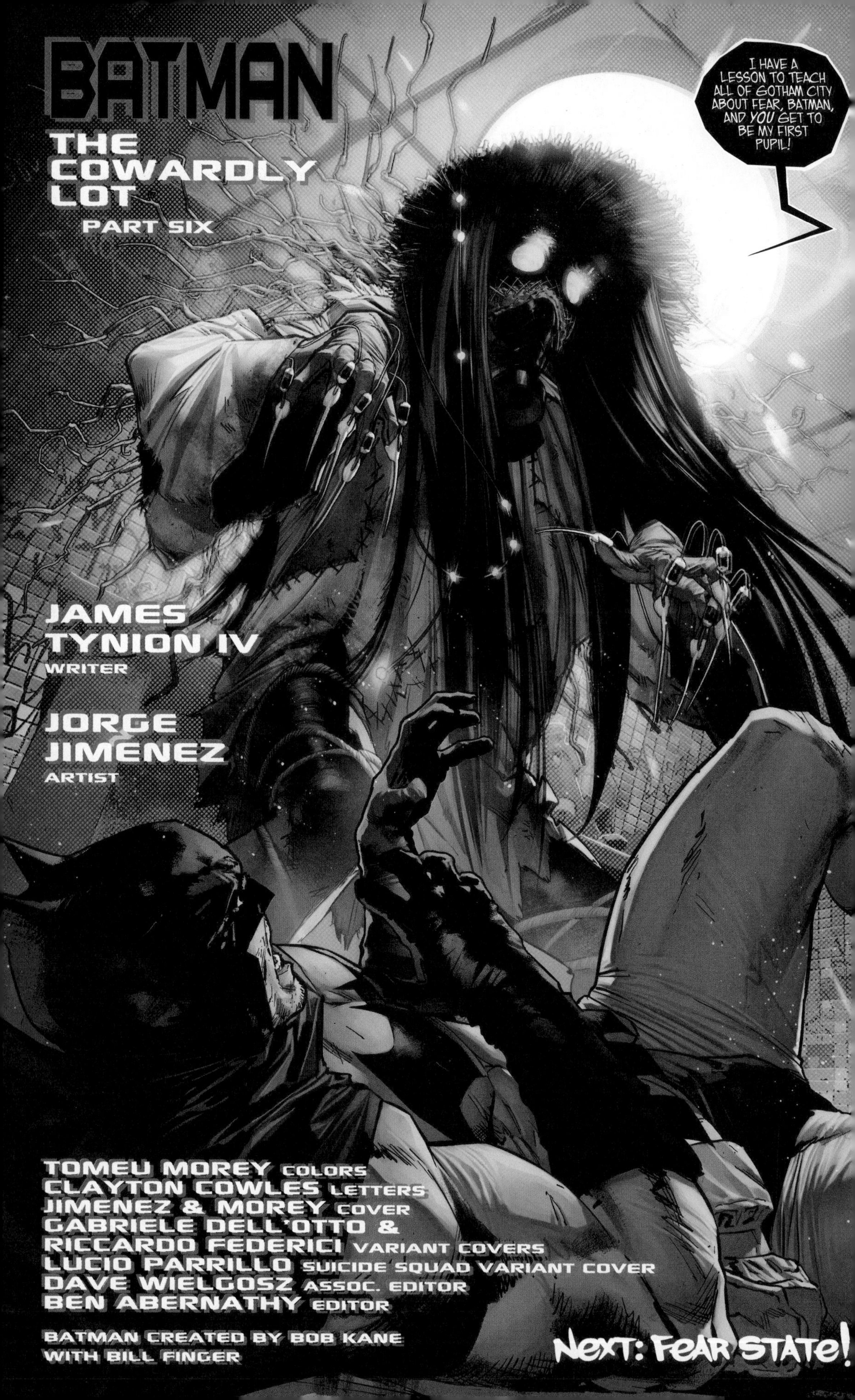
BATMAN
THE COWARDLY LOT
PART SIX
I HAVE A LESSON TO TEACH ALL OF GOTHAM CITY ABOUT FEAR, BATMAN, AND YOU GET TO BE MY FIRST PUPIL!
JAMES TYNION IV WRITER
JORGE JIMENEZ ARTIST
TOMEU MOREY COLORS
CLAYTON COWLES LETTERS
JIMENEZ & MOREY COVER
GABRIELE DELL'OTTO & RICCARDO FEDERICI VARIANT COVERS
LUCIO PARRILLO SUICIDE SQUAD VARIANT COVER
DAVE WIELGOSZ ASSOC. EDITOR
BEN ABERNATHY EDITOR
BATMAN CREATED BY BOB KANE WITH BILL FINGER
NEXT: FEAR STATE!

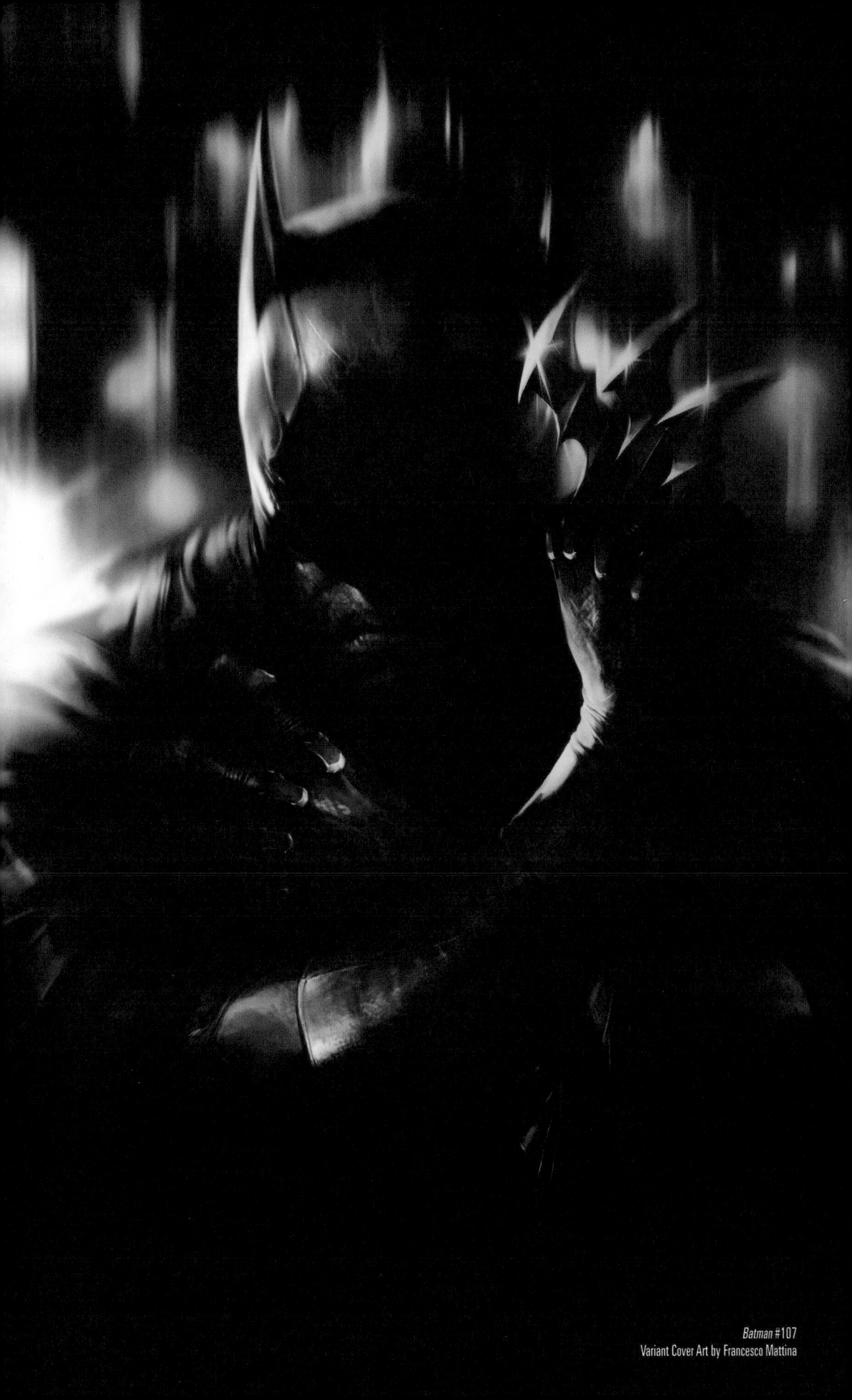

Batman #107
Variant Cover Art by Francesco Mattina

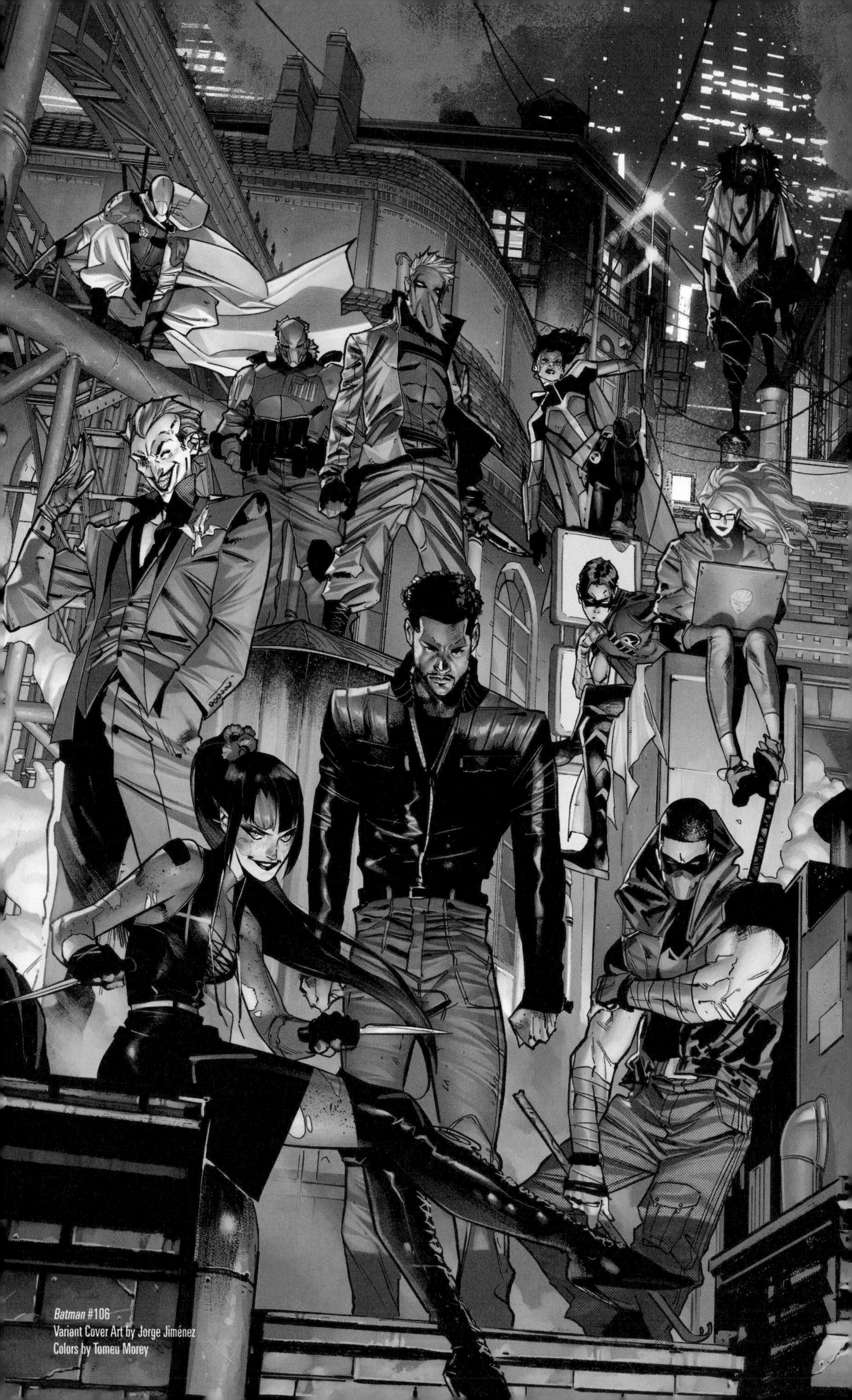

Batman #106
Variant Cover Art by Jorge Jiménez
Colors by Tomeu Morey

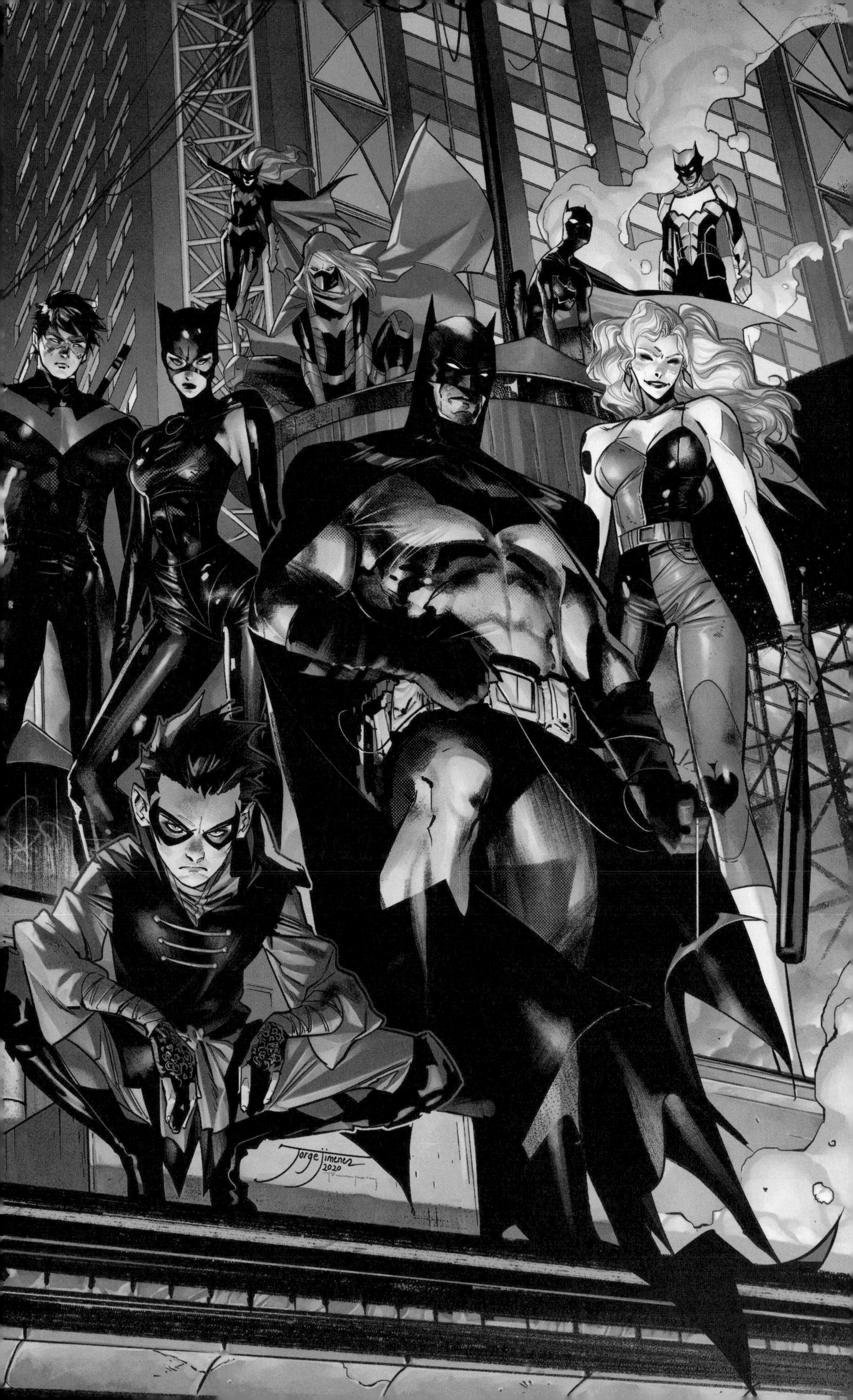
Jorge Jimenez
2020

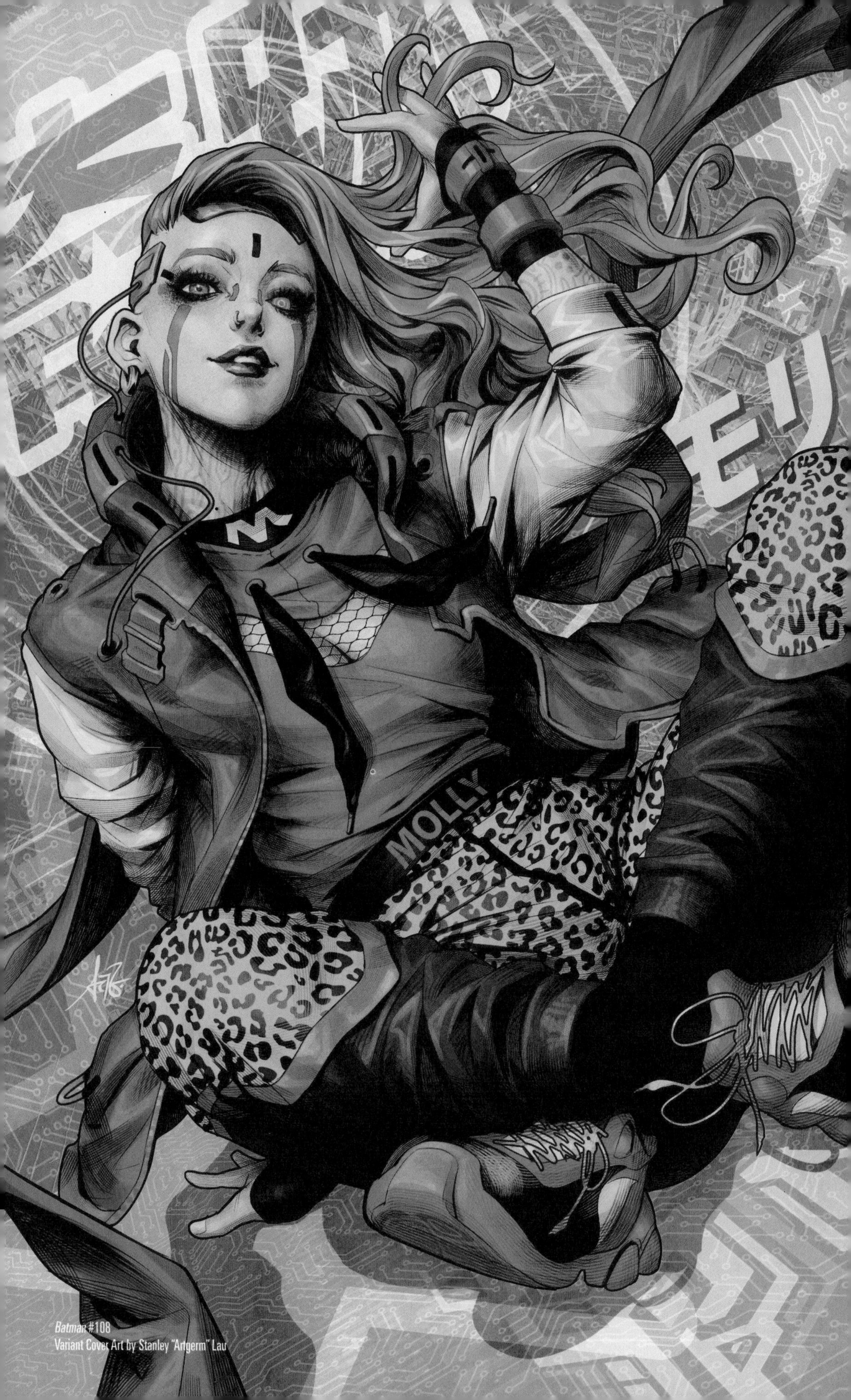
MOLLY

Batman #108
Variant Cover Art by Stanley "Artgerm" Lau

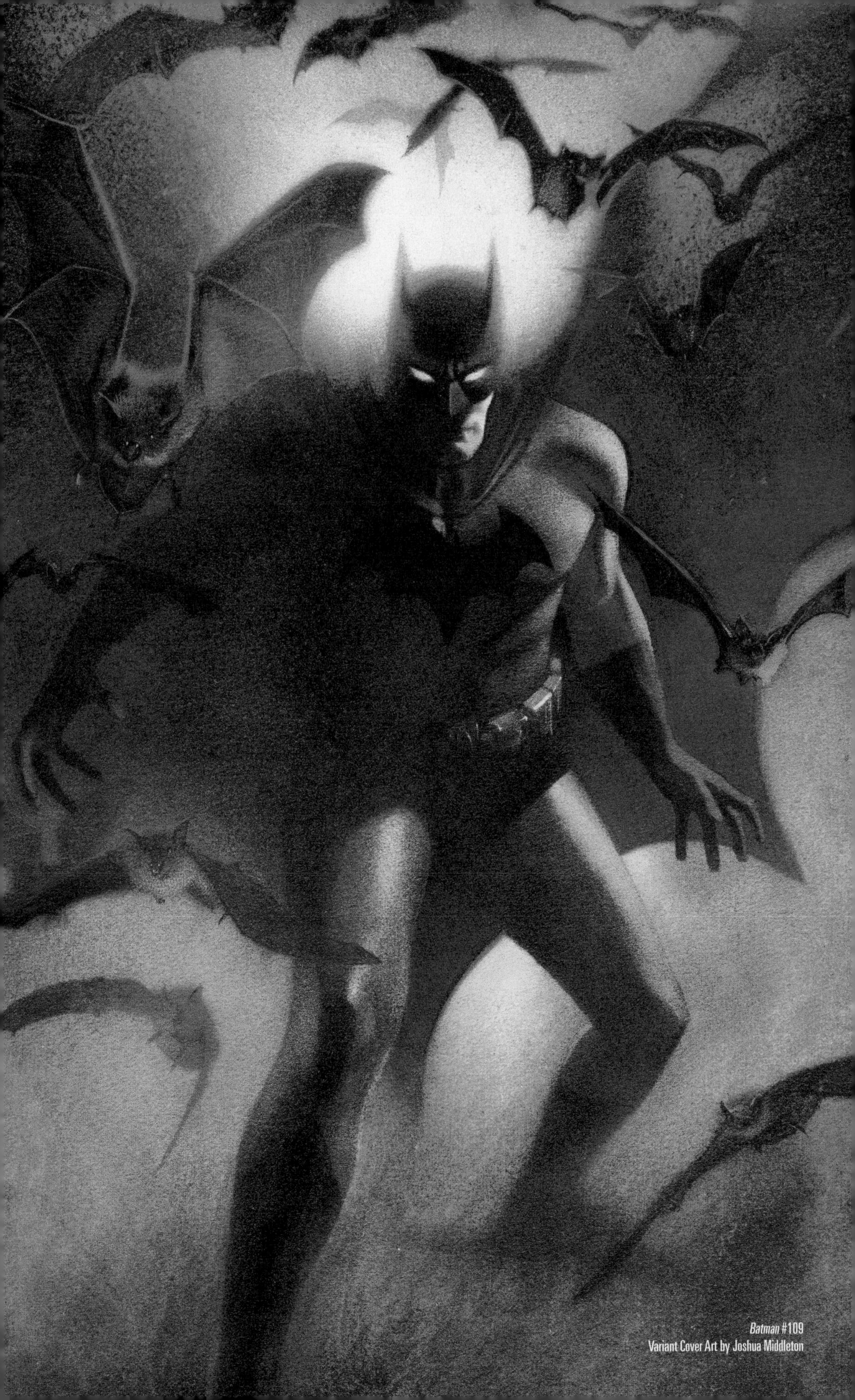

Batman #109
Variant Cover Art by Joshua Middleton

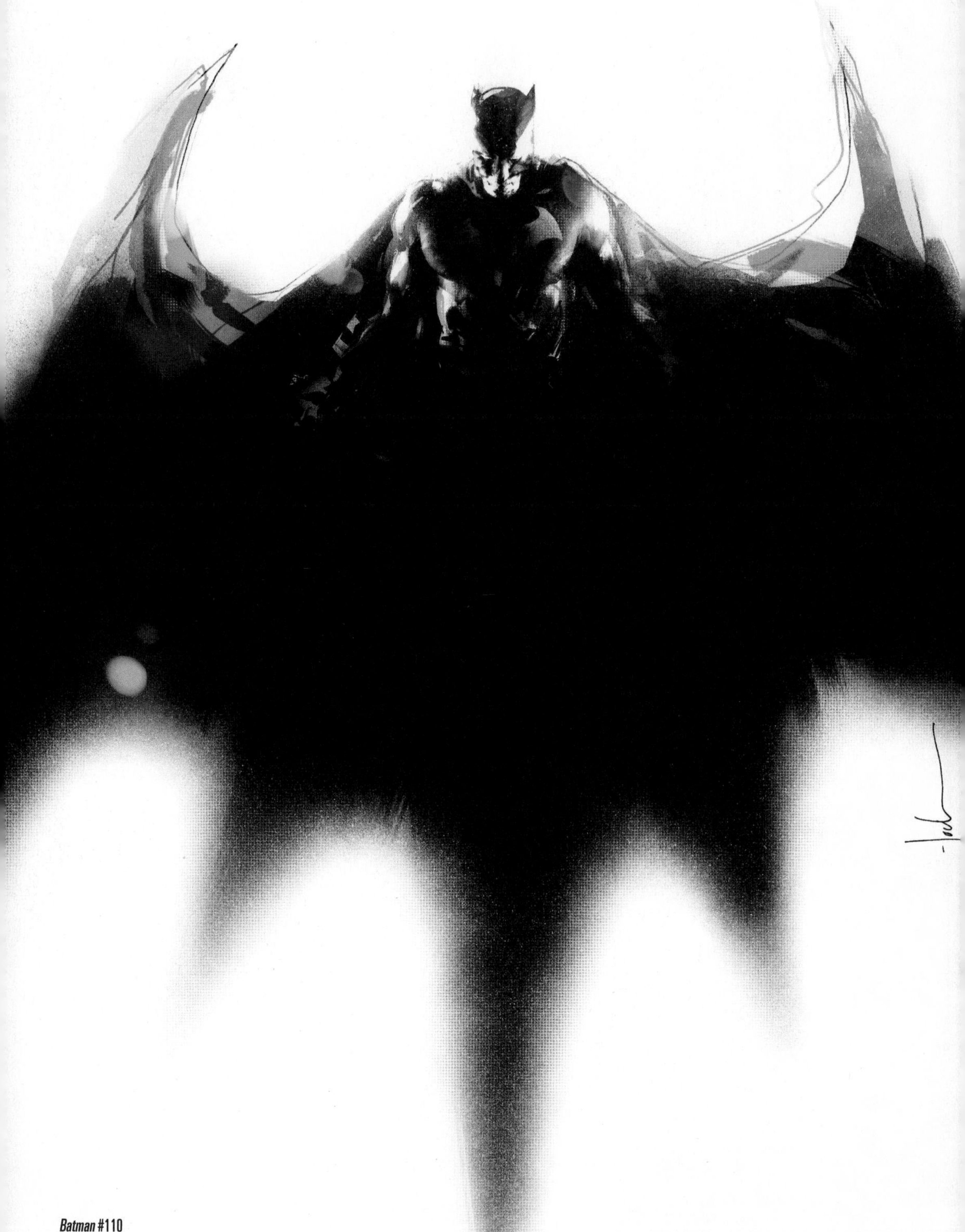

Batman #110
Variant Cover Art by Jock

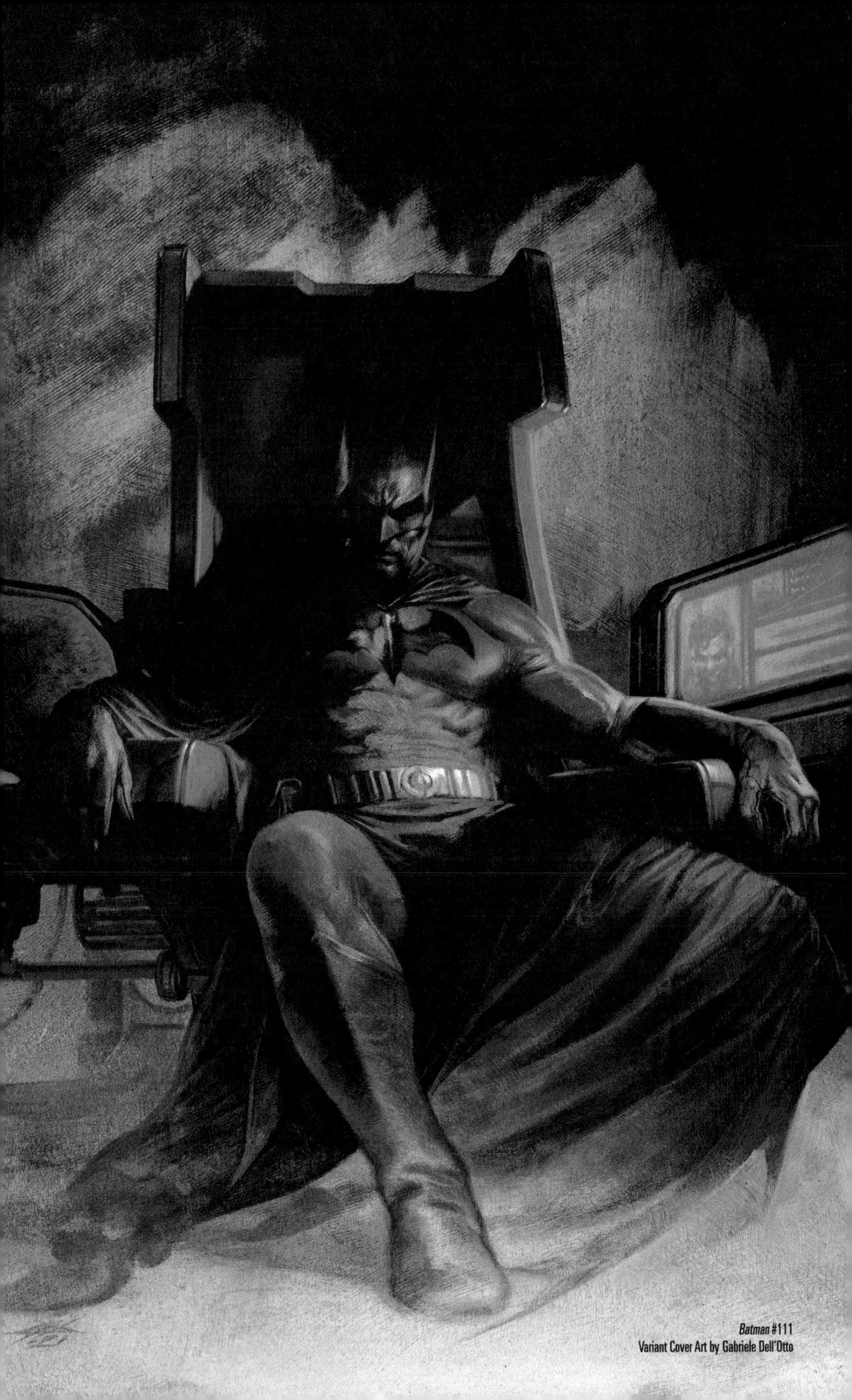

Batman #111
Variant Cover Art by Gabriele Dell'Otto

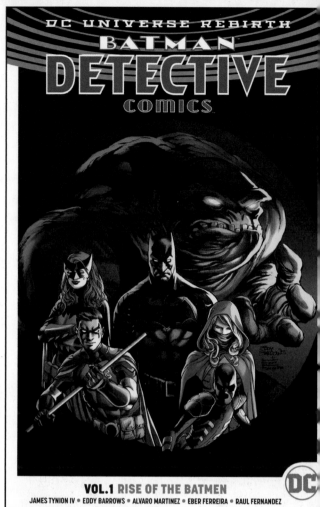

"Tynion, Barrows and company have delivered the single strongest book of DC's Rebirth era."
—NEWSARAMA

"Dramatic, suspenseful, and full of gorgeously detailed artwork. What more could a Bat-fan ask for?" **—IGN**

DC UNIVERSE REBIRTH
BATMAN
DETECTIVE COMICS
VOL.1 RISE OF THE BATMEN
JAMES TYNION IV • EDDY BARROWS • ALVARO MARTINEZ • EBER FERREIRA • RAUL FERNANDEZ

BATMAN: DETECTIVE COMICS

VOL. 1: RISE OF THE BATMEN

JAMES TYNION IV,
EDDY BARROWS,
ALVARO MARTINEZ and more

DC UNIVERSE REBIRTH
BATMAN
DETECTIVE COMICS
"DETECTIVE COMICS is my favorite DC title right now." io9
VOL.2 THE VICTIM SYNDICATE
JAMES TYNION IV • ALVARO MARTINEZ • EDDY BARROWS • BEN OLIVER

BATMAN: DETECTIVE COMICS VOL. 2: THE VICTIM SYNDICATE

DC UNIVERSE REBIRTH
BATMAN
DETECTIVE COMICS
NEWSARAMA
VOL.3 LEAGUE OF SHADOWS
JAMES TYNION IV • MARCIO TAKARA • CHRISTIAN DUCE

BATMAN: DETECTIVE COMICS VOL. 3: LEAGUE OF SHADOWS

READ THEM ALL

BATMAN: DETECTIVE COMICS VOL. DEUS EX MACHIN

BATMAN: DETECTIVE COMICS VOL. A LONELY PLACE OF LIVIN

BATMAN: DETECTIVE COMICS VOL. FALL OF THE BATME

BATMAN: DETECTIVE COMICS VOL. BATMEN ETERNA

Get more DC graphic novels wherever comics and books are sold!